From Autos to Architecture

From autos to architecture

Fordism and Architectural Aesthetics
in the Twentieth Century

David Gartman

Princeton Architectural Press | New York

For my daughters Greta and Hanna—
to whom I leave these seeds of time past, in the hope that they
may help them cultivate a better future.

And again for my wife, Betty—
whose daily cultivations continue to give me hope.

Published by
Princeton Architectural Press
37 East 7th Street
New York, NY 10003

For a free catalog of books,
call 1-800-722-6657
Visit our website at www.papress.com

Editor: Lauren Nelson Packard
Designers: Paul Wagner and Bree Apperley

Special thanks to: Nettie Aljian, Sara Bader,
Nicola Bednarek, Janet Behning, Becca Casbon,
Carina Cha, Penny (Yuen Pik) Chu, Carolyn
Deuschle, Russell Fernandez, Pete Fitzpatrick,
Wendy Fuller, Jan Haux, Clare Jacobson,
Aileen Kwun, Nancy Eklund Later, Linda Lee,
Laurie Manfra, John Myers, Katharine Myers,
Dan Simon, Andrew Stepanian, Jennifer
Thompson, Joseph Weston, and Deb Wood
of Princeton Architectural Press
—Kevin C. Lippert, publisher

Library of Congress Cataloging-in-
Publication Data
Gartman, David, 1950–
From autos to architecture : Fordism and
architectural aesthetics in the twentieth century /
David Gartman.
     p.   cm.
Includes index.
ISBN 978-1-56898-813-9 (alk. paper)
1. Architecture, Modern—20th century.
2. Architecture and society—History—
20th century.
I. Title. II. Title: Fordism and architectural
aesthetics in the twentieth century.
NA680.G38 2010
724'.7—dc22
                                    2009014437

CONTENTS

preface

The title of this book, *From Autos to Architecture*, describes not merely a causal path of aesthetic influence but also a career path of research development. I first became interested in architecture while researching my book on American automobile design. I discovered that in the 1920s avant-garde European architects like Le Corbusier took Ford's Model T as the aesthetic exemplar for the modern architecture they were pioneering. They declared that they wanted to build houses like Ford built cars, through mass production, thus giving their architecture the same standardized, utilitarian look as the Model T. And these architects made these declarations with a revolutionary fervor, for they believed that creating a new, mass-produced architecture would help to create a new world.

It struck me as odd that these European architects, who lived on a continent still dominated by craft production, were more enthusiastic about mass-produced autos than Americans, who had possessed them for over a decade. To be sure, Americans loved the Model T, for its cheap price brought automobiles to the masses and allowed them to move quickly and efficiently from here to there. But they never idealized its plain, black, rectilinear looks as beautiful. I knew from my study of automotive history that by the 1920s many Americans saw the Model T as ugly, and were deserting it for the more stylishly curved and decorated cars of General Motors. American architects did not seem to think that the look of mass production was beautiful either. Even though they pioneered the use of standardized, mass-produced buildings, they generally disguised their new techniques under historical decoration.

I did not mention this difference in the aesthetic assessment of mass-produced cars by Europeans and Americans in my history of auto design, but it haunted me. What accounted for this difference? My neo-Marxist sympathies led me to look for explanations of culture and aesthetics in the economic structure of society. But in this case there seemed to be a disjuncture, not a continuity, between economy and culture. The European pioneers of the modern architecture that idealized mass production lived in societies that had not introduced this technique, while in America, which had, architects avoided its aesthetic. A cursory look at the architectural literature unearthed another conundrum. I discovered that sometime in the 1970s the modern architecture created by Europeans began to be replaced by a style called postmodernism, which discarded the sober, functional aesthetic of the former for a glitzy eclecticism of superficial decoration. But to me these postmodern buildings resembled the wild and whimsical designs of American automobiles during the 1950s. Autos and architecture obviously developed at different paces, but why? Was it because one was popular art and the other high art?

To answer these questions, I shifted the focus of my research from autos to architecture. When I told one of my former professors of this shift, he wryly quipped: "That's a pretty big step for a working-class boy." I had to agree. I grew up in a working-class family in the 1950s and was thus steeped in the popular culture of automobiles. When I went to college and became an academic, however, I lost personal interest in automotive mass culture and acquired knowledge and interest in the high arts. But while my knowledge of cars and mass culture was deeply ingrained and almost intuitive, my knowledge of architecture and high culture was that of a parvenu, acquired solely through study. I came to understand through the sociology of Pierre Bourdieu, however, that my ambiguous position between the two realms of high and low culture had advantages for both studies. In the auto design study, I combined a theoretical knowledge of culture and art that few working-class auto enthusiasts have with a practical sense about cars that few academics have. In the architecture study, I combined a working-class skepticism toward high culture that few raised in it have with a formal knowledge and interest in high art that few working-class people have. Because I had to formally and consciously learn what those steeped in high culture naturally take for granted, I was better able to expose artistic practices and sensibilities to scholarly analysis.

Further, having knowledge of both realms, although different types of knowledge, I was in a better position to see the influences of one on the other. Both Theodor Adorno and Pierre Bourdieu, the major theoretical influences on this study, have noted that high and low culture have been inextricably intertwined since the beginning of modern society. And both of these great critical thinkers have also recognized that the relation between elite and mass culture is conditioned by the relations between the social classes that these cultural realms represent. There are substantial differences between Adorno and Bourdieu on how cultural artifacts like autos and architecture are related to class. But it is one of the foremost goals of this study to bring their insights together and show empirically that both are indispensable to understanding the development of mass-produced cars and high-art architecture in the last century.

This book has been fourteen years in the making, and it is not at all what I originally intended to write. But it is a much better book for having thwarted my initial intentions. Projects like this take on a life of their own, dragging their unwitting authors along for the ride, like a leaf in a gale. During this long and tumultuous trip I have received helpful assistance from some who crossed my path on the way to different destinations. From others I have received rejection, indifference, and hostility. To mention the latter would be mean-spirited and impolitic. Not to mention the former would be impudent.

As readers for another press, Jeffrey Meikle, Terry Smith, and Katherine Solomonson provided insightful suggestions and wisely pushed me in directions I needed to go. Jeffrey Meikle provided a particularly meticulous reading, and suggested the epilogue on 9/11. Mauro Guillén provided in his own book a critique of my arguments that helped to sharpen them. At Princeton Architectural Press Nancy Eklund Later served officially as my acquisition editor, but this title does not come close to describing her role. With her knowledgeable eye she pored over the manuscript line by line, making corrections, suggestions, and demands that saved this newcomer to architecture more than a few embarrassments. And my editor, Lauren Nelson Packard, whom Ms. Later described as "a gentle soul and master collaborator," certainly lived up to the part by genially and skillfully steering my manuscript through the publication process. Academic authors striving for autonomy from the pecuniary demands of the market require substantial amounts of institutional support, and I have received that from the University of South Alabama. The Department of Sociology, Anthropology, and Social Work and the College of Arts and Sciences granted me sabbaticals and release from teaching duties to pursue this research, as well as funds to acquire photos. And the Interlibrary Loan department of the University of South Alabama Library patiently tracked down often obscure sources. The photos in this book also lean heavily on the generosity of numerous public and semipublic agencies, who granted me permission to reproduce their images gratis. A special thanks goes to Meredith Clausen of the University of Washington, whose Cities and Buildings Online Database proved an invaluable resource. Finally, many architect's offices took the time to track down requested images and provided them free of charge. I fear, however, that the galloping commodification of all aspects of art and culture is making the use of images for the sake of knowledge, not profit, increasingly difficult. When an individual or corporation claims exclusive ownership of an image that is part of the cultural heritage of society and controls its use and sale, then the whole concept of a shared culture is endangered.

In the dedications of my books I have been paying my debts to the successive generations of my family. These personal debts to my parents, wife, and children are representative of the broader historical debts that each generation owes to past, present, and future generations. People make their own history, but not under circumstances of their own choosing. They make history under the circumstances that they encounter, circumstances transmitted from the past. Through their struggles and labors, each generation plants the seeds of circumstance for the next, creating the historical opportunities and contradictions that facilitate and constrain its history-making efforts. My parents, Doyle and Laura Gartman, were part of a generation whose anonymous efforts during World War II and after created the world that my baby-boom generation inherited. We seized the opportunities and freedoms they helped to create, and stormed the remaining barriers, sometimes naively and without a historical sense of our efforts. My wife, Betty Gartman, and many others of our generation continue this struggle, cultivating these seeds of hope and opportunity against the grain of our time. But I sense that the time of my generation as historical actors is fading. The point is rapidly approaching when we must leave the seeds of time we have planted to be cultivated by the generation of my daughters. For Greta, Hanna, and others, I can only hope that we have sown more opportunities for history's progress than obstacles. To them I dedicate this effort to understand history, in the hope that it will contribute in a small way to their efforts to change it.

1

Introduction:
The Problematic Aesthetics of Fordism

NO NAME IS MORE EMBLEMATIC or evocative of the changes suffered by societies in the twentieth century than Ford. This mark of a man, a company, and a car was for much of the century the foremost sign of modernity, as both a promise and a threat. As the producer of the first affordable automobile, the Model T, Henry Ford promised to bring to masses of consumers the essential freedom of modernity—mobility. But as the father of mass production, he threatened to simultaneously enslave these masses in skilless, repetitive work along the assembly lines that produced their cheap vehicles of freedom. During the last century, the word "Fordism" came to stand for a new economic system that encompassed this contradictory couplet of autonomous consumption and heteronomous production. But, as the Italian Marxist Antonio Gramsci realized, it also stood for a new cultural system—new ways of thinking about, living in, and seeing the world—that sought to cope with, accommodate, and overcome the problematic schism at the heart of the Fordist economy.[1] This study focuses on the effect of this contradiction on one part of the culture of Fordism—the art of architecture, one of the most important aesthetic pursuits in the new economy.

———

Fordism and the Visual Order

Fordism transformed the visual order and sensibilities of society through its revolutionary mass-production process, the defining principle of which was the subordination of all ends to the efficiency of means: what was produced was secondary to how it was produced. Cheap, quick production process required, above all, standardization of products. If automakers, for example, manufactured many models, their general-purpose machinery would have to be adapted to different models by highly skilled workers, who were not only expensive but also independent. Ford decided to produce one standardized, unchanging car, the Model T, allowing him to use specialized machines that required only unskilled workers. He built the pace of their labor into the machines themselves; especially into the assembly lines, which moved at a speed that gave workers a bare minimum of time to perform their tasks.

Ford's revolutionary production process took its toll on the aesthetics of early automobiles, however. The craft production process that preceded mass production had lavished hundreds of hours of skilled labor on car bodies, molding them into stylish, curving forms that were hand-varnished in a wide variety of colors. But the production of curved panels and varnish finishes was difficult to mechanize, so following the dictates of efficiency, not aesthetics, Ford body engineers designed a Model T that eliminated curves and chromatic variety. The result was a flat, rectilinear body mechanically painted in one color, black. And since there was little time along speeding assembly lines for the detail work of fit and finish, Model Ts were thrown together with abrupt transitions and crude joints, producing a crude, fragmented appearance.

By 1924, sixteen years after the Model T's introduction, Ford had flooded the world with ten million copies of this black, square, undecorated, fragmented car, comprising a full half of the autos existing on the planet. The visual impact of these cars alone on the American landscape was substantial, but it was increased exponentially by masses of other consumer goods—telephones, clothing, cameras, clocks, furniture, sewing machines, electric irons, dishes— that were similarly standardized and mass produced following Ford's model. Mass production created a new look that was synonymous with modernity, a look dominated by standardization, repetition, rectilinearity, and lack of ornamentation. It thus consolidated a visual order of efficiency and instrumentalism that had been emerging in the United States for some time.

The objects that increasingly dominated the vision of Americans in the 1920s announced loudly that they were tailored for use, not ostentation. Products were designed not for the aesthetic contemplation of the elite but for the efficient use of the masses. And the efficiency that these new consumer goods exuded was one not only of ultimate use but also of initial manufacture. If goods had to be stripped of decoration, curves, and color to produce them cheaply and bring their prices down to a level affordable for common folk, then so be it, as long as their usefulness was not impaired. Prosperity for all took precedence over beauty for the few. Thus, for many the appearance of these mass-produced cars and other products became symbolic of freedom and democracy, either as realized fact or idealized aspiration.

The visual order of Fordist instrumentalism was not confined to consumer goods but also spilled over into the built environment. The emerging economy of mass production and mass consumption demanded new spaces—new factories to produce commodities, new stores to sell commodities, new homes to consume commodities, and new roads to drive the quintessential commodity of Fordism, the automobile. To quickly and cheaply satisfy the voracious appetite of the new economy for commodified accommodations, many of these spaces were themselves mass-produced. New construction methods were invented that employed unskilled workers to quickly assemble standardized, factory-made materials into the new spaces of commerce. Not surprisingly, then, these buildings often shared the instrumental look of mass production's most famous exemplar, the Model T. This was especially true of the factories of mass production such as Ford's Highland Park plant in Detroit, which was designed by industrial architect Albert Kahn (1869–1942) for no other end than to provide a bare-bones, efficient building-machine for the manufacture of the bare-bones, efficient automobile-machine. Like the Model T built in it, the plant was a rectilinear and largely undecorated repetition of standardized industrial parts.

Emergence of the Machine Aesthetic

It was to these American factories and the mass-produced machines coming out of them that European architects of the interwar period looked to create a new architecture, a modern architecture for the modern age. In 1923 the Swiss-born architect Charles-Édouard Jeanneret (1887–1965), who was known by the pseudonym Le Corbusier and would soon become a leader of the modern movement, embraced the mass production of housing, declaring the house a machine for living in that should be designed and manufactured like Ford's Model T. He illustrated his argument by printing photographs of automobiles and American factories, including Ford's Highland Park, declaring that the engineers who built them were the true artists of modern society. Their work exuded beauty and harmony because it was driven by the economic law of utility. American architects, on the other hand, worked in "styles," erecting historical souvenirs that wasted money and had no place in the efficiency-driven machine age.[2]

Le Corbusier and other European architects thus used the instrumental look of mass production pioneered in the United States to develop a new aesthetic for modern architecture. Variously labeled the machine aesthetic, the International Style, or *Neue Sachlichkeit* (German for "new objectivity"), this architectural aesthetic eventually became almost synonymous with modern architecture. There were, of course, other architectural styles that also claimed the right to be called modern—expressionism, art deco, streamline moderne, etc. But by about 1950 advocates of the machine aesthetic had successfully monopolized the label. Their modernism mimicked the look of mass production in several ways, as can be seen in the photo of Le Corbusier's Villa Stein, built in 1927. Incidentally, the car in front is the architect's own, parked there specifically to emphasize the aesthetic similarities between the house and a mass-produced car. It is not a Model T, however, but a French car, a Voisin. Nevertheless, several similarities are evident. First, and perhaps most

Le Corbusier and Pierre Jeanneret, Villa Stein, Garches, France,1927 (© 2006 Artists Rights Society, NY/ADAGP, Paris/ FLC L1(10)19)

obvious, is the house's absolute absence of decorative detail—just flat, smooth, unadorned surfaces, as if it had been stamped out on Ford's gigantic metal presses. Second, the Villa Stein, like the Model T, is insistently monochrome, but the single color is white, not black. White was the preferred color of many modernists, for it symbolized the pristine purity they were seeking and also made their forms stand out in the sunlight.[3] Third, the lines of the house are rigidly rectilinear—even the roof is flat, in defiance of the traditionally peaked form. Finally, as in mass-produced sedans and the factories in which they were manufactured, the windows of the Villa Stein are arranged in continuous strips of glazed openings that wrap around the structure, interrupted only by sup- porting posts and mullions. This house is thus the epitome of a machine for living in, modeled on the most advanced production process in the world— American mass production.

Le Corbusier's Villa Stein certainly *looks* mass-produced, but its looks are deceiving. The smooth, white, continuous facade looks like a monolithic frame of poured-in-place, reinforced concrete, the type European modernists praised in American factories like Ford's Highland Park. But in reality it is composed of hand-laid brick and concrete block that was cemented, plastered, and painted to look like this industrial material.[4] The Voisin car parked in the garage of the villa was not mass-produced either. It is a luxurious, custom-made, highly finished vehicle that was designed by the architect André Noël-Lelmont.[5] In Le Corbusier's France of 1927, as in most of the rest of Europe, industrial building materials were rather scarce, and mass-produced automobiles were absolutely nonexistent. The techniques of mass production pioneered in the United States in the first decade of the twentieth century had yet to be adopted in European industry by the end of the third decade. In Europe, mass production was not a reality but an aesthetic dream, an unrealized ideal.

While European modernists were dreaming of a future they had yet to achieve, American architects were dreaming of a past they had already surpassed. In the land where mass production was an established fact, there was no aesthetic movement that venerated the forms of the machine. During the same period in which Le Corbusier and other Europeans idealized the mass-produced Model T as a thing of beauty, Americans were ridiculing it as the epitome of ugliness.[6] To be sure, Americans celebrated the mass-produced Model T, but for its low price and utility, not its beauty. As their incomes increased in the mid-1920s, more and more Americans traded their ugly, utilitarian Model Ts for autos with sleek, stylish curves and decorative embellishments that covered over all signs of standardized mass production. Similarly, American architects pioneered mass-production building techniques, but they generally concealed these under historic styles or organic ornamentation on all but the most utilitarian buildings. While the European avant-garde was exposing simulated machine forms as part of a movement to promote mass production, American builders and manufacturers were covering over the real look of mass production to please increasing demanding consumers. Thus, mass production as a cultural ideal and aesthetic did not emerge in synchrony with mass production as an economic system. In Europe the aesthetic considerably preceded the economy, while in America the aesthetic lagged decades behind, with modern architecture becoming influential only after the Second World War.

A Class Model of Aesthetic Development

This disjuncture between mass production and the machine aesthetic based on its products serves as a warning against accepting a simplistic reflection model of the relation between economy and culture. The history of architectural aesthetics in the early twentieth century reminds us that the relation between a society's economic system of production and its cultural system of symbols is much more complex that the some simplistic Marxists suspect. What they often forgot is that economy and culture are not things that mechanically influ-ence each other like natural forces, behind the backs of human beings. Both exist in the realm of social relations and affect one another through the actions of the humans who participate in them—these actions, however, are con-strained by the structure of their relations to one another. To understand the contradictions and disjunctures between economic production and cultural aesthetics, it is necessary to map the influence of the relations of one sphere on the relations of the other. In this study I follow the Marxist insight that class relations of the economic sphere are generally primary and thus condition the relations under which architects in the cultural sphere produce their aesthetic creations. However, these cultural relations cannot be reduced to artists' class interests that are imported into and directly reflected in their work, as postu-lated by some Marxist instrumentalists who see culture as merely ideology.[7]

Developing a more complex model, both Marxist literary critic Fredric Jameson (b. 1934) and French sociologist Pierre Bourdieu (1930–2002) argue that the influence of class on culture is indirect and unconscious. For these scholars, a particular type of economic structure creates problems or contra-dictions that shape the experiences of all living within it. Artists unconsciously grapple with and seek to resolve these contradictions in their aesthetic forms, but the nature and type of these resolutions are shaped by their class positions and conflicts with other classes in history. An artist's class and its struggles provide the cognitive limits to her forms by rendering her unable to conceive of aesthetic resolutions that contradict her real class interests.[8] Bourdieu calls these unconscious cognitive structures that shape an artist's productions a "habitus," a set of durable, embodied dispositions inculcated by early socializa-tion in a particular position in the class structure. These class-specific habitus give rise to specific cultural tastes, which in turn influence the forms of art that people produce and consume. Thus, in advocating or creating a particular aes-thetic, an artist unconsciously and symbolically asserts the superiority of her class over others in society.[9] Bourdieu calls such cultural acts "symbolic vio-lence,"[10] while Frederic Jameson calls them the "political unconscious."[11] Both, however, agree that all artistic productions intervene symbolically in the social struggles of the day, but these political interventions are most often uninten-tional and unconscious. Bourdieu and Jameson also agree that aesthetic form cannot be explained simply by the artist's class and its unconscious interests. One must also take into account that class's changing relations to class oppo-nents in a contest for power. Like the moves in a game of chess, actions in class conflict are largely determined by the positions and strategies of one's opponents. Nothing less than a full-scale, historical study of the changing class conflicts of a period can yield an explanation of the aesthetic forms that symbolically respond to and seek to resolve them.

The emergence of a machine aesthetic in Europe rather than the United States must thus be explained by the different class structures and class conflicts of these regions. In America, the new mass-production economy revolutionized not only production methods and the visual order but also class relations and conflicts. Ford's de-skilling machines and assembly lines reduced the skill differentials within the working class and leveled it to a homogeneous mass with similar wages, working conditions, and interests. The economies of scale demanded by these methods also produced huge, centralized factories like Ford's Highland Park and River Rouge, which concentrated thousands of workers into close proximity and facilitated their communication and organization. In other words, mass production also created the proletarian masses, which quickly began to pose a threat to the class power of its capitalist creators.

By 1913, the year that the assembly line was introduced, Ford had already faced an attempt to organize his workers by the radical anarcho-syndicalist group the Industrial Workers of the World. This, combined with the informal resistance presented by worker turnover, absenteeism, and output restriction, motivated Ford to make a drastic move countering this class opponent early in 1914—the introduction of the Five Dollar Day. This program promised to almost double the average daily wage of his workers, allowing them to participate in the culture of mass consumption that the economy of mass production was creating. In return, however, Ford demanded that his workers adopt a new, consumption-based lifestyle of sobriety and stability at home that supported the discipline and docility he demanded at work. And to enforce this trade-off of autonomous consumption for heteronomous production, the company created the Sociological Department, a personnel department staffed with middle-class social workers, ministers, and psychologists charged with investigating and cajoling workers into the stable, consumption-oriented lifestyle that Ford demanded.

Ford's Sociological Department illustrates another sea change that mass production instigated in American class structure—the creation of a professional-managerial class of corporate employees to help contain the threat posed by proletarianized workers to capitalist employers. The initial revolution of mass production had already created new corporate positions for managers, engineers, and technical professionals, who centralized the knowledge and skills confiscated from workers through the new machinery. Now Ford and other mass-producers added to them a layer of social professionals to patch up the human damage done by mass production with corporate-administered programs known in the day as "welfare work." Most of these programs aimed to create a realm of consumer autonomy in workers' leisure hours to compensate them for the heteronomy and monotony of their working hours, thus containing the incipient class conflict against Fordism.

In order for consumption to provide substitutes for lost freedom and individuality, its products had to help workers forget the Fordist labor responsible for their loss. Such soothing amnesia was impossible, however, as long as mass-produced consumer goods carried with them into the domestic retreat the visual reminders of the oppressive workplace, and this was exactly what the instrumental look of products like Ford's Model T did: the rigid rectilinearity was a reminder of the unbending regimentation of work; the fragmented appearance recalled the fragmented and degraded division of labor; and the drab, black finish was reminiscent of the forced monotony of effort. Consequently, as the class bargain of higher wages and consumption in exchange for worker acquiescence to production took hold in the 1920s, consumers increasingly demanded dissimulating product designs that disguised the marks of oppressive labor under unified and individuating surfaces. Sales of Ford's utilitarian T declined, while those of the superficially integrated and differentiated models of General Motors rose. To implement its new policy of aesthetic deception, mass-production corporations like General Motors had to add to their growing bureaucracies a new knowledge-based profession— industrial designer. As it became clear during this period that appearance, not substance, sold things, corporations also began to employ other aesthetic professionals such as ad illustrators and copywriters to lend their wares a semblance of beauty. And to cater to consumer demands that the ugliness of standardized and heteronomous mass production be disguised, corporations also employed architects to design their public buildings. The corporate headquarters building increasingly became a monumental advertisement, designed by an architect to project the image of a business anxious to meet consumer demands for excitement, glamour, and individuality.[12] Many of these artistic professions had, of course, been established before the emergence of the consumer society of the 1920s. Corporate demand for their services transformed them, however, not merely by increasing their numbers but also by integrating them into business bureaucracies, where profits—not aesthetic standards— were the measure of success.

Intraclass Conflict and Aesthetic Autonomy

This transformation of art in America alerts us to the fact that a class analysis of aesthetics is insufficient if it is confined to the major classes recognized by traditional Marxists, such as aristocracy, bourgeoisie, and proletariat. Bourdieu has insightfully argued that the dominant bourgeois class is itself divided into two fractions that are often at odds. One is the group that is generally thought to solely constitute this class—those who own and control capital, or money invested in profit-making enterprises. Bourdieu labels this fraction the economic bourgeoisie and concedes that its major resource—economic capital—makes it the dominant fraction of the dominant class. The other fraction he labels the "cultural bourgeoisie," which is engaged in the production of art and culture and whose major resource is cultural capital, or assets of the mind such as knowledge, taste, and education. Bourdieu argues that a society's culture and aesthetics are determined not merely by interclass relations between the major classes but also by the intraclass relation between these two fractions of the bourgeois class. There is an inherent potential for conflict and contention between them, because each struggles to make its kind of capital the basis for the social distribution of power and wealth. The economic fraction believes that money should rule, while the cultural fraction is vehement that knowledge should play this role. When a specific field of art is autonomous from the money-making demands of the market and governed by its own cultural standards, its artists generally produce aesthetic forms that reflect the interests and struggles of the cultural bourgeoisie and are potentially antagonistic to the economic bourgeoisie.[13] It is my argument that the International Style of modern architecture was such an aesthetic, for its technological and rational forms idealized the cultural capital of the knowledge professions and symbolically challenged the rule of moneyed industrialists. But when many American artists and architects went to work for Fordist industries, they lost this autonomy and began to cater to the monetary demands of their corporate employers. Because the class bargain of higher wages for workplace discipline made workers important consumers in mass markets, making money required that corporations and their aesthetic professionals cater to worker demands for products and buildings that aesthetically obscured, not displayed, the technology and instrumental rationality of work. Consequently, the beginnings of an American machine aesthetic in the early twentieth century were quickly quashed by architects working for corporate clients, who gave the masses historical or moderne decoration that provided the obfuscation and entertainment necessary to placate their incipient revolt against Fordist work.

In Central Europe, by contrast, the machine aesthetic in architecture took root and flourished because both the interclass and intraclass conflicts were different. Here the aristocracy persisted into the twentieth century, providing a powerful opponent to the economic bourgeoisie and its struggle for dominance. In most of Europe, industrialists compromised with aristocratic power, making them weak and opponents of the Fordist modernization of industry pioneered in America. The cultural bourgeoisie of managers, engineers, and intellectuals thus found no home for their modernizing ambitions within regressive European businesses. Consequently, they mounted an independent push for modernization, a technocratic movement that vehemently juxtaposed the rationality and objectivity of their knowledge to the venality and selfishness of moneyed industrialists. In the aftermath of the First World War this movement gained momentum, especially in Central Europe, where workers' movements toppled Old Regimes and installed democratic states. The professional-managerial class, along with some factions of the workers' movement, looked to Fordism as the solution to the problems of these societies. The architectural proponents of the machine aesthetic led the aesthetic wing of this technocratic movement, glorifying in their forms the technology of mass production and the instrumental rationality on which it rested. But because capitalists were still reluctant to modernize, these modern architects and other professionals allied with social-democratic state managers to mount a state-led industrial rationalization program modeled on Fordism. This program promised workers increased consumption, but unlike in America, this consumption was delivered through the state, not the market. Thus, workers' buying power had little effect on the aesthetics of consumer goods, especially housing, which was provided in the form of state-financed worker apartments. Because state patronage gave the architects of these worker estates autonomy from the market, they were able to employ their machine aesthetic, which symbolized their own technocratic interests rather than worker demands for escape from Fordist work.

Fordism and Modern Architecture: An Overview

This misplaced origin of the machine aesthetic, which is treated in chapter 2 of this study, was only the beginning of the complex and circuitous relation between Fordist mass production and modern architecture in the twentieth century. After this powerful beginning in Europe in the 1920s, the machine aesthetic suffered an international setback in the 1930s, as revealed in chapter 3. As the Great Depression seized the world economy, the promise of mass prosperity through Fordism lost its allure, along with the modern architecture that symbolized it. The collapse of mass consumption gave birth to deep doubts about the system of mass production that it legitimated, and ultimately instigated popular movements of the left and right that were fueled by desires for collective unity and control over the economy. In America, strong capitalist opposition displaced popular revolt into futuristic dreams of a technological utopia. In Germany, however, an antiquated class structure diverted popular dreams of wholeness into nostalgic longings for a fictitious past. Both political programs found aesthetic expression in a rejection of modern architecture, in its moderne and International styles. In the United States this rejection gave rise to an aesthetic of romantic modernism, which was supplemented by neo-classicism in state buildings and nostalgic populism in individual housing. In Germany, popular longings for a premodern past were aesthetically expressed in neoclassical monumentalism for the Nazi state and a *völkisch* aesthetic for public housing. But Nazis supplemented these reactionary styles with romantic modernism in their mass-production programs, of which automobilization was especially important.

After this serious retreat in the 1930s and early 1940s, the modernist machine aesthetic triumphed internationally in the 1950s, as the Fordist system emerged from the Second World War stabilized by state demand management. Chapter 4 tells the story of this dual triumph of Fordism and modernism. Even America, which had previously rejected the International Style, now embraced the severe machine aesthetic of Mies van der Rohe for the urban headquarters of Fordist corporations, due to changes in the structure and geographic distribution of classes. The postwar emphasis on economic planning in government and industry shifted the balance of class power from entrepreneur-owners to technocratic managers and professionals, whose interests were symbolized by the instrumental rationality of the machine aesthetic. And working Americans also became more accepting of modern architecture in urban centers as they moved away to the new suburbs. There builders mass-produced single-family homes that accommodated popular tastes by covering the reminders of mass production with historical decoration. Other parts of the suburban culture of consumption, especially those associated with automobiles, adopted a more modern aesthetic, but one that disguised the harshness of the machine under futuristic fantasies of a technological utopia. Americans tolerated technocratic modernism in their urban workplaces because they could escape to this entertainment aesthetic in their leisure lives. In postwar Europe, however, the slower consolidation of Fordism and its bifurcated aesthetic created the space for an architecture of opposition that rejected both insular modernism and nostalgic historicism.

As chapter 5 reveals, however, modern architecture's triumph was short-lived, coming under attack in the tumultuous 1960s as the institutions of Fordism fell into crisis. The intensification of the entertainment aesthetic in this decade led to the public exposure of the deceptions of mass consumption, and industry's attempts to address this problem undermined mass production. In the fields of art and architecture, the influx of a youthful cohort of new producers with new habitus increased competition and the pressure for innovation. Thus, young architects rejected established modernism, and found an sympathetic audience in a broad populace challenging the Fordism that it symbolized. These architectural rebels criticized the International Style as elitist, meaningless, environmentally destructive, and technologically obsolete, then pioneered alternative aesthetics to remedy these problems. Against modernism's elitism, they offered a populist aesthetic; against meaninglessness, a historicist aesthetic; against environmental destruction, a natural aesthetic; and against technological obsolescence, a technological expressionism. These counteraesthetics of the 1960s, several of which drew inspiration from America's automotive culture, provided the innovations from which a postmodern architecture was constructed in the last quarter of the century.

Beginning in the early 1970s continuing social struggles resulted in the dismantling of Fordism and the gradual construction of a new system of post-Fordism, the topics of chapter 6. This regime of production and consumption greatly increased the flexibility and mobility of capital, thus drastically restructuring both the classes and landscapes of capitalist societies. A new cultural bourgeoisie of symbol manipulators grew in power as the industrial working class was decimated by the movement of production to low-wage areas. Post-Fordism spatially concentrated this new cultural bourgeoisie in a few global cities, along with legions of low-paid workers to serve them. This new economic regime transformed architecture by creating both new clients and new problems. Cuts in public-sector spending, especially for urban areas, forced the majority of architects into the private-construction market, thus undermining the autonomy of the field. There they encountered the dual ideological demands of the new cultural bourgeoisie struggling for dominance on two fronts. This new class sought to convince the restless working class of their democratic intentions by offering images from popular culture, especially automobiles. At the same time they sought to assert their cultural superiority to the old bourgeoisie by treating this popular content in high-art forms. These dual demands produced the double-coded aesthetics of the new postmodern architecture, which combined high and popular art and was epitomized by the buildings of Disney's new entertainment venues. However, as post-Fordism became stabilized and its dominant class more confident, the largely backward-looking aesthetic of postmodernism was replaced by the more forward-looking architectural aesthetic of deconstructionism, which boldly celebrated the post-Fordist world of hypermobility and fragmentation. These economic and architectural changes were epitomized by the tragedy of September 1, 2001.

These chapters thus trace a complex story of economic and aesthetic change that began with automobiles and eventually revolutionized architecture—twice. "From autos to architecture" describes not only the direction of an aesthetic influence but also a slogan under which architectural revolutionaries remade the twentieth century and laid the groundwork for its successor.

NOTES

1. Antonio Gramsci, "Americanism and Fordism," in *Selections from the Prison Notebooks*, eds. Quintin Hoare and Geoffrey Nowell Smith (New York: International Publishers, 1971), 279–318. The quote is on 302.

2. Le Corbusier, *Towards a New Architecture* (New York: Dover, [1923] 1986), 4, 264, 42.

3. On the meaning of whiteness, see Charles Jencks, *Le Corbusier and the Continual Revolution in Architecture* (New York: Monacelli Press, 2000), 71–72; Le Corbusier, *Towards*, 29.

4. Jencks, *Le Corbusier*, 169.

5. Penny Sparke, *A Century of Car Design* (Hauppauge, NY: Barron's Educational, 2002), 89–90.

6. David L. Lewis, *The Public Image of Henry Ford* (Detroit: Wayne State University Press, 1972), 121–25.

7. On the Marxist instrumentalist conception of culture, see Herbert Marcuse, *The Aesthetic Dimension* (Boston: Beacon Press, 1978), 1–6; Frederic Jameson, *The Political Unconscious* (Ithaca, NY: Cornell University Press, 1981), 281–99.

8. Jameson, *The Political Unconscious*, 75–102; Pierre Bourdieu, *The Rules of Art* (Stanford, CA: Stanford University Press, 1996), 100–9.

9. Pierre Bourdieu, *Distinction: A Social Critique of the Judgement of Taste* (Cambridge, MA: Harvard University Press, 1984).

10. Pierre Bourdieu and Jean Claude Passeron, *Reproduction: In Education, Society and Culture* (Beverly Hills, CA: Sage, 1977), 4–10.

11. Jameson, *The Political Unconscious*, 17–20.

12. Katherine Solomonson, *The* Chicago Tribune *Tower Competition* (New York: Cambridge University Press, 2001), 99–106.

13. Bourdieu, *Distinction*, 114–25; Bourdieu, *The Field of Cultural Production* (New York: Columbia University Press), 37–46.

2

Modernism and the Model T:
The Misplaced Development of the
Machine Aesthetic

MODERN ARCHITECTURE EMERGED as a self-conscious movement in 1923, when it found its voice in Le Corbusier's impertinent manifesto, *Vers une Architecture*. Brazenly articulating the infatuation of the interwar artistic avant-garde with mechanization and mass production, the Swiss-born architect declared that "a house is a machine for living in" and should be designed and manufactured "on the same principles as the Ford car I bought," that is, the standardized, utilitarian Model T. Le Corbusier thus demanded that architects throw off the outmoded decorative and historical styles and create simple, functional architecture for the machine age. To illustrate his argument, he shockingly juxtaposed photos of the Parthenon and automobiles, implying that each constituted the standard of beauty in its age.[1]

Le Corbusier enhanced the urgency of his message by appending to his artistic arguments a social rationale. The machine age, he insisted, had thrown society "out of gear," had left the human animal "breathless and panting before the tool that he cannot take hold of...[and to which] he feels himself to be a slave." The only way that society could reconcile the working masses to this alienating reality and avoid the revolutionary turmoil that loomed at Europe's eastern doorstep was to offer them "intellectual diversion" and physical recuperation from their labor in new homes. And the only way to build enough of these homes was for architects to design for mass production. "Architecture or Revolution," he concluded threateningly. "Revolution can be avoided."[2]

Le Corbusier's manifesto became the rallying cry of a group of architects who carefully insinuated their machine aesthetic into the tumultuous social atmosphere of interwar Europe. They were part of a broader movement of artists, intellectuals, engineers, and politicians who saw the solution to social problems in the techniques of mass production pioneered in the United States by the likes of Frederick Taylor and Henry Ford. But even though America pioneered the economy of mass production in the early years of the twentieth century, it gave rise to no aesthetic movement venerating the forms of the machine. Americans celebrated the mass-produced Model T for its low price and dependability, not for its beauty. On the contrary, the simple, cheap car was widely ridiculed as the epitome of ugliness. As soon as most Americans attained sufficient means, they traded in their ugly, utilitarian Model Ts for autos with sleek, stylish curves and decorative embellishments that covered over all signs of standardized mass production. Similarly, American architects pioneered the use of standardized industrial materials like steel and concrete, but they generally concealed these machine-made materials under historic

styles or organic ornamentation. While the European avant-garde was exposing machine forms as part of a movement to promote mass production, the
American builders and manufacturers who pioneered this system were busy
covering them up to please increasingly demanding consumers.

Thus, the machine aesthetic was geographically misplaced, emerging as an aesthetic ideal in European societies which had yet to develop its
economic foundation of mass production. This misplaced development can
be understood only if we view art and aesthetics not as a direct reflection of
economic structures, but as often unconscious interventions in social struggles
specific to country and region. Le Corbusier specifically tied his architectural
struggle for the machine aesthetic to the social struggle against revolution in
Europe. But what was the revolutionary force threatening Europe, and with
whom was Le Corbusier proposing an alliance to quash it? Why was there no
similar force threatening revolution in the United States in this period, motivating similar aesthetic alliances? Only a careful historical analysis of the imbri-
cations of class and aesthetic struggles in America and Europe can answer
these questions.

___

America: The Social Foundations of Functionalism

Early America was the land of unadulterated capitalism, where no feudal past
stood in the way of the pursuit of profits and new methods of production
were invented incessantly. This capitalist imperative was reflected in America's
material culture, which was marked from the beginning by a bare-bones utili-
tarianism. In feudal Europe the decorative arts were lavishly embellished with
hundreds of hours of craft labor, testifying to a highly stratified society in which
labor was not yet commodified. Even as Europe entered the industrial age, the
new products were marketed mainly to a wealthy few, who demanded the decorative excesses still symbolic of high station.[3] In the United States, however,
human labor was commodified early on, and the scarcity of this commodity
combined with the lack of an aristocratic leisure class to discourage the costly
embellishment of goods. American products consequently gained a reputation
for stark, utilitarian simplicity. When Europeans accustomed to contrived lux-
uries saw these simple goods at the 1851 International Exposition in London,
they were astonished. The official catalog stated: "The expenditure of months
or years of labour upon a single article, not to increase its intrinsic value but
solely to augment its cost or its estimation as an object of *virtu*, is not common

in the United States. On the contrary, both manual and mechanical labour are applied with direct reference to increasing the number or the quantity of articles suited to the wants of a whole people...."[4]

Early American architecture also reflected this imperative to use scarce labor efficiently in a budding capitalism oriented to the broad populace. While the public buildings of the young republic were produced in classical styles to claim an ancient pedigree for the new democracy, structures of residence and commerce were built simply to accommodate new labor-saving machines and methods. In the 1830s Americans pioneered balloon-frame construction, which replaced the mortised and tenoned timber frame that required skilled carpenters. The balloon frame was made of standardized, machine-cut lumber assembled quickly by unskilled workers using manufactured nails. This, as well as other labor-saving construction methods, produced the predominance of flat, undecorated walls in most early buildings. Such aesthetic simplicity persisted when, around the middle of the nineteenth century, cast-iron fronts and frames were introduced on commercial buildings. While Europeans used this new material to imitate historic styles, Americans like James Bogardus (1800–1874) cast the metal into standardized parts in factories and assembled them on site using "the most ignorant workmen," as Bogardus wrote. Although there was some historical decoration on these cast-iron buildings, the sheer repetition of standardized columns and bays on four or five stories lent them a taut, rectilinear look. The weight-bearing iron frame also allowed the use of greater areas of glass for illumination and display, turning these buildings into light, dematerialized frameworks that could accommodate almost any commercial activity.[5]

Also contributing to the early functionalist aesthetic in American architecture were factory buildings of the nineteenth century. In the 1820s there was a rationalization of factory and mill design in America, dictated largely by the economies of construction and use. Factory buildings were multistoried to minimize land costs and narrow in section both to accommodate the transmission of power through shafting and also to minimize the distance of work stations from light-delivering windows. Topped with a flat roof that maximized inhabitable space, the typical factory was a long narrow box constructed of brick walls and an internal frame of iron or wood. These factories bore a remarkable resemblance to the urban tenement buildings that also arose in American cities in the middle of the nineteenth century to house industrial workers. Driven by similar economic pressures to maximize profitable space and to deliver a bare minimum of light and air to human occupants, urban landlords built long, rectangular "railroad tenements" with similar methods and materials. As the century wore on, the windows that delivered the necessities of life to workers in their tenement houses remained stingily small, while those in their factory workplaces grew to generous proportions to admit the light that fueled labor productivity. By the turn of the century, the older type of factories with solid-brick walls punctured by small windows had been replaced by buildings constructed of brick piers separated by expansive areas of glass that delivered more daylight to workers inside. Like the retail capitalists of this period, who built dematerialized, glazed frameworks of stores to better display commodities, industrial capitalists built increasingly transparent factories to better produce them.[6]

Such empty frameworks of standardized, rectilinear proportions were not new to the American landscape. They had emerged early on as a symbol of America's ambition to turn the space of nature into a standardized commodity for human exchange. The entire Western wilderness was mapped in a standardized grid of land sections to facilitate its conquest and commodification. Disregarding the heterogeneous features of the topography, the surveyor's transit slashed the land into a grid of homogeneous units of exchange value. On a smaller scale, new American cities carved out of the virgin land a grid of right-angle streets and standardized lots, like that on Manhattan Island, which, New York City commissioners argued, facilitated "the buying, selling, and improving of real estate." These grids controlled space by turning its natural use value into a commodity with an abstract and measurable exchange value. As capitalism boomed in the second half of the nineteenth century, the buildings placed on these city grids were also constructed in a standardized rectilinearity in order to control and commodify human labor. The use of standardized lumber and metal sections manufactured in factories allowed builders to employ cheap, unskilled labor under their rigid control.[7]

The utilitarian appearance of early America's architecture and landscape cannot, however, be explained solely by the economic imperatives of saving labor and commodifying nature, as design historians sympathetic to modernism's form-follows-function ethic have asserted. From the beginning, these forms also embodied an aesthetic dimension that expressed cultural aspirations as well as economic realities. As Gwendolyn Wright has argued, early Americans sought to symbolize in their plain dwellings the new social order they were creating and its break with the old order of Europe. In contrast to the architectural extravagance of unequal, aristocratic Europe, America's plain building aesthetic testified to the egalitarian, democratic aspirations of its people. The most popular residential aesthetic in early nineteenth-century cities was the Federal style, whose flat planes, repeated openings, and restrained ornament were dictated not by the economic imperatives of the balloon frame, which was yet to be invented, but by symbolic necessities. When lined up along straight urban streets of uniform lots, Federal style row houses emphasized an orderliness and uniformity that symbolized civic unity and equality. Reyner Banham has also suggested that the sober, boxy, brick-and-glass factories of this period were aesthetically influenced by the neoclassicism of Europe's Enlightenment architecture, as American industrial architects unconsciously sought to associate these satanic mills with the reason and democracy of the earlier age. The United States was unequal and imperfectly democratic from its inception, and both problems increased as industrialization progressed in the nineteenth century. But the nation's simple, egalitarian architecture obscured these divisions and allowed the winners of progress to persuade themselves, as well as the losers, that America retained its legacy of revolutionary freedom and democracy.[8]

It was not long, however, before economic changes shattered these aesthetic illusions of equality and gave rise to a new American architecture that testified to and justified growing class inequality. By the middle of the nineteenth century, rapid industrialization had created a class of industrial wage workers as well as a class of nouveau-riche industrialists who employed them, both of which undermined the myth of America as an equal society of small property holders. Industrial cities concentrated the growing working class, evoking in capitalists and the petty bourgeoisie fears of a rabble that would threaten property and order. Consequently, these cities became defined as "dangerous" and "unhealthy," and the simple aesthetic that characterized the built environment was also redefined. The plain, boxy architecture of the urban tenements and factories that concentrated workers symbolized to the "respectable classes" of America the contagious threat of unrest by the "dangerous classes." Even repetitive and rectilinear office and retail buildings came to represent a cold, competitive, commercial culture that threatened the human qualities of love and spirituality cultivated in the bourgeois home. As Marx recognized long ago, the commodification of the world is alienating not only for workers but also for capitalists, who must also subject themselves to the ruthless logic of the market. Consequently, around the middle of the nineteenth century the nouveau-riche industrialists began to flee the mechanical grids of urban centers to the winding lanes of the rural periphery, creating the first suburbs. There they constructed a natural refuge from urban standardization, where they sought to recapture a lost innocence and individuality.[9]

In their suburban retreats the rich built mansions that eschewed the simple, rectilinear style of commercial buildings and embraced a variety of historical styles that spoke of preindustrial craft work. Commissioning architects with training in Paris's École des Beaux-Arts, like Richard Morris Hunt (1827–1895), Henry Hobson Richardson (1838–1886), and Charles Follen McKim (1847–1909), the retreating robber barons built monuments to their wealth in a mélange of historic styles that denied its industrial origins. Pierre Bourdieu has argued that the high bourgeoisie has a socially determined taste for such abundantly decorative but tastefully restrained styles. Abundant economic capital removes this class from concern with the immediate necessities of life, and engenders a habitus that predisposes its members to a "pure aesthetic," that is, cultural products that are stylized and formalized. This aesthetic lifts goods above mundane materiality and distinguishes the bourgeoisie from and makes them appear superior to the lower classes, who are forced by lack of resources into a concern for economy and function. Through consuming cultural goods that are "disinterested," that is, removed from venality and selfishness, members of the bourgeoisie display their taste and sophistication and thus convert their economic capital into cultural capital, that is, symbolic resources like taste, knowledge, and lifestyle. Consequently, they appear to others as superior individuals who deserve their greater economic capital. Such an unconscious legitimation process seems to have been at work in the Beaux-Arts suburban residences of mid-nineteenth-century capitalists. In contrast to the boxy, economical appearance of other Americans' residences, as well as the standardized and repetitive look of factories and commercial buildings, their elaborately stylized castles lifted the newly rich industrialists above the crass material concerns of other classes into the pure realm of disinterested art. By retreating from the city and its aesthetic reminders of the increasingly rationalized economy into the bucolic suburbs and their Beaux-Arts mansions, American capitalists simultaneously legitimated and consolidated their power in the very economy they aesthetically escaped.[10] After the Civil War, a growing and changing American middle class began following the wealthy to the suburbs and building miniaturized versions of their elaborately decorated historical mansions, a development also explained by Bourdieu's theory class distinction. The latter argues that the petty bourgeoisie has a taste for pretension. Members of this class of moderate means aspire to the cultural distinction of the grand bourgeoisie, but have neither the economic capital nor habitus to achieve it. Consequently, they are forced to settle for cheap imitations of the prestigious goods consumed by their class betters.[11] But there was more than simple emulation motivating these middle-class suburban minimansions. This class underwent a profound transformation during the Victorian period that drove their aesthetic demands. The consolidation of large corporations and their bureaucracies of technicians, salespeople, and clerical workers was undermining the old middle class of business entrepreneurs and independent professionals and creating a new middle class of dependent white-collar employees.[12] Their loss of power and income relative to wealthy industrialists induced these middle-class employees to seek refuge from the urban sources of these discontents in suburban residences, where they sought to restore a semblance of security, togetherness, and individuality. Since they could not afford to hire the professional architects who designed tastefully restrained historical splendor for the rich industrialists, the new middle class employed mass-market builders of moderately priced homes. The stylistic differences between these two classes of suburban Victorian architecture were ostensibly minimal. Both relied largely on Gothic and Italianate Revival styles, loosely adapted and combined in a complex hodgepodge of bay windows, turrets, dormers, towers, and porches stuck onto the basic box to lend it individuality. Houses of both classes also dripped with an abundance of elaborate, decorative moldings, which were mass-produced in factories by steam-powered machinery. Ironically, both the middle and upper classes tried to escape from the increasingly standardized and rationalized industrial system in houses individualized with standardized, machine-made decoration. But the suburban houses of the nouveau-riche industrialists and the new middle class were distinguishable, and not by quantitative differences in scale and ornament alone. Those with sufficient cultural capital, like architects, insisted that they could distinguish the integrated forms and restrained elegance of the mansions of the wealthy from the unrefined abundance and fragmentation of the merely middle class.[13]

The Rise of America's Compromised Modernism

Beginning in the 1890s, however, this Victorian ideal of the home as a privatized retreat and the aesthetic of obscuring historicism which expressed it was challenged by the same middle-class that had been their erstwhile champion. Newly organized into a vast array of political and civic organizations, the new middle class launched the Progressive movement to reform America by putting its institutions on a more rational, scientific, and efficient foundation. A crucial part of this Progressive crusade was a program for housing reform, which criticized individualized and decorated Victorian architecture and advocated simple, similar, and efficient houses so as to make them available to all Americans. Middle-class Progressives thus embraced the standardized, functionalist architecture of industry and commerce that they had previously sought to escape. This abrupt aesthetic about-face can be explained by the shifting position of the middle class in the extraordinary social struggles of fin de siècle America.

Social tensions in the U.S. had been rising since the slowdown in economic growth in the mid-1870s, to which industrialists responded by consolidating into trusts, intensifying labor, and cutting wages. These measures touched off movements by small capitalists, farmers, and workers that challenged the growing power of corporations. These mounting conflicts came to a head in the 1890s, when the depression of 1893 drastically increased unemployment, bank closings, and agricultural miseries. An explosion of political activity against big business followed, organized into new political forces like the Socialist Party, the Populist Party, and the Progressive Party. This period also jolted the heretofore quiescent new middle class into action. The depression made this class aware of its economic dependence on corporations and the growing inequality between it and the rich industrialists. Consequently, middle-class Progressives were highly critical of the abuses of the big industrial trusts. They were also threatened by the growing power of the organized working class, whose struggle against these industrialists grew more militant and violent in the 1890s. For the new middle class, whose economic position now depended not on property but on education and intellectual skills, this conflict and disorder called for fundamental reforms, conceived and administered by a mediating force wielding the neutral weapons of science and professional knowledge to engineer a more rational and efficient society. This class of professionals, managers, and technicians—Bourdieu calls it the cultural bourgeoisie due to the predominance of its cultural capital over its economic capital—offered itself as just such a mediating force that would restore order and prosperity to America and, in the process, restore power and status to itself. The Progressive movement was thus born. In industry, professional engineers like Frederick Taylor, Harrison Emerson, and Henry R. Towne developed a system of scientific management that promised to overcome the conflict of labor and capital by rationally reorganizing work and management to the benefit of both. In politics, Progressive activists similarly offered to balance conflicting interests through efficient bureaucracies that neutrally administered government for the public good. But housing was also a central focus for Progressives, who argued that new homes that were efficient, simple, and scientifically designed could help create a new America. They held out this model of the home not only for the middle and upper classes, but also for the working class, and sought to instill their housing ideals in poor families through settlement houses like Jane Addams's Hull-House in Chicago. The Progressive middle class believed deeply in the power of the environment to shape human behavior, and was convinced that building the right kind of houses for the restive working class could quell their discontent.[14]

The ideology that legitimated the Progressive movement of the professional-managerial middle class was technocracy, which sought to redefine the legitimate basis for the distribution of power and wealth. Vigorously contesting the capitalist principle of distribution based on private property, aspiring technocrats argued for the rule of knowledge, education, and reason. The most vociferous advocate of the technocratic ideology in America was Thorstein Veblen, a professor of economics at the University of Chicago, a hotbed of Progressive activism. His first book, *The Theory of the Leisure Class*, published in 1899, denounced the holders of private property as wasteful drones and championed the "industrious classes"—i.e., the new middle class—as society's saviors. Veblen argued that humanity's instinct for productive activity was perverted by the rise of private property, which created a leisure class that valued conspicuous inactivity and consumption. Progress in industrial society required the replacement of this leisure class by professionals and engineers engaged in intelligent and productive work. Veblen's technocratic treatise included a direct attack on the aesthetics adopted by the leisure class of his day, the nouveau-riche industrialists. With their lavish Beaux-Arts mansions in mind, he argued that this class's "pecuniary tastes" measured beauty as directly proportionate to an object's uselessness and conspicuous waste of labor and materials. Veblen argued that the appropriate aesthetic for an industrial society based on efficient technique was a simple and unadorned functionalism. "This expression of economic facility or economic serviceability in any object—what may be called the economic beauty of the object—is best served by neat and unambiguous suggestion of its office and its efficiency for the material ends of life."[15] Veblen's voice was merely one in a rising chorus of Progressive discontent with the wealthiest Americans, whose ostentatious, architect-designed homes were said to be indicative of their general irrationality and wasteful disregard of the common good. As Herbert S. Stone, editor of *The House Beautiful*, summed up the Progressive case against the rich's aesthetics in 1905, "costly ugliness is a crime."[16]

Bourdieu has called the type of sober and unadorned aesthetic advocated by the Progressives "aristocratic asceticism," and argues that it is specific to the cultural bourgeoisie. This fraction of the dominant class has more knowledge (cultural capital) than money (economic capital), and is thus driven to contest the dominance of the economic bourgeoisie, which has more money than knowledge. The plain and simple aesthetic does this by symbolically asserting the superiority of the technician's rationality and efficient technique over the rich's monied extravagance. The Progressive cultural bourgeoisie of the 1890s pioneered the first architectural expression of aristocratic asceticism in America, the Chicago school, which emerged in this city known as a center of the Progressive movement. The major architects of this school, Louis Sullivan (1856–1924) and Frank Lloyd Wright (1869–1959), came from the cultural petty bourgeoisie—that part of the middle class with proportionally more cultural capital—and were thus sympathetic to the movement that asserted the importance of intelligence and technology over money. In the architectural field, their class backgrounds and consequent aesthetic preferences placed Sullivan and Wright on the periphery, attacking the established elite of Beaux-Arts architects providing wealthy industrialists with the legitimating aura of high culture.[17]

Louis Sullivan, the son of an Irish dance-school owner, started Beaux-Arts training in architecture twice but lasted a year or less each time, probably because his class habitus was unsuited for the hidden curriculum of this high-culture education.[18] He went on to study engineering on his own and ended up as an apprentice to architect/engineer William Le Baron Jenney (1832–1907) in Chicago. This booming industrial city was being rapidly rebuilt after the great fire of 1871, and office space in the downtown area was in short supply. To provide more space Jenney pioneered steel-frame construction, which allowed higher buildings. Sullivan learned the new technique of high-rise construction and went on to work with Dankmar Adler (1844–1900), another architect known for his engineering skills. While helping Adler design such innovative structures as the Chicago Auditorium (1889), Sullivan also developed an ideological justification for the aesthetic resulting from the new technique. He coined the slogan "form follows function," arguing that the building's "outward appearances [should] resemble inner purposes," that is, its technical structure of supports. This new functional style, he asserted, was "a monument to trade, to the organized commercial spirit, to the power and progress of the age, to the strength and resource of individuality and force of character." Sullivan loved commerce and invention but, like Veblen, condemned accumulated

wealth, for it stood in the way of the technical progress pioneered by the educated and intellectual class. "For of what use is money alone," he asked rhe-
torically, "without a chastened guiding spirit,...when not impelled by carefully
selected brains[?]" Monied interests undermined democracy, Sullivan wrote,
and wrapped themselves in outmoded aristocratic styles. The virile democracy of America must express itself through simple, utilitarian architecture.
"Democracy in its heart would abolish all human wastages....It would, in its
efficiency, its thorough-going knowledge and understanding, establish universal productiveness and racial poise...."[19]

Sullivan's application of technocratic principles was not as bold as his pro-
nouncements, however. Although he routinely disparaged historical decoration, his buildings were always enriched by a florid ornamentation tacked onto
the surface. For example, while the upper floors of Sullivan's Carson, Pirie,
Scott and Company department store in Chicago (1904) clearly expressed the
rectilinear steel frame through the unadorned repetition of standardized bays,
the first two floors were covered with cast-iron panels decorated with ornate
art nouveau motifs. Sullivan was reluctant to expose the severe standardization
of the new capitalism because he knew that it was deeply disturbing to many
Americans. Rationalized, bureaucratized capitalism created, he argued, "psychic discords whose disturbing influences we must resolve." Sullivan wrote of
the necessity of reconciling the contradiction between the objective reality of
this new age, which entailed heteronomy and standardization, and the subjective spirit of Americans, who expected autonomy and individuality. Referring
to the unadorned tall buildings constructed under the imperatives of efficient

Louis Sullivan, Carson,
Pirie, Scott and Company
department stores, Chicago,
1904 (Library of Congress,
Prints and Photographs Division,
Historic American Buildings
Survey, HABS, ILL, 16-CHIG-
65-1)

engineering and real-estate speculation, he asked: "How shall we impart to this sterile pile, this crude, harsh, brutal agglomeration, this stark, staring exclamation of eternal strife, the graciousness of those higher forms of sensibility and culture that rest on the lower and fiercer passions?"[20]

For Sullivan the only way to reconcile the objective fragments of standardized buildings with human subjects was what he called "organic ornamentation." In the harmonious, curvilinear lines of nature he found what the abstract grids of the city and tall building lacked: "the peace of perfect equilibrium, the repose of absolute unity, the serenity of a complete identification." While other architects turned to the historical styles of preindustrial societies to provide the semblance of peace and stability, Sullivan looked back even further to a romanticized "Nature" existing before and outside of the grip of exchange value. He wagered that importing the image of nature into the city would cover over the lacerations left on buildings by the galloping process of commodification.[21]

Sullivan's decorated functionalism was a product of the ambivalent position and culture of the new middle class of bureaucratic employees. On the one hand, they celebrated the rational knowledge and technical skills they wielded in managing and administering the new corporate bureaucracies, and asserted these assets symbolically with a sober, rational aesthetic focused on efficiency. But on the other hand, they realized that their knowledge and skills did not make them the rulers of these new bureaucracies but merely their employees, important but ultimately dependent on the monied capitalists at the top. Such subordination created, as Sullivan realized, "psychic discords," especially in the context of the middle class's traditional Protestant ethos of salvation through autonomous, self-denying work. In order to overcome this tension between the expectation of autonomy and the reality of dependence there emerged in the late nineteenth and early twentieth century among this class a new therapeutic ethos of self-fulfillment through leisure and consumption, as T. J. Jackson Lears has argued. To recover from the rigid rationalization they faced at work, the new middle class began to embrace a vigorous and healthy leisure life facilitated by consumer purchases, especially the suburban home. Integral to this new culture was the idealization of nature and rural life, which were believed to be healthier than life in the crowded and diseased city. So the new class of professionals and managers who worked in urban bureaucracies sought out suburban residences as part of their therapeutic lifestyle. In the aesthetics of their suburban homes of the 1890s, the new middle class now embraced a simple and efficient look to symbolize their responsible and parsimonious rationality and distinguish themselves from the profligate rich. But to distance themselves from the reminders of the standardized subordination of their jobs in the city, they also relieved the frugal simplicity of their homes with pastoral symbols, embracing healthy nature against degraded urbanity. Sullivan's steel-framed functionalism relieved with naturalistic decoration struggled to deliver this ambivalent aesthetic in the heart of the city. But the privileged venue for this aesthetic became the suburbs, and another group of Chicago architects, known as the Prairie School, emerged in the 1890s to give the fleeing new middle class their soothingly natural but rational escape from the city. Foremost among these was Frank Lloyd Wright, the other giant of the Chicago school, whose work of this period would define the quintessential suburban style in America for decades to come.[22]

A country boy from rural Wisconsin, Wright, like Sullivan, came from a petty-bourgeois family with cultural aspirations. His father, a preacher and music teacher, abandoned the family when Frank was fifteen. To help support the family Wright worked for a local building contractor, while simultaneously taking civil engineering courses at the University of Wisconsin. He ventured to Chicago at eighteen to become an architect, and ended up in the office of Adler and Sullivan, where he became the protégé of the latter. Imbued with a love of his native Wisconsin countryside and a lifelong hatred of the city, Wright was naturally drawn to Sullivan's concept of organic architecture, adopting it as his own. But while Sullivan used the look of nature merely to relieve the psychic discords of the rationalized city, Wright's organic architecture was an attempt to destroy the city and create a decentralized, rural utopia. Although his grand scheme proved infeasible, Wright's antiurban aesthetic did provide the soothing escape and sense of rootedness for which new-middle-class refugees from cities were searching.[23]

While working with Sullivan on urban projects like the Chicago Auditorium, Wright developed a lucrative sideline designing suburban houses for the new middle class. Like Sullivan, he held a class habitus and peripheral position in the architectural field that inclined him to this class's Progressive crusade to cast itself as capitalism's savior. Wright also took up the technocratic crusade, denouncing the corrupting influence of uncontrolled capitalism and touting the moderating potential of the class of knowledge and education. He railed against the "plutocratic class" that appropriated unearned rents by concentrating people in urban factories and tall buildings. This "sterile urban verticality," he wrote, was a "volcanic crater of confused energy bred by money-power,...forcing *anxiety* upon all modern life." For Wright, these problems could be solved only by the "the man of ideas....He is by nature (and by office) the qualified leader in any society.... Not only is he way shower but, with experienced command of modern ways and means, he is our natural leader toward a coveted culture of our own...." This technocratic elite, which included artists, architects, engineers, and scientists, understood that the "ugly commercialism" of the machine age had to be humanized and beautified. With Sullivan, Wright thought this could be achieved with an organic aesthetic, one that used the order and stability of nature to counter the chaos of the machine. Unlike Sullivan, however, he argued that this required not just adding some stylized vines and leaves to hide the urban building's verticality, but building a decentralized suburbia where the union of humans with nature was more real than contrived.[24]

The organic aesthetic that Wright developed in the 1890s was initially part of a larger Arts and Crafts movement among Chicago Progressives. This movement, which was also active in England and Scotland during this period, was heavily influenced by the writings of John Ruskin (1819–1900) and William Morris (1834–1896), both of whom denounced the effects of the industrial division of labor on workers and their crafts and sought to revive individualized craftsmanship by involving workers in the design process. Middle-class Progressives in the United States conveniently ignored the anti-industrialism and socialist politics of the British Arts and Crafts movement and advocated merely improving the design of machine-made goods by turning it over to artists, who would ensure that these possessed the high quality and simple lines of handcrafted goods. In 1897 Chicago Progressives founded the Chicago Arts and Crafts Society, which met in Jane Addams's Hull-House and had Frank Lloyd Wright as a charter member. Influenced by the ideas circulating there, Wright moved from his earlier aesthetic, which was more akin to Victorian complexity and clutter, to a simple and rectilinear style that he characterized in a 1901 lecture to the society as fit for a machine-age, democratic society. Wright thus led a group of other Chicago architects, including Myron Hunt (1868–1952), Robert Spencer (1864–1953), and Charles White (1876–1936), in pioneering the Prairie School of architecture, which combined machine-age simplicity with naturalistic siting and details to give the new middle class the look of both rationality and bucolic escape.[25]

This new Prairie style designed by Progressive-influenced architects was initially patronized by the new middle class that was moving to Chicago suburbs like Oak Park, as has been documented by Leonard Eaton's empirical survey of Frank Lloyd Wright's clients. Most of those for whom Wright built homes between 1890 and 1913 were middle-class businessmen—not Chicago's industrial elite but owners and managers of smaller businesses. The majority did not attend college, but those who did, like Frederick Robie, had engineering degrees. Whether or not they were college-educated, however, these businessmen were generally involved in the technical side of manufacturing firms and had an abiding interest in technology—so much so that most were tinkerers and inventors in their spare time. Like the rest of the new middle class, their major resource was thus their technical knowledge, not their economic capital. A surprising majority also had aesthetic interests—not in the high or formal arts of the grand bourgeoisie, but in middle-class applied arts and practical crafts like photography and music-playing. While most were not directly involved in Progressive politics, compared to wealthy capitalists a disproportionate number were members of liberal faiths, like Unitarianism and Christian Science, and had wives who were suffragettes.[26]

In the Prairie style homes that he built in Oak Park and elsewhere, Wright gave his new-middle-class clients ahistorical simplicity and machine-like rectilinearity that testified to their interests in technology and efficiency. But he also softened these mechanical forms by blending them into the natural landscape, which served as a counter to urban artificiality. Wright's Prairie style houses were long and low, stressing horizontality—"the true line of human freedom on earth," he asserted—in contrast to the city's verticality. They hunkered down into the landscape and often incorporated natural materials into the structure. Wright centered these houses on a large hearth, often built of stone from the

Frank Lloyd Wright, Robie House, Chicago, 1910 (Library of Congress, Prints and Photographs Division, Historic American Buildings Survey, HABS, ILL, 16-CHIG-33-4)

construction site, symbolizing an attempt to reassert a family togetherness that was being threatened by urban bureaucratization and rationalization.

Wright's Prairie style houses also incorporated nature by opening up to their natural surroundings. The interior spaces, which were generally flowing and unencumbered by traditional walls, flowed freely out into the exterior spaces through large window areas, terraces, and patios. But Wright's open, flowing spaces were not exposed or empty, as were the abstract grids of urban streets and tall buildings. The architect went to great pains to create a sense of protection and shelter, for he conceived the home as a "modern sanctuary," a "refuge for the expanding spirit of man the individual." Wright thus gave his Prairie style houses wide, overhanging eaves that he called "broad protecting roof shelters." And his houses never conveyed the uniform emptiness of the urban office building but were full of rich decoration and detail, often derived from exotic, preindustrial societies like Japan, China, and Egypt. Wright also sought to achieve an individuality that countered the uniformity of the machine age. Each of his Prairie style houses gave its occupants the difference and distinction that they sought in a world of growing bureaucratic uniformity and factory standardization.[27]

Wright's Prairie style was popularized in 1901 by plans he published in *Ladies' Home Journal*, a magazine that advocated new-middle-class ideas on domestic reform. Indeed, many elements of the Prairie style, like open spaces, built-in furniture, natural materials, and large window areas, were drawn directly from the suggestions of Progressive domestic scientists, public health workers, and Arts and Crafts enthusiasts. But Wright's architecture was distinguished by its uncanny translation of the Progressive agenda into concrete aesthetic principles. Before long the middle-class suburbs were covered with homes incorporating his pioneering elements. His growing popularity also led to a number of urban projects, but these were generally less successful. Wright had to struggle to adopt his horizontal, open, suburban style to the vertical grids of urban office space. In the Larkin Administration Building in Buffalo (1904), he was able to translate his ideal of open interior space into a multi-storied building, arranging the offices in open galleries around a central, four-story light well. The walls inside and out were brick, flat and smooth. But the supporting brick piers were relieved of their rectilinear monotony by capitals with Japanese ornament. There was, however, little communication between the exterior and interior spaces, for the building was visually sealed from the sights of the surrounding factories. Windows were scarce, with light provided primarily from the light well. As in the suburbs, the architect's intent was to

Frank Lloyd Wright, Larkin
Administration Building,
Buffalo, New York, 1904
(Courtesy The Frank Lloyd
Wright Foundation, Taliesin
West, Scottsdale, AZ)

insulate occupants from the harsh realities of urban capitalism. But whereas in the suburbs this insulation was provided by incorporating the beauty of the natural landscape, in the midst of this ugly industrial city Wright sealed his building against the disturbing and alienating sights of production.[28]

During the 1890s and early 1900s, as Progressive architects on the periphery of their profession created radical innovations for the new age, the established elite in architecture grew more insular and conservative, further bifurcating the field. The attacks by reformers led these traditional architects to raise professional boundaries against outsiders by reasserting academic styles like the Beaux Arts and advocating laws requiring a license to design structures bigger than a single residence. Such laws, in conjunction with the decline of low- and moderate-priced construction during the depression, led these architects to concentrate on large monuments and grand city plans, and to organize their offices into large, specialized bureaucracies. All of these developments pushed the established architectural elite even more completely into the arms of the wealthy, who alone could afford large-scale projects during this period. One such project that attracted the attention of not only the grand bourgeoisie but Progressive reformers as well was Daniel Burnham's (1846–1912) White City, a grand Beaux-Arts composition built by the city of Chicago for the

World's Columbian Exposition of 1893. What Progressives found especially appealing about this project was not the classical and Renaissance styles, but the vision of an efficiently planned, orderly industrial city that used aesthetics to quell unrest and restore equilibrium to society. The Exposition spawned the City Beautiful movement, which sought to use the order and symmetry of historical styles to create a semblance of unity in America's tumultuous industrial cities. But when Burnham turned his Exposition principles into a Chicago plan to develop the lakeshore site into a grand civic center, the Progressives, faithful to their social principles, criticized it for the lack of housing and recreation areas for the poor. The class divide between the architectural visions of the new middle class and the grand bourgeoisie remained. As the new century wore on, however, and approached its second decade, the aesthetic divisions between middle-class reformers and elite industrialists began to wane, symbolizing a more fundamental rapprochement of interests between the previous class combatants.[29]

The Social Sources of Modernism's Demise

The tide of America's reform-minded architectural modernism began to ebb around 1910. Sullivan gained few substantial commissions after this date. Wright's practice was also trailing off at this time, and in 1909 he left for Europe, leaving his office in charge of the more conservative Herman von Holst (1874–1955). In California, pioneering modernists like Irving Gill (1870–1936) and the Greene brothers, Charles (1868–1957) and Henry (1870–1954), also began to lose their middle-class clients and the backing of professional journals. Prairie School architects who were left in Chicago became more conservative, embracing historical styles such as Colonial Revival and Tudor Revival. Ironically, the modern aesthetic of efficiency and simplicity declined because the Progressive movement of the new middle class whose interests it symbolized was an overwhelming success, and success changed the position and struggles of this class relative to industrial capitalists and workers. Briefly put, this American modernism was feeble and stillborn because the new middle class that it ideologically represented gained power and status within corporate capitalism and became part of the status quo it once denounced.[30]

As Robert Wiebe has written in explanation of the decline in reformist zeal among this new middle class dependent upon knowledge and expertise, "many of these one-time challengers had simply won too much to fight on. Recognition, place, and at least a share of power had drawn them into a system with which they identified, one they could now defend as good and just.

Former progressives were gradually becoming spokesmen for the status quo." By the 1910s the corporate capitalists of America had begun to embrace at least part of the Progressive agenda in response to the crisis conditions of the long economic downturn. Searching desperately for ways to contain working-class struggle and meet heightened competition, industrialists followed the advise of the new middle class and began to rationalize production—that is, to divide labor, specialize and professionalize management, and place all operations on a precise, rule-governed basis. By 1912, the efficiency principles pioneered by Frederick Taylor were championed not just by reforming engineers, domestic scientists, and housing crusaders but also by capitalists, who increasingly placed the everyday running of their industrial empires in the hands of experts with rational, scientific knowledge. In the words of Alfred Chandler, the "managerial revolution" triumphed in American business, creating millions of new corporate positions for engineers, technicians, accountants, and middle managers. Outside the workplace, the changing corporations also supported attempts by Progressive reformers to bureaucratize and centralize government as well. The growing strength and organization of the working class, expressed especially through the Socialist Party, had begun to bring it considerable power in the patronage politics of many cities. Corporations saw in the efforts of reformers to bureaucratize and professionalize government a way to insulate power from the influence of workers. Finally, although many big businesses were skeptical about Progressive reforms aimed at the urban lower classes, some saw them as a vehicle to wean workers off "foreign ideologies" and integrate them into the "American way of life." [31]

The new middle class thus began to be securely and lucratively integrated into corporations controlled by the economic bourgeoisie, and no longer needed a separate justification for its project of technocracy. As this new class accumulated power and money, it dropped the ideological distinction between idle wealth and productive knowledge found in Veblen, Sullivan, and Wright. It based its legitimacy increasingly on the capitalist ideology of the marketplace—that is, wealth and power are rewards for an individual's contribution to the market, and thus testify to effort and ability. This alliance of parts of the new middle class—or cultural bourgeoisie, in Bourdieu's terms— with industrial capitalists undermined the market for modern architecture. Protomodernists like Sullivan and Wright looked to this class for clients, for it had some money and occupied a position in the field of power homologous to their position in the architectural field—outsiders challenging an established elite. But when engineers, managers, and scientists were accepted into an alliance with corporate capitalists, they lost their autonomy from the market and consequently their interest in the technocratic ideology. These professions forsook the aesthetic of asceticism and rationality and adopted an aesthetic of bourgeois luxury and historicism similar to their capitalist allies. So around the turn of the century large parts of the American cultural bourgeoisie converged with their new allies of the economic bourgeoisie on an architecture of Beaux-Arts classicism and revival styles. As Leonard Eaton reports, by the 1920s Chicago residents of this class that previously provided clients for Wright were commissioning houses from Howard Van Doren Shaw (1869–1926), an architect with formal training in the Beaux Arts who was the favorite of the city's industrial elite.[32]

The alliance between industrial capitalists and the newly incorporated professions of the cultural bourgeoisie cannot, however, explain why American architecture ultimately moved beyond Beaux-Arts historicism to an aesthetic of mass entertainment and obfuscation. To understand this, the influence of the working class in the emerging process of mass production and concomitant markets of mass consumption must be taken into account. No American industry played a larger part in the development of mass production and mass consumption than the automobile industry. The class and cultural struggles surrounding this pioneering industry provide the key to understanding both the demise of America's early modernism and the rise of its unique mass-consumption aesthetic of entertainment and obfuscation in architecture and other consumer goods.

Fordism and the Rise of the Mass-Consumption Aesthetic

Elements of mass production emerged in the late nineteenth century as part of the first wave of depression-induced industrial rationalization. But these elements were not forged into an integral system until the 1910s, when Henry Ford was struggling to produce a cheap car for the masses with a recalcitrant work force of skilled craft workers. Drawing on the widely circulated efficiency ideas of Progressive engineers and reformers, Ford first divided and specialized labor, fragmenting skilled crafts into specialized, detail work. Once craft workers were thus eliminated, Ford and his staff replaced the general-purpose machines they traditionally used to perform a variety of tasks with specialized machines built to perform one task alone. These machines incorporated the skill and discretion previously controlled by workers into technology designed and controlled by engineers and managers, allowing Ford to hire unskilled laborers who could be trained in their operations in a matter of days. Finally, and most importantly, Ford controlled the production pace of his unskilled workers by a spatial reorganization of work that ensured uninterrupted continuity between their tasks. His engineers crowded work stations close to one another in the order of their succession in the production process. Then they ensured the quick transmission of work between stations by mechanical conveyance, first through slideways and rollways, then increasingly by power-driven production and assembly lines. These moving lines removed the pauses and lapses in the production process, forcing workers to labor at the rapid and continuous pace set by managers. Thus, the niggardly compression of space and its orderly rearrangement into continuous flows allowed Ford managers to correspondingly contract the time of production, reducing necessary labor time and astronomically increasing the rate of surplus value. In the process, the skill and discretion of the direct labor was confiscated and centralized into a growing bureaucracy of white-collar engineers, technicians, and managers who conceived, built, and controlled the efficiently spaced machinery of production.[33]

In order, however, to achieve mass production and reap its incredible increase in productivity, Ford and other automakers had to alter the design and appearance of cars to accommodate the new work process. First, to make use of specialized machines, the product had to be standardized to one unchanging type—in Ford's case, the infamous Model T. Ford produced this sole model, with minor alterations, from 1908 until 1927. Further, engineers drastically transformed the traditional finishing process, which entailed the hand-application of up to twenty coats of slow-drying varnish paints and occupied a crew of workers for a month. To eliminate this bottleneck, Ford designed a

Ford Model T, 1910
(From the collections
of The Henry Ford,
P.833.10187)

largely automated process that dipped body panels in vats of enamel and conveyed them through baking ovens, completing the finish in a few hours. But the high temperatures in the ovens changed all pigments except black, leading Ford to discontinue all other Model T colors. Mass producers were also forced to design bodies with predominately flat panels, for curved parts tended to stick in the dies of the metal presses used to stamp them out in the millions. Finally, the careful hand-assembly of body parts was eliminated in favor of the mechanical processes of welding and riveting, which could be accomplished quickly along speeding assembly lines. To ensure that mass-produced cars met these demands of mass production, their design was taken away from bodybuilding craft workers, who followed long-held aesthetic traditions, and given over to body engineers, whose detailed blueprints were dictated solely by the utilitarian criterion of cost-cutting, mechanical production. Consequently, mass-produced cars like the Model T had a distinctly plain, rectilinear, fragmented look. The flat panels and parts were quickly slapped together at right angles with little attention to joints and cracks. These cars thus bore direct testimony to a fragmented, mechanical labor process, in which human labor was rigidly controlled and standardized in the name of profit-producing efficiency.[34]

Fordist mass production had a direct impact not only on the design of cars flowing out of factories in the millions, but also on the design of these factories themselves. As we saw above, the design of factories and other commercial buildings were altered in the late nineteenth century by the cost-cutting use of standardized industrial materials assembled with increasingly unskilled labor. But the rise of mass production early in the twentieth century further revolutionized factory construction to render it congruent with the revolutionary production imperatives. Between 1902 and 1906 pioneering American industrial architects like Ernest Ransome (1844–1917) and Albert Kahn replaced brick pier and glass in-fill construction with the concrete-framed factory. Kahn partnered with his engineer brother Julius, who invented a bar truss system for reinforced concrete, to build innovative factories for automakers, such as Packard's plant No. 10 (1905) and Ford's Highland Park (1910), the birthplace of mass production. Two cost-cutting imperatives of mass production favored this new type of construction—the efficiency of factory construction and the efficiency of factory production. First, factories with reinforced-concrete frames were quicker and cheaper to construct than those with brick-pier frames. Especially when assembled from precast, standardized components, concrete frames required fewer skilled trades and yielded substantial savings. Second, the strength of reinforced concrete allowed for longer spans between supports, thus maximizing the sunlight flowing into the building and the work flowing through the building, both of which increased production. Mass production demanded above all a rapid, unimpeded flow of production past closely spaced work stations. The open, unobstructed interior space of the concrete-framed factory allowed for the close packing of workers and machines and the free flow of work between them along production and assembly lines.

Kahn was largely responsible for developing this new architecture of mass production in his work for the pioneer of this production technique, the Ford Motor Company. What he achieved in his two great works for Ford, the Highland Park plant and the River Rouge plant (begun 1916), was nothing less than the completion of the rationalization of space begun by the Chicago School. Here architecture became nothing more than a means to an external end, an instrument for the efficient production of cars and ultimately profit, with no regard whatsoever for aesthetics, human accommodation, or the natural landscape. Thus, the Highland Park plant was a massive, rectilinear concrete frame with glass in-fill whose structure was dictated solely by the sequential flow of work functions in the production process. Ford specified the space requirements and order of the production process, and Kahn merely designed a functional container for it. The building was a four-story, glass-and-concrete conduit for work—production began on the top floor, to which raw materials were hoisted from rail lines, and flowed down through chutes and conveyors to the bottom, where the finished Model T emerged. But a few years after its completion even this empty, snaking conduit for capital flows proved too restrictive. The incessant, expansive changes Ford made in its production process to squeeze the last drop of surplus value out of men and machines soon

Albert Kahn, Original Building, Ford Motor Company, Highland Park, Illinois, 1910 (From the collections of The Henry Ford, P.188.5258)

encroached on walls and floors, necessitating constant cutting and gouging through concrete. With the irresistible force of a mighty river, the powerful production flows cut a path of least resistance through man-made stone, creating their own space. It became clear to Ford and Kahn that mass production required not specialized space for particular purposes but flexible space infinitely expandable and adaptable to any purpose. Thus, merely three years after completing a new, six-story building at Highland Park, Kahn began construction on the River Rouge, Ford's massive production complex on a sprawling suburban site remote from the congestion of downtown Detroit. There Kahn built Ford a single-story, steel-framed work shed that was infinitely expandable in all directions, allowing production flows to meander and seek their own paths on the flat landscape. An additional advantage of the site was its ability to connect production flows with the supply flows of raw materials from around the globe through the deep-water port Ford built on the River Rouge. Once materials like rubber, iron, coal, and lumber arrived at the Rouge by ship or rail, they flowed smoothly and incessantly through the empty, flexible space of the sheds until completed cars rolled out the other end. Since the spatial organization of flows was the quintessential characteristic of mass production, one could say that Kahn's factories for Ford were themselves production machines—work was done not in them, but by and through them.[35]

These open, flowing, transparent factories of concrete or steel and glass were also places of a new kind of power, exercised by and through spatial organization. The transparency and continuity of space within them facilitated the surveillance of workers and enforcement of work pace by the new managerial/technical class of Fordism. The very concentration of masses of workers in open space made it easy for supervisors to oversee their work. And because every worker was tied to a particular position in the flow, anyone out of place was easily detected. Finally, the closely spaced and timed flows of production enforced a uniformly high pace of work and made immediately visible any "shirkers" or recalcitrant workers. As two engineering journalists wrote of the introduction of production lines in Ford's Highland Park plant: "the floor was cleared, and all the straw boss had to do to locate the shirk or operation tools in fault was to glance along the line and see where the roll-way was filled up." This timed and coordinated flow of work was conceptually created by the new managerial class in the flowcharts of engineers and inventory records of accountants. But to achieve the desired control, these abstract symbols had to be translated into real spaces of surveillance—transparent, open spaces created by the new industrial architecture.[36]

As we will see in the second part of this chapter, this new architecture of mass production pioneered in America was a crucial influence on the modernist machine aesthetic created by European architects. Yet in the United States, these innovative factories had little impact on the broader profession of architecture. That is to say, these mass-production factories did not stimulate an *aesthetic*, with a symbolic significance in and for itself, beyond the mere utility of their spaces for efficient production. One reason for this, as Reyner Banham has suggested, is that these buildings and their architects were remote from the metropolitan centers of architecture like New York and Chicago, where competition for professional status was based on innovations in formal beauty for the cultured, not concrete utility for businessmen. These industrial architects were located in provincial industrial towns like Detroit and Buffalo, where success was measured in the number and worth of commissions from industrial clients who had no use for beauty, at least in their businesses. For their residences they may have commissioned a local Beaux-Arts architect to erect a castle that displayed their wealth and impressed the public, but in their factories they wanted nothing but cost-cutting utility, and that's what industrial architects like Kahn gave them. These industrial buildings produced a new *look* that was prominent in the landscape, but it was not a consciously cultivated look, created in and for itself. Kahn and other industrial architects did not themselves value this look, as demonstrated by their tendency when designing spaces for public consumption, not private production, to hide their innovative construction under a veneer of traditional decoration. For example, in the back of his first building at Highland Park Kahn baldly displayed the concrete frame, but on the public face of the factory along Woodward Avenue he timidly concealed it with brick cladding and decorative tiles, and broke up the monotony of its repetitive bays with a modillion cornice and turrets with ornate crestings. And when he designed homes for the pioneers of mass production, he disguised the brutal efficiency and power of the factories in which their money was made with the preindustrial craftwork of historical styles, as in the English Gothic mansion Kahn built in Grosse Pointe for Ford's son Edsel.[37]

The look of mass production that emerged in cars and factories did stimulate an aesthetic in some fields of American high art, especially photography and painting. Photographers like Alfred Stieglitz and Paul Strand created a modern aesthetic in their stark, cropped photographs of mass-produced cars. And precisionist painter and photographer Charles Sheeler aesthetically validated Ford's River Rouge plant in a series of paintings and photographs portraying its machines and buildings as manifestations of a new, harmonious order of civilization. Why, then, did not this aesthetic spill over into the art of architecture in America? As we have seen, the new middle class initially embraced just such an architectural aesthetic of simplicity and functionality to symbolize their rational, scientific knowledge in the Progressive movement for power and recognition. But they increasingly abandoned this aristocratic ascet-icism as they were integrated into mass-production corporations. They did so not merely because they no longer had a political need for it, but also because they confronted in their new corporate homes another struggling class whose aesthetic needs contradicted it, the working class of mass production. Workers contested the power of the new managerial/technical class, which conceded higher wages and benefits to compensate them for their lost workplace power. These concessions inadvertently added to the emerging mass market millions of new working-class consumers, who exercised their marketplace power to demand a new aesthetic of entertainment and obfuscation. Both automobiles and architecture became part of this mass market and were forced to march to the aesthetic drumbeat of the consumer dollar.[38]

Like early victims of capitalist attempts to rationalize industrial labor in the Progressive Era, auto workers at Ford and other companies did not supinely accept the new methods of mass production. From the beginning they resisted, at first through individual forms like turnover and absenteeism, but increas-ingly through collective efforts at organization. Shortly after Ford introduced the moving assembly line in 1913, his company and other Detroit automak-ers were rocked by a unionization drive mounted by the anarcho-syndicalist Industrial Workers of the World that challenged the entire mass-production regime with radical demands for worker control. Unwilling to concede such control, Ford and others offered workers concessions in consumption that left intact the balance of class power in production. With a dramatic announce-ment early in 1914, Henry Ford introduced his Five Dollar Day program, which doubled the average daily wage of most of his workers. He thus offered to inte-grate his workers into the culture of therapeutic consumption pioneered by the upper and middle classes in return for their acquiescence to the new methods of mass production.

Ford realized, however, that only a specific type of consumption was com-patible with the workplace subordination that he sought. The increased wages had to support a privatized, rationalized realm of consumption in the home that complemented and compensated for the rationalized work in the Fordist factory. In Ford's own words, the Five Dollar Day served as an "incentive to bet-ter living…a man who is living aright will do his work aright." To enforce this connection between production and consumption behavior, Ford recruited another contingent of the Progressive new middle class, the "helping" or social professions, to assist his engineers, technicians, and managers. He formed the Sociological Department and staffed it with social workers, ministers, psychologists, and others to investigate the private lives of his workers and certify them fit for the new wage. Through these cajoling intrusions, Ford encouraged workers to abandon their collectivist culture of tenements, saloons, and ethnic organizations for a life of privatized consumption of durable goods in single-family homes. Such consumption habits not only rendered workers dependent on their higher wages, thus discouraging quitting and recalcitrance, but also provided the recuperation required by the exhausting demands of mass production.[39]

Ford's efforts were part a wave of industrial reform in the period just before and after the First World War that ultimately incorporated more Progressive professionals into corporate bureaucracies. Large industrial employers sought to stabilize their work forces and head off the incipient revolt against new production methods by a variety of programs that went under the heading of welfare work. Through such programs employers like Ford sought to mold the leisure lives of workers to the bourgeois ideal of privatized, home-based consumption. Consequently, they and their Progressive allies focused on housing as central to the labor question. Ownership of a single-family home was believed not only to make workers dependent on their wages and discourage turnover but also to provide a safe place for socializing and entertainment, removed from the corrupting atmosphere of the saloon, movie house, and ethnic club. While some employers provided their workers with company-built housing, most merely facilitated home ownership through real-estate services, legal assistance, and low-interest loans. Reformers were not, however, content to stop at the threshold of the new worker-owned homes but intruded into the interior to instruct families in "American" standards of housekeeping, food preparation, and hygiene. Domestic reformers like Christine Frederick applied scientific management to the home, rationalizing the domestic tasks of reproduction in the same way that Ford and Taylor had rationalized factory production. Kitchens became one focus for domestic reformers, who sought to turn this room into a small, efficient factory for food preparation modeled on a steamship's galley. They also criticized the working-class practice of socializing in the kitchen, arguing for the removal of this family function to a separate parlor, in accordance with middle- and upper-class practice. In this and other ways the new middle class sought to separate and individualize family members and their functions. Although their ostensible concerns were the elimination of crowding, dirt, and disease, these "dangers" were merely metaphors for the perceived impurities of the working class and the contagion of class consciousness that these middle-class reformers feared.[40]

A crucial component of this program of reforming working-class consumption focused on domestic aesthetics. Progressive housing reformers argued that workers should be provided with suburban single-family retreats to escape from the urban ugliness of factory production. But these homes had to be smaller and more community-oriented than earlier suburbs. By the 1910s Progressive reformers had abandoned the radical style of the Prairie School for more historically based aesthetics, like their erstwhile Beaux-Arts enemies. But both groups agreed that the new century called for historical styles that were simple and avoided the ornately decorated, individualized Victorian dwellings. They also argued that these homes should be built in carefully planned communities, which would not merely reduce costs by allowing for standardization of design and construction but also instill a sense of order and discipline in residents. So architects and social scientists began collaborating to design large-scale, moderately priced developments of Tudor bungalows and Colonial Revival cottages. And to train workers to live and consume aright in their new houses, reformers pushed their domestic aesthetic of simplicity, efficiency, and hygiene on workers. Through settlement-house classes and welfare-work investigations they encouraged workers to buy unupholstered wood furniture in Mission and Craftsman styles instead of overstuffed and elaborately decorated Victorian pieces, and to rely on built-in storage units instead of ornate case pieces. Reformers also advocated wooden floors to replace dust-collecting carpets and rugs, and plain, painted walls to replace decorative wallpaper. Although most American workers accepted the middle-class ideal of the suburban home as an insulated retreat from the increasingly rationalized world of work, they rejected the reformers' aesthetic asceticism and molded their retreats to their own style. First, they obstinately resisted functional separation within the home. Even when their houses had parlors and dining rooms, working-class families continued to eat and socialize in the close conviviality of the kitchen. Unlike most middle-class people, who opened their homes to entertain professional and business acquaintances, workers entertained only close friends and family, and for them the kitchen was sufficient. Further, workers ignored the bourgeois advice to construct an antiseptic, functional interior, embracing instead a domestic aesthetic of decorative surfeits. Drawing upon the mass market for cheap, machine-made furnishings, they covered their floors with carpets, their windows with curtains, and their walls with elaborately decorated wallpaper. Rejecting built-ins, working-class families bought heavy case pieces like bureaus, chiffoniers, and buffets. Instead of simple Mission furniture, they acquired plush, upholstered chairs and sofas in the Victorian style once embraced by but now anathema to the middle class.[41]

In his sociology of taste, Bourdieu has argued that the working class has a socially ingrained preference for simple, functional goods that make no attempt at pretense or show. Workers' low economic capital is said to determine a habitus that inclines them to goods that merely meet material needs and swear off aesthetic form. But American workers' preference for elaborately decorated domestic goods during this period disproves Bourdieu's theory. Some historians, like Lizabeth Cohen, have suggested that this preference may be explained by the culture of workers' native countries in Southern and Eastern European, where such decorative excesses were symbolic of aristocratic status. But I believe that this aesthetic is more fully explained by workers' contemporary class position in America than by their cultural past. As the Frankfurt School's theory of mass culture has suggested, workers, like the new middle class, sought in consumer goods an escape and respite from the increasingly alienating and heteronomous workplace produced by Fordist rationalization. Unlike the new middle class, however, which exercised some discretion within the newly rationalized labor process, the working class was subjected to its full alienating force. Further, most workers still lived in cities near factories, being economically unable to seek refuge in the rural idyll of suburbia. For both reasons, they needed more symbolic insulation from the new workplace than did the new middle class, and they could not find it in the unadorned styles pressed on them by the latter. Even though preindustrial in origin, starkly simple historical styles looked too much like the niggardly efficiency of the mass-production factory to workers. As one design historian has written of working-class taste in mid-nineteenth-century Britain: "A plain, functional form generally signified the often harsh necessities of work, and as such was tolerated in its place, but art, in the form of decoration and ornament, presented for many people a deep aspiration for a better life." The domestic realm of consumption followed, in the words of another design historian, "the basic requirement that the environment should kill all associations with work." Working-class Americans thus demanded an aesthetic of obfuscation and decoration, in which reminders of the fragmented, standardized mass-production process was covered with varied, unified decoration in order to provide escape from industrial drudgery.[42]

The dynamics of the mass market ensured that this popular aesthetic would ultimately win out over the fading functionalism of the new middle class, as well as the renewed Beaux-Arts historicism. In the 1920s the wages of working Americans rose, and they became an increasingly important market for the products of mass-production industries. To sell goods to this expanding market, mass-production corporations were forced to eschew standardized, utilitarian goods in favor of products with the look of diversity and decoration. To supply this demand for aesthetic obfuscation, mass producers hired artistically trained designers, many of whom came from working-class and petty-bourgeois backgrounds. Thus, the profession of industrial design was born, and the industry most responsible for its gestation was automobiles.

As we have seen, the mass-produced Model T was the epitome of a simple, functional car, designed by engineers to accommodate cost-cutting techniques. Because of its cheapness and reliability, the car was widely revered during its twenty-year production, and became the object of an admiring folklore among Americans of modest means, including a growing number of workers. At the same time, however, the Model T was popularly regarded as an ugly car. Jokes sprang up to ridicule its undesirable aesthetic qualities. One asked why a Model T was like a mistress. The answer: because you hate to be seen on the streets with one. As car ownership became more common during the 1920s, consumers turned their attention away from utility and economy toward aesthetics, and the Model T was definitely lacking in this department. Earnest Elmo Calkins, a pioneering advertising agent, wrote that this car "did violence to the three senses, sight, hearing, and smell" and constituted an "intrusion of more ugliness into a world that was losing peace and silence and the beauty that inheres in old things." For Calkins and others, the utilitarian T was too reminiscent of the ugliness of standardized mass production to be acceptable, especially in comparison with the cars driven by the upper classes. In the 1920s the cheap, square, mass-produced cars shared the roads with the large, expensive craft-built cars like Packard, Cadillac, and Lincoln, whose carefully integrated, curvilinear forms testified to a life of luxury, unsullied by necessity or routine. By comparison, cars like the Model T connoted a degraded class position, a fragmented life dictated by mechanical and bureaucratic necessity, subject to the cost-cutting concerns of supervisors and assembly lines.[43]

As American consumers in the early twentieth century constructed a domestic refuge of consumption to shut out the unpleasant reminders of work, they began to demand cars that obscured the connotations of the mass-production factory. Market competition ensured that they got what they wanted. In the early 1920s Alfred Sloan, the new head of General Motors, was desperate to break Ford's dominating 50 percent share of the automobile market. Realizing that it was impossible to compete on the basis of price with Ford's awesome mass-production machine, he decided to tap the emerging demand for variety and style that obscured the standardized ugliness of the factory. Instead of offering one universal car for the masses, Sloan's GM began to market a variety of makes arrayed in a price hierarchy, thus providing consumers a sense of individuality in their purchases. In all its makes, from the cheapest to most expensive, GM tried to achieve a more unified, organic look that obscured mass-produced fragmentation and rectilinearity. This organic look, however, was achieved mainly in the surfaces of the body and did not extend to the fragmented functional parts beneath. Body parts and panels were carefully integrated, and all signs of assemblage were suppressed. And this more unified body was enlarged to cover over previously exposed functional parts like the gas tank, engine, and frame members. Further, to prevent these bodies from appearing too plain, decorative features like chrome strips and moldings were attached to the surface, giving consumers something to look at. GM also pioneered the use of inexpensive, fast-drying lacquer paints that added a variety of bright colors to the car body. Finally, to obscure the look of the unchanging standardization required by mass production, Sloan introduced the annual model change. Each year the models were changed slightly in appearance by altering the body surfaces and accessories, while the mass-produced parts underneath remained the same for decades to ensure economies of scale.

By giving consumers the variety, beauty, and change that offered escape from the standardized ugliness of mass production, Sloan dealt Ford a withering blow. By 1927 GM's Chevrolet was outselling the Model T, forcing Ford to concede to the market imperative for style. In this year he discontinued the T and introduced the more stylish and integrated Model A. Other automotive companies also rushed to compete in the new style game, but to do so required the addition of a new profession to their growing corporate bureaucracies, industrial designer. In the same year that he triumphed over Ford, Sloan created a new department at GM to implement his aesthetic policies, the Art and Color Section. To head this first styling department in the industry he hired Harley Earl (1893–1969), a Hollywood custom coachbuilder. Earl had grown up in his father's carriage shop building spectacular vehicles for the movies and their stars. He had learned early on to think of cars as entertainment for the masses, and Sloan sensed correctly that it was just such escapist fantasies that consumers wanted. To staff the new department, GM, like other automakers, hired just about anyone with artistic talent—coachbuilders, draftsmen, architects, interior decorators, advertising illustrators.[44]

In the 1920s this profession of industrial design exploded into prominence under the competitive pressures of the day. Most mass producers were facing markets nearing saturation, and many followed the auto industry's policy of distinguishing their products through appearance. The industrial designers recruited by companies to "style" products became so important to the economy that many like Raymond Loewy (1893–1986) and Norman Bel Geddes (1893–1958) became celebrities. And most in this new profession understood clearly what the public demanded of them. As American designer Paul Frankl (1886–1958) wrote, the task of the industrial designer was "the domestication of the Machine," that is, eliminating the fear people felt for machines and their products due to their incomprehensible complexity. The industrial designer's job was to obscure the complex mechanism with an "organic look" of simplicity and order, which, according to Frankl, could "cover up the complexity of the machine age...or at least divert our attention and allow us to feel ourselves master of the machine." To this end Frankl, Loewy, and others attached obscuring sheet-metal shells to refrigerators, stoves, and other appliances to make them acceptable in the domestic retreats of American consumers. And again following the auto stylists' lead, they tacked onto these obscuring surfaces differentiating color and ornament to hide the mechanical standardization underneath and give them the appearance of individuality.[45]

Slowly during this period, the majority of Americans with artistic training and aspirations were drawn into the large, mass-production corporations, just like the technical and social professions of the cultural bourgeoisie before them. This fact is well-illustrated by Sinclair Lewis's novel of 1922, *Babbitt*, a scathing critique of the American middle class and its business culture of this period. Babbitt owns a successful real estate firm but is proud to count among his friends a number of "intellectuals," with whom he gets along famously for they are businessmen too—a PhD economist who works as a publicity counsel for the streetcar company, a professor who teaches public speaking in his own business school, and a poet who writes advertising copy for everything from automobiles to tobacco. In one of his booster addresses to the local real estate board, Babbitt praises this peculiarly American integration of intellectuals into pecuniary business.

> In other countries, art and literature are left to a lot of shabby bums living in attics and feeding on booze and spaghetti, but in America the successful writer

or picture-painter is indistinguishable from any other decent business man; and I, for one, am only too glad that the man who has the rare skill to season his message with interesting reading matter and who shows both purpose and pep in handling his literary wares has a chance to drag down his fifty thousand bucks a year, to mingle with the biggest executives on terms of perfect equality, and to show as big a house and as swell a car as any Captain of Industry.[46]

In Bourdieu's terms, most American artists came to be employed in the large-scale or mass subfield of cultural production, where the goal of making economic profits forced them to cater to the demands of the masses of consumers. Consequently, they lost—or more likely, never experienced—the autonomy that Bourdieu argues comes from a position in the restricted or high-art subfield of cultural production, where the goal is making not economic but symbolic profits, that is, receiving recognition from other artists on the basis of strictly aesthetic criteria. In the large-scale subfield, the new industrial designers, ad illustrators, copywriters, and others were compelled to abandon any remaining allegiance they might have felt to a functionalist aesthetic and meet the popular demand for obscuring ornamentation. But like the technical professions of their class, the very employment of these artists by corporations undermined their *need* to assert an opposition to the economic bourgeoisie through a distinctive aesthetic symbolizing their cultural capital, for they were also acquiring more economic capital. Thus, the integration of the majority of the cultural bourgeoisie and, increasingly, the working class into the economic bourgeoisie's system of Fordist mass production and mass consumption resulted in the blurring of the class-distinctive aesthetics postulated by Bourdieu, and the rise of a broadly shared aesthetic of mass consumption of the type postulated by the Frankfurt school.[47]

The Architecture of Mass Consumption

The mass-consumption aesthetic of insulation, obfuscation, and decoration began to spill over from manufactured goods into the built environment during this same period, for architecture was not immune to the enticements of the emerging mass market. As a cultural field, the art of architecture is inherently hybrid in nature. It has one foot firmly planted in the high-art subfield of culture, with its autonomous aesthetic standards and traditions defining the worth of a practitioner's efforts. Yet architecture has its other foot in the mass subfield of culture, where the economic profit of a work is the standard of evaluation. A building is an expensive material product that requires for its realization substantial economic resources that must, in a capitalist society anyway, be compensated by those consuming the building. The emergence of the mass market in America provided even architects in the high-art subfield with new sources of capital to realize their designs. But with these economic opportunities came the aesthetic stricture of accommodating the demands of the masses for escape from and compensation for their increasingly rationalized and heteronomous work lives. The result was a uniquely American style of architecture that was neither functionalist nor historicist, the aesthetic poles that defined the European field.[48]

As we saw above, Chicago-style modernism was already in retreat by the beginning of the twentieth century, displaced by the rising popularity of Beaux-Arts classicism, which had been dominant in New York for years. It was in this city that the collision of this tradition of classicism with the demands of the emerging mass culture produced the architectural aesthetic of mass consumption. While Sullivan, Wright, and other Chicago architects were pioneering a new aesthetic for the steel-framed tall building in the late nineteenth century, New York architects, who were their rivals in technical innovations, wrapped their new skyscrapers in old forms of Renaissance and Romanesque derivation. This aesthetic was determined in part by their main clients, banks and insurance companies, which sought to project to their generally upper-class customers an image of security, stability, and established wealth. The historical forms of these tall buildings connoted endurance and heritage by hiding innovative technology under layers of obscuring ornamentation. The pioneering metal-grid construction was buried under stone and terra-cotta cladding, and the exciting new heights were suppressed by accentuating the horizontal dimension with belt courses, cornices, and a classical tripartite division.[49]

By 1910, however, this staid tradition of classicism seemed out of step with the emerging Fordist America. The serene symmetry of these Beaux-Arts skyscrapers did not express the dynamic growth and progress that the economy evidenced. Nor did their elitist pretensions capture the increasingly mass nature of American production and consumption. There was, however, one part of America's built environment that did reflect the exuberant escapism of the emerging mass-consumption society—the empires of entertainment built by cultural entrepreneurs to capture the rising income of working Americans. Opulent movie theaters arose in many cities, decorated in a wild pastiche of historical styles and patronized mainly by working-class people. Both the architecture and the films of these movie houses constructed a temporary dream world in which workers could escape the everyday monotony of their rationalized work and the rectilinear urban grid that symbolized it. But probably more important in pioneering the new entertainment aesthetic in architecture were the amusement parks that were emerging in the open land on the edges of urban America. Many of these parks were built by urban streetcar companies at the end of their lines to stimulate pleasure-riding. Chicago had its Riverside; Memphis, its Fairgrounds and East End Park; and Oakland, its Idora Park. But the model for all suburban amusement parks was Manhattan's Coney Island. This sandy spit of land at the mouth of New York's harbor had served in the mid-1800s as a nature retreat for Manhattan's upper class. But by 1883 the Brooklyn Bridge was bringing the working masses to the island, transforming it into their own image of fantastic escape from the city. Here the entertainment entrepreneurs gave the masses not soothing nature but otherworldly exhilaration, which was offered in the main attractions as well as the architecture. At his Luna Park, built in 1903, architect Frederic Thompson (1873–1919) treated visitors to a simulated lunar surface occupied by fantastic, randomly placed towers in a dizzy mélange of oriental, classical, and Renaissance styles.[50] Although he used historical styles, Thompson, a drop-out from architecture school, defied the order and symmetry of the Beaux-Arts school to create a wildly disorienting dreamscape that stimulated the imagination and obliterated unpleasant earthly realities. A year later another park was built on Coney Island that baldly admitted its escapist intent, Dreamland. This park offered a wide array of manufactured spectacles, most of which were staged in fantastic towers, domes, and globes. The crown jewel of Dreamland was Beacon Tower, a 375-foot observation tower with a powerful search light that soared above all but one of Manhattan's skyscrapers, advertising an escape route from the latter's ubiquitous grid. While elaborately decorated in regional and period styles, these structures had as their main function to erase any sight or memory of the city, leaving visitors with a tabula rasa on which to inscribe the compensating spectacles.[51]

Just like the entertaining domestic aesthetic that working Americans enjoyed, Coney Island's fantastically decorated insulation from urban capitalism quickly ran afoul of Progressive reformers. Appalled by the cheap wooden construction and monstrous diversity of fantastic buildings, the middle-class humanitarians demanded that the island be turned into a natural park, their own idea of escape. This effort was part of a larger parks-and-playground movement during this period aimed at controlling the disorder and degeneracy of working-class leisure. Seeking to impose their own therapeutic ethos on the masses, the moral crusaders advocated constructing scenic parks where common people could be refreshed by the contemplation of nature and engage in the type of structured and disciplined play that supported rationalized work. Ironically, however, instead of the new middle class's sober and rationalized aesthetic infiltrating the entertainment enclaves of the masses, the aesthetic of the latter spread to engulf the architecture of the city itself, as urban areas became the home of commercialized mass culture and the corporations that produced it.[52]

In the early years of the twentieth century, mass entertainment venues began to move to the city, in closer proximity to the consuming masses. In New York, Madison Square Garden, Frederic Thompson's Hippodrome, and other buildings appeared to house Coney-Island-type spectacles. The growing corporations that produced and sold the commodities of mass culture also began to build prominent headquarter buildings in cities, not merely to provide office space but also to symbolize and advertise their products. In Manhattan, the demand of mass-production corporations for commercial space and attention-grabbing trademarks pushed skyscrapers to soaring heights in a brash competition for symbolic prominence. The newly rich heads of these corporations knew that the design of their buildings, as well as their products, had to cater to the tastes of their consumers, more and more of whom were working-class Americans. Unlike the wealthy clients of banks and insurance companies, these consumers craved excitement and stimulation, not the staid serenity and stability of bourgeois culture. Yet, at the same time these powerful corporations did not want to seem *too* commercial, to be driven solely and selfishly by pecuniary gain. In the early twentieth century they were still under attack by Progressive reformers, who criticized corporate abuses and advocated the regulation of business to ensure the public good. Consequently, mass-production corporations also wanted to appear civic-minded, the repositories of nonpecuniary, spiritual values that transcended crass commercialism, or, as Bourdieu would put it, to express a distance from economic necessity that conferred on them distinction. By so doing, they could position themselves as the enlightened and benevolent elite of a new society of consumer democracy. The challenge of architects, especially those in New York, during the first two decades of the twentieth century was to find a style that reconciled these imperatives of mass exuberance and disinterested civic responsibility.[53]

Initial efforts to find a form for the soaring new skyscrapers seemed to borrow from Coney Island's fantastic architecture. For example, when the Singer company, mass-producer of sewing machines and other appliances, decided to expand its New York headquarters, architect Ernest Flagg (1857–1947) placed on top of the existing fourteen-story block a narrow tower that soared thirty-two stories and culminated in a domed roof topped with a beacon, reminiscent of Dreamland's Beacon Tower. But this audacious grab for commercial attention, completed in 1908, was clothed in a heavily ornamented and pretentious Beaux-Arts style, making the building look like a gorilla in a tuxedo. Although the Singer Tower soared to record-breaking heights, its horizontal divisions deflated the vertical dimension and tamed its excitement. And the clear visibility of the identical windows in the tower, which were dictated by the economics of rental space, made the building *look* commercial, like an efficient agglomeration of standardized units that, like the standardized Model T, symbolized in the public mind the rationalized work of the Fordist corporation. The next great monument to mass production in Manhattan, however, pointed toward an aesthetic reconciliation of mass excitement and elite distinction. The Woolworth Building of 1913, designed by Cass Gilbert (1859–1934), was a conscious attempt by the retailer to top the Singer Tower and create an upscale image for its downscale five-and-ten-cent stores. But in this 792-foot building with a soaring central tower reminiscent of Singer, Gilbert abandoned the serene horizontality of the Beaux-Arts style for the soaring verticality of the Gothic, at the request of F. W. Woolworth himself. Dubbed the "Cathedral of Commerce" for its resemblance to a medieval

Cass Gilbert, Woolworth
Building, New York, 1913
(Archive Timothy McCarthy/
Art Resource, NY)

church, the Woolworth Building blended the excitement of mass consumption with the higher values of spirituality. The excitement was in the bold celebration of height, which was accentuated by continuous piers and mullions that ran up the structure and were interrupted only by the jagged staccato of the four setbacks. These vertical elements stood out in front of the numerous windows, which seemed to disappear into their depths, suppressing the standardized openings and floors. Thus, these repetitive elements, which could dampen the excitement of consumption with reminders of rationalized production, were rendered invisible. The spirituality of the building was the transcending beauty and religious connotations of its Gothic ornament. During this period, American intellectuals like Henry Adams and Ralph Adams Cram popularized John Ruskin's idea that the Gothic style represented spiritual values that were antithetical to the rampant mechanization and industrialization of the day. By combining in this skyscraper mechanical excitement with spiritual transcendence, the corporate elite suggested that commercialism and spirituality could be reconciled in a society unified by a cultured, benevolent elite.[54]

Over the next two decades, the Gothic skyscraper gained increasing popularity. But in the process it was slowly stripped of its historical ornament and transformed into an unabashedly modern aesthetic that created excitement in the overall form of the building. Several forces were at work in this transformation, not the least of which was economic. These tall buildings were very expensive to build, and the market for rental space in them was very competitive. There thus emerged a tendency to save money by eliminating nonessentials like superficial decoration. Besides, as buildings rose higher and higher, only the biggest and boldest exterior decoration was visible past the first few floors. Consequently, economics exerted pressure to achieve distinction in overall form, not tacked-on decoration. This pressure was increased by an important political force, the New York zoning law of 1916. Shaped by a public increasingly critical of the congestion and lack of fresh air and light created by the close packing of skyscrapers on Manhattan Island, the ordinance mandated that at a certain height buildings had to step back from the plot line at an angle determined by a line extending diagonally from the street's center. The height of buildings was unlimited, as long as they covered only 25 percent of the site. The zoning law thus popularized the bold setbacks evidenced in the Woolworth Building, and architects quickly embraced their expressive potential, for their zagged edges seemed to capture the exciting, staccato rhythms of jazz music and urban life in America in the 1920s.

Finally, the aesthetic trend toward overall sculptural form was furthered in architecture, as in automobiles, by the necessity of obscuring the increasing rationalization of production. During the 1910s and 1920s, economics drove the construction of office buildings toward standardization and mechanization. To save design and construction costs, all of the office floors were exactly alike—standardized, mass-produced units replicated story after story to the top. And they generally appeared as standardized units from the exterior as well. The window openings that marked each floor were numerous, evenly spaced, and identical in number and size, and this was not merely to allow for mass production and create aesthetic unity. Lots of small, similar windows also allowed the interior to be quickly divided and redivided by nonbearing partitions to accommodate diverse and changing tenants. All these identical openings on identical floors stacked one atop another to the heavens not only connoted the standardization of these building themselves but also the standardization and rationalization of the work being done in them. But, as I have argued, it was just this look of standardized, monotonous mass production that the working masses were rejecting as an aesthetic in their consumer goods, including automobiles, for it was a reminder of the degraded work that they were seeking to escape in consumption. Thus, if the moguls of mass production wanted advertisements that attracted the favorable attention of the working masses to whom they sold their goods, they would have to obscure this look. The auto designers were already pointing the way in the early 1920s, as they hid their standardized parts under a unified and obscuring body. Under similar pressures from mass-production corporations, increasingly their main clients, American architects followed.[55]

The architectural aesthetic that emerged at the New York conjuncture of these forces was called, variously, moderne, modernistic, and art deco. All denoted, however, the same stepped-back, upward thrusting, tall building with minimal historical decoration. The overriding concern of the new style was to create an aesthetic unity to obscure the fragments of production. To obscure the disunity of the standardized stacked floors, the exteriors of these buildings displayed a unifying sculptural form. Instead of displaying the functions and structure of the interior, in accordance with Sullivan's functionalist doctrine, the exterior of the moderne skyscraper was a facade for disguising the interior, creating a disjuncture or forgetting between inside and outside that Rem Koolhaas has called "the Great Lobotomy." In his pioneering design of the Barclay-Vesey Building for the New York Telephone Company (1926), architect Ralph Walker (1889–1973) established an obscuring idiom that would

Ralph Walker, Barclay-Vesey
Building, New York, 1926
(Reprinted from Le Corbusier,
Toward a New Architecture, trans.
Frederick Etchells. New York:
Dover, 1986, ii)

become standard in the moderne style. Borrowing from the Gothic vocabulary of Gilbert's Woolworth Building, he disguised the separate floors by a series of continuous piers, separated by recessed spandrels, that ran up the entire height of the building. This device, along with the separate towers placed on the legally mandated setbacks, gave the whole composition a unifying upward thrust, just as the continuous, horizontal body moldings on cars unified and obscured the separate body panels and gave the vehicle a forward thrust. Although much less decorated than the Woolworth, Walker's massive skyscraper did have some simplified Gothic ornament at the crests of the setbacks, as well as naturalistic art nouveau embellishments on the interior to relieve the rectilinearity. Lewis Mumford wrote that this "decoration is an audacious compensation for the rigor and mechanical fidelity of the rest of the building; like jazz, it interrupts and relieves the tedium of too strenuous mechanical activity."[56]

Another pioneer of the moderne style was Raymond Hood (1881–1934), a New York architect with Beaux-Arts training who rose from obscurity to prominence in the profession by collaborating with John Mead Howells (1868–1959) on the winning entry in the Chicago Tribune Tower competition of 1922. Completed in 1925, this Gothic-style building had a shaft of upthrusting piers and mullions that unified the form and obscured the floor and window divisions. But the sculptural unity was disrupted by the tiered crown of elaborate Gothic ornament, including nonfunctional flying buttresses. However, in Hood's next major commission, New York's American Radiator

William Van Alen, Chrysler Building, New York, 1930 (Archive Timothy McCarthy/ Art Resource, NY)

Building of 1924, he moved toward the lobotomized moderne. In what seemed an intentional effort to conceal the dark window openings that testified to the separate floors, he used black brick in the continuous piers. The Gothic ornament on American Radiator was less elaborate than that on the Tribune Tower, and half-heartedly two-dimensional, as if a parody of itself. And Hood rendered this ornament not in serious stone but in glitzy gold in a gaudy attempt to simulate and advertise the company's product, automobile radiators, which during this period were usually framed in bright brass. Another skyscraper-cum-advertisement for an automobile corporation was the Chrysler Building (1930), designed by William Van Alen (1882–1954) as a publicity vehicle for the Chrysler Corporation in the spectacular skyline of Manhattan. Van Alen also gave this skyscraper a metallic crown to attract attention, but unlike Hood's historical ornament the Chrysler crown was insistently modern. The six-story, stainless-steel spire, with its six gleaming arches punctured by triangular windows, was abstractly reminiscent of curving auto forms and bright chrome trim, and also helped relieve the monotonous rectilinearity of its seventy-one other stories. At the thirty-first floor, however, the auto symbolism was more literal. A brickwork frieze depicted wheels, hubcaps, and fenders, and the abstract chrome eagles that projected from this floor resembled the Chrysler radiator ornament. In the lobby of the Chrysler Building, murals portrayed automobiles, dirigibles, and airplanes in a paean to the brave new world ushered in by mass-produced transportation. No signs of Fordist machines or assembly lines were in evidence, however, so as not to interrupt this dream of consumer freedom with cruel reminders of the heteronomy of production.[57]

The culmination of America's moderne style was Rockefeller Center, in which concealment and lobotomy spilled beyond the individual building to become the scheme for urban planning on a monumental scale. In a 1927 essay Hood had already proposed rebuilding Manhattan as a "city of towers," conceiving the island as a forest of freestanding needles separated only by sufficient space for the circulation of light, air, and traffic. This became the theory behind Rockefeller Center, but only after the collapse of the initial elitist scheme under the economic exigencies of the mass market. The project began as a new building for the Metropolitan Opera, but it was quickly discovered that such a high-culture venue could not pay for itself on Manhattan's expensive real estate. This caused the opera's architect, Benjamin Wistar Morris (1870–1944), to expand the project to a three-block complex that included enough commercial space to make the opera house financially feasible. In 1928 he designed a strictly symmetrical Beaux-Arts composition, placing the opera at the end of a long plaza

Hood, Godley & Fouilhoux;
Reinhard & Hofmeister;
Corbett, Harrison & MacMurray,
RCA Building, Rockefeller
Center, New York, 1932
(Library of Congress, Prints and
Photographs Division, Gottscho-
Schleisner Collection, LC-G612-
T-21012-AX)

flanked by four skyscrapers and two longer, lower buildings. The commercial space in these latter buildings would generate the dirty cash to support the pure, disinterested cultural activity.

But even this cultural mongrel was financially unviable in Manhattan's ruthlessly pecuniary grid, causing John D. Rockefeller Jr. to step in and reformulate the project into an unrepentant Mecca of consumer culture, "a commercial center," explained *Fortune* magazine, "as beautiful as possible consistent with a maximum of income." The opera house of high culture was excised entirely, and the Beaux-Arts serenity of the symmetrical plaza was slashed by the insertion of a huge office shaft leased to the giant of mass communication, Radio Corporation of America (RCA). To disguise this capitalist engine of profit and render it acceptable to the consuming masses, Rockefeller brought in the master of the lobotomy, Raymond Hood. Just as automakers used a hood to cover the ugly mechanicals of the car, Rockefeller used a beautifying Hood to cover the ugly mechanicals of his real-estate engine.[58]

Hood and his team of architects designed for consumers a composition exemplifying the obscuring exuberance of America's consumer culture. The jazzy, jagged step-downs on the RCA slab expressed the expansive optimism of mass consumption, while masking the stacking of standardized floors that betrayed the homogenization and heteronomy underlying mass production. Further relieving the rigid rectilinearity were rooftop gardens on the lower buildings, bringing the organic dream of suburbia into the heart of the city, and the Gothic ornament that Rockefeller instructed the architects to attach atop the RCA slab. More innovative, however, than this obfuscation of the vertical grid of skyscraper floors was the masking of the horizontal grid of standardized blocks in this urban project. Because Rockefeller Center covered three blocks, the architects could offer a large, aesthetically unified composition that counteracted the fragmentation of the street grid. Instead of each block containing an aesthetically distinct monument to its private owner, like the rest of Manhattan, Rockefeller Center offered a unified urban composition that seemed to symbolize an urban public interest. The buildings were physically separate but united in style. The original plan also called for the ground level of all three blocks to be unified by a complex of five theaters that shared an enormous suspended lobby bridging 49th and 50th Streets. Eventually this complex was reduced to one venue for mass-produced spectacles disguising the realities of the Manhattan grid and the rest of Fordist America, the Radio City Music Hall.

This huge, mechanical complex for mass escape brought the fantastic technology of Coney Island downtown, promising urbanites that "a visit to Radio City Music Hall is as good as a month in the Country." Run by master showman Samuel Rothafel, or "Roxy," Radio City offered such narcotizing illusions as the famous Rockette dancers, whose plotless theatrical routines epitomized unthinking escapism. Such consumerist illusions came just in the nick of time, for between the conception of Rockefeller Center in 1928 and start of construction in 1931, America had been plunged into the depths of depression by an unequal consumption machine unable to absorb the goods of its production machine. The illusions of limitless consumerism were beginning to wear thin for many unemployed Americans, and thus required even thicker layers of obfuscation. Despite this, some Americans saw through the illusions, as revealed by the controversy over one of the decorations for Rockefeller Center.[59]

Intent, it seems, on injecting a bit of high culture into his mass-entertainment complex, Rockefeller commissioned artists to provide didactic murals and sculptures, most on themes of scientific and technological progress. In 1932 his son, Nelson Rockefeller, invited Pablo Picasso, Henri Matisse, and the Mexican muralist and communist Diego Rivera to provide works on the theme of "man at the crossroads" for the lobby of the RCA Building. Only Rivera accepted after lengthy negotiations with Hood and Rockefeller. His planned mural contained some optimistic images of technology and science, but also revealed some of the ugly results of their capitalist misuse in depictions of chemical warfare, exploited and unemployed workers, and a May Day demonstration. The furor that arose, however, centered on the portion of the mural portraying Lenin uniting the hands of a worker, a farmer, and a soldier. After viewing the portrait of the communist leader in the almost-finished mural, Nelson Rockefeller wrote to Rivera demanding its removal. When Rivera refused, he was ordered to stop work, paid in full, and then his mural was smashed off the wall. So the high-art cover for Rockefeller's capitalist real-estate venture came crashing down.[60]The aesthetic vicissitudes of Rockefeller Center epitomized the state of culture in America as it moved into the tumultuous years of the Depression. The country's capitalists still had some pretensions to high culture, which they used to legitimate their growing wealth by lending it an aura of disinterestedness. However, these pretensions were undermined by pressures from both the new middle and working classes. As part of a campaign to insinuate its technical knowledge into the political and economic institutions of America, the former challenged the aesthetic historicism of the upper classes, offering a simpler aesthetic praising technology and rationality. But from the beginning the machine modernism championed by these technocrats was softened by organic decoration. Their early incorporation into corporate America made a militant technocratic aesthetic unnecessary, and they escaped from the aesthetic consequences of their victory in soothing suburban retreats adorned by the look of nature. The working class was also a counter-force to the technocratic aesthetic. With increased wages wrested from large corporations, workers registered in the mass market their preference for decoration and obfuscation that hid the reminders of the mass-production factories in which they toiled. Both capitalist manufacturers and the professionals and managers that worked for them gave the masses what they wanted in order to make money, thus altering their own aesthetic preferences in the process. They put up little cultural resistance to this aesthetic of mass consumption, for neither class faced much of a challenge to its legitimacy. Capitalists faced no preexisting aristocracy and its traditional culture, and professionals and managers faced no entrenched capitalist opposition to their rationalizing project. The line-up of classes was different in Europe, however, giving rise to the paradox that this technologically backward continent pioneered a technocratic aesthetic that adulated the mass-produced machines that Americans had already rejected as an art exemplar.

Blocked Modernization and the European Technocratic Project

Arno Mayer's influential book, *The Persistence of the Old Regime*, provides an analysis of the line-up of class forces that produced Europe's unique modern movement. Unlike the United States, where the absence of an aristocratic order gave the modernizing industrial bourgeoisie a free rein, in Europe capitalists confronted an entrenched class of landed aristocrats intent on maintaining power and molding industrialization to their own designs. Economic production was still predominantly agricultural, and although industrialization had made major economic inroads, the majority of manufacturing concerns were small or midsized and craft-based, with only a few engaged in large-scale mass production. The antiquated class structure dictated that most goods were produced for high-income and export markets. The political order was also dominated by landed and public-service nobilities, who were adamant about retaining power and bending any parvenu bourgeois to their purposes. Legitimating the power of this Old Regime was a traditional culture entrenched in state-sponsored academies, conservatories, and universities, which promoted an academic historicism that established the pedigree and inevitability of the aristocratic order. By controlling school curricula, salaried appointments, and official subsidies, these cultural reactionaries ensured that any modernist challenges were weak.[61]

This entrenched opposition to modernization effectively blocked the development of an independent class of industrial capitalists. Instead of actively contesting the old order, bourgeois capitalists developed a symbiotic relationship with it. The aristocrats retained power and in return protected the economic interests of capital with government contracts, tariffs, and colonial preferments. The state also used its coercive apparatus to protect industrialists from the rising labor movement at home and rival powers abroad. Finally, the sons of the great bourgeois were admitted into the highest offices of state and civil service, provided that they passed through the certifying process of higher education, which inculcated them with the culture of the aristocracy. This dependency on the old order prevented industrialists from whole-heartedly pursuing not merely political liberalism and cultural modernism but also economic modernization. When the prolonged depression of 1873 to 1896 struck, instead of pursuing a program of rationalization as American industrialists did, European capitalists sought state aid and protection from foreign competition.[62]

This class of capitalists reluctant to modernize left the emerging professional-managerial class in a tenuous position. This bourgeois fraction dependent on its knowledge and technical expertise had been growing in Europe in the late nineteenth century, but its power and prestige lagged behind its counterpart in America. The culture of the Old Regime valued the classical knowledge of the leisured aristocracy and denigrated any knowledge connected to commercial or industrial pursuits. The established universities trained students in a classical curriculum and resisted modernization. Most countries were thus forced to open separate schools for the sciences and engineering. But their graduates were denigrated in the status order. So unlike their class counterparts in America, who were embraced by modernizing capitalists and incorporated into their programs of economic and political rationalization, the European new middle class was stunted and stigmatized.[63]

Blocked from a livelihood by the regressive economic and aesthetic policies of a supine bourgeoisie more intent on aping the lifestyles of the aristocracy than rationalizing its industries, the professional-managerial class developed a technocratic ideology to further its interests. Like Veblen and others in the United States, the propertyless intelligentsia in Europe railed against the dead weight of property and argued that salvation lay in reorganizing society around a ruling group of neutral professions, whose useful skills and knowledge would ensure progress for all. Such a technocratic ideology had a long history in Europe, dating back to the Restoration in France (1815–30), when Henri de Saint-Simon and Auguste Comte offered a vision of rule by a scientific elite to cut through class stalemate. This dream of a society organized by useful intelligence, not rank or property, gained momentum in early twentieth century Europe, and then exploded into prominence in the years after the First World War. This was a period of both great promise and grave threat in many European countries, but especially Germany. Across Eastern and Central Europe the political tumult in the wake of the war toppled the Old Regimes, creating the potential for liberal regimes and economic modernization. But this potential was accompanied by what the privileged classes saw as the new threat of a mobilized working class. In Germany, Russia, and Austria workers organized in socialist parties were instrumental in toppling the Old Regimes and gained substantial power in the new governments. In Germany, Social Democrat Friedrich Ebert was elected the first president of the Weimar Republic in 1919 and was immediately besieged by radical workers to his left and radical nationalists to his right. In such societies marked by tumultuous class struggle, rampant inflation, and mass unemployment, young representative governments seemed unable to restore order, and the technocratic program of the intelligentsia gained widespread appeal.

Promising escape from the zero-sum conflict of classes, engineers, psychologists, sociologists, and artists offered workers and capitalists alike a program of "rationalization," objective, scientific measures administered by professionals to create economic growth and prosperity for all. Beginning in 1925, with the stabilization of the currency and the rise of more moderate coalition governments, Germany became particularly enthralled with the promise of technocratic rationalization, or, as it was sometimes called, *Fordismus* (Fordism). Germans of all classes looked to America's combination of mass production and mass consumption as the solution to all problems. And its pioneer, Henry Ford, was widely viewed as the messiah of the modern world. Industrialists, trade-union officials, engineers, politicians, professors of sociology and psychology all made pilgrimages to America that invariably included a visit to Ford's Highland Park plant. They were all fascinated with the size, speed, and mechanization of the Ford factory, as well as its labor and marketing policies. Ford's book, *My Life and Work*, was also enormously popular in Germany, where it was read and admired by Social Democrats, Communists, and future Nazis like Adolf Hitler.[64]

Fordism or rationalization appealed to a broad range of groups because each laid hold of that specific part of the whole that served its interest. For the technical intelligentsia, industrial rationalization meant a program of technological efficiency and social engineering that brought them jobs and status. German industrialists showed little enthusiasm for the technological innovations of Fordism, for they believed these would be too expensive and create price competition that would undermine their protective cartels. Industrialists were, however, interested in attaining Fordism's high level of labor productivity, and argued that this was achieved mainly through increased work intensity, not technology. Fordism for industrialists, then, was an instrument with which to force workers to work harder. The Social Democratic and trade-union leaders of workers emphasized the mass-consumption side of Fordism, arguing that higher wages would increase consumption and create the volumes required for mass-production technology. Conversely, higher consumption would compensate workers for any loss of skill and control under Fordist technology. Further, because these leaders feared rank and file militancy, collaboration with industrialists to rationalize industry seemed safer to them than mobilizing workers to achieve change.[65]

Since capitalists were reluctant to pursue technological rationalization, the professional-managerial class saw as its best chance for success an alliance with Social Democratic politicians and trade unionists to push a state-sponsored program of industrial restructuring. So working-class leaders became the main champions of state programs that benefited largely capitalists and the new middle class. During this period, the Weimar state established eighty-five offices and sixty-seven research and testing institutes to work on problems related to rationalization. But most state funds and expertise were channeled through a network of six hundred private organizations, many of which were controlled by industrialists who used public money for their private interests. The result was a timid rationalization effort, which increased industrial efficiency but also created unemployment, de-skilling, and stagnant wages for the working class. But the professional-managerial class participated enthusiastically, and no part of it benefited more that the modern architects employed by the state to design the products and buildings of rationalized production.[66]

The Origins and Vicissitudes of Modern Architecture

During the interwar period in Europe, modern architecture became the aesthetic wing of the growing technocratic movement of educated professionals, managers, and technicians. The machine aesthetic developed by this new school of architecture and design was an unconscious attempt to aesthetically reconcile the era's social contradictions in the interests of this new class of technocrats. But this affinity between modern architecture and technocracy was not a predetermined inevitability but the contingent accomplishment of the struggles of this period—both the class struggles in the broader society and the aesthetic struggles within the architectural field.

The entire field of art in Europe was in a rather precarious position since at least the end of the nineteenth century. Due to the rise of a prosperous bourgeoisie and the spread of education, there had been an expansion of the market for cultural goods, drawing to this field an unprecedented number of new producers. Many of these were the educated children of the petty bourgeoisie and working class, who were denied administrative and professional positions by the domination of the aristocracy. The consequent crowding in the field of art intensified competition and encouraged aesthetic innovation in order to stand out and gain recognition. New styles and genres proliferated, many based on the class habitus of the newcomers. But just as the artistic field was expanding, its sources of support were contracting. The decline of full-blown feudalism had undermined the patronage artists formerly received from aristocrats, forcing them to rely on either the open market or state support. But both these sources became more tenuous in the early twentieth century. The prosperous bourgeoisie bought art that conformed to a narrow classicism endorsed by the Old Regime, and the state similarly supported a small coterie of artists ensconced in the academies and conservatories. Architecture was hit particularly hard by these changing circumstances. Artists whose work required meager resources to create—e.g. painters and writers—could practice while supporting themselves with other jobs and cultivating low-cost, bohemian markets for their work. But architects required substantial amounts of money to realize their buildings. Few beyond the aristocracy and the grand bourgeoisie could buy architecturally designed buildings, and both were supporting a narrow historicism that lent ancient legitimacy to new wealth. The state also patronized only a small group of neoclassical architects working in official art academies, such as France's École des Beaux-Arts.[67]

In such a stultifying climate for the arts, industry provided a glimmer of hope in the first years of the twentieth century. Like Louis Sullivan and Frank Lloyd Wright in America, the artists and architects of Europe were aware of the social problems caused by rapid industrialization, especially the fragmentation of work that tore crafts asunder and stripped workers of their skill and discretion. The result, they held, was not only misery for workers but also a plague of ugliness in industrial products and the landscape. These middle-class artists and architects believed, however, that such problems could be overcome by changing aesthetics rather than economic or social realities. They argued that artists could work within industry, accepting its technical realities but providing the aesthetic improvements to industrial goods that would mitigate industrial ugliness and improve sales. This would, of course, create a new avenue of employment for artists outside of the stultifying old order.

This program for allying art with industry was particularly strong in Germany, which was in the early twentieth century playing catch-up in the increasingly competitive industrial markets of Europe. Some nationalist politicians like Friedrich Naumann argued that German competitiveness depended upon merging art with industry to provide high-quality, artistically designed goods. To this end he and other officials joined with artists and industrialists to establish the Deutsche Werkbund in 1907. This attempt to blend art and industry was soon torn apart, however, by feuds among artists about how best to accomplish this task. Hermann Muthesius (1861–1927), an architect driven primarily by the economic exigencies of large-scale mass production, argued for eliminating individualistic design and decoration and creating standardized, functional types. His position was opposed by the expressionist wing of the Werkbund represented by Henry van de Velde (1863–1957) and Peter Behrens (1868–1940). They rejected the functional determination of style by technique and argued for individuality achieved by artistic expression. Van de Velde developed simple forms decorated with art nouveau ornamentation that closely paralleled the style of Sullivan in America. Behrens, head architect and designer for the German Electric Company (AEG), abjured the directly functional to wrap his buildings and objects in a style that used classical and other premodern elements to clothe the brutality of industrial function.[68]

Despite some limited successes, however, neither wing of the Werkbund was able to achieve much industrial patronage. The major obstacle was the fact that most European firms were not sufficiently large or rationalized to need the services of industrial designers. Up to and through the First World War manufacturing was dominated by small and midsized family enterprises staffed by skilled craftsmen. Design and production remained unitary, with the craftsmen adding the aesthetic touches that made their goods distinctive. Only the larger firms like AEG needed designers to lend style to mass-produced goods. And due to the traditional taste of the bourgeoisie, these designers usually wrapped their new goods in old styles.

This traditional bourgeois taste particularly rankled the struggling architects working in the modern idiom, who angrily pointed out the aesthetic discrepancy between the functional factories owned by the bourgeoisie and the historical styles of their domiciles. Adolf Loos (1870–1933), an Austrian architect who equated ornament with crime, satirized the bourgeois-dominated Ringstrasse in Vienna as a Potemkin village that placed an aristocratic facade on common burghers. Applying the economic calculus of factory production to their homes, he argued that "it is a crime against the national economy that it [ornament] should result in a waste of human labour, money, and material." Le Corbusier, the dean of the modern movement, wrote that big businessmen at work created "an accumulation of very beautiful things in which economic law reigns supreme." But "away from their businesses in their own homes... everything seems to contradict their real existence—rooms too small, a conglomeration of useless and disparate objects, and a sickening spirit reigning over so many shows—Aubusson, Salon d'Automne, styles of all sorts and absurd bric-a-brac."[69]

Thus, on the eve of the First World War, European architects who were seeking outlets for new styles forged in the competitive heat of an overcrowded field were in dire straits. They found few takers for their work in the Old Regimes, in which the bourgeoisie had forsaken its role of revolutionizing industry and looked to the cultural past to legitimate its lethargy. However, the ensuing world war destroyed these Old Regimes and, in the process,revolutionized the field of architecture by providing the modernists with important political allies. And these new alliances were strongest in the country that, apart from Russia, experienced the greatest postwar tumult: Germany.

The German revolution of 1918 toppled the Old Regime of the Hohen-zollerns and placed a left-wing government led by Social Democrats at the helm of the new Weimar Republic. Modern architects were enthusias-tic supporters of the revolution and the new regime, seeing the fall of the Old Regime as a devastating blow to its outmoded culture. Architects like Bruno Taut (1880–1938) and Walter Gropius (1883–1969) argued that the polit-ical revolution had to be completed with a spiritual revolution to create a new culture. Because the devastation of the war had created a disastrous housing shortage, they argued, architects would take the lead in constructing this new culture, building with a new aesthetic that would restore spiritual unity to soci-ety. To this end, artists in various cities formed radical "art soviets," the most important of which was the Arbeitsrat für Kunst (the Workers' Soviet for Art), organized by Taut and Gropius. Their aesthetic vision for the new culture was expressionistic, reflecting the optimism and exuberance of the era. Taut devel-oped an anarchistic plan for decentralizing cities based on glass architecture. Old urban centers would be broken up and their populations spread over the land in small communities supported by agriculture or handicrafts. The spiri-tual center of each community would be a crystal cathedral, a glass pavilion in prismatic shapes symbolizing openness and enlightenment. In such commu-nities a "socialism above politics" would be created, Taut argued, "the simple straight-forward relationship of men to one another [which] bridges over the gap between warring classes and nations and binds man to man." Thus, a spatial utopia created by architects would resolve all remaining social and polit-ical contradictions.[70]

Gropius, who became a leading figure in modern architecture, was simi-larly caught up in the utopian fervor of the revolution. But unlike Taut, his fer-vor was institutionalized in the foremost school of modernism, the Bauhaus. Established in 1919 by the Social Democratic government of the state of Saxe-Weimar, this school was initially the vehicle for Gropius's vision of spiritual unity through small-scale craft communities. Evoking Taut's idea of class unity through art, Gropius wrote in the founding proclamation of the Bauhaus: "Let us create a new guild of craftsmen, without the class distinctions which raise an arrogant barrier between craftsmen and artist. Together let us conceive and create the new building of the future, which will embrace architecture and sculpture and painting in one unity and which will rise one day toward heaven from the hands of a million workers like the crystal symbol of a new faith." The

Bauhaus curriculum required each student to study a craft as well as art, thus symbolizing the alliance of artists with workers that was the ambition of these architects in a period in which revolutionary hopes were high. The artistic output of the early Bauhaus conveyed this hope in expressionistic designs of sharp angles and dynamic movement.[71]

By 1922, however, the utopian enthusiasm of German architects was waning under the pressure of shifting economic and political winds. The devastating inflation and unemployment of this period dampened schemes for utopian communities funded by the state. And the political balance shifted back to the right, away from the ardent socialism of early Weimar toward moderate proposals for industrial rationalization. In this climate young German architects shifted their political strategy and their aesthetic to match. Taut and Gropius spoke less of worker-artist alliances and more of integrating art into industry. Rationalization and Fordism, not socialism, were now the solutions. Talk of egalitarian cooperation between classes was replaced by advocacy of a new hierarchical order in which architects and engineers benevolently ruled deskilled proletarians.[72]

This political shift toward technocracy was clear in a 1923 essay by Gropius, in which he defined the main purpose of the Bauhaus as "a reunion between creative artists and the industrial world." Gropius now declared that the skilled crafts could not be revived, for the mechanization and division of labor were destroying them and reducing workers to unskilled laborers. Artists, however, could now provide the skill and creativity required in the work force, becoming the new craftsmen "responsible for the speculative preliminary work in the production of industrial goods." Their creative work would ensure that products were designed for the most efficient methods, thus increasing productivity for capitalists. But workers would be compensated for their losses in skill and control with the lower prices and increased consumption that accompanied mass production. Industrial artists would also ensure that these mass-produced products that workers consumed in their homes would be beautiful, thus alleviating the disquieting ugliness of the machine age. Gropius declared that the role of the Bauhaus was now training these new craftsmen of industry, who would "avert mankind's enslavement by the machine by giving its products a content of reality and significance, and so saving the home from mechanistic anarchy." He thus proposed that artists join engineers and other industrial technicians to form a new industrial hierarchy to assist capitalists in rationalizing industry and subordinating workers. Under his leadership, the Bauhaus established contacts with industry, entered contracts to design industrial products, and placed students in factories to gain industrial experience.[73]

Gropius was representative of a trend among modern artists and intellectuals in Germany and other European countries away from revolutionary fervor of the immediate postwar period toward a sober recognition of the "harsh realities" of their times. This attitude became known as *Neue Sachlichkeit*, the new objectivity or matter-of-factness, and it was also prevalent among artists in Holland and Switzerland. It entailed a sober recognition of, even a resignation to, certain material facts of the age, such as scarcity, unemployment, and conflict. Such problems, it was believed, could be overcome not with class struggle and socialism but with material progress through rationalized production. The new objectivity was thus the artistic manifestation of the technocratic movements that were emerging across Europe in the mid-1920s. In the Soviet Union, a similar transition from revolutionary fervor to the hard task of industrializing a backward country produced a related artistic movement called productivism, which also embraced industrial technology and engineering. France was not in such dire economic straits as Germany or Russia, but it too felt the chilling mood of matter-of-factness, which manifested itself in the aesthetic movement of purism.[74]

The political shift of modern architects toward the technocratic project of the professional-managerial class and away from the socialism of the working class was not motivated by simple opportunism. Although this strategy was in their immediate economic interests, it was also engendered by these modern architects' underlying positions in both the class structure and the field of architecture. With respect to class structure, they shared a similar position vis-à-vis capitalists as the other professionals, managers, engineers, and technicians of the technocratic movement. All were occupations that depended on their cultural capital or knowledge for a livelihood, which united them in opposition to the industrialists, whose livelihood depended on economic capital or property ownership. Consequently, all had a similar class interest in changing the basis for distributing industrial power and wealth from property to knowledge. Their interests also determined an opposition to the working class, whose members' lack of cultural capital subordinated them to the educated and knowledgeable in cultural institutions and, if technocracy was successful, in economic institutions as well. However, modern architects' affinity with the cultural bourgeoisie's crusade for technocracy was also the result of their position in the cultural field of architecture. They were on the periphery of the field, low-status newcomers who were marginalized and dominated by an established elite of traditional architects working in historical styles. Thus, their position in the architectural field was homologous to the position of the cultural-bourgeois industrial professions in the industrial field—both were subordinated outsiders and newcomers. Bourdieu argues that such homologous field positions generate common outlooks and alliances between groups.[75]

This analysis, however, begs the larger question of how modern architects came to be positioned on the periphery of the field to begin with. Why did these newcomers not adopt the established style of the architectural elite, instead of pioneering a new style that consolidated their outsider position? The answers are found, as Bourdieu argues, in the class positions from which these architects originated and their consequent habitus. Many, though not all, modern architects came from working-class or petty-bourgeois backgrounds, which determined habitus that entailed peripheral status in the architectural field. Le Corbusier, for example, was the son of a watch-case engraver who worked in the shops of the Swiss watch-making town of La Chaux-de-Fonds. Ludwig Mies van der Rohe (1886–1969), another pioneer of modern architecture, was born in the German Rhineland to a humble mason. Although both were exposed early to the arts or architecture, their experiences were with the applied arts, instilling a habitus valuing the functional and practical. Their modest resources as well as their habitus disqualified them from the elite art academies, which privileged the formal over the functional. Le Corbusier was trained at his hometown École d'Art, a school for the technical trades of the watch industry. Mies briefly studied the building trades at a local trade school, but his real education came from the job site, where he assisted his father and other construction workers. European modern architects as a group were, like Americans Frank Lloyd Wright and Louis Sullivan, much more likely to study engineering than attend traditional art schools and academies. They also tended to apprentice with architects known more for their engineering and industrial achievements than their aesthetic innovations. Le Corbusier, Gropius, and Mies all apprenticed with Peter Behrens. Le Corbusier also learned much from his stay in the office of the French pioneer in reinforced concrete construction, Auguste Perret (1874–1954).[76]

The backgrounds and education of modern architects predisposed them to more practical and technical styles, privileging function over form. But their modernist inclinations were exacerbated by the heightened competition of the architectural field, which encouraged radical innovation to stand out in the crowd. Consequently, these newcomers to architecture pioneered a new style that, without intention, validated the technical knowledge of the professional-managerial class and also consigned them to the periphery of their field, a position homologous to the latter in industry. Modern architecture and technocracy were thus a match made in the social heaven of structural homologies. No architect better articulated these affinities than the rhetorical leader of the modern movement, Le Corbusier. Born in Switzerland as Charles-Edouard Jeanneret, this budding architect moved to Paris in 1917 and associated with avant-garde circles, changing his name in 1920. His book *Vers une Architecture*, published in 1923, legitimated with prophetic arguments the trend of European artists toward a technocratic alliance with the professional-managerial class around a program to rationalize industry. In a masterful ideological balancing act, he appealed simultaneously to workers, industrialists, and the new-middle-class intelligentsia to help architects construct a new society of mass production and consumption. Although his program was almost identical to that of Gropius in Germany, Le Corbusier's rhetorical and ideological deftness in presenting his vision of technocratic capitalism immediately made him the leader of the modern movement.

Le Corbusier's politics have often been characterized as socialistic, but even a cursory examination of *Vers une Architecture* reveals that he was seldom critical of big capitalist industry. Toward the end of the book he declared that "the majority of industry has been transformed: big business is today a healthy and moral organism.... [It has] created new tools...[that] are capable of adding to human welfare and of lightening human toil." Le Corbusier referred here to the new mass-production industries and their standardized, mechanized production methods. He heaped lavish praise on Frederick Taylor, Henry Ford, and other engineers who were responsible for these techniques that had the potential to liberate humankind. However, at the same time he praised capitalists, Le Corbusier also threatened them with an ultimatum on the behalf of his own profession: "Architecture or Revolution." Industrialization was, he argued, throwing society "out of gear." Tools which once were controlled by humans "have been entirely and formidably refashioned and for the time being are out of our grasp. The human animal stands breathless and panting before the tool that he cannot take hold of;...he feels himself to be the slave of a frantic state of things and experiences no sense of liberation or comfort or amelioration."[77]

Le Corbusier thus described aptly the alienation felt by mass-production workers, who were divorced from the objective products and processes of their own work. But, like Gropius and other modernists, he believed that this alienation could be resolved by aesthetic form, without changing the organization of production. Capitalist mass production needed only to be balanced with a new realm of mass consumption based in the home. "Man feels today that he must have intellectual diversion, relaxation for his body, and the physical culture needed to recuperate him after the tension of muscle or brain which his labour—'hard labour'—brings." Such diversion could only be had in safe, modern housing, which, Le Corbusier declared, was woefully scarce. The solution to this housing shortage that threatened to turn into revolutionary demands was architecture. "It is a question of building which is at the root of the social unrest of today: architecture or revolution." But not just any architecture would forestall revolution. Building clean, wholesome housing on a large scale required mass produced, standardized buildings "built on the same principles as the Ford car I bought." This rationalization of building required the guiding hand of architects who knew the requirements of mass production and could design "machines for living in." And Le Corbusier made it clear that his technocratic scheme would require not democracy but a despotism of professional knowledge. "The despot is the Plan, the correct, realistic, exact plan, the one that will provide your solution once the problem has been posited clearly, in its entirety, in its indispensable harmony. The Plan has been drawn up well away from the frenzy in the mayor's office or the town hall, from the cries of the electorate or the laments of society's victims. It has been drawn up by serene and lucid minds.... And this plan is your despot: a tyrant of the people,...a product of technology."[78]

"The Plan" was the authority of experts and professionals, hiding under the guise of neutral, scientific fact. The result of this technocratic dictatorship, Le Corbusier believed, would be a society run with the "admirable order [that] reigns in the interior of markets and workshops, [which] has dictated the structure of machines...and conditions each gesture of a gang of workmen." He envisioned an entire society run with the authoritarian precision of a mass-production auto plant. When Le Corbusier visited Ford's River Rouge plant outside Detroit in 1936, he had nothing but praise. "In the Ford factory, everything is collaboration, unity of views, unity of purpose, a perfect convergence of the totality of gesture and ideas." The famous architect seemed blind to the brutal repression lurking behind the "unity of purpose" at Ford Motor Company. In these Depression years the resistance of auto workers against the alienating precision of the assembly line was growing. Four years before Le Corbusier's visit workers and communists had organized the Ford Hunger March to protest mass lay-offs at the company. They were met with the "admirable order" of tear gas, fire hoses, and bullets from the Dearborn police and Ford's security force. Five protestors were killed in this "collaboration." Inside the factory the repression was almost as bad. Under the threat of a growing union movement, Ford had turned over his factories to the Service Department, a security force run by Harry Bennett, an ex-boxer thug with mafia ties. He and his squad of toughs spied on, brutalized, and intimidated the entire work force to achieve the "unity of views" that Le Corbusier observed.[79]

Le Corbusier was partially correct, however, in proclaiming the political neutrality of his project. Although it was a blatant attempt to advance the rule of the middle-class intelligentsia, the technocratic project was flexible with respect to its "politics," in the narrow sense of governmental authority. It could and did appeal to any centralized authority capable of granting it power. In *Urbanisme*, Corbu lavished praise on strong, authoritarian rulers like Louis XIV, Louis XV, and Napoleon, who possessed "that spirit which is able to dominate and compel the mob." And, as we will see in the next chapter, during the 1930s modern architects throughout Europe declared themselves willing and able to collaborate with fascism and Nazism. The modernists' technocratic project was thus compatible with any authoritarian regime, whether of the left, right, or center.[80]

The Ends of the Machine Aesthetic

In the 1920s modern architects like Walter Gropius, Mies van der Rohe, and Le Corbusier pioneered a new aesthetic to support and testify to their technocratic project to rationalize industry and place artists, engineers, and other professionals in positions of power. This new aesthetic, known as the new objectivity or machine aesthetic, was characterized by simple, geometric forms, usually of severe rectilinearity. Any and all surface decoration was stripped off in favor of plain, unadorned surfaces. Industrially produced building materials like steel, glass, and concrete were preferred over traditional materials like wood and stone. And open, free-flowing space, both inside and outside of the structure, was privileged over space enclosed by barriers and walls. The architects and ideologists of the modern movement offered two reasons for their machine aesthetic. The practical rationale argued that the mass production of housing required simple, unadorned forms, like Ford's Model T. But this excuse collapses under close scrutiny, exposing a more complex symbolic rationale. The machine aesthetic did not merely accommodate the rationalization of industry but also ideologically promoted it as the resolution of all social problems.

All modernists resorted to practical, functionalist arguments to justify their aesthetic preferences. One of the first to do so was Adolf Loos, who advanced an economic justification for unadorned architecture as early as 1908.

He declared that "omission of ornament results in a reduction in the manufac-turing time and an increase in wages....Ornament is wasted labour power and hence wasted wealth." The economic straits of postwar Europe strengthened this economic argument. Gropius asserted that limiting buildings to a few stan-dard types allowed them to be assembled from mass-produced industrial com-ponents without the necessity of expensive, skilled handwork. Le Corbusier similarly argued that mass production in building required standardization and lack of variety, which achieved "a maximum output and a minimum use of means, workmanship and material, words, forms, colours, sounds." He cited the mass-produced auto as the example of such standardization. Le Corbusier also argued that mass-produced housing generated a unique aesthetic form: "to use the resources of the modern industrial 'yard' to advantage demands the exclusive employment of straight lines, square-set." In this he also drew on the experience of the auto industry, which found that it was cheaper for machines to produce straight parts than curved components. Le Corbusier put this pre-cept to use in his mass-housing project at Pessac, completed in 1926. The entire development of fifty-three units was built on a set of standardized, square mod-ules that allowed him to use mass-produced components and pour machine-made concrete on site.[81]

Some modern architects argued that functionalism eliminated the neces-sity for art in architecture entirely. Mies van der Rohe bordered on such extrem-ism early in his career, writing in 1923 that: "We refuse to recognize problems of form, but only problems of building. Form is not the aim of our work, but only the result." Perhaps the most uncompromising functionalist was Hannes Meyer (1889–1954), who took over the directorship of the Bauhaus when Gropius resigned in 1928. He immediately changed the name of the architec-ture department to the building department, and focused exclusively on the economics of construction and the technical problems of building. In support of their arguments for architecture dictated by the exigencies of fast, efficient construction stringently adapted to the internal uses of space, these militant modernists pointed to American industrial architecture, which they held up as a model of undecorated functionality. Thus, in *Vers une Architecture* Le Corbusier published photos of American grain elevators and concrete-framed factories, including Kahn's Highland Park plant, as exemplars of the new archi-tecture he advocated. However, a closer examination of European modern-ists' use of these factories reveals that they were more fascinated with their look than their construction or use. As Reyner Banham has pointed out, they were initially familiar with American industrial buildings almost exclusively through photographs published in books and journals, so they knew little about the details of their construction or function. They imitated the flat roofs of factories, for example, despite the fact that their copies, unlike the American originals, often leaked due to their ignorance of the actual construction techniques. In fact, many early modernist buildings, like the Villa Stein, achieved their machine-made look through laborious hand-made construction. Further, in order to make the functional American factories conform to the European ideal of functionalism, a bit of deception was often necessary. For example, Le Corbusier's photo of Ford's Highland Park plant was doctored to remove the decorative turrets above the staircases on the Woodward Avenue facade. Finally, while American industrial architects confined their stark functionality to factories, where efficiency was the desideratum, European modernists transferred the functional look to all building types, including residences, in which efficiency of production was not the real function. It is clear, then, that while in the United States functional architecture was dictated by the exigencies of efficient mass production, in Europe functionalism was an aesthetic, a look cultivated in and for itself to serve a symbolic purpose.[82]

Many creators of European modernism readily admitted this aesthetic aspect of their work, asserting that their role was not merely to house people economically but also to inspire them aesthetically. Gropius wrote that "the achievement of a new spatial vision means more than structural economy and functional perfection....Only perfect proportions and colors in a well-balanced harmony deserve that title of honor: beautiful." Le Corbusier also protested the totally functionalist attitude, declaring that architecture also deals with beauty, "the imponderable...[the] capacity for achieving order and unity by measurement and for organizing, in accordance with evident laws, all those things which excite and satisfy our visual senses to the fullest degree." If the unadorned forms and open spaces of modern architecture were not merely functional adaptations to mass-production methods but constituted an aesthetic realm that symbolized something else, what was it? The aesthetic dimension of modernism promoted the technocratic project by ideologically symbolizing the domination of instrumental reason over humans and nature with beautiful forms that reconciled alienated subjects to this oppressive objectivity.[83]

Modern architects sought to resolve the contradictions of the emerging technocratic capitalism at the aesthetic level, leaving their real basis in economic production unscathed. Following America's example, Le Corbusier, Gropius, and others hoped that workers could be integrated into mass production by offering them a compensating realm of mass consumption in the home. But they sensed that not just any sort of houses and goods could provide this compensatory relief. These mass-produced products had to symbolize and glorify the instrumental reason and technology that dominated them at work, while at the same time alleviating some of its worst human consequences. The ugly exigencies of heteronomous mass production embodied in consumer goods had to be beautified, aesthetically altered so as to slip unobtrusively into the sanctuary of the home. The task of modern architects and designers was nothing less than the spiritualization of technique to facilitate both the acceptance of and relief from its consequences.

This ideological goal of the modernist machine aesthetic was best expressed by Mies van der Rohe, the acknowledged leader of modern architecture in Germany during this period. His short, succinct writings and speeches captured the essence of modernism, especially the *Sachlich* (objective) attitude. In an essay written in 1930 upon accepting the directorship of the Bauhaus, Mies wrote: "Let us accept changed economic and social conditions as a fact. All these take their blind and fateful course. One thing will be decisive: the way we assert ourselves in the face of circumstance. Here the problems of the spirit begin." For Mies the era of industrial mechanization and standardization was an inevitable fact that people could not modify. In the spirit of Auguste Comte's positivism, he resigned himself to these facts, which he defined as neutral. The role of art was to establish the spirit or values commensurate with the facts, to express the spirit of the age in its creations. As Mies once stated in an interview: "I am not a reformer. I don't want to change the world. I want to express it." For him the technology of modern production was more than a means of building; it was a spiritual value in itself that had to be expressed in the art of architecture. Architecture fulfilled technology by expressing it in its purified form, by spiritualizing its sometimes disorderly and confusing material manifestations.[84]

These ideological moves by Mies were nothing less than an attempt to make acceptable to society the socially produced "facts" of modern technology and the instrumental reason that underlay them. He did so first by reifying the repressive regime of mass production, postulating it as an objective fact, determined by the inexorable march of technical progress in history and beyond the control of human subjectivity.[85] Then he declared this fact to be the embodiment of a value-free rationality that could be put to any purpose or end. Reason and progress, he implied, lie not in debating the ends of technology but in perfecting the means, from which all benefit. Art would assist this perfection by beautifying technology in order to facilitate its acceptance by human subjects.

The Frankfurt school of critical theory labels this type of thinking instrumental or technological reason, and argues that it is not neutral but inherently oppressive. Instrumental reason fetishizes the means to ends, focusing rationality on determining the efficiency of means, not the desirability of ends. Max Horkheimer, Theodor Adorno, and Herbert Marcuse argue that by ignoring the inherent ends of human beings and nature, instrumental reason allows those who control the technological means to turn them into objective means for alien ends. The entire world is transformed into things-without-ends in order to be manipulated by a dictatorship of means with no ends except domination and exploitation.[86]

Fordist technologies furthered instrumental reason in production by reducing human workers to abstract, homogeneous things manipulated by others for their own ends. Mies van der Rohe, Le Corbusier, and other modernists sought to extend the same logic into the realm of consumption and culture. They believed that the consumption of products that aesthetically glorified instrumental reason and its technology could control workers and induce them to accept their rationalized, alienated existence on the job. It is clear from an examination of modernists' writings that they consciously tried to achieve the look of instrumental reason in their work. Le Corbusier, for example, argued in *Urbanisme* that rectilinear street grids were superior to layouts of curving lanes, for the straight line represented the mastery of reason over nature and humankind. "Man governs his feelings by his reason; he keeps his feelings and his instincts in check, subordinating them to the aim he has in view. He rules the brute creation by his intelligence.... [Consequently] Man walks in a straight line because he has a goal and knows where he is going." In contrast to this disciplined, means-end rationality of the straight street, Le Corbusier writes, "the winding road is the result of happy-go-lucky heedlessness, of looseness, lack of concentration and animality." Reason controlled nature and that part of humanity that surrendered to its natural instincts, the "rabble." The straight line in streets and buildings captured and subordinated both to instrumental reason.[87]

If the street grid and orthogonal building were expressions of the technological rationality of the machine age, so too was the abstract space that they captured. Between the straight streets and steel frameworks lay an open and empty space, delimited but ready to be filled with any and every activity. Mies argued that the steel-framed building "gives you a lot of freedom inside....

Inside you can do what you like." It was his goal to create this virtually empty space, this "almost nothing" (*beinahe nichts*), as he called his architecture. Such space was required, he argued, by the fast-paced urban real estate market, in which abstract capital moved much faster than the fixed materiality of buildings. The rapid turnover of business tenants necessitated that space be flexible enough to accommodate any activity. And because labor was also a commodity that had to be malleable and mobile to accommodate capital, residential buildings also had to be nonspecialized, ready to facilitate the rapid turnover of workers of any sort. The "almost nothing" space of modern architecture was thus the space of the commodity, that empty vessel of abstract exchange value that is indifferent to the actual use values within it. Such a space was inherent in the capitalist economy from the beginning, but its realization required the new technologies of this period. The machines of mass construction and transportation reduced the qualitative, differentiated *place* of the landscape to an abstract, empty *space*, quantitatively measured by money in the marketplace.[88]

Modern architects understood, however, that their forms could not directly express the technology of the age. To facilitate its acceptance by humans, especially those of the working class, technology had to be purified, stripped of its often fragmented appearance and given the look of order and unity. As Gropius stated: "Since my early youth I have been acutely aware of the chaotic ugliness of our modern man-made environment when compared to the unity and beauty of old, preindustrial towns." The role of modern art, he continued, was not to change society but "to rebalance our life and to humanize the impact of the machine." As Mies stated in his own succinct style, the "single goal" of creative work in the modern age must be "to create order out of the desperate confusion of our time." Le Corbusier also argued that the purpose of architecture was to create "a state of platonic grandeur" and "mathematical order" that conveyed "a feeling of calm, order, and neatness, and inevitably imposes discipline on the inhabitants." Without this aesthetically inspired sense of discipline and order, he feared that workers' increased leisure time under Fordist mass production would pose an "imminent threat to the machine age of society."[89]

The Means of the Machine Aesthetic

Modern architects pursued this general principle of purifying technological rationality so as to reconcile it to humans through specific aesthetic means on both small and large scales. At the small or micro level they elaborated an aesthetic of the mass-produced house, while at the large or macro level they

Le Corbusier and Pierre Jeanneret, Villa Savoye, Poissy, France, 1929
(Mary Ann Sullivan, Bluffton University)

developed principles for planning entire cities. But regardless of scale, they sought to create an environment that not only physically incorporated mass-production technologies but symbolically legitimated them as well.

The Aesthetics of the House

Modern architects created a new aesthetic of the house that incorporated conceptions of time and space that reconciled subjects to the exigencies of capitalist mass-production. On the dimension of time, modern architecture symbolized a radical break with the past and the dawn of a new era of technological progress. The modernists vehemently rejected historic styles as unfit for the new machine age. Echoing Henry Ford's infamous assertion that "history is bunk," Le Corbusier declared that use of historical styles "is a respectful and servile salute to the past: disquieting modesty! It is a lie…." By stripping their buildings of soothing historical referents such as pillars and classical cornices, modernists registered the radical disjuncture of the new machine age.[90]

The progress of the machine age was also symbolized simply by borrowing the forms of technology. This technological symbolism was often direct, as in Le Corbusier's famous Villa Savoye, where the metal railings and columns referred to the promenade decks of ocean liners. The curved concrete screens of the roof were also a direct analogy to the smokestacks of a ship. But most of the technological symbolism in modern architecture was indirect, adapting only the idealized forms of machines. Modernists preferred pure, elementary shapes like the cube and cylinder because they believed them to be the result of "the law of mechanical selection," which stated that objects tend toward a standardized type determined by economy of manufacture and use.[91] Le Corbusier saw the automobile as an example of such a mechanically determined type, and argued that architecture should follow its lead. Detecting the prominence of the right angle in early cars, as well as airplanes and ocean liners, he and other modernists used it almost exclusively in their architecture. Because machine-made goods generally had smooth, unadorned surfaces, modernists preferred these as well. Most modernist exteriors in the 1920s were a combination of plate glass and finely finished stucco. Since most early modernist houses were not actually mass-produced but custom-built villas for people of means, these materials and finishes were not a requirement of mass production but an attempt to symbolize it as a panacea for social ills.

Finally, technological progress and the instrumental reason underlying it were symbolized by an aesthetic of domination over nature. For the modernists, progress was measured by humanity's separation from and conquest over nature, which they registered aesthetically with several devices. Modern architects raised all or parts of their buildings off the ground, where they hovered "to deny the law of gravity," as Gropius put it. This light, buoyant architecture symbolized human reason in defiance of nature. Le Corbusier invariably raised his buildings on pilings or pilotis, declaring that the "natural ground" harbored dirt and disease and was consequently "the enemy of man." But once he abolished nature on the ground, Le Corbusier reproduced it in the sky in a carefully controlled and rationalized form. He was fond of roof gardens, where plants and trees were carefully arranged in pots and planters and meticulously clipped in precise geometric shapes. This architect of instrumental reason was not even content to leave uncontrolled the view of nature. Around the roof garden of the Villa Savoye Le Corbusier placed a concrete wall with carefully spaced slots that framed the surrounding landscape. Unwilling to let nature speak for itself, he captured and controlled it within his architectural grid of rectilinear voids.[92]

This aesthetic of technological progress in time was complemented by an aesthetic of open space, in which the distinction between inside and outside was erased. Traditional architecture created a sharp disjuncture between the public facade of the building and the private interior space, enclosing and protecting inhabitants against nature and other people outside. Modern architects were convinced that such segregation had to be destroyed. In the interdependent society of mass industrialism, the individual had to be integrated into the cooperative group, both at work and at home. At work the barriers of privacy had to be eradicated to integrate the individual worker into the collective machine for efficient production. This was achieved by tearing down internal walls and opening up exterior walls with extensive use of glass. Le Corbusier, for example, praised the openness of the glass walls in the Van Nelle factory in Holland, designed by Dutch architects J. A. Brinkman (1902–1949) and L. C. van der Vlugt (1894–1936). He believed that the resulting visibility of each by all created a new collective subject. "Everything is transparent; everyone can see and be seen as he works.…This deflection of the egoistic property instinct toward a feeling for collective action leads to a most happy result: the phenomenon of personal participation in every stage of the human enterprise." Glass was also used in public buildings to connote the new openness of government to the scrutiny of all. For example, in his proposal for the League of Nations building in Geneva in 1927, Hannes Meyer consciously used extensive glazing inside and out to symbolize the collapse of the Old Regimes and the rise popular democracies. "No pillared reception rooms for weary monarchs but hygienic workrooms for the busy representatives of their people. No back corridors for backstairs diplomacy but open glazed rooms for public negotiation of honest men." For modernists, glass symbolized Enlightenment in human affairs, the opening of previously private interests to scrutiny by the collective.[93]

Most modernists, however, conceived their "collective" as not egalitarian but hierarchical, as a graded organism in which the educated and credentialed class ruled benevolently over all others. "Openness" allowed constant surveillance not only of the rulers by the ruled, but also of the ruled by these new rulers. In his 1923 design for a concrete office building, Mies created an open, undivided space in the center of each floor, thus permitting free visibility. As he stated: "The office building is a house of work, of organization, of clarity, of economy. Bright, wide workrooms, easy to oversee, undivided except as the undertaking is divided." Just as in Kahn's concrete factories, the wall-less space of Mies's concrete office building allowed the gaze of the supervisor to penetrate and control all, obliterating any privacy for workers. Modernists sought to extend the same objective gaze of power even to workers' homes. By designing residential complexes with few internal dividing walls and extensive glazing on the exterior, they submitted individuals to the same collective surveillance in the realm of consumption that they experienced in their work lives. To be truly integrated into collective production, people also had to be collectivized in consumption, consuming standardized, mass-produced goods. The privacy and inwardness of the individual ego were thus battered down architecturally to allow the invasion of the mass-produced, technocratically administered society.[94]

Walter Gropius, Bauhaus Dessau, Dessau, Germany, 1926 (Reprinted
from Sigfried Gidieon, *Walter Gropius*. New York: Dover, 1992, 127)

Modern architects also erased the barrier between inside and outside in
order to reveal the technological framework supporting the structure. Long
after buildings began to employ modern supports like steel beams and concrete posts, traditional architects hid these artifacts of the machine age under
archaic materials like stone and brick. In their campaign for honesty and
morality in architecture, the modernists demanded that deceptive facades be
stripped off to reveal industrial materials doing the real work of support. As
Walter Gropius wrote in 1923: "We want to create a clear, organic architecture
whose inner logic will be radiant and naked, unencumbered by lying facades
and trickeries." One way to reveal the supporting structure inside the building
was the glass wall. Gropius made dramatic use of this principle in the work-
shop wing of the Bauhaus complex at Dessau, where the completely glazed
exterior revealed the set-back framework of reinforced concrete. Even when the

frame was not behind but coplanar with the exterior walls, modernists sought to clearly reveal it by separating it from the nonfunctional in-fill elements. For example, in Mies's famous proposal for a concrete office building of 1923, he set the windows back behind the concrete parapets of outer wall, thus foregrounding the supporting frame. By exposing the supports of industrial materials, the modernists were celebrating mass-produced technology and the engineers and technicians who were responsible for it. The "inner logic" of the gridded structure was an advertisement for their instrumental reason, which grasped nature and humanity and forced it into a homogeneous structure of means that could be manipulated for their end of domination.[95]

The space created by the technological grids of modernist architecture was not merely open but also abstract and homogeneous, undifferentiated and mobile. Although the grid of supports captured and subdued space for exploitation, it did not fix the space for a specific use but merely opened it up for the ebb and flow of exchange value. The modernists prided themselves on creating space that was empty and facilitated the free movement of capital and labor. Office buildings of steel or concrete frames eliminated internal load-bearing walls, which limited the uses of space. Light partitions or screens could temporarily tailor the space for a particular tenant. In residential apartments modernists facilitated the rapid mobility of workers in the labor market by supplying built-in cabinets and furniture, eliminating the need to move heavy case pieces. Le Corbusier wrote that with his concept of the house-machine, "the idea of the 'old home' disappears, and with it local architecture, etc., for labour will shift about as needed, and must be ready to move, bag and baggage."[96]

To symbolically express such mobility, modernists created space that was never at rest but flowed and moved constantly. As Gropius stated: "It is evident that motion in space, or the illusion of motion in space produced by the artist's magic, is becoming an increasingly powerful stimulant in contemporary works of architecture.…The buildings seem to hover, space seems to move in and out." One way that this movement was achieved was the asymmetrical placement of volumes in the landscape. Eschewing the stasis of classical symmetry, the modernists created a decentered space that expanded into the landscape. At the Bauhaus complex in Dessau, Gropius designed an asymmetrical composition of three buildings, placed at right angles to one another and connected by a raised bridge and a low wing. The composition created the impression of a pinwheel with three radiating arms, rotating and reaching out into the landscape.[97]

Mies achieved a similar movement of space by the careful placement of planes that slid past one another into the landscape. In his Barcelona Pavilion, an exposition building for Germany at the 1929 International Exposition in Spain, the walls refused to be contained under the roof but slid freely out into the surrounding grounds. And to relieve these walls of any real or symbolic burden of bearing the roof, Mies placed a row of thin, cruciform chrome columns in front of the wall planes. As many commentators have noted, the Barcelona Pavilion closely resembled a De Stijl painting by Mondrian, with sliding planes reaching out to define an infinite, abstract space. Yet, although Mies's space was open and infinite, it was also defined by a rational structure that "opened" it up to human occupation and exploitation. The space of Frank Lloyd Wright's Prairie houses was also open, but it flowed out into a landscape full of uncontained nature. Mies's external space was, like his internal space, open but empty, measured but unspecified in use. In Mies's meticulously detailed ground plans for his buildings, the wide, empty outdoor spaces of patios and courtyards were invariably covered with grids, which often represented the squares of floor tile or paving stones. Both the representational grid and the rectilinear materials symbolized for Mies the imposition of rational structure on space, a technological, "almost nothing" structure that could be filled with any activity—any, that is, except a noninstrumental activity whose end was contained in itself, not in the technological means to achieve it.[98]

Mies van der Rohe, Barcelona Pavilion at the International Exhibition, Barcelona, 1929 (Digital Image © The Museum of Modern Art/Licensed by SCALA/Art Resource, NY/Artists Rights Society, NY)

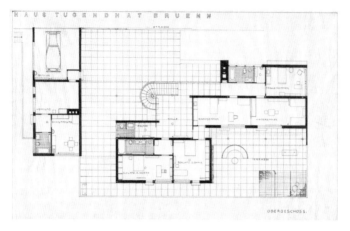

Mies van der Rohe, Tugendhat House, Brno, Czech Republic, 1930
(Digital Image © The Museum of Modern Art/Licensed by SCALA/Art Resource, NY/
Artists Rights Society, NY)

This constantly mobile, abstract space of the machine aesthetic did not leave human occupants much comfort or rest. As one critic stated: "The emphasis on space *per se* and on spatial variety, on movement and violent shifts in orientation inside and out all but killed any ability of a space or an occupant to be at rest." Modernist houses were notoriously impractical and unpleasant to live in. Glass curtain walls allowed too much solar heat in during warm months and too much interior heat out during cold ones. Open floor plans with few dividing walls proved impractical for family living. But that did not deter the modernists, who did not believe that people should be comfortable in their homes. German architect Adolf Behne (1885–1948) wrote in 1918: "The European is right when he fears that glass architecture might become uncomfortable.... [But] the European must be wrenched out of his coziness." Le Corbusier called the notion of a permanent, protective house a "sentimental hysteria." "The house will no longer be an archaic entity, heavily rooted in the soil by deep foundations, built 'firm and strong,' the object of the devotion on which the cult of the family and the race has so long been concentrated... it will be a tool as the motor-car is becoming a tool." Like the mass-produced car, the mass-produced house was a tool to facilitate the relentless motion of a society obsessed with commerce.[99]

This machine aesthetic developed by modern architects was not, however, a straightforward reflection of the system of mass production and the autos that issued from it, as they claimed. Le Corbusier made the boldest claims, juxtaposing photos of automobiles and classical Greek architecture, asserting that both reflected beauty purified by economy of production and use. But for all his praise of Henry Ford and the Model T, Le Corbusier reproduced not one photo of the mass-produced American car, including instead illustrations of expensive European cars, all of which were produced in small volumes by craft-workers using extensive handwork. These low, sleek machines were indeed as elegantly proportioned and integral as the Parthenon or one of Le Corbusier's own purist villas, but none of them bore much resemblance to the Model T. Ford's car, like most mass-produced vehicles of the day, was short and high, lending it an ungainly appearance. And the Model T was not a smoothly inte-grated mass but a fragmented assemblage of disjointed parts. The quickly manu-factured components did not fit together precisely, and there was no time along rapid assembly lines for careful fitting and finishing. Nor did the functional parts that were visible have the smooth, precision finishes of Le Corbusier's pilotis or Mies's chrome columns, but were generally crudely finished stampings or castings. The precision-machining praised by the modernists was reserved for internal engine parts, which were not visible. In sum, these early mass-pro-duced cars had rather inelegant ostensible forms, whose fragmentation and ugliness bore direct testimony to the fragmented, heterogeneous work that produced them.[100]

Modern architecture did not directly reflect this alienated production process but purified and idealized its forms. The fragmented forms were uni-fied into an integral smoothness. In Le Corbusier's Villa Savoye, for example, the smooth, white stucco surface showed no signs of assembly work, as if the cube had floated down from the ethereal realm of reason instead of being con-structed by physical labor from the ground up. Mies insisted that the steel frameworks of his buildings be revealed, but at the same time he concealed their assembly by specifying that joints be welded, not bolted, and then ground flat and painted so as to hide their connectivity. Mies and other modernists suppressed not only the work of assembly but also the work of support. Both the Barcelona Pavilion and the Villa Savoye employed thin columns, of steel and concrete respectively, without capitals or bases, which seemed to deny their work of bearing weight. In the Pavilion Mies further thinned the columns visually by constructing them of two crossed steel plates and covering them with a chromed casing, which effectively reduced them to ethereal shafts of light. Technology was visible in these buildings, but it did not work, nor was it worked upon. The mass-produced technology of the modernists was the abstract, dematerialized idea of work, not its physical reality.[101]

The modernists' class position and its relation to technology caused this denial of the materiality of work. For the professional-managerial class, technology was not so much a material reality as a conceptual system. Because its members conceptually created and manipulated machines with engineering diagrams, accounting books, and managerial directives, technology appeared to them as an effortless system of symbols, not a recalcitrant material reality. Artists and architects were even further removed from actual factory production than the industrial professions, so their experience of technology was even more idealized, an empty framework of abstract means. Architects were also aware that the new system of mass production was frightening to the classes who stood to lose from it. For those workers and petty bourgeois who stood, as Le Corbusier put it, breathless and panting before the tools that they could not control, this technology was chaotic and unwelcome in their homes in the forms of mass-produced goods and mass-produced housing. Modernists remade the technology into an orderly aesthetic that concealed the physical realities of work in order to render it acceptable to those imperiled by it.

The Aesthetics of the City

The architects of the machine aesthetic realized that for society to function efficiently not only individual houses but entire cities had to be transformed into rational machines. The unregulated urban real estate market had created a jumble of spaces that prevented the new technologies of production and consumption from realizing their potentials. Le Corbusier argued in the Athens Charter, a document written under the auspices of the International Congress

Le Corbusier, The Voisin Plan of Paris, 1925 (Reprinted from Le Corbusier, *Une Maison, Un Palais*. Paris: G. Crès, 1928, 83)

of Modern Architecture (CIAM), that: "The preeminence of private initia-
tives, inspired by personal interest and the lure of profit, is at the bottom of
this regrettable state of affairs. Up to now, no authority, conscious of the nature
and importance of the movement toward mechanization, has taken steps to
avert the damage." He proposed to remedy this situation through urban planning, whose goals were "to organize our cities, to police and discipline them, to
keep them efficient for production, and lift them out of the chaos which stifles
them." To achieve this he and other modernists sought not to eliminate private property but to adapt it to the machine age by collectively planning urban
commerce and consumption. This was to be done by an authority "who pos-
sesses a perfect knowledge of man," that is, the technocratic authority of architects themselves.[102]

The aesthetic principles that modernists applied to create an efficient, orderly
city were similar to those employed at the small scale of the house: open space,
functionalism, and movement. Here, however, their utilitarian intent was often
as strong as their symbolism. One of the primary principles of modernist city
planning was open but defined spaces. Le Corbusier, for example, advocated
high-density housing in large skyscrapers separated by vast expanses of empty
green space and wide roadways. His speculative Ville Contemporaine plan
(1922) for three million inhabitants showed a business center dominated by
twenty-four sixty-story office towers, which were separated by wide spaces.
Occupying most of these intervening spaces were broad, elevated superhighways, shrines to the modernist god of the car. So central to Le Corbusier's city
planning was the automobile that he approached the heads of France's major
automakers for money to finance his 1925 proposal for rebuilding Paris, and
named it the Voisin Plan after the only company that agreed. He believed that
"business demands the greatest possible speed in regard to traffic," and to create it city centers had to be torn down and rebuilt to accommodate more and
faster cars. If the empty but gridded spaces of modernist houses symbolized the
movement of capital, the empty urban centers filled with road grids facilitated
this movement in reality.[103] The open, empty urban space that Le Corbusier and
other modernists advocated allowed not merely the circulation of capital but
also the accommodation of the working population to this flow. Le Corbusier
cited approvingly the "great openings" in Paris made by Louis XIV, Louis XV,
and Napoleon, calling them embodiments "of that spirit which is able to dominate and compel the mob." Sigfried Giedion, the premier historian of early modern architecture, also praised the wide, straight boulevards that were plowed
through many of Paris's working-class quarters by Georges-Eugène Haussmann,

agreeing with him that they "permit the circulation not only of air and light but also of troops...so that they [people] will be rendered less disposed to revolt." Modernists were appalled by the crowding in the poor quarters of cities, arguing that it bred contagious diseases. But the disease they aimed to clear out with their plans was often just a metaphor for the dreaded contagion of class consciousness that working-class concentration created.[104]

The modernists proposed to clear out class contagion not only by the force of troops but also by the palliative of nature. The open spaces of the modernist city were to be filled with parks as well as arteries of commerce and coercion. Recognizing that "modern life requires the recuperation of the forces which are used up in pursuit of it," Le Corbusier looked to nature to provide this recuperation. Specifically, recreation in parks and playing fields would relieve tension and induce joy. And, on an aesthetic level, the organic forms of trees and foliage would provide an antidote to the mechanical forms of the skyscrapers. "The tree modifies a scene that is too vast, and its casual forms contrast with the rigid forms which we have conceived and made by the machinery of our epoch.... Its presence in the city is a sort of caress." Like Frank Lloyd Wright, Le Corbusier realized that humans subjected to a rationalized production process must be given some relief in the organic forms of nature. But while Wright thought it necessary to transport people to the suburbs to do so, Le Corbusier would provide them with nature in the center of the city. And while Wright and other American architects felt they had to make buildings more organic, Le Corbusier and the European modernists would only plant some grass and trees among structures that remained rigidly dictated by the logic of the machine.[105]

Once urban space was opened up and cleared of congestion, the modernists held that efficiency demanded that it be functionally specialized. Just as Ford specialized jobs and assigned each its separate space along a moving line, modernist city planners sought to segregate land uses into specialized spaces connected by corridors of movement. Obsessed with purity and order, they were appalled by the messy mixture of various people and activities that the urban real estate market had created. Le Corbusier wrote, for example, that "Paris is a dangerous magma of human beings gathered from every quarter by conquest, growth, and immigration; she is the eternal gypsy encampment." This racist fear of mixing with immigrants was also overlain by a deep class bigotry. In *Space, Time and Architecture*, Sigfried Giedion expressed disgust at the "intermingling of different functions" (read: classes) in the nineteenth-century Parisian apartment house. The apartments of "upper-middle-class tenants" on the main floors shared the same building with the "congested slums" on the attic floor. Making a similar argument for the segregation of industry in the outskirts of the city, Le Corbusier wrote in analogy that "in a decent house the servants' stairs do not go through the drawing room—even if the maid is charming."[106]

The major goal behind the functionalist specialization of urban space seems to have been class segregation. An orderly, efficient city required that the dangerous classes be moved away from the center of power. In the nineteenth-century industrial city, the concentration of rail and other transportation arteries in city centers concentrated industry there as well. Industrial workers usually lived close by in densely packed quarters that facilitated quick mobilization and easy access to centers of industrial and political power. The working-class struggle for power in the nineteenth century was conducted in the narrow streets of the core, where a few makeshift barricades paralyzed state and industry. This fact, combined with the abysmal housing conditions in poor neighborhoods, led middle-class reformers to advocate as early as the middle of the nineteenth century the decentralization of industry and workers to the rural outskirts. The most influential of these was Ebenezer Howard (1850–1928), a British reformer who founded the Garden City movement. Le Corbusier and the modernists picked up this idea and made it the center of their urban planning.[107]

Le Corbusier's Ville Contemporaine plan of 1922 revealed an intent to suppress class conflict through segregation. At the center of Le Corbusier's city, dominating the entire plan aesthetically and politically, were twenty-four cruciform skyscrapers containing offices for the technocratic administrators of government, finance, and industry. In the open spaces around these cathedrals of technocracy were parks and places of entertainment for this elite. Close on to this center Le Corbusier placed the residential housing for the elite in two concentric rings. The first ring of "luxury dwellings" contained the city's top technocrats, while the second ring of more modest apartments housed the lower-middle-class clerks and bureaucrats. The blue-collar workers in Le Corbusier's city were confined to garden-city suburbs located beyond a "protected zone" of open space. Also ostracized from the city center was industry, which was segregated into separate industrial centers to which the workers commuted. In these garden cities Le Corbusier provided the working class with mass-produced apartments, each with its own outdoor area for gardening and rest. "The inhabitant comes back from his factory or office, and…sets to work on his garden. His plot, cultivated in a standardized and scientific way, feeds him for the greatest part of the year."[108]

So Le Corbusier not only segregated workers in rural areas away from urban seats of power, but also made them produce their own food, thus transforming utopian socialist plans for cooperative work into a scheme for capitalist exploitation. One of his heroes, Henry Ford, was implementing a similar scheme in America at this time. Noting that concentrations of industry in urban centers led to "violent plagues of upheave and unrest," Ford developed a network of village industries beginning in 1918. Located in rural Michigan, these small-parts plants employed farmers who not only provided much of their own subsistence by farming but also knew little about unions and class conflict.[109]

Once modernist planners like Le Corbusier had corralled the proletarian savages on reservations far removed from the centers of technocratic civilization, they faced the problem of controlling these working-class concentrations. To ensure that suburban concentration would not lead to class consciousness and mobilization these architects designed mass housing that spatially privatized and individualized working-class residents. Le Corbusier proposed that his working-class apartments be constructed as self-contained cells, each carefully insulated from its neighbors. Opaque walls were used throughout, with the only glass facing individual patios and gardens. Each apartment would also be totally soundproofed, ensuring that, as Le Corbusier wrote, "even a hermit in the depth of a forest could not be more cut off from other men." Although Le Corbusier envisioned the provision of collective services like laundering, cleaning, and food preparation in each building, these would be delivered to individual apartments, not consumed in common. The hotel, not the commune, was his model. Even entertainment would take place in isolation, away from the contagious comradery of saloons and movie houses: "The gramophone or the pianola or wireless will give you exact interpretations of first-rate music, and you will avoid catching cold in the concert hall, and the frenzy of the virtuoso."[110]

In an attempt to further individualize and isolate all residents, not merely workers, modernist planners declared a war on the street. For them the public space of the street, with its free mixing of people and traffic, work and commerce, was a dangerous environment. They also believed that most streets were far too narrow, thus slowing down commerce. So the modernists declared "Death to the Street!" The narrow lanes and sidewalks along which people congregated had to be abolished. Vehicular traffic in the city center would be relegated to below-grade corridors for deliveries and raised expressways for through traffic, while pedestrians would have a separate grade. All residential housing would face toward green areas, turning blind backsides to the street. And internal walks and stairways in large apartment blocks would replace surface sidewalks and streets as corridors of circulation, for they were much easier to control than the open, public space of the traditional street. Thus, the modernists sought to destroy the public space of the street and replace it with private space that segregated and individualized city inhabitants.[111]

The ideal city of the modernist planners was thus a space of class hierarchy and segmentation, with the technocratic elite of business and government at the center, succeeded by concentric rings of successively lower classes. Yet, within this hierarchical space there was a type of equality as well. In the cities of feudalism and early capitalism, class inequality was marked out by the different aesthetics of buildings, which were believed to testify to the inherent inequalities of taste on which rank rested.[112] The modernist city, by contrast, was to be a hierarchy of equals, with people ranked solely by their function in the mechanical process. Le Corbusier marveled at the "egalitarianism" of the Van Nelle factory in Holland, where workers and managers alike dressed neatly, ate together, and looked healthy. "There is no proletariat here," he wrote, "simply a graduated hierarchy, clearly established and respected." This hierarchy was based solely on one's function within the factory, as determined by knowledge and skill. Similarly, in the modernist city all dwellings were aesthetically equal. From the skyscrapers occupied by the technocratic brains to the garden-city apartments occupied by the working-class brawn, all buildings were united by a machine aesthetic of unadorned economy, mass-produced standardization, and machine-like rectilinearity. The only distinctions between the parts of the city were their functions within the urban process, as marked by their position in the spatial hierarchy. In contrast to previous urban forms, the modernists were symbolizing in their new city the basic equality of culture and taste. This urban ideology of technocracy thus promised to hide the continuing inequalities of class within rationalized capitalism behind the unifying facade of a common aesthetic. Modernists could thus appear as champions of equality against the culturally retrograde bourgeoisie, while simultaneously seeking to place their technocratic class in a position of greater authority.[113]

Utopia Realized? The Modernist Housing Estates

The symbolic crusade of modern architecture for the rationalization of city and factory met with reluctance and suspicion among the European bourgeoisie, especially in Germany, where the modernist movement was strongest.

Industrialists were afraid of the large costs involved in rationalization and its potential to undermine protective cartels. They were also suspicious of the intentions of crusading engineers, technicians, architects, and other educated professionals. The main support for this technocratic project came from the politicians and trade union representatives of the Social Democratic party, who in the period from 1925 to 1930 still wielded considerable power at the national and local levels in Germany. The rationalization program that received the greatest state backing was the construction of massive housing estates for Germany's ill-housed population. The right of German citizens to "a sound dwelling" had been established back in 1918, along with a system of state loans and governmental agencies to fund and oversee construction. But the housing program of the Weimar Republic did not become effective until 1924, when a new tax on rents provided the federal government with a sizable fund for new construction. This money was lent on affordable terms to building societies, which were cooperative, limited-profit organizations that built low-cost housing for their members. Although many had originally been established by trade unions and professional associations, municipalities eventually came to wield almost complete control over these building societies. Thus, local municipal administrations, many of which were dominated by Social Democrats, controlled the planning and design of most of these housing estates.

The Social Democrats had several objectives for these Weimar housing estates. First and foremost, this housing was part of a reformist scheme to compensate workers with greater consumption for their acquiescence to industrial rationalization. But officials of the labor movement also wanted workers' housing to promote the rationalization of working-class domestic life as well. Like the middle-class reformers in America, SPD leaders sought to eliminate what they considered the evils of the older proletarian culture, such as taking in boarders, frequenting saloons, and participating in mass culture. They wanted a working-class culture that was rationalized and disciplined in order to support the rigors of rationalized factory work. And fearing a return to the mass mobilizations that might threaten their positions, these leaders also wanted a privatized and individualized lifestyle, focused on the nuclear family and the home. These goals were also supported by a number of large capitalists, as well as bourgeois feminists, educators, and social workers. Progressive reformers in the United States promoted similar goals, but the means of achieving them were different. While efforts in the United States were channeled mainly through the private sector, in Germany the main vehicle was the state-sponsored housing program.[114]

Between 1919 and 1932 various public and semi-public authorities in Germany built 2.5 million apartments that housed 9 million people, or 14 percent of the population. To accomplish this ambitious program many of these regional and municipal politicians and bureaucrats turned to modernist architects, convinced that only mass-production methods could provide affordable housing in sufficient quantities. So in German cities like Frankfurt and Berlin during this period, modernists got their first opportunities to realize their ideas on mass-produced housing and city planning on a large scale. In Berlin a building society controlled by SPD trade unions hired Bruno Taut to direct a massive building program, while in Frankfurt the mayor hired modernist architect and planner Ernst May (1886–1970) to do likewise. Similar state-sponsored housing programs were undertaken in other European countries, especially Austria and Belgium.[115]

Following established modernist precepts, nearly all of these housing developments or *Siedlung*, as they were called in Germany, were built on the outskirts of cities, for both practical and ideological reasons. On a practical basis, land was cheaper and more plentiful outside of crowded urban centers, where the private real estate market drove prices beyond the reach of public entities. But for ideological reasons, the modernists also wanted these suburban housing projects to stand apart from the irrationality of urban centers as models of rational social planning. As Bruno Taut, wrote, "they [housing estates] cannot stand in the metropolis because the latter, rotten in itself, will disappear along with the old power. The future lies on the newly developed land, which will feed itself." Whether or not they intended it, however,

Ernst May, Bornheimer Hang settlement, Frankfurt, 1927
(Photograph Thorsten Scheerer/courtesy Ernst May Gesellschaft
e.V., Germany)

one consequence of the modernists' preference for the urban periphery was to politically weaken the working class by geographically dividing it. Despite heavy state subsidies, apartments in the new German estates were so expensive that only the middle class and the upper tier of the working class could afford to live there. The more affluent skilled workers were thus segregated from the poorer and less skilled, who remained behind in working-class neighborhoods near urban centers.[116]

These housing estates exemplified the emergence not of socialism, as some claimed, but of rationalized capitalism, as revealed both by the methods of construction and the lifestyle cultivated there. Modernists largely succeeded in adopting mass-production methods in the construction of their housing developments. Both May and Taut used standardized building sections and precast concrete slabs, which eliminated the need for most skilled construction labor. Gropius used Taylorist time and motion studies to cut labor costs at his Dessau and Praunheim housing estates. Le Corbusier also embraced mass-production methods at his Pessac housing settlement outside of Bordeaux, even though he realized these would undermine the skilled trades. He bragged that his design for the concrete houses was "capable of being erected by unskilled labor." The entire project was based on a standardized 5 x 5 meter cell, which allowed him to use factory-built, standardized windows and precast concrete T-beams. However, some workers at the Pessac site, especially the masons and cement workers, refused to work under the new methods, and

Le Corbusier and Pierre Jeanneret, Pessac housing estate, near Bordeaux, 1925 (© 2006 Artists Rights Society, NY/ADAGP, Paris/FLC L2(15)141)

construction went forward only after Le Corbusier himself took control of the site and eliminated, in his words, "all doubtful elements from the work force." So in the name of helping the working class, the modernists introduced construction methods that de-skilled and weakened it.[117]

Modern architects designed workers' estates to standardize and Taylorize the work of not merely those building them but also those living there. In their attempts to rationalize workers' consumption, modernists introduced new spatial principles in these apartments. Foremost among these was the niggardly use of space. Rooms were designed to facilitate the performance of domestic functions in the most efficient manner and in the least possible space. Such modernist designs were part of a broader movement for household rationalization supported by SPD and trade union officials, middle-class reformers, and industrialists. All believed that to save resources and promote economic recovery, the home, like the factory, had to be rationalized to lower the reproduction costs of labor. Unlike the American domestic reform movement, however, which promoted the purchase of new household technologies, German reformers sought to achieve efficiencies through scientific organization alone. To save time, they conducted Taylorist time studies of everything from potato peeling to floor mopping. To save space, modernist architects like May undertook research to determine an "existence minimum," the absolute minimum amount of space required for human existence. He and others designed minuscule rooms no bigger than necessary to perform functions efficiently, and then downsized furnishings and fittings to fit into these cramped spaces. The kitchen received the most attention, for in Germany, as in the United States and elsewhere, the large kitchen was usually the center of the old working-class domestic culture. In their housing estates modernist architects broke up this inefficient communality by designing tiny kitchens, where the housewife, now isolated from the rest of the family, undertook her lonely, Taylorized tasks. Space for eating was provided in a small dining room, while socializing was confined to the small parlor provided in most apartments.[118]

Writing in 1929 on the "minimum dwelling of urban industrial populations," Gropius offered an interesting justification for these tiny, hygienic apartments in multistory buildings. While the large, single-family dwelling was still suitable for the "wealthier classes," he wrote, the industrial class was better suited to the small apartment because of the changing structure of the family. Citing rising rates of divorce and employed women, Gropius argued that women were being liberated from the patriarchal family. The state was taking over the burden of domestic work with socialized services, so women's work in the home shrank, requiring less room. Large homes weighed women down with cleaning and maintenance, while small apartments lightened their load and liberated them for employment outside the home. Under the guise of women's liberation, Gropius thus gave German industrialists an expanded low-wage work force and relieved them of the responsibility of paying men the traditional family wage. He further justified small apartments in massive estates by the similarly dubious working-class "freedom to move." While the single-family home was suited to higher-income families who were permanently settled, "the rented dwelling in an apartment house is better adapted to the needs of the more mobile working class." To fully render workers a malleable commodity ready to move at the beck and call of capital, they had to be warehoused in small, efficient boxes that facilitated their quick, cost-efficient entry and egress.[119]

At the same time that the housing estates sought to reduce workers to an abstract, mobile commodity, they also sought to provide them with relief from these dehumanizing conditions of production. The magazine of the Britz-Berlin housing project stated that the "objectivity" (*Sachlichkeit*) of the spaces would create "the truly appropriate healing factors to escape from the unrest and nervousness of modern life and to preserve one's inner strength and lightness of heart, the eternal protection of our (human) nature." This escape was to be found in private consumption within the sanctuary of one's own apartment. Modernists concentrated on isolating the individual apartments from one another, visually and socially. At Pessac, Le Corbusier privatized his rows of attached terrace houses by reversing the floor plans of adjacent dwellings, ensuring that the open spaces of one house would be next to the closed spaces of the next. Further, there were few provisions for any public life on most estates. Historian Adelheid von Saldern has stated that there were few if any meeting rooms or community centers in the typical German *Siedlung*, although some had schools, shops, and restaurants. Residents normally had to leave their estates to participate in cultural or political activities. Neither did the SPD or trade unions in Germany promote tenants' participation in housing administration. The building societies and city governments argued that since they were public bodies, there was no need for tenants' participation. Von Saldern argues that collective activity was discouraged because top SPD leaders feared that any worker activism would benefit the Communist Party, not themselves. So they privatized and demobilized tenants, constructing an insulated realm of consumption that merely compensated for and in no way challenged the rationalized realm of production.[120]

There were similarities between the German and American new-middle-class movements for reforming working-class domestic life. In both countries reformers drawn from the professional-managerial class sought to rationalize working-class consumption to better adapt it to the demands of Fordist production. Both groups advocated simple, utilitarian styles in furnishings and decoration, and sought to force the economies of the factory into women's domestic work. In both countries the focus was also on consumption in the nuclear family, while extended-family ties were discouraged. Although these rationalization programs had similar ends, however, their means diverged due to national differences in socioeconomic circumstances. In the United States rationalization occurred in a period of general prosperity, which encouraged domestic programs focused on the compensating consumption of individual commodities. Labor shortages in mass-production factories encouraged worker turnover, which induced capitalists like Ford to pay higher wages to attract and keep workers. To further stabilize this restive work force, Ford and other capitalists, with the help of middle-class reformers, encouraged ownership of single-family homes, which tied workers to a mortgage and made them dependent on their high wages. Wives and children were discouraged from working, making males even more dependent on their wages. Working-class families were also cajoled to purchase durable domestic goods, further stabilizing this class and absorbing the glut of consumer goods flooding off assembly lines. The consequence of these conditions was a rationalization program focused on marketplace consumption, and an alliance of the educated middle class with the industrialists that supplied these commodities.

In Germany conditions were vastly different. After the 1918 revolution the new Weimar Republic undertook ambitious public programs that, under conditions of a devastated industrial infrastructure, led to rampant inflation. The economy was stabilized after 1924 with austerity measures that created large-scale unemployment and general depression. The rationalization programs that emerged during this period thus focused on efficiency and austerity in factory and home, not the consumption of new technologies. Labor markets were glutted with workers as industries slashed employment, and wages fell. Mindful of the recent revolutionary activity, government officials knew the working class had to be pacified and incorporated into the emerging regime of rationalized capitalism. But because industry was unwilling to take steps to mass produce consumer goods and increase wages, officials launched, with the help of middle-class professionals and architects, an austerity-minded public program of worker consumption, the focus of which was the provision of

existence-minimum housing. This explains the preference of German state officials and architects for mass-produced apartment blocks over the more expensive single-family dwellings encouraged in the United States. Further, unlike
labor-stabilizing mortgages, rented apartments facilitated the worker mobility
that industry required in this period of lay-offs, cutbacks, and restructuring.
And domestic efficiency measures not dependent upon new appliances helped
contain and cut the reproduction costs of labor. The modernist architecture
of these state-subsidized housing estates both symbolized and facilitated this
austerity-minded rationalization of working-class consumption. Even if
German industrialists were reluctant to adopt mass production, the rationalizing professional-managerial class could establish a front for efficiency and
standardization in working-class homes.[121]

Class Reactions to the Machine Aesthetic

The German case provides greater insight than the American one into the reactions of the various classes to the modernist machine aesthetic. In the United
States modernism was cut short by an emerging mass marketplace for consumer goods, through which the populace could express their aesthetic preferences. Thus, the American public never confronted a full-blown machine
aesthetic. In Germany, by contrast, the modernists were unconstrained by consumer preferences and realized their aesthetic in public housing estates that
dominated the outskirts of major German cities. Nearly all Germans perceived
these and other examples of modern architecture as symbolic of the rapid
political and economic changes of this period, especially industrial rationalization, since architects promoted it as such. The specific responses to this symbolic association varied, however, by class position.

As we have seen, the various fractions of the technocratic middle class—
SPD and trade union leaders, architects, engineers, technical professions—
supported modern architecture enthusiastically. The reaction of the capitalist
class, however, was mixed and complex. Some large industrialists supported
these aesthetic innovations, both as a symbol of and a vehicle for the rationalization programs they supported, but the smaller capitalists who owned the
majority of businesses were threatened by industrial rationalization and often
attacked the modern architecture associated with it. The Weimar Bauhaus and
its collaboration with large industry came under sharp attack by this class at
the regional level. During a heated political campaign in 1924, tradesmen
and small manufacturers took out advertisements claiming that the Bauhaus
and its Social Democratic supporters aimed to destroy them by attacking

individualized enterprise and fostering large-scale "communalized" trades and industry. In a diatribe against modern architecture, conservative architect Alexander von Senger argued that the modernists' use of industrial materials and techniques "destroys and proletarianizes hundreds of thousands of self-sufficient building tradesmen; it liquidates the heart of the petty bourgeoisie." Further, the fact that both socialist and communist leaders in Germany were avid supporters of modern architecture was enough to turn many capitalists, large or small, against it on political grounds, regardless of their immediate economic interests.[122]

Perhaps the largest threat to the bourgeoisie posed by modern architecture, however, was neither economic nor political, but cultural. German bourgeois, along with other Europeans of this class, rested their legitimation on the high culture created by the still powerful aristocracy, instead of cultivating an independent bourgeois culture. The modernist cult of rationality and efficiency undermined this borrowed legitimacy and threatened to expose the bourgeoisie's naked economic interests. Thus, many bourgeois attacks on modern architecture were aimed at defending their cultural capital against devaluation. Prominent bourgeois scholars, politicians, and artists worried that mass production in general and industrialized building in particular would level the class-specific consumption patterns of German society, resulting in a culturally homogeneous "mass man." And the modernists' materialist stress on technology and practicality was said to threaten the spiritual values celebrated in German *Kultur*. One critic, himself a traditional architect, wrote that modernist aesthetics expressed only the qualities of the workplace, which were inadequate because "men require warmth and rejoicing, splendor and brilliance,... the qualities of life appropriate to the hours after work is done." Nationalist critics pointed out that modernist buildings had the look of transience and rootlessness and undermined the traditional bond with "blood and earth." One argued that the houses of the modernists "are the work of the nomads of the metropolis, who have lost entirely the concept of the homeland."[123]

Unlike the bourgeoisie, the working class had no high-cultural legitimation or small businesses to protect, but it too was threatened by economic rationalization and was suspicious of the modern architecture that symbolized it. Workers in the construction trades rightly saw modernism as a threat to their jobs and their skills. The Bauhaus encountered opposition as well from industrial craftworkers, who feared that its designs for mass-produced products would accelerate the decline of already precarious skills. But the economic threat of modern architecture and design to the vast majority of the working class in Germany and elsewhere was more symbolic than real. In the 1920s all workers were worried by the German industrialists' program of rationalization, which focused on lay-offs, wage-squeezing, and work intensification. In Erich Fromm's large-scale survey of German workers in 1929, the overwhelming majority of both skilled and unskilled workers held negative opinions of economic rationalization. Because modern architecture was symbolically associated with rationalization, rank and file workers were understandably suspicious, even as their political and trade union leaders enthusiastically embraced it.[124]

One would expect these negative opinions to be reflected in complaints by working-class residents of the German housing estates, where modernist architects practiced their machine aesthetic. Yet people there expressed surprisingly few objections. For example, a recent study of the modernist housing of Weimar concludes that, despite some complaints, most inhabitants adjusted quickly to their new quarters. But these findings must be qualified for several reasons. First, given the severe housing shortage of this period, most workers must have been delighted to have any sort of dwelling, and were not disposed to look a gift horse in the mouth. More important still was the fact that, due to the relatively high rents in these estates, only the middle class and the upper working class could afford to live there, both of which were more favorably disposed to household rationalization. Finally, residents were probably a self-selected group, with those favorably disposed to modern architecture more likely to move there to begin with. A better gauge of worker reactions to modernist housing estates is found in Le Corbusier's Pessac project near Bordeaux, France, which was different from the German estates in several respects. First, due to larger state subsidies, this housing attracted a much lower fraction of the working class. Second, most units were sold, not rented, to workers, allowing the owner-occupants to undertake alterations to their houses, a practice strictly forbidden in the German estates. In these alterations and their rationale we can detect the true reactions of a broad stratum of the working class to modernist architecture.[125]

Many Pessac residents made alterations due to practical objections to the spatial arrangements of Le Corbusier's houses. Like most modernist projects, Pessac provided residents with a tiny, one-person kitchen, with eating confined to the adjacent dining room and sociality to the parlor. One popular alteration was the expansion of the kitchen into the parlor, thus asserting the working-class preference for the informal sociality of the kitchen over the bourgeois formality of the parlor. Other Pessac alterations, however, seemed directed at aesthetic objections, not practical ones. For the worker and bourgeois alike, the machine aesthetic symbolized the threatening economic changes of rationalization. Just as Americans objected to the standardized look of the Model T in the domestic realm, so did these French workers reject the look of mass production in their homes. Residents quickly filled the austere spaces reminiscent of the efficient factory with symbols of cozy domesticity. Le Corbusier's flush ribbon windows were given sills, pediments, shutters, and planter boxes. Nearly all residents also divided these long, metal-framed windows into traditionally narrow windows with wooden frames. Pessac residents thus reasserted the comforting continuity of the area's traditional building vernacular against the disturbing newness of the machine aesthetic, because, as one stated, "things are moving a bit too fast nowadays."[126]

Another characteristic of the modernist aesthetic addressed in alterations was the eradication of the barrier between inside and outside. Le Corbusier, like most modern architects, sought to open the inside spaces of domesticity to the outside space of public surveillance. Consequently, Pessac residents frequently complained that their houses were unprotected and exposed to outside threats. Although residents usually perceived these threats as natural, they were actually symbolic of the social intrusions that they felt. One resident complained that "there's no protection for the building," citing the lack of eaves and awnings to deflect wind and rain. But these missing elements were more symbolic than functional, representing the traditional protection of the domestic realm from the "winds of change" and the "hard rain" of economic restructuring raging outside. This is clear in another common complaint about the open roof terraces on the houses. One resident complained that sonic booms from jets shook his house. "I'm not asking for a mansion,... but I would like to be under a roof." A peaked roof would not have prevented sonic booms from shaking his house, but it would have offered symbolic insulation from the intrusion of the machine age from above. Many residents consequently roofed over the terraces and enclosed the space.[127]

Through these and other alterations the working-class residents of Pessac expressed their opinions on Le Corbusier's "machines for living in." In contrast to Le Corbusier's modernist worship of machine forms, standardization, and abstract space, the actual victims of the instrumental rationality that these symbolized resisted the intrusion of the commodity logic into their lives, turning Le Corbusier's concrete boxes into cozy domestic bunkers in which reminders of the invading forces outside were carefully eradicated.

The Dialectical Progressivism of Modern Architecture

The modern architecture that arose in Europe in the interwar period was part of a technocratic ideology that justified the intervention of the new cultural bourgeoisie of professionals, managers, and engineers into capitalism in order to rationalize and stabilize its operation. For Pierre Bourdieu, who cynically holds that all culture is inevitably tainted by class interests, this aesthetic can be judged no better or worse than the American aesthetic of mass consumption, which was more attuned to the mass market dominated by the popular classes. Frankfurt school theorists, however, hold that there are standards whereby the progressive nature of socially influenced art may be judged. The aesthetic judgments of these theorists are based on a dialectical conception of reason in history.

Although these Frankfurt philosophers are heavily critical of instrumental reason, their intent is not to undermine the concept of reason as such and justify a retreat to irrationalism. For them history is still the story of reason's progress, but it is marked by dialectical reversals. Instrumental reason initially emerges to advance reason's progress by freeing humans from the blind forces of nature. But at the same time, this form of reason also enslaves people and nature to the new, social necessities of production and the market. Real freedom, they argue, lies not in returning back before instrumental reason, but in moving beyond it to a new, emancipatory reason that no longer treats humans or nature as mere means but as ends in themselves.[128]Applied to the present case, this theory conceives of the new technologies and knowledge introduced by educated professionals in this period as manifestations of instrumental reason and its contradictions. On the one hand, these techniques were employed to enhance the power of the dominant class and further enslave humanity to the demands of the market. On the other hand, however, these techniques also embodied a progressive element that could be used to better meet the material needs of all humanity. The technocratic project contained the potential for a more democratic control of these techniques. Its focus on the rational planning of production by those with knowledge and education undermined the power of individual property owners and, consequently, the blind forces of the marketplace produced by private ownership.

Frankfurt theorists hold that art should assist the dialectical development of reason in history, undermining oppression and enhancing the liberating potential of knowledge and technology. Art does so by revealing in its aesthetic forms the potentials for a rational, emancipated society, while simultaneously criticizing the oppressive irrationality of the existing society. Authentic art,

Theodor Adorno writes, exposes people to the contradictions of the existing society and refuses to offer them comfort and illusion. But neither does it
reify or eternalize these contradictions. Art performs a delicate balancing act
between promising utopia and denying its existence with a dialectic of beauty
and ugliness. The beauty of its forms, which evokes an ideal of happiness, is
disrupted by the ugliness of the existing world, which prevents this happiness
from being realized. In faithfully reflecting on its surface the scars and lacerations inflicted on beauty by social antagonisms, art keeps faith with utopia but
prevents its immediate use as a comforting illusion for the masses.[129]

Adorno makes it clear that in order to realize this authentic aesthetic, art
must be totally autonomous from the capitalist marketplace, whose demand
for immediate gratification turns art into kitsch. But he does not identify the
social basis for such cultural autonomy. Adorno has lost the traditional Marxist
faith in the ability of the industrial proletariat to ideologically transcend capitalist reification, and seems to deny a class basis for any transcendence. For
him artists seem to constitute a class unto themselves, capable of willing themselves free of the determinations of the market. Bourdieu's sophisticated class
analysis provides a more satisfactory method of sociologically grounding artistic autonomy and the resulting authentic aesthetic. He shows that under specific social conditions a fraction of the cultural bourgeoisie achieves autonomy
and develops an interest in a field whose logic is opposed to the market, even
though he denies that this logic is totally disinterested.

The art of the modern architects of Europe meets Adorno's criteria for
authenticity, especially in comparison to the consumer-responsive architecture of the Unites States. In America the progressive part of the technocratic
project—the demand for the rational organization of society—was compromised by the closeness of the professional-managerial class and its artists to
the capitalist market. Confined largely within capitalist corporations designing
commodities that would sell, American artists offered consumers comforting
illusions that covered over the ugliness of a rationalized capitalism. Disguising
the rectilinearity, standardization, and heteronomy of the Fordist factory, they
designed buildings and goods that ideologically announced that the utopia
of individuality, autonomy, and reconciliation was to be found in *this* society,
through the capitalist marketplace.

In Europe, by contrast, modern architects found autonomy from the
market through state commissions. Consequently, they were free to express
the logic of technocracy in its veritable form, revealing both the beauty and
the ugliness of their project and denying immediate reconciliation with the

existing society. Although Adorno is critical of this modern architecture, he also recognizes its authenticity as art, for it displays the social antagonisms of technocracy rather than seeking to cover them over.[130] The buildings of the best modernists possessed beauty, for they took the often fragmented forms of machines and industrial products and shaped them into harmonious proportions, reflecting the unifying potential of human reason. But at the same time these modernists unconsciously reflected the ugliness of the machine age and the instrumental form of rationality that underlay it. The unbending rectilinearity of their architecture testified to the unforgiving discipline of the specialized machines that absorbed workers' skills and subjected them to mind-numbing routine. The standardized similarity of their designs proclaimed the mass-production factory's destruction of the individual. The plain, unadorned surfaces of modernist boxes, as well as their stingy internal accommodations, symbolized the niggardly economy of effort and material imposed by the market on capitalists and workers alike. The empty, open spaces reminded occupants that they were just interchangeable commodities to be stored temporarily until the market again mandated their movement. Finally, the rigid segregation of classes in modernist city planning, with the working class relegated to a peripheral location, could not help but keep the insult of class degradation alive in the minds of the system's victims.

By faithfully reflecting the damage done to people within the rigidly authoritarian and dehumanized mass-production process, modern architects undermined their own intentions to reconcile workers to this society with a beautiful world of home consumption. Workers found it difficult to find peace and comfort in domestic surroundings disrupted by the ugliness of the instrumental rationality of work. By boldly bringing this ugliness into the domestic refuge, modernists prevented consumption from becoming a substitute for and sublimation of human needs denied in the workplace. Despite their intentions, modern architects did not preclude revolution but kept revolutionary hopes alive through their uncompromisingly alienated aesthetic. But the dynamics of Depression-era Europe determined that these surviving hopes of deliverance from instrumental reason and its Fordist techniques would be channeled into the reactionary delusions of fascism.

1. Le Corbusier, *Towards a New Architecture* (New York: Dover, 1986). The quotes are on 4, 264.

2. Ibid., 289, 271, 277–78.

3. Stuart and Elizabeth Ewen, *Channels of Desire: Mass Images and the Shaping of American Consciousness* (New York: McGraw-Hill, 1982), 117–28; Stuart Ewen, *All Consuming Images: The Politics of Style in Contemporary Culture* (New York: Basic Books, 1988), 111–16.

4. International Exhibition catalog quoted in Arthus J. Pulos, *American Design Ethic: A History of Industrial Design to 1940* (Cambridge, MA: MIT Press, 1983), 110. See also Sigfried Giedion, *Space, Time and Architecture*, 5th ed. (Cambridge, MA: Harvard University Press, 1967), 336–42; John Heskett, *Industrial Design* (New York: Oxford University Press, 1980), 50–58.

5. Bogardus quoted in Pulos, *American Design Ethic*, 107; Giedion, *Space*, 195–204, 347–63.

6. Reyner Banham, *A Concrete Atlantis: U.S. Industrial Building and European Modern Architecture, 1900–1925* (Cambridge, MA: MIT Press, 1986), 39–49; Gwendolyn Wright, *Building the Dream: A Social History of Housing in America* (Cambridge, MA: MIT Press, 1983), 114–34.

7. New York City Commissioners' Report quoted in Rem Koolhaas, *Delirious New York* (New York: Monacelli Press, 1994), 18. See also Kenneth T. Jackson, *Crabgrass Frontier: The Suburbanization of the United States* (New York: Oxford University Press, 1985), 73–75.

8. Wright, *Building the Dream*, 24–40; Banham, *Concrete Atlantis*, 49–56.

9. Jackson, *Crabgrass Frontier*, 20–32; Gwendolyn Wright, *Moralism and the Model Home: Domestic Architecture and Cultural Conflict in Chicago, 1873–1913* (Chicago: University of Chicago Press, 1980), 97–98; Wright, *Building the Dream*, 94–97; Karl Marx, "Economic and Philosophical Manuscripts of 1844," in Karl Marx and Frederick Engels, *Collected Works*, vol. 3 (New York: International Publishers, 1975), 306–26, esp. 314–15.

10. Pulos, *American Design Ethic*, 190–97; Ewen, *All Consuming Images*, 116–20. On Pierre Bourdieu's explanation of bourgeois taste, see his *Distinction: A Social Critique of the Judgement of Taste* (Cambridge, MA: Harvard University Press, 1984), 176–77, 292–94.

11. Bourdieu, *Distinction*, 318–71.

12. C. Wright Mills, *White Collar* (New York: Oxford University Press, 1951).

13. Wright, *Moralism and the Model Home*, 25–45, 79–81, 97–102; Wright, *Building the Dream*, 94–113.

14. Robert Wiebe, *The Search for Order, 1877–1929* (New York: Hill and Wang, 1967); James Weinstein, *The Corporate Ideal in the Liberal State, 1900–1918* (Boston: Beacon Press, 1968); Alfred D. Chandler, *The Visible Hand: The Managerial Revolution in American Business* (Cambridge, MA: Harvard University Press, 1977).

15. Thorstein Veblen, *The Theory of the Leisure Class* (New York: Modern Library, 1934), 115–66. The quote is on 151–52. On technocracy in general, see Charles Maier, "Between Taylorism and Technocracy: European Ideologies and the Vision of Industrial Productivity in the 1920s," *Journal of Contemporary History* 5, no. 2 (1970): 27–51.

16. Wright, *Moralism and the Model Home*, 145–49. The Stone quote is on 147.

17. On aristocratic aestheticism, see Bourdieu, *Distinction*, 214, 287–91, 317.

18. On the importance of class habitus in architectural education, see Garry Stevens, *The Favored Circle: The Social Foundations of Architectural Distinction* (Cambridge, MA: MIT Press, 1998), 186–201.

19. Louis Sullivan, *Kindergarten Chats and Other Writings* (New York: George Wittenborn, 1947), 170, 43, 30, 28, 21, 163. On Sullivan and the Chicago School, see also Giedion, *Space*, 368–93; Kenneth Frampton, *Modern Architecture: A Critical History*, 3rd ed. (London: Thames and Hudson, 1992), 51–56; and Sherman Paul, *Louis Sullivan* (Englewood Cliffs, NJ: Prentice-Hall, 1962), 1–23.

20. Sullivan, *Kindergarten Chats*, 115, 202.

21. Ibid., 189, 195.

22. T. J. Jackson Lears, "From Salvation to Self-Realization: Advertising and the Therapeutic Roots of the Consumer Culture, 1880–1930," in *The Culture of Consumption*, eds. Richard W. Fox and T. J. Jackson Lears (New York: Pantheon, 1983), 1–38.

23. Peter Blake, *The Master Builders: Le Corbusier, Mies van der Rohe, Frank Lloyd Wright* (New York: Norton, 1976), 287–301.

24. Frank Lloyd Wright, *The Living City* (New York: Bramhall House, 1958), 51, 36, 144. See also Frank Lloyd Wright, "The Art and Craft of the Machine," in *Roots of Contemporary American Architecture*, ed. Lewis Mumford (New York: Dover, 1972).

25. Wright, *Moralism and the Model Home*, 126–49. On the Arts and Crafts movement, see also Frampton, *Modern Architecture*, 42–50.

26. Leonard K. Eaton, *Two Chicago Architects and their Clients: Frank Lloyd Wright and Howard Van Doren Shaw* (Cambridge, MA: MIT Press, 1969).

27. Wright, *Living City*, 40, 20, 125, 208; Wright quoted in Giedion, *Space*, 409. See also John Peter, *The Oral History of Modern Architecture* (New York: Harry Abrams, 1994), 84; and Blake, *Master Builders*, 301–22.

28. Wright, *Moralism and the Model Home*, 134–40; Frampton, *Modern Architecture*, 59–62; Blake, *Master Builders*, 333–35; Giedion, *Space*, 418–22.

29. Wright, *Moralism and the Model Home*, 119–227; Ewen, *All Consuming Images*, 204–6.

30. Wright, *Moralism and the Model Home*, 273–91; Eaton, *Two Chicago Architects*, 229–35.

31. Wiebe, *Search for Order*, 292–93; Chandler, *Visible Hand*; Weinstein, *Corporate Ideal*. For a study of the integration of the engineering profession into corporations, see David F. Noble, *America by Design: Science, Technology, and the Rise of Corporate Capitalism* (New York: Knopf, 1977).

32. Pulos, *American Design Ethic*, 204–10; Ewen, *All Consuming Images*, 204–6; Eaton, *Two Chicago Architects*, 231. On the aesthetic affinities between cultural producers and consumers in homologous positions, see Bourdieu, *Distinction*, 230–44.

33. David Gartman, *Auto Slavery: The Labor Process in the American Automobile Industry, 1897–1950* (New Brunswick, N.J.: Rutgers University Press, 1986); David Hounshell, *From the American System to Mass Production, 1800–1932: The Development of Manufacturing Technology in the United States* (Baltimore: Johns Hopkins University Press, 1984); Terry Smith, *Making the Modern: Industry, Art, and Design in America* (Chicago: University of Chicago Press, 1993), 15–33.

34. David Gartman, *Auto Opium: A Social History of American Automobile Design* (London: Routledge, 1994), 43–49.

35. Banham, *Concrete Atlantis*, 56–107; Smith, *Making the Modern*, 34–40, 57–80.

36. Horace L. Arnold and Fay L. Faurote, *Ford Methods and the Ford Shops* (New York: Arno Press, 1972), 279–80; Gartman, *Auto Slavery*, 83–101; Smith, *Making the Modern*, 40–46.

37. Banham, *Concrete Atlantis*, 98–103; Smith, *Making the Modern*, 79–92, 141–44.

38. Smith, *Making the Modern*, 109–35; Gerald Silk, "The Automobile in Art," in *Automobile and Culture*, ed. Gerald Silk (New York and Los Angeles: Harry Abrams and The Museum of Contemporary Art, 1984), 91–100.

39. Henry Ford, *My Life and Work* (London: Heinemann, 1923), 128. See also Gartman, *Auto Slavery*, 203–14; Stephen Meyer III, *The Five Dollar Day: Labor Management and Social Control in the Ford Motor Company, 1908–1921* (Albany: State University of New York Press, 1981).

40. On welfare work in general, see Stuart D. Brandes, *American Welfare Capitalism* (Chicago: University of Chicago Press, 1976). For the attack on working-class culture, see Roy Rosenzweig, *Eight Hours for What We Will: Workers and Leisure in an Industrial City, 1870–1920* (New York: Cambridge University Press, 1983). On domestic reform, see Susan Strasser, "The Business of Housekeeping: The Ideology of the Household at the Turn of the Twentieth Century," *Insurgent Sociologist* 8 (Fall 1978): 147–63; and Lizabeth Cohen, "Embellishing a Life of Labor: An Interpretation of the Material Culture of American Working-Class Homes, 1885–1915," in *Material Culture Studies in America*, ed. Thomas J. Schlereth (Nashville: American Association for State and Local History, 1982), 289–305.

41. Cohen, "Embellishing a Life," 292–305; Pulos, *American Design Ethic*, 215–19; Wright, *Building the Dream*, 175–91; Wright, *Moralism and the Model Home*, 231–64.

42. Bourdieu, *Distinction*, 372–96; Cohen, "Embellishing a Life," 301–4; Heskett, *Industrial Design*, 49; Adrian Forty, *Objects of Desire* (New York: Pantheon, 1986), 101. For the Frankfurt School's theory of mass culture, see Max Horkheimer and Theodor Adorno, "The Culture Industry: Enlightenment as Mass Deception," in *Dialectic of Enlightenment* (New York: Herder and Herder, 1972), 120–67.

43. Model T joke is from David L. Lewis, *The Public Image of Henry Ford* (Detroit: Wayne State University Press, 1976), 125; Earnest Elmo Calkins, "Beauty the New Business Tool," *Atlantic Monthly* 140 (August 1927): 146; Gartman, *Auto Opium*, 39–67.

44. Gartman, *Auto Opium*, 62–99.

45. Paul Frankl quoted from his book *Machine-Made Leisure* (New York: Harper and Bros., 1932), 13–14, and in Jeffrey Meikle, *Twentieth Century Limited: Industrial Design in America, 1925–1939* (Philadelphia: Temple University Press, 1979), 153. On the organic look, see also Walter Dorwin Teague, *Design This Day* (London: Studio Publications, 1947), 26, 89.

46. Sinclair Lewis, *Babbitt* (New York: New American Library, 1961), 150.

47. For Bourdieu's subfields of cultural production, see his "The Field of Cultural Production," in *The Field of Cultural Production* (New York: Columbia University Press, 1993), 29–73. For a

comparison of Bourdieu's theory of culture with that of the Frankfurt school, see David Gartman, "Culture as Class Symbolization or Mass Reification? A Critique of Bourdieu's *Distinction*," *American Journal of Sociology* 97 (1991): 421–47.

48. On the hybrid nature of the architectural field, see Magali Sarfatti Larson, *Behind the Postmodern Facade* (Berkeley: University of California Press, 1993), 12–20.

49. Sarah Bradford Landau and Carl W. Condit, *Rise of the New York Skyscraper, 1865–1913* (New Haven, CT: Yale University Press, 1996).

50. On movies as working-class leisure, see Rosenzweig, *Eight Hours*, 191–221. On amusement parks, see Jackson, *Crabgrass Frontier*,112–13.

51. Koolhaas, *Delirious New York*, 29–79.

52. Ibid., 62–79; Rosenzweig, *Eight Hours*, 127–51; Robert Goldman and John Wilson, "The Rationalization of Leisure," *Politics and Society* 7, no. 2 (1977): 157–87.

53. For the aesthetic demands on the tall building during this period, see Katherine Solomonson, *The Chicago Tribune Tower Competition* (New York: Cambridge University Press, 2001).

54. Landau and Condit, *Rise of the New York Skyscraper*, 354–61, 381–91; Solomonson, *Chicago Tribune Tower*, 178–89, 226–32.

55. Landau and Condit, *Rise of the New York Skyscraper*, 293–94; Solomonson, *Chicago Tribune Tower*, 205–11; Koolhaas, *Delirious New York*, 107–9.

56. Mumford quoted in Manfredo Tafuri, "The New Babylon: The 'Yellow Giants' and the Myth of Americanism," in *The Sphere and the Labyrinth: Avant-Gardes and Architecture from Piranesi to the 1970s* (Cambridge, MA: MIT Press, 1990), 183. See also Richard Guy Wilson, Dianne H. Pilgrim, and Dickran Tashjian, *The Machine Age in America, 1918–1941* (New York: Harry Abrams, 1986), 150–55; and Koolhaas, *Delirious New York*, 100–4.

57. Wilson et al., *Machine Age*, 156–65; Koolhaas, *Delirious New York*, 165.

58. Koolhaas, *Delirious New York*, 162–207. The *Fortune* quote is on 178.

59. Ibid., 208–19.

60. Bertram D. Wolfe, *The Fabulous Life of Diego Rivera* (New York: Stein and Day, 1963), 297–340.

61. Arno J. Mayer, *The Persistence of the Old Regime* (New York: Pantheon, 1981).

62. Ibid.

63. Ibid., 253–72.

64. Charles S. Maier, "Between Taylorism and Technocracy: European Ideologies and the Vision of Industrial Productivity in the 1920s," *Journal of Contemporary History* 5, no. 2 (1970): 27–61; Mary Nolan, *Visions of Modernity: American Business and the Modernization of Germany* (New York: Oxford University Press, 1994).

65. Nolan, *Visions of Modernity*, 17–82.

66. Ibid., 131–78.

67. Ibid., 189–244; Anthony Jackson, *Reconstructing Architecture for the Twenty-First Century* (Toronto: University of Toronto Press, 1995), 20–34. On the changing position of artists in society, see also Pierre Bourdieu, "The Market of Symbolic Goods," in *The Field of Cultural Production* (New York: Columbia University Press, 1993), 112–41; Pierre Bourdieu, *The Rules of Art: Genesis and Structure of the Literary Field* (Stanford, CA: Stanford University Press, 1996), 47–112.

68. John Heskett, *Industrial Design* (New York: Oxford University Press, 1980), 85–92; Frampton, *Modern Architecture*, 96–99, 109–15; Reyner Banham, *Theory and Design in the First Machine Age* (New York: Praeger, 1967), 69–82.

69. Adolf Loos, "Ornament and Crime," in *Programs and Manifestoes on Twentieth-Century Architecture*, ed. Ulrich Conrads (Cambridge, MA: MIT Press, 1970), 21; see also the Loos quote in Frampton, *Modern Architecture*, 92; Le Corbusier, *Towards*, 18–19.

70. Barbara M. Lane, *Architecture and Politics in Germany, 1918–1945* (Cambridge, MA: Harvard University Press, 1985), 41–49. The Taut quote is on 48–49. See also Frampton, *Modern Architecture*, 116–22; Franz Schulze, *Mies van der Rohe: A Critical Biography* (Chicago: University of Chicago Press, 1985), 83–87.

71. Walter Gropius, "First Proclamation of the Weimar Bauhaus," in *Bauhaus: 1919–1928*, eds. Herbert Bayer, Walter Gropius, and Ise Gropius (New York: Museum of Modern Art, 1938), 18.

72. Lane, *Architecture and Politics*, 65–68.

73. Walter Gropius, "The Theory and Organization of the Bauhaus," in *Bauhaus: 1919–1928*, eds. Herbert Bayer, Walter Gropius, and Ise Gropius (New York: Museum of Modern Art, 1938), 23; Walter Gropius, *Scope of Total Architecture* (New York: Harper and Brothers, 1955), 11; Walter Gropius, *The New Architecture and the Bauhaus* (Cambridge, MA: MIT Press, 1965), 54.

74. Maier, "Between Taylorism and Technocracy."

75. Pierre Bourdieu, *Homo Academicus* (Stanford, CA: Stanford University Press, 1988), 165–66.

76. On the educational backgrounds of modern architects, see Mauro Guillén, "Scientific Management's Lost Aesthetic: Architecture,

Organization, and the Taylorized Beauty of the Mechanical," *Administrative Science Quarterly* 42 (1997): 704–7.

77. Le Corbusier, *Towards*, 283–84, 289, 271.

78. Ibid., 277–78, 8, 264, 4; Le Corbusier, *The Radiant City* (New York: Orion, 1967), 154.

79. Le Corbusier, *Towards*, 54; Le Corbusier, *When Cathedrals Were White* (New York: Reynal and Hitchcock, 1947), 168.

80. Le Corbusier, *City of Tomorrow*, 282; Le Corbusier, *Radiant City*, 1. See also Jean Jenger, *Le Corbusier: Architect, Painter, Poet* (New York: Harry Abrams, 1996), 74–75; Schulze, *Mies*, 185–86; Frampton, *Modern Architecture*, 184–85.

81. Loos, "Ornament and Crime," 22; Le Corbusier, *Towards*, 137, 238–39. See also Gropius, *Scope*, 30–40; Walter Gropius, *Rebuilding Our Communities* (Chicago: Paul Theobald, 1945), 34–37; Philippe Boudon, *Lived-In Architecture* (Cambridge, MA: MIT Press, 1972), 10–11, 193–95.

82. Ludwig Mies van der Rohe, "Aphorisms on Architecture and Form," in Philip Johnson, *Mies van der Rohe* (New York: Museum of Modern Art, 1947), 183–84; Hannes Meyer, "Building," in *Programs and Manifestoes*, 117–20. On the aesthetic use of American industrial architecture by European modernists, see Banham, *Concrete Atlantis*, 3–21, 215–30.

83. Gropius, *Scope*, 4; Le Corbusier, *Towards*, 143.

84. Ludwig Mies van der Rohe, "The New Era," in Johnson, *Mies van der Rohe*, 190; Mies interview quoted in Schulze, *Mies*, 270. See also Ludwig Mies van der Rohe, "Technology and Architecture," in *Programs and Manifestoes*, 154; Kenneth Frampton, *Studies in Tectonic Culture* (Cambridge, MA: MIT Press, 1996), 205–6.

85. On reification, see Georg Lukács, *History and Class Consciousness* (Cambridge, MA: MIT Press, 1971).

86. On instrumental or technological rationality in general, see Max Horkheimer and Theodor Adorno, *Dialectic of Enlightenment* (New York: Herder and Herder, 1972); Max Horkheimer, *Eclipse of Reason* (New York: Seabury, 1974); Herbert Marcuse, *One-Dimensional Man* (Boston: Beacon Press, 1964).

87. Le Corbusier, *City of Tomorrow*, 5, 12.

88. Mies quoted in John Peter, *The Oral History of Modern Architecture* (New York: Harry Abrams, 1994), 168. See also Peter Blake, *The Master Builders* (New York: Norton, 1976), 236–38; M. Gottdiener, *The Social Production of Urban Space* (Austin: University of Texas Press, 1985), 124–31.

89. Gropius, *Scope*, xiii, 175; Ludwig Mies van der Rohe, "Inaugural Address as Director of Architecture at Armour Institute of Technology," in Johnson, *Mies van der Rohe*, 194; Le Corbusier, *Towards*, 110, 17, 242–43.

90. Le Corbusier, *Towards*, 94.

91. Banham, *Theory and Design*, 211.

92. Gropius, *Rebuilding*, 46; Le Corbusier, *Radiant City*, 55; Blake, *Master Builders*, 58–61. On the way that Le Corbusier's architecture frames and dominates nature with an objectifying gaze, see also Beatriz Colomina, "The Split Wall: Domestic Voyeurism," in *Sexuality and Space*, ed. Beatriz Colomina (New York: Princeton Architectural Press, 1992), 110–28.

93. Le Corbusier, *Radiant City*, 177, 179; Hannes Meyer quoted in Frampton, *Modern Architecture*, 134. On a different interpretation of this erasure of the barrier between inside and outside, private and public, see Beatriz Colomina, *Privacy and Publicity: Modern Architecture as Mass Media* (Cambridge, MA: MIT Press, 1994), 1–15, 283–335.

94. Mies quoted in Frampton, *Modern Architecture*, 163. On the destruction of privacy, see Max Horkheimer, "Authority and the Family," in *Critical Theory* (New York: Continuum, 1972), 47–128.

95. Gropius, "Theory and Organization," 29.

96. Blake, *Master Builders*, 236–38, 249; Le Corbusier, *City of Tomorrow*, 231.

97. Gropius, *Scope*, 36–37; Giedion, *Space*, 491–97.

98. Banham, *Theory and Design*, 322; Johnson, *Mies*, 30, 58; Schulze, *Mies*, 109–16, 157–58. On Mies's ground plans, see Frampton, *Studies*, 159–207.

99. Jaquelin Robertson, "Machines in the Garden," *Architectural Forum* 138 (May 1973): 53; Behne quoted in Kenneth Frampton, "Industrialization and the Crisis in Architecture," *Oppositions* 1 (1973): 73; Le Corbusier, *Towards*, 237, 263.

100. Le Corbusier, *Towards*, 129–48. On the aesthetics of early mass-produced cars, see Gartman, *Auto Opium*, 39–67. For a critique of the technological basis of modern architecture, see Banham, *Theory and Design*, 325–29; Reyner Banham, "Machine Aesthetic," *Architectural Review* 117 (April 1955): 224–28.

101. Frampton, *Studies*, 175–78, 203–7.

102. Le Corbusier, "Charter of Athens," in *Programs and Manifestoes*, 137–38; Le Corbusier, *City of Tomorrow*, 108.

103. Le Corbusier, *City of Tomorrow*, 116, 277–78, on plans for the Ville Contemporaine, see 163–78.

104. Ibid., 282; Giedion, *Space*, 744–54. The quote is on p. 746.

105. Le Corbusier, *City of Tomorrow*, 84, 237.

106. Ibid., 25; Giedion, *Space*, 767–69; Le Corbusier quoted in Banham, *Theory and Design*, 253.

107. Edward Soja, *Postmoderm Geographies* (London: Verso, 1989), 176–80; Frampton, *Modern Architecture*, 47–48; Giedion, *Space*, 782–85.

108. Le Corbusier, *City of Tomorrow*, 170–78. The quote is on 206.

109. Ford, *My Life and Work*, 192.

110. Le Corbusier, *Radiant City*, 113; Le Corbusier, *Towards*, 123. See also Le Corbusier, *City of Tomorrow*, 215–20.

111. Le Corbusier, *Radiant City*, 124; Le Corbusier, *City of Tomorrow*, 167, 70.

112. On the ideology of taste, see Bourdieu, *Distinction*.

113. Le Corbusier, *Radiant City*, 179.

114. Lane, *Architecture and Politics*, 87–90; Nolan, *Visions of Modernity*, 119–20, 206–7; Adelheid von Saldern, "The Workers' Movement and Cultural Patterns on Urban Housing Estates and in Rural Settlements in Germany and Austria during the 1920s," *Social History* 15 (Oct. 1990): 333–54.

115. Lane, *Architecture and Politics*, 90–124.

116. Bruno Taut, "A Programme for Architecture," in *Programs and Manifestoes*, 42; Manfredo Tafuri, "Sozialpolitik and the City in Weimar Germany," in *The Sphere and the Labyrinth* (Cambridge, MA: MIT Press, 1990), 197–233; Von Saldern, "Workers' Movement," 352.

117. Lane, *Architecture and Politics*, 102, 109; Tafuri, "Sozialpolitik and the City," 200–2; Le Corbusier quote from the text of a speech given at the inauguration of the Quartiers Modernes Fruges at Pessac, June 13, 1926, reproduced in Boudon, *Lived-In Architecture*, 194.

118. Boudon, *Lived-In Architecture*, 121–22; Nolan, *Visions of Modernity*, 206–26; Heskett, *Industrial Design*, 81–84; Sigfried Giedion, *Mechanization Takes Command* (New York: Norton, 1969), 522–27.

119. Gropius, *Scope*, 104–18. The quote is on 125.

120. Von Saldern, "Workers' Movement," 342–46. The quote is on 343; Boudon, *Lived-In Architecture*, 38.

121. On the difference between American and European programs of household rationalization, see Victoria de Grazia, *Irresistible Empire: America's Advance through Twentieth-Century Europe* (Cambridge, MA: Harvard University Press, Belknap Press, 2005), 423–38.

122. Lane, *Architecture and Politics*, 69–86, 125–45. The Senger quote is on 141.

123. The quotes are in Lane, *Architecture and Politics*, 131, 139. See also Nolan, *Visions of Modernity*, 108–26.

124. Lane, *Architecture and Politics*, 135–36; Bayer et al., *Bauhaus*, 92; Erich Fromm, *The Working Class in Weimar Germany* (Cambridge, MA: Harvard University Press, 1984), 98–104; Nolan, *Visions of Modernity*, 175–78.

125. Lane, *Architecture and Politics*, 103, 122; Nolan, *Visions of Modernity*, 226; Von Saldern, "Workers' Movement," 348–49.

126. Boudon, *Lived-In Architecture*. The quote is on 104.

127. Boudon, *Lived-In Architecture*. The quotes are on 100–1, 78–79.

128. Horkheimer and Adorno, *Dialectic of Enlightenment*.

129. Thedor Adorno, *Aesthetic Theory* (London: Routledge, 1980). For a more extensive exposition of Adorno's aesthetic theory, with an emphasis on architecture, see Hilde Heynen, *Architecture and Modernity: A Critique* (Cambridge, MA: MIT Press, 1999), esp. 148–225.

130. Theodor Adorno, "Functionalism Today," in *Rethinking Architecture*, ed. Neil Leach (London: Routledge, 1997), 6–19.

3

Displaced Dreams of Wholeness:
The Depression-Era Retreat of Modernism

FORD AND THE FÜHRER—the relationship between the father of Fordism and the father of Nazism embodied the contradictory responses to the economic disaster of the Great Depression. Hitler assembled popular support for his Nazi Party by railing against mass production and calling for a return to agrarianism and the crafts. After coming to power, however, the Führer praised Ford, sending German engineers to study his methods and awarding him the Grand Cross of the Supreme Order of the German Eagle. Hitler came to realize that his nostalgic vision of an organic community rooted in the land could be achieved only by building roads into the countryside and mass producing cars to take people there.

For his part, Henry Ford realized shortly after pioneering mass production that the urban concentrations of capital and labor required by it created dangerous class discontents. He began in the 1920s to build small, rural plants, and by the 1930s Ford was pushing as a cure for the Depression the return of workers to the land, where they could grow their own food to supplement their wages. But Ford also advocated a system of superhighways, on which workers could drive their streamlined cars to the country. Ultimately, both Ford and the Führer converged on an idea that was increasingly popular among the powerful of this period—alleviating the discontent caused by the breakdown of mass production by creating an accelerated and decentralized realm of mass consumption. Both also realized that the landscape, homes, and products of this compensating realm of consumption would have to cover the fragmentation of machine production celebrated by modernism with an aesthetic of wholeness.

———

Anti-Fordist Struggles and Diversionary Dreams

These Depression-era promises of machine-made wholeness were responses to the popular reaction against Fordist rationalization and the machine aesthetic that symbolized it. The Depression raised questions about the ability of unfettered Fordism to deliver the goods to the masses. Left to the fitful regulation of the market, the rationalized machinery was capable of producing far more commodities than consumers could buy with their wages. In the early 1930s, the popular image of Fordism was transformed from the savior of humanity to its curse, both in America and abroad. In 1939 a Gallup poll of Americans on relief found that the most frequently mentioned cause of unemployment was the increased use of machinery. In Germany most parties lost their enthusiasm for *Fordismus*, and most rank and file workers blamed the unprecedented levels of unemployment directly on industrial rationalization. This loss of faith in Fordist capitalism touched off social movements that, although politically diverse, were united by their collectivism and populism. From communism and industrial unionism on the left to fascism and Nazism on the right, all movements pushed for greater collective control over the vicissitudes of the market. And they all paid at least political lip service to the interests and power of "the people." In recognition of the mobilized masses of workers, unemployed, aged, and others, all parties downplayed talk of experts, intellectuals, and capitalists, and paid homage to the common man and woman, variously defined.[1]

The popular, collectivist struggles of the Depression encountered opposition from the established classes with a stake in rationalized capitalism. The political outcome of these clashes was determined largely by the stage of Fordist development in which each country found itself at the onset of the 1930s. In the United States, where Fordist production and a placating culture of mass consumption were already well established, the revolt was displaced into the market for mass consumption. A strong class of capitalists and their technocratic allies beat back popular challenges with the argument that America could consume its way out of the Depression with products that were "humanized" to better serve the needs of consumers. Fordist corporations promised America a utopia of streamlined machines that facilitated movement out of troubled cities into the peaceful countryside. In Germany, where Fordism was still in its infancy, dreams of a mass-consumption utopia were unable to bear the burden of popular desires for wholeness. Because there remained sizable contingents of craftworkers and petty bourgeois with fond memories of a proximate past of small-scale capitalism, people dreamed not of a leap into the future but a return to the past. Hitler cleverly mobilized this dream of a fictitious past for a state-led program of reaction.

The aesthetic movements of this tumultuous period reflected these contradictory dreams of past and future, of nature and machines. All were united, however, by a rejection of modernism as it had come to be defined by Europe's avant-garde. The militant celebration of the machine and its instrumental rationality was clearly unwelcome by Fordism's Depression-era victims. Even the moderate angularity of America's modernistic architecture seemed out of place in the depressed 1930s. Corporate purveyors of the streamlined consumer utopia realized that selling their vision to machine-weary consumers required even greater obfuscation of the aesthetic reminders of the Fordist workplace. Architects and designers pursuing this vision redoubled their previous efforts to humanize the machine by rounding off angular protrusions and lending objects the soft, organic look of nature. I will call this trend in American architecture and design romantic modernism, for although it retained the mechanical connotations of speed and efficiency, this aesthetic obscured the harsh rationality of production with the romance of consumption.

Although this romanticized modernism predominated in America, two subsidiary aesthetics were also apparent, representing different facets of the emerging system of mass consumption. Because the state played an expanding role in collectivizing and regulating consumption through Keynesian demand management programs, it was necessary to express this role in state architecture. Here, a stripped and monumental neoclassicism emerged. Oblique references to classical architecture created a reassuring heritage for this new state role, while the symmetry of the style lent public institutions an aura of order in these tumultuous times. The imposing scale also gave the state an image of power, enveloping the individual in a collective spectacle of the nation. The final aesthetic of the period was nostalgic populism, a symbolic concession to the importance of "the people." Prevalent in individual housing, this style symbolically promised a return to a simple past by aping the vernacular architecture of different regions. Although formally diverse, this aesthetic was unified by antiurban references and an obsession with reuniting people with nature.

These same aesthetic dreams of wholeness were present in Europe, especially in Germany, but in a different proportional mix determined by the different response to depression. The Nazi Party channeled popular longings for a premodern past into a reactionary program in which the militarized state, not corporate capital, played the central role. Thus, architecture was dominated by a neoclassical monumentalism that glorified and eternalized the Nazi state apparatus. Going beyond the milder monumentalism of America and other parts of Europe, Nazi state architecture was dedicated to the regimentation of society, reducing all individuality to a mass absolutely subordinate to the all-powerful Führer. But once Nazi monumentalism had leveled individuals, it then enveloped them in an irrational community of race and *Volk* (folk) with a trumped-up heritage of greatness. A similar escape into the premodern past was provided by the populist or *völkisch* aesthetic, which was confined largely to public housing and regional state buildings. This style celebrated the rural past of the common people and their unity with the soil. Finally, the Nazis employed the humanized style of romantic modernism in their programs of Fordist mass production and motorization, which they realized were required to capture the glories of a premodern past. Hitler's program of mass motorization provided both the means of escape to the purifying countryside and the industrial basis for the military might to capture more living space for the Aryan masses. In order to reconcile their program of industrial domination with their antimodern ideology, the Nazis adopted romantic modernism for their machines and factories.

Although distinctly different in many ways, both the American market-led program of futuristic consumption and the German state-led program of reactionary recovery furthered the progress of capitalist rationalization by putting a pretty face on this Moloch. Popular demands for a collectively controlled and just society were ultimately diverted into fantasies of consumption based on reconfigured, organic space. As Americans and Germans alike dreamed dreams of spatial fulfillment, the nightmare of history proceeded unimpeded.

Europe Pioneers the Aesthetic Reaction

The most radical reactions to the collapse of the Fordist promise came from Europe, where mass production and mass consumption were least developed. Unlike in America, Fordist rationalization had yet to fundamentally transform either the class structure of production or the culture of consumption. State-led rationalization programs had threatened but not eliminated large contingents of craftworkers and petty bourgeois, who retained vivid memories of a recent past of power and prosperity. Nor had a mass-consumer culture emerged to provide narcotizing escape from the exigencies of rationalized production. A still viable premodern high culture rooted in the Old Regime was ready to confront a weak modernist culture of technocracy discredited by economic collapse. Consequently, the economic debris of the Depression fueled the existing fires of reaction to state-led rationalization and its aesthetic symbol in modern architecture.

In Germany, in particular, a strong critique of rationalization and modernism emerged in the late 1920s, as the ravages of state programs intensified. This critique crystallized around *völkisch* ideology, a right-wing combination of populism and nationalism. Its advocates believed that industrialization and urbanization were undermining the foundation of German culture and community—the racially pure peasant. Big industry, it was said, attracted a racially degraded working class and replaced the organic ties of the rural community with materialistic connections. *Völkisch* ideologues argued that modern architecture reflected this racial and social degradation, and it became their favorite cultural target. Paul Schultze-Naumburg (1869–1949), architect and founding member of the *völkisch* cultural organization Der Block, argued that traditional

German rural architecture reflected the rural rootedness of the Aryan race, while modern architecture was "the work of the nomads of the metropolis, who have lost entirely the concept of the homeland....We feel that something irreplaceable is annihilated, either intentionally or unintentionally, while, as a substitute, a soulless, godless, and mechanical world threatens to rise, in which life has lost its inmost meaning." Alfred Rosenberg, another *völkisch* ideologue and the founder of the Kampfbund für Deutsche Kultur (Militant League for German Culture), similarly denounced modern architecture as "engineer art," and asserted that architecture rooted in the blood of Germany's "Nordic race" should resemble that of the classic Greeks, from which it was descended. Regardless of these divergent racial mythologies, the *völkisch* movement was clearly united in criticism of the destruction of human bonds by the instrumental rationality of the market and mass production. But instead of looking forward to create new noninstrumental bonds for the industrial age, it searched the past for a lost community to restore, constructing myths of race and nation. These myths were confined to small circles of nationalists until the onset of the Depression, when the Nazis seized the *völkisch* critique of modern architecture and used it to channel the rising tide of popular frustration toward their movement.[2]

German *völkisch* ideology was, however, only an extreme form of a general questioning of Fordist rationalization and its machine aesthetic in Depression-era Europe. Outside the increasingly volatile politics of Germany, many modern artists sought to temper technocratic enthusiasm for the machine with humanistic and collectivist impulses that did not resort to racist nostalgia. By the late 1930s even the preeminent historian and diplomat of modern architecture, Sigfried Giedion, had become, in his words, "conscious of the limits of logic and rationality" embodied in modernism. He wrote that industrial production had split the human personality between reason and emotion, and that it could be made whole again only by subordinating the rational machine to the organic, feeling human. "The machine must be guided in such a way that its products stem directly from a human point of view, fundamentally growing out of a humanistic atmosphere." Giedion identified several surrealist artists as pioneers of this Depression-era attempt to humanize a mechanical society with organic forms. The undulating, curvilinear but abstract forms of painter Joan Miró and sculptor Hans Arp attempted to dredge up reminders of an untamed world of unconscious human desires just beneath the surface of manufactured objects, which in Europe had not been totally rationalized by mass production.[3]

Foremost among the architects developing this surrealist sensibility was Alvar Aalto (1898–1976). In fact, this Finnish architect incorporated in his work all three of the aesthetic tendencies of this period—populism, classicism, and romantic modernism—that sought to humanize machine civilization. But unlike other architects, who used these styles to create an artificial wholeness that reconciled humanity to existing industrialism, Aalto created buildings in which his organic elements stood in stark, unreconciled tension to modern ones, testifying to the unfulfilled promise of a genuinely human industrial civilization. As an artist in Finland, Aalto stood in a unique position to accomplish this consciously incomplete synthesis. Finland compressed into one decade three modern developments that other countries required a century or more to accomplish: national independence, democratic government, and industrial development. Consequently, the aesthetic symbols of these struggles were complexly superimposed on one another. In the early 1920s, shortly after Finland achieved national independence from the Soviet Union, Aalto and other Finnish architects were still expressing nationalist impulses with national romanticism, an aesthetic dating back to the turn of the century that combined a timber vernacular with indigenous medieval architecture. But with national unity on a firm basis by the mid-1920s, Finnish architects turned increasingly to classicism to express and bolster the country's new democratic government. By the late 1920s, when Finland was beginning to industrialize, Aalto led the country's architects in adopting modern architecture to symbolize this transition, designing several notable buildings in a rectilinear, rationalized style.[4]

By the early 1930s, however, Finland's preeminent modernist was backpedaling, compromising his machine aesthetic with curvilinear, organic elements reminiscent of the surrealists. The first manifestation of this synthesis was the tuberculosis sanatorium at Paimio, completed in 1933. The stark white exteriors, long ribbon windows, and rectilinear concrete frame were clearly modernist. Yet, these elements were juxtaposed to a number of curving, organic elements, especially in the separate wing of sunning balconies. Unlike the squared-off balconies at the end of the rectilinear patient's wing, the balconies of this wing were smoothly rounded on the corners. And the entire wing of sunning balconies was connected to the patient's wing with an undulating curve. The entrance to the lobby of the building was also covered with a canopy in a curving, grand-piano shape.[5]

Aalto articulated the intentions of his more romantic, curvilinear modernism in his writings of the 1930s, in which he criticized the "technical rationalization" of architecture and called for a rationality based upon human functions. "We all know that we are living in an age which is involved in a continuous battle against mechanization and machines....We say we should be masters of machines whereas in fact we are their slaves....The main duty of the architect is to humanize the age of machines." This duty involved introducing variety into the standardized schemes of machine modernism, in order to protect "the single human being against large groups of people and the pressure from the collectivity." After the Paimio Sanatorium, Aalto gradually turned away from his romantic modernism and back to the vernacular wooden architecture of Finland to achieve such individualism and privacy. But unlike the *völkisch* ideologues, who completely covered over the brutality of the machine with fictionalized visions of a preindustrial past, Aalto maintained a tense balance between the promise of humanization and its continued denial in the existing industrial society.[6]

Such was the achievement of the Villa Mairea (1939), a private residence for a Finnish industrialist. The house was a complex combination of the cold artificiality of the machine and the warm organicism of nature. The main mass was rendered in mechanical rectilinearity, while the entrance canopy, plunge pool, and attached studio had the curvilinear forms of nature. On the exterior, public rooms were clad in rough wooden siding, while private rooms were

Alvar Aalto, Villa Mairea, Noormarkku, Finland, 1939 (Photograph Gustaf Welin/ Alvar Aalto Museum)

finished in smooth, white stucco. Inside, the main staircase was supported by irregularly spaced, slender wooden poles, while the living room was interrupted by two thick steel columns in black enamel. But even the latter expressed an internal contradiction by being wrapped intermittently with delicate caning. Open and flowing spaces were combined with quiet, private areas. And on and on the stark juxtapositions revealed themselves.[7]

At Mairea Aalto revealed, but refused to resolve, the contradiction between the human subject and the mechanical object of rationalized capitalism. The cane weaving and wooden siding revealed the labor of assembly in a craft process in which humans consciously shaped natural materials to their needs. But instead of using these organic touches to cover over the brutality done to craft labor by Fordist machines, Aalto confronted one with the other, revealing the human price paid for mass production. Industrial ugliness confronted craftwork beauty, each denying the other. The objective machine forms refused a nostalgic retreat to a sanitized past, and the subjective craft forms refused to let the machine portray itself as the fulfillment of humanity. The unresolved aesthetic tension provided no home in the present, no end to or retreat from history, but goaded it on to a different, more humane future.

Also maintaining a tense balance between the organic and the mechanical during the 1930s was one of the most militant modernists of the 1920s, Le Corbusier. In his writings of the Depression era, he continued his bent toward corporatist technocracy, but his expression of this program was transformed from an objective modernism to an abstract populism and organicism. With his ear always to the ground, Le Corbusier heard the low rumble of change approaching from the east. In 1931 he and other leading modernists were invited by Soviet authorities to submit entries for a competition to design the Palace of the Soviets, a public building that would represent the achievements of the Russian revolution. Seeing the Soviet experiment as part of an international trend toward rationalization and technocracy, Le Corbusier's entry was a militant exercise in the machine aesthetic, featuring a Great Hall with a roof suspended from a parabolic arch and a totally transparent skin. But under Stalin, Soviet policy was changing from an expansive internationalism to a defensive nationalism. Consequently, Le Corbusier's design was rejected and denounced by Soviet authorities in *Pravda* for its "spirit of 'naked industrialism.'" The jury awarded first prize to a Russian, Boris Iofan (1891–1976), whose entry was a neoclassical wedding cake of tiered colonnades culminating in a monumental statue of a worker, which was replaced in subsequent alterations by the figure of Lenin. The Soviet elite evidently thought that Le Corbusier's

Le Corbusier and Pierre Jeanneret, Swiss Pavilion at the Cité Universitaire, Paris, 1932 (© 2006 Artists Rights Society, NY/ADAGP, Paris/FLC L2(8)24)

machine aesthetic did not represent the increasingly embattled and isolated state around which it sought to rally the common people with socialist realism. Officially endorsed by the party in 1932, this nationalist and populist aesthetic was thought to appeal to the people by incorporating traditions comprehensible to them.[8]

Although shaken by this rejection from a country he counted as an aesthetic ally, Le Corbusier drew an important lesson from defeat, and gradually forsook the purism of his machine aesthetic for a more humanistic style that drew on organic and popular elements. In several vacation houses built in France in the mid-1930s, he used vernacular styles and natural materials, revealing a new sensitivity to landscape and tradition. The Villa de Mandrot (1931) had some concrete elements, but its bearing walls were of native stone and the roof was pitched. The Mathes house (1935) was made entirely of stone and wood in a traditional post-and-beam pattern. Departing even further from the flat roof, Le Corbusier gave this house a butterfly or V-shaped roof. In another weekend house near Paris, built in 1935, he used a sensuously curved barrel-vaulted roof.[9]

While Le Corbusier's domestic architecture of the 1930s used vernacular styles of common construction, his urban and institutional works were contradictory compounds of monumental modernism and natural organicism. Such was the case in the pivotal Swiss Pavilion of 1932, a hostel for Swiss students at the Cité Universitaire in Paris. In many respects typical of Le Corbusier's machine aesthetic, the building was a white, steel-framed rectangle raised on pilotis and faced with a glass curtain wall. But a careful eye encountered numerous contradictory details. The pilotis were no longer slender steel columns of spiritualized support but massive ovoid structures of concrete that visibly bore the building's weight. The rectilinear slab of rooms was contradicted by the free-formed block of communal areas, with its sensuously curved, rubble-stone wall. Similar contrasts were present in Le Corbusier's Depression-era design of an automobile. While in the 1920s he praised the functional rectilinearity of the Model T, his Voiture Minimum design of the 1930s abandoned the right angle and substituted a sweeping curve that began at the top of the windshield, swept over the passenger compartment past the rear-mounted engine and then down to the bumper. The organic curves of the roof and rear were contradicted, however, by the straight mechanical line of the front, which slashed down to complete the slope of the windshield. Once again the pioneer of the modern movement was making concessions to a more organic aesthetic, but without totally erasing reminders of machine rationality.[10]

In their work of the 1930s, Aalto and Le Corbusier reflected the dilemmas of the European modernists and their technocratic allies, whose social position was altered substantially by the decade's developments. The already heavy dependence of European architects on state commissions increased during the decade, since the Depression severely limited the availability of private funds for building. But the ideological agenda of state architecture changed sharply in the 1930s, reflecting its changed role in capitalist society. The Depression severely discredited the state programs of industrial rationalization of the 1920s and their technocratic promulgators, on which most workers blamed the economic downturn. The latter joined other classes, especially the petty bourgeoisie, to demand that the state provide not facilitation of but collective protection from the ravages of economic rationalization. To ideologically testify to this new role, the state needed an architecture that spoke of the power and heritage of the nation-state and the importance of "the people" in its eyes. Yielding to the demands of their state patrons, many modernists like Aalto and Le Corbusier were willing to compromise the machine aesthetic with elements of populism, organicism, and classical monumentalism. Even the few private patrons with money to build during the Depression, like Aalto's Finnish industrialist, did not seem to want to confront others with aesthetic reminders of the industrial machinery that had broken down, preferring more popular and organic forms.

The political opportunism of modern architects and their technocratic project became more evident than ever during the depression. Many like Le Corbusier actively courted authoritarian regimes of the left and right. Le Corbusier dedicated his 1935 manifesto on city planning, *La Ville Radieuse*, "to Authority," and promptly sent complimentary copies to Stalin, Mussolini, Nehru, and Pétain, the latter of which went on to head the collaborationist French Vichy government. And under Vichy France he accepted an appointment to a committee charged with the reinvigoration of the building industry. In Nazi Germany Walter Gropius, Martin Wagner (1885–1957), and Hugo Häring (1882–1958) privately appealed for support from Goebbels's Propaganda Ministry, with Gropius arguing for the inherent "Germanness" of the new architecture. When the Nazis shut down the Bauhaus in April of 1933, then director Mies van der Rohe pleaded with Alfred Rosenberg, Minister of Culture, to reopen it, arguing that the school was not interested in politics but merely the aesthetics of technology and industrial development. In the United States Philip Johnson (1906–2005), a curator at the Museum of Modern Art and admirer of Mies, wrote an article indirectly appealing to the Nazis to accept his hero, arguing "Mies has always kept out of politics" and "is respected by conservatives." In Italy the indigenous modernists, known as rationalists, organized the Movimento Italiano per l'Architettura Razionale and appealed directly to Mussolini for support in a 1931 pamphlet, arguing "our movement has no other moral aim than that of serving the Revolution in the prevailing harsh climate."[11]

Despite the willingness of many modern architects to politically compromise with far-right regimes, those who remained true to their aesthetic principles found little acceptance in the changed social climate of the 1930s. In Germany, the Gestapo gave Mies permission to reopen the Bauhaus, but it remained closed due largely to lack of financial support from the state. Mies staid in the country four more years, until Nazi interference in one of his few commissions motivated his emigration to the United States. For him, like many modernists, it was not the Nazis' politics but their restriction of artistic autonomy that was decisive. In fascist Italy modernism was tolerated temporarily, but eventually the classicists were victorious over the rationalists. Even Le Corbusier and his more organic modernism found little success beyond a few commissions. The personal politics of modernists mattered little. Their real failing was a technocratic aesthetic that idealized technical expertise and technology and thus symbolized their interests as members of the cultural bourgeoisie. But a growing number of workers and petty bourgeois saw this class and its technology as responsible for the economic debacle of the 1930s. For a state that was seeking to contain the rising discontent of these classes with visions of collective unity, the machine aesthetic was anathema. An aesthetic acceptable to both would have to completely obliterate reminders of the ahistorical efficiency of the machine and replace them with the historical togetherness of nation and people. No country was more inventive in this aesthetic of trumped-up collectivism and populism than Nazi Germany.[12]

Nazi Architecture: The Aesthetic Reaction as Mass Deception

Hitler's National Socialist German Workers' Party was slow to join the *völkisch* critique of modern architecture. In fact, before 1930 Alfred Rosenberg's party-affiliated cultural organization, Kampfbund für Deutsche Kultur, published several articles praising the modernist housing estates. But in this year the Nazi Party realized that a campaign against modernism, which was already associated in the public mind with industrial rationalization and unemployment, could take advantage of the sentiment against these problems exacerbated by the Great Depression. Consequently, it began to take a harshly critical stance toward both modern technology and the architecture that symbolized it. The *völkisch* critic Paul Schultze-Naumburg and his racist theories of art became influential on Nazi cultural policy, and the party sponsored popular lectures by him. By early 1933 Nazi cultural propaganda was dominated by criticism of modern architecture. Much of it appealed to unemployed workers in the building trades, arguing that modernist mass-production techniques threw them out of work and promising that the Nazis would revive craft production and restore construction activity.[13]

The Nazi attack on modern architecture also appealed to workers and the petty bourgeoisie by denouncing the intellectual bourgeoisie, whose interests were symbolized and advanced by the style. Some critics called modernism the mere musings of intellectuals that were unrelated to the real needs of the German people. Engineers, the professionals most closely associated with industrial rationalization, came in for the most bashing. Alfred Rosenberg denounced modern architecture as "engineer art," arguing: "This movement exclusively emphasizes rationalism of a mere purposelessness. Therefore it only appeals to the schematizing brains of engineers." These attacks were part of the broader anti-intellectualism of Nazism, which probably had its origins in Hitler himself. The Führer had little use for people with credentials or education. As an aspiring architect, he was rejected by the Vienna Academy School of Architecture in 1907 for lack of talent. Without a credential, he was unable to practice but remained interested in the field, sketching and producing plans for rebuilding entire cities. Hitler later wrote resentfully of education: "It's all wrong that a man's whole life should depend on a diploma that he either receives or doesn't receive at the age of seventeen." He argued that self-taught architects from the common people best reflected the will of the race.[14]

This attack on modern architecture seemed to help the Nazi Party gain support among the petty bourgeoisie, as well as workers outside of big industry, that is, those in agriculture, the public and service sectors, and the handicrafts and small workshops. (During the Depression many industrial workers were drawn to the German Communist Party, which also grew rapidly because it was highly critical of industrial rationalization, if not modern architecture.)[15] But given the Nazis' late entrance into the debate around modern architecture, it is necessary to ask whether the Nazi movement was genuinely opposed to industrial rationalization, technology, and intellectuals, or merely used these popular criticisms opportunistically to win support. Albert Speer (1905–1981), the major architect of the Third Reich and later armaments minister, argued after the war that Hitler was genuinely antimodern, and polemicized against the "soulless machine" and mass production in the name of artisanal production. Otto Wagener, Hitler's economic adviser until 1934, also argued that the Führer truly believed that the individual "had become enslaved by industrialisation, was in bondage to capital and the machine." Speer and others argued that only the necessity of rearmament for war and pressure from powerful industrialists and financiers forced Hitler to eventually endorse the Fordist rationalization of industry.[16]

It is fruitless, however, to ask what Hitler really believed about mass production and rationalization in his heart of hearts, for the answer would not help to explain the actions of the Nazi Party in Germany. The political rule of Nazism must be understood not as representing the ideology or interests of a particular class or class fraction but as an instance of the relative autonomy of the state. Heightened class conflict during the Weimar Republic prevented the bourgeoisie as a class from ruling democratically, and allowed the emergence of an independent state power that detached itself from society and subordinated all classes to its rule. Having no specific social base or interests, apart from gaining and holding power, the Nazis were free to manipulate their ideas to appeal to whatever group seemed strategically important at the time. Nazi architectural policy was part of this opportunistic, shifting pastiche of ideas that served as a direct vehicle for the political ambitions of the party-state. This motive was unequivocally expressed by Speer, the main architect of Nazi state buildings and one of Hitler's closest confidants. He wrote, in retrospect: "[Critics are] right to detect Hitler's desire for power and the submission of others in my buildings....Our means had no ideological grounding, but were politically demonstrated: they were inspired by the experience of the political struggle for power."[17]

By subordinating architecture directly to politics, the Nazis destroyed the relative autonomy that the field had won in early capitalism. This autonomy had always been partial, since architects required economic capital from either capitalists or the state to build. But before this period, market and state patronage had been channeled through an arena of artistic competition governed by autonomous aesthetic principles. The battle between architects for commissions was a battle of ideas tied to positions in the architectural field, which were indirectly tied to positions in the social field of classes. The Nazis, however, put an end to this relatively autonomous field by directly subordinating architecture to the battle for power, eliminating the mediating architectural principles. Nazi architecture, as Speer stated, had no ideology, no set of ideas that mediated the interests and problems of a particular social group. It was a mere weapon, the expression of the will to domination of a relatively autonomous state gang.[18] When the National Socialists assumed power in 1933, they undertook a huge building program faithful to the significance they attributed to architecture in their rise to power. This program also was intended to stimulate economic activity and fulfill Nazi promises to the building trades. But while the scale of the building program lived up to the prepower propaganda, its aesthetics was a disappointment to committed *völkisch* ideologues. Having reaped the propaganda value of this movement for his rise to power, Hitler cooled to its constricting ideology and ignored the recommendations of its advocates. Alfred Rosenberg's Kampfbund organization was eased out of power, and control of architectural commissions was turned over to the Reichskulturkammer (Reich Culture Chamber), a part of Goebbels's Propaganda Ministry. Goebbels, like Hitler, took a pragmatic view of architecture, and developed an eclectic program determined strictly by political opportunism. State architecture was dominated by a neoclassical monumentalism that expressed the power of the state and the collectivity on which it supposedly rested. For domestic architecture, however, *völkisch* and vernacular styles were deemed appropriate to give the individual respite from the demanding collectivity with rural illusions of unity with the soil and landscape. Concessions were made to modernism in industrial architecture, however, symbolizing the Nazi rapprochement with industrial technique, instrumental rationality, and the big capitalists that championed these. This Nazi return to an architectural typology based on purpose countered one of the most objectionable features of technocratic modernism—the erasure of the barrier between the public and private worlds. This erasure, exemplified by private residences that looked like factories, symbolized for many the colonization of the world of consumption and family by the relentless logic of industrial technique. Nazi architectural policy assured Germans, however falsely, that they would restore the protective barriers.[19]

Völkisch *Style: The False Aesthetic of Rural Escape*

Although *völkisch* or populist architecture did not dominate in the Third Reich, as its advocates had hoped, this style was tolerated in domestic housing, especially that in rural areas. But domestic architecture was probably the least important facet of the Nazi building program. Before 1933 the Nazis often expressed a concern with public housing for workers, but once in power they built relatively little workers' housing. And what was built seemed more motivated by antiurban propaganda than real improvements in workers' living conditions. The party transferred control over public housing construction from states and municipalities to a centralized authority, whose new Kommissar stated that the purpose of his program would be "the dissolution of the metropolis, in order to make our people be settled again, to give them again their roots in the soil." The city was held to be the source of communism, Jewish capitalism, and pollution of the German race. Salvation lay in dispersing urban populations into the countryside, where they would be unified with German soil and their racial heritage. In this way, Nazis hoped to offer the common people battered by political conflict and economic rationalization a sense of security and community.

The Nazis built several hundred rural housing settlements, most of which housed workers for new factories in these areas. All employed *völkisch* styles that evoked images of a simple, rural life in harmony with nature and community. These developments also differed from the modernist estates of multistoried apartment buildings by being composed of small, single-family houses, which gave residents a sense of individuality and privacy. Also prominent were the steeply pitched roofs, which, in contrast to the visually open, flat roofs of modernism, were, according to one writer, "a symbol of the strong, protective strength of the Nordic feeling for the home." These roofs were often handcrafted of natural materials, thus revealing a harmonious unity of humanity and nature. Beyond these common elements, rural housing developments often varied, adopting details from the local vernacular—thatched roofs in the

Labor Front housing settlement, Wurmevier, Germany, 1938 (Library of Congress, Prints and Photographs Division, LC-USZ61-1141)

North Sea, half-timbering and gable roofs in Lower Saxony, Tyrolean roofs and white stucco in South Germany's mountains.[20]

The openings of these *völkisch* settlements were always accompanied by a barrage of propaganda touting Nazi efforts to return the German race to handicrafts and the soil. But this publicity was deceptive in two regards. First, it created the impression of a greater volume of housing than was actually built. Second, the propaganda surrounding the rural settlements disguised the fact that most Nazi-built housing consisted of urban apartment buildings. But even though the latter shared with modernist estates a stacking of small, standardized apartments, Nazi architects disguised this mass-produced urbanism with touches of rural craftsmanship. Steeply pitched roofs with overhanging eaves replaced the flat roofs of modernism, and vertical windows with picturesque shutters were used instead of the endless, factory-like ribbon windows preferred by modern architects. Inside, traditionally divided rooms replaced modernist open plans.[21]

Whether found in rural settlements or urban apartment blocks, *völkisch* housing sought above all to create a reassuring sense of "home," a feeling of individual security and rootedness. The modernist machine aesthetic cultivated the connotations of movement and transience inherent in the emerging society of rationalized capitalism. The empty spaces and standardized appearance

of modernist housing estates were routinely criticized as symbolic of a civilization of urban vagabonds, workers who moved constantly to the beck and call of
technological change. The Nazis wanted to offer workers traumatized by economic rationalization not an empty machine to live in but a comforting home
full of reminders of handicraft and rural work, in which people were united
with nature's resources. Martin Heidegger's existential philosophy, which arose
in Germany during this period, also expressed this desire for home, an authentic existence rooted in a space where humans and nature lived in harmony, and
registered the fear of the rationalized technology that denied humanity this
home. Technology and its scientific reason, Heidegger wrote, defined space
as abstract extension, a "homogeneous expanse, not distinguished at any of its
possible places, equivalent toward each direction, but not perceptible with the
senses,...[which] challenges modern man increasingly and ever more obstinately to its utter control." Humans do not dwell authentically in such abstract,
endless space (*spatium*), but in a place (*Raum*), a location that brings together
harmoniously mortal humans with the earth, the sky, and the divinities. Only
in such a place do humans have an authentic dwelling. To build, Heidegger
asserted, is to create such places for dwelling, and he tipped his architectural
and ideological hand when he exemplified authentic building by a two-hun-
dred-year-old farmhouse in the Black Forest.

> Here the self-sufficiency of the power to let the earth and heavens, divinities and
> mortals enter in simple oneness into things, ordered the house. It placed the farm
> on the wind-sheltered mountain slope looking south, among the meadows close to
> the spring. It gave it the wide overhanging shingle roof whose proper slope bears
> up under the burden of snow, and which, reaching deep down, shields the cham-
> bers against the storms of the long winter nights....A craft which, itself sprung
> from dwelling, still uses its tools and frames as things, built the farmhous.[22]

Although Heidegger wrote these words in 1954, after the war, they
reveal the unreconstructed *völkisch* ideology that the Nazis used to mobilize
the masses, and which drew Heidegger into a collaboration with National
Socialism. Both Heidegger and the Nazis were sensitive to the dehumanizing effects of instrumental rationality and the economic rationalization that
it drove. Yet both offered a home of comforting rootedness and authenticity *in this world*, in a segregated realm within a society that continued to be
dominated in its other parts by the instrumental rationality and technology
they renounced. Consequently, these ideas of an authentic, human space for

dwelling merely put a pretty face on an ugly regime and diverted attention from the real changes in the political and economic structure of society that would be required to realize such a space. This is why during the darkest days of the war against Nazism, exiled German philosopher Theodor Adorno declared, countering Heidegger, that "dwelling, in the proper sense, is now impossible.... It is part of morality not to be at home in one's home."[23]

Neoclassical Monumentalism: The Aesthetic of the Massified State

The real heart of the Nazi building program was not this *völkisch* fantasy of rural domesticity but a neoclassical monumentalism that glorified the Nazi party-state. As a relatively autonomous entity unsecured by a social base, this state apparatus required its own mythology to legitimate its domination over an entire nation. Architecture played the leading role in this state legitimation, objectifying and reifying Nazi mythology in physical space. Like *völkisch* housing, Nazi state architecture looked to the past to register its claims to rule. But it looked back before medieval ruralism to a classical urbanism for the mythology of a state representing nation and race. Above all, Nazi state buildings were symbols of a community, a *Gemeinschaft* of ancient ties and traditions, not a *Gesellschaft* of material ties between individuals. Monumental, neoclassical buildings were testimony to Germans and the rest of the world of the power and permanence of this racial community.

Because of its centrality to the legitimacy of his regime, Hitler himself took a direct interest in state architecture. Public buildings, he believed, had to be large and impressive, and imply that the community was superior to the lives of its individuals. One of his main criticisms of industrial capitalism in Germany was that its "niggardly" concern for costs had discouraged large public buildings and undermined the representative character of urban centers. Hitler's model for returning the symbolic character to cities was the baroque urban center, with its imposing cathedral and state buildings that, in his words, created "a mysterious gloom which made men more ready to submit to the renunciation of self." Because Hitler hated the religious symbolism of baroque architecture, however, he turned to classicism for his urban monumentalism, legitimating it by a racial mythology that asserted a common "Nordic" heritage for ancient Greeks and Germans. The architectural imitation of ancient Greeks helped the Nazis lift their regime out of vulgar history and into a realm of timeless, eternal completeness often associated with classical civilization. Nazi neoclassicism asserted that history had culminated in the Third Reich, the true heir of the Greek polis.[24]

In 1933 Hitler appointed as the main architect of National Socialism Paul Ludwig Troost (1878–1934), a leader of the prewar historicist movement seeking to revive nineteenth-century German neoclassicism, especially that of Karl Friedrich Schinkel (1781–1841). His first and only major building for Hitler, the House of German Art in Munich (1937), revealed Schinkel's concern for symmetry and love of long colonnades. But Troost's classicism was stripped of the tasteful ornament and delicate proportions that lightened the blocky masses of Schinkel's architecture. The flat surfaces of Troost's massive limestone walls and the uninterrupted march of his rigid colonnade gave the building a durability and weight that seemed to defy the vicissitudes of time and proclaim the eternity of the Nazi regime. This architectural obsession with durability and substance continued under Albert Speer, the architect appointed to replace Troost upon his death in 1934. Speer had apprenticed with Heinrich Tessenow (1876–1950), a *völkisch* architect, before becoming commissioner for technical and artistic organization of rallies in the Nazis' Reich Propaganda Bureau. He came to Hitler's attention because he shared the Führer's vision of architecture as a grand spectacle that gave individuals a relief from, in Speer's words, "the ugliness of our industrial world" and enveloped them in the security of a primordial community outside of history.[25]

Speer's first important buildings for Hitler were the Nazi Administration Building and Führer Palace in Munich (1935), which created an image of protection and organic rootedness to contrast with industrial ephemerality and transience. Both buildings were long and low, giving them an earthbound appearance not unlike Wright's Prairie style. Also emphasizing the horizontal were the seemingly interminable colonnades on their facades. Speer added visual weight with heavy cornice lines, which, in contrast to the light, cornice-free walls of modernism, seemed to hold these buildings to the ground. The heavily recessed reveals on windows and doors also testified to thick, protective walls, and countered the light, depthless feel of modernism's flush windows and doors. Finally, both buildings adamantly refused industrial materials for natural stone—pale-yellow Danubian limestone on the exterior, and dark-red Saalburg marble and yellow Jura marble on the interior. These materials lent the structures durability and earthiness, and, in the words of one party commentator, "radiated comfort and serenity."[26]

The culmination of Speer's neoclassical architecture was the new Chancellery building in Berlin, completed in 1939 after a mere nine months of frenetic construction. The entire building was designed to exude an air of disciplined, military order, for one defining criterion of Nazi architecture was

Albert Speer, Chancellery building, Berlin, 1939 (Photograph U.S. National Archives, reprinted from Robert Taylor, *The Word in Stone: The Role of Architecture in the National Socialist Ideology*. Berkeley: University of California Press, plate 17)

held to be *Ordnung* (order). The Nazis proclaimed that their rule brought Germany an authoritative, disciplined way of life, and demanded that architecture reflect this. Speer's Chancellery expressed the obsession with order in its rigid symmetry. While modernists used asymmetry to set their buildings in motion, Speer used classical symmetry to settle space into a profound and eternal stillness. Orderliness was also expressed by the repetition of identical architectural elements, like the deeply set windows that Speer placed on each side of the Chancellery's central portal. He delighted that these windows gave the wings an appearance of "severe, disciplined organization and order."[27]

Also rigidly disciplined and orderly was the procession of spaces through which visitors entered the Chancellery, for Hitler proclaimed that "one should have the feeling that one is visiting the master of the world." To fulfill this edict, Speer created a theatrical promenade designed to awe visitors with its overwhelming scale and opulence. Spectators entered the building through the Court of Honor, then proceeded through a portal dominated by four soaring columns and two large neoclassical statues. The procession then led through an antechamber into the opulent Mosaic Room, a huge, high-ceiling chamber covered with mosaics of militaristic Nazi symbols. Next, the awed visitor proceeded through the Round Room of inlaid marble walls into the Marble

Gallery, where the door and window surrounds and floors were of pink and green marble. Finally, the privileged visitor would be led into Hitler's office, a huge, sparsely furnished but elegant room with walls of dark-red Limbourg marble, floor of Ruhpoldinger marble, and ceiling of coffered wooden panels.[28]

This egregious spectacle of elegance and opulence was meant to testify not only to the Third Reich's power and cultural refinement, but also to its revival of the handicrafts. While the modernists' use of mass-produced industrial materials testified to an alienated and rationalized labor process, the neoclassicism of the Nazis displayed copious amounts of human handwork and natural materials to hide any evidence of mechanical processes. As Speer wrote of his buildings, "they were a romantic protest against technology." The lavish craftwork displayed in the Chancellery testified to the Nazis' antitechnological pledge to revive the crafts and protect them against rationalization. The construction of the Chancellery employed 8,000 artists and craftworkers, and one Nazi writer argued that it alone revived the craft of quarry workers. Party ideologues also stressed that the building was the result not of an individual creator but of the cooperative work of many craftsmen, obviously seeking to capture the desire to return to the cooperative, organic labor of the past.[29]

Nazi public architecture also symbolically expressed the predominance of the general community over the individual, reflecting a popular desire for belongingness that had been denied by the rapid spread of market egoism. Modern architects also sought to envelope the individual in a community, but their community was a functionally segmented, hierarchical machine, in which the specialized parts were united solely by the cool efficiency of means and dominated by a spiritless technical/intellectual elite. This modernist vision and its architectural expression threatened many petty bourgeois and skilled workers with a decline of skills and independence. National Socialism appealed to them and other Germans with a different version of community, in which individuals were enveloped in an undifferentiated mass, united by organic ties of race and nation, and led by a charismatic visionary. Such a leveled, mass community bound by irrational ties was more susceptible to regimentation and militarization than the differentiated, functional community. It was just such a massified community that the Nazis sought in their "community architecture." They cleverly captured the longing for authentic community for their political ambitions to subordinate an entire nation.[30]

The characteristics of Nazi public architecture that symbolized and created this militarized mass community were repetition and scale. These buildings were dominated by the repetition of elements like columns and piers, the sheer number of which was overwhelming and testified to the power of the undifferentiated mass when marshaled by some ordering demiurge. The latter, always identified as the party/Führer, arranged the massified architectural elements into an order that went beyond the gentle rhythms of their classical models to form an intimidating drumbeat of regimentation. Modern architects also used repetition, but their repeated elements were organized rationally to serve and represent different building functions—e.g., ribbon windows to illuminate, concrete piers to support. Nazi elements, by contrast, were irrationally massed in numbers exceeding any functional purpose to reveal the sheer power of assembled masses. Thus, for example, the Great Hall, an unbuilt project by Speer to hold 180,000 spectators for Nazi political events, was ringed inside with 100 white marble pillars, a number far beyond the engineering requirement of support. These pillars, each of which stood 24 meters high, echoed the size, power, and regimentation of the assembled throng.[31]

Perhaps more important, however, in symbolizing and producing the undifferentiated, regimented mass community was the sheer scale of Nazi public buildings. Hitler demanded, and Speer designed, gargantuan structures on a scale rarely contemplated before. "Why always the biggest?" Hitler asked the workers assembled to dedicate the Chancellery. "I do this to restore his self-respect to each individual German....I want to say to each of you: we are not inferior, on the contrary, we are completely equal to every other nation." The size of "community architecture" was thus meant to reflect the greatness and power of the community. It was also meant, Hitler implied in other remarks, to distinguish this new community from the rationalized, industrial society it was displacing. He stated of several projects that they should not be built on a "niggardly scale" as in the past, obviously referring to the modernist housing estates and their existence minimum determined by efficiency. Hitler proclaimed that the Nazis would reveal a society ruled by a greatness beyond petty efficiency: "The eyes of the children must be weaned from the niggardly, and trained on the grandiose."[32]

The scale of Nazi public buildings revealed not only the size and strength of the new community but also its nature. These structures were spacious, but not spaceless like modernist buildings. Modernism created abstract, rationalized, endless *space—spatium*, in Heidegger's terms—with which humans found it difficult to identify. This space of technical means, unrelated to human ends, seemed simply immeasurable, and hence monotonous. The Nazi monumental buildings, by contrast, were grandiose and concrete *places—Raum*, in Heidegger's vocabulary—spaces invested with human meaning through the use of common symbols of life. But these ordinary symbols of life were transformed into extraordinary symbols of community by their superhuman scale. Thus, for example, the column or post is a primordial architectural element symbolizing the common experience of living under a supported roof, dwelling between the sky and the ground in a height defined by the human body. When, however, the column was expanded from 2 meters to 100 meters in height and repeated in colonnades of almost interminable length, it created a place that was human, but far beyond the scale of the individual. Such a place spoke of a *Lebensraum*, a living place for a great and expansive community, of which the individual was an insignificant part.[33]

The Nazi architecture of monumentality was often used as a theatrical set for mass assemblies whose intent was precisely to achieve such deindividuation that facilitated mass domination. The grandest such set was the Zeppelinfeld at Nuremberg, part of a vast Nazi party complex built in 1935 for rallies. The field was built to hold 90,000 on the field proper, 60,000 in the principal stand, and another 64,000 on the earthen banks on the sides. The principal stand was rigidly symmetrical, with a massive central block containing the speaker's rostrum and on either side a long colonnade terminating in a pylon. The composition was centered on the speaker's rostrum, or "the place of the *Führer*," below

Albert Speer, The Zeppelinfeld, "Cathedral of Light" rally, Nuremberg, 1937
(reprinted from Robert Taylor, *The Word in Stone: The Role of Architecture in the National Socialist Ideology*. Berkeley, University of California Press, 1974, plate 44)

which the masses of spectators were leveled in an anonymous homogeneity. One Nazi commentator, Wilhelm Lotz, wrote that the Zeppelinfeld was the architectural incarnation of the "leadership principle": "Leadership is present everywhere, for in each meeting space and on each parade square is the place on which the *Führer* stands, especially prominent architecturally." The rest of the field was surrounded with sixty-six closely spaced stone bastions, each with six flagpoles flying the Nazi standard.[34]

The Zeppelinfeld spectacle unifying Führer and *Volk* was not consummated, however, until after nightfall, when most of the massive party rallies were held. The darkness of night allowed Speer to complete his material architecture of massification with the ethereal effects of light. Always attuned to the importance of stage lighting for his Nazi dramas, Hitler's architect placed around the perimeter of the field 130 searchlights that shot a beam of light fifteen kilometers up into the night sky. Called the Cathedral of Light, this lighting effect surrounded the Zeppelinfeld with a gargantuan colonnade dwarfing all individual participants. Blocks of light also shined a patchy pattern across the field, revealing massed ranks of troops within which no individual was discernable. These nighttime assemblies were above all Durkheimian rituals of collective conscience, overwhelming and enveloping the individual in a forest of symbols testifying to the power of the racial community and the insignificance of the person. As one Nazi writer described a Zeppelinfeld rally: "Great crowds of people had gathered, not in unruly mobs, but rather in response to the call of a 'form-giving will,' surrendering to a strong original form of communal existence, following a traditional soldierly precedent. It was wonderful to see the masses saved from disorder and formlessness, and individuals saved from atomization."[35]

Had not war interrupted their efforts, Hitler and Speer would have rebuilt the entire center of Berlin as one big set on which to stage mass spectacles. In the late 1930s the two worked together closely on a plan for a monumental city center, in which gargantuan public buildings dominated an emptied out space that provided vast, dramatic vistas. Plans called for the reorganization of the city around two axes composed of grand boulevards. For the dominant north-south axis Hitler himself designed a classically inspired triumphal arch that stood 100 meters high, through which was visible the grandeur of the Great Square, standing at the axes' intersection. There alongside the Führer Palace and new Chancellery would stand the Great Hall, the huge dome of which would reach the height of 200 meters and dominate vistas from all directions. The grand scale of such buildings and the vast expanses of space around them were reminiscent of Le Corbusier's Radiant City plan, which also symbolically testified to the power and grandeur of a central ruling class. But Le Corbusier's central skyscrapers spoke of the rule of industrial technology and a techno-cratic elite, which stood in tension with concentric rings of housing differenti-ated by class function. Hitler and Speer's Radiant Berlin, by contrast, covered over all traces of modern technology with a neoclassical grandeur that sym-bolized a political elite, which dominated an undifferentiated mass community united by bonds of race and nation. In this vision of utopia there was no ten-sion between individual and community, and no progress propelled by it. The serene Nazi metropolis obliterated history and its dialectic, not by realizing the promise of individuality in a new form of community, but by destroying indi-viduality altogether within an undifferentiated, primordial community. This disturbing, totalitarian utopia of Nazism held a powerful sway over the people of Germany and other countries only because of the failure of the modernist utopia of technology to resolve this historical contradiction of individual and society, as both Erich Fromm and Theodor Adorno have argued.[36]

Romantic Modernism: Reconciling Humanity and the Machine
Despite the predominance of this neoclassical program of antimodern regres-sion back before individuation, another element of Nazi aesthetics sought to mobilize remaining modernist impulses for the Third Reich. The dream of individual freedom through the machine could not be ignored by the Nazis for strategic reasons. First, Hitler and party officials realized that to consolidate power they needed the support of industrial capitalists, which was contingent on the state's stimulation of industrial production. Second, the regime's impe-rial ambitions required a massive war machine, built efficiently and quickly by mass production. As Speer argued, preparation for war impelled a Nazi pro-gram for rationalizing and mechanizing German industry, including the build-ing sector. Third, and perhaps most importantly, despite the best efforts of common Germans to escape from individual freedom in the undifferentiated, primordial community, they could not reverse the individuation produced by modern society. People retained a painful desire for individual freedom, which was only temporarily alleviated in mass ceremonies.[37] The Nazis realized that this desire had to be assuaged, while simultaneously diverting it away from the regime's monopoly on economic and political power. Individual consumerism proved the palliative for freedom least threatening to the Nazi will to power. If the Nazis could keep the promise of consumer abundance broken by Weimar, then they could contain the dangerous desire for freedom and demonstrate the

superiority of their regime. Such consumer goods would have to be mass produced, but in ways that did not awaken the fears of dehumanization that the
Nazis had used against Weimar rationalization programs.

The industrialization program that fulfilled these imperatives of stimulating production, preparing for war, and pacifying consumers was the automobilization of Germany. Mass producing automobiles would provide to German
consumers this symbol of individual freedom that was already displacing
broader conceptions of economic and political freedom in the modern world,
while building highways on which to drive them would unify people with
the beloved landscape of the fatherland. Both road building and auto making
would also stimulate economic activity and simultaneously furnish the industrial infrastructure for the Nazi war machine.

With these strategic benefits in mind, Hitler announced the initial steps
toward automobilization at the Berlin Motor Show in February of 1933, declaring "a nation is no longer judged by the length of its railways but by the length
of its highways." He called for the construction of a network of superhighways
across Germany and the production of a small car for the masses to drive on
them. In subsequent statements, the Führer made it clear that the main purpose of mass motorization was to unify and placate the *Volk*, to overcome the
class struggles associated with Weimar by offering all Germans the diverting joys of individual consumption. This was the main benefit of Fordism for
Hitler, who declared in 1933 that "the motor car, instead of being a class dividing element, can be the instrument for uniting the different classes, just as it
has done in America, thanks to Mr. Ford's genius." The Nazis conceived of the
car as an object of consumption to be driven on holidays on joyous highways,
not an object of production to be manufactured on workdays on monotonous
assembly lines. Consequently, the company that was formed to design and
build Hitler's small car for the masses, the Volkswagen Development Company,
was funded and controlled by the German Labor Front's Strength through Joy
branch, which was charged with organizing recreation for workers. Thus, automotive consumption was to be controlled and orchestrated by the collective,
preventing the individual competition and invidious distinctions that plagued
Weimar. The Nazis promised the German people progress through industrial
machines, but a harmonious and peaceful progress which benefited the entire
Volk. The autobahns built to carry the cars were also said to unify the community by eliminating the local consciousness of Germany's various regions. Nazi
mass motorization thus sought to offer individuals the pseudofreedom of geographic movement within the bounds of a repressive pseudocollective.[38]

In order to achieve these artificial solutions to real problems, the Nazis once again made clever use of aesthetics. The car, the roads over which it drove, and the factories that produced it were all designed to disguise the ugly reality of regimented industrial rationalization beneath soothing signs of organic unity. The Volkswagen, or, as it was officially named, the Strength through Joy car, was conceived as the German equivalent of the Model T, but unlike Ford's car its design sought to reconcile mass production with a romantic vision of organic unity. The car originated as an ultra-light, rear-engine racing car that Austrian-born engineer Ferdinand Porsche designed for the German Auto Union firm. But Porsche, like Hitler, dreamed of producing a small car for the masses, so in the early 1930s he redesigned his racing machine for mass production, calling it the *Volksauto*. Porsche peddled his prototype first to the Soviets, but their negotiations quickly broke down. So when Hitler approached him late in 1933 about a mass-produced car, he offered the design to him. The Führer demanded for his Volkswagen a technically advanced closed car capable of carrying four adults and selling for under 900 marks (about $360). The contract signed with Porsche also stipulated that the car be capable of carrying three soldiers and a machine gun, showing that military applications were important from the beginning. In 1938 Porsche delivered the final prototype, a 1600-pound, 94.6-inch-wheelbase car with a central-tube frame and a four-cylinder, rear-mounted, air-cooled engine developing twenty-five horsepower.[39]

The appearance of Porsche's Volkswagen bore little resemblance to Ford's Model T. The latter had exposed mechanicals and rigidly rectilinear lines that

Ferdinand Porsche, with Adolf Hitler, Volkswagen prototype, 1938
(Photograph Heinrich Hoffmann/Hulton Archive/Getty Images)

spoke of the unbending heteronomy of the machine and assembly line. The Volkswagen, by contrast, carefully covered these connotations with the fullness of a curvilinear body, on which there was scarcely a straight line. While designing race cars, Porsche had learned the importance of aerodynamic bodies for speed, but the Volkswagen's streamlining carried cultural connotations beyond functional exigencies. The soft, bulging curves gave the car the organic look of nature, thus humanizing this machine. Its lines blended into the landscape, reuniting the *Volk* with nature and thus recapturing a simpler, preindustrial past. Further, this curvilinear aesthetic testified to Hitler's attempt to overcome class antagonisms through automobilization. The Volkswagen brought the curvilinear, streamlined look characteristic of luxury sedans and roadsters to the masses, simultaneously closing the technological and the aesthetic gap between the classes and superficially uniting the German *Volk* behind Hitler's leadership.[40]

In 1937 the Volkswagen Development Company was formed to manufacture the Volkswagen, and before one car was built it launched a massive propaganda campaign to promote it. One part of the campaign was a layaway plan whereby workers could reserve a Volkswagen by paying five marks a month toward the purchase price of 990 marks. But none of the 336,668 Germans who paid into the plan ever got a car. Preparations for the production of civilian cars were canceled with the invasion of Poland in 1939, and the Volkswagen plant began producing military versions of the vehicle. One part of Hitler's motorized plan was realized, however—the autobahns—and they also revealed his dream to use the modernist promise of the machine to create a romantic, organic community.[41]

Construction began on this network of superhighways in the same year that Hitler came to power, and results were almost immediate. A major motive of autobahn construction was putting the unemployed back to work on a state project that incorporated them into the "national community." By 1936, 130,000 workers were directly employed in autobahn construction, and another 270,000 in related trades also benefited. Since camps to house workers had to be built near construction sites, the Nazis used these to create a small-village atmosphere that overcame alienation and to provide amenities not available to most at home. Advocates of the *völkisch* movement argued that another practical benefit of autobahn construction was the decentralization of crowded and dangerous cities into the healthy countryside. One *völkisch* scholar wrote that the autobahns revealed a Nazi dedication to the reagrarianization of Germany and the reversal of the development of an industrial state. But the Nazis' dedication to deurbanization was more ideological than real, and the autobahns were meant mainly to provide the German masses with temporary escape into the countryside and consequent relief from the Nazis' regimented, industrial society. But to provide this escape, the roads as well as the cars moving on them would have to disguise their mechanical nature under an aesthetic veneer of organicism. By careful attention to autobahn design, the Nazis came close to achieving just this sort of false reconciliation of technology and nature.[42]

From the beginning the Nazis declared that their autobahns would be a different type of road, symbolizing their commitment to a different type of modernization and technology. Fritz Todt, inspector general of German roads and head of the autobahn program, stated: "In the conception of National Socialist technology, roads are works of art, just like architectural structures.... From this will to culture results as well our relationship to the landscape; therefore we fit the roads into the landscape with care for the trees and shrubs!" The autobahns were not merely efficient machines for transportation but aesthetic statements of Nazi culture's organic relation to nature. They were planned to be scenographic, to create an aestheticized space that transported motorists into the idealized environment of a preindustrial past rooted in blood and soil. In each construction district a *Landschaftsanwalt*, or counsel for the landscape, was appointed to supervise landscaping and ensure that the autobahns did not spoil the natural spectacle with a mechanical appearance. On bridges and overpasses natural materials like hand-carved stone were used to blend these technological structures into the landscape. And landscape architects and engineers selected routes for their beauty, not efficiency. For example, the highway between Munich and Salzburg was routed through Irschenberg, a twenty-kilometer detour, to give motorists a scenic view of the Alps. Flat, straight road segments, which for Le Corbusier symbolized rationality and efficiency, were eschewed in favor of rolling curves that blended into the terrain and eliminated monotony. Along the autobahns reminders of industrial civilization were also minimized, with billboards and advertisements forbidden and all buildings but gas stations banned from the roadside.[43]

The architecture of all buildings visible from the autobahns was also tightly controlled. Most hotels, restaurants, and gas stations were constructed in the *völkisch* style, which emphasized organic unity with nature. Yet there were conspicuous exceptions. One gas station near Chiemsee had a distinctly modern look, with white stucco, ribbon windows, and a flat canopy that covered both service building and open drive. But the station departed from the rectilinear lines of the machine aesthetic in the softly ovoid shape of the building. The station's aesthetic was what came to be known as "streamline style," a modernism with the edges rounded off that was accepted, even encouraged, on purely functional buildings and objects as an emblem of the progress achieved by Nazi-engineered technology. To emphasize the human goals of technology, the style bent technology to conform to the curves of organic bodies. Like the sweeping curves of the Volkswagen and the autobahns, this architectural style sought to reconcile technology and nature, to use the liberating movement of the machine to accomplish the human goal of returning to an agrarian paradise.[44]

This type of romantic modernism also infected the functional buildings of the Third Reich, aesthetically obscuring the brutality of Nazi rationalization. This style took on greater importance after 1936 when the Nazis launched their program of industrial rationalization, which extended state control over labor and industry and mandated the predominance of military production. The focus of the Nazi construction program then shifted from state to industrial buildings, a change accompanied by an ideological shift. The industrial technology the Nazis originally portrayed as dominating humans was increasingly glorified, and the small-scale, artisanal production previously celebrated now assumed an aura of backwardness. Nazi propaganda now emphasized that productive efficiency and machine technology were neutral means that could be divorced from the evil ends of capitalism and employed to create the racial community.

This hybridized ideology blending modern efficiency and primordial community created a hybridized architecture. There was a cautious incorporation of some modernist principles in the new Nazi factories. To reflect the military gravity and importance of the work performed within, industrial buildings were generally bereft of ornamentation. And modern building materials like glass, steel, and concrete were embraced as more efficient than archaic materials like stone and wood. But the Reich's industrial buildings were softened with a touch of organicism, and never as harshly angular and coldly efficient as the machine aesthetic. Thus, for example, the laboratory buildings of the Air Force German Experimental Station (1935) had exposed steel beams and large expanses of glass, but they were also surfaced in warm, red brick, giving the structures an earthy look, and the roofs were gently pitched as opposed to flat.[45]

More important in reconciling the new drive for industrial efficiency with the *Volk* community, however, was the conscious manipulation of aesthetics that was going on inside these new factories. Leaders of Hitler's National

Socialist German Workers' party were astutely aware of the alienating effect upon workers of the Weimar program of industrial rationalization, since they used it to win the support of some workers. They had to ensure that their own rationalization program did not rekindle these fears but somehow reconciled workers to the new production demands. This task fell to the Beauty of Labor office, founded as part of the German Labor Front in 1933 and charged with, according to the Front's head, Robert Ley, ending the "joyless compulsion" of labor and restoring to the worker "the feeling for the worth and importance of his labour." This was to be accomplished not through changing the nature of work or increasing the power of labor, but by creating a more beautiful work environment. The real subordination of workers increased under the Nazis, with the National Law of Labor establishing absolute hegemony of management within the industrial enterprise. But this fact was obscured by an aesthetic image carefully crafted to extinguish any class consciousness or struggle under the smothering mantle of the national community. As the editor of the *Beauty of Labor* journal Wilhelm Lotz wrote, praising the success of the program: "The proletarian coloring of the concept of 'laborer' and the fighting attitude toward another rank has been extinguished....There is only one culture and one life form, that of the German people. It is clear that from all the efforts to transform the plant into a cell of community life, a life style of the German worker must emerge."[46]

To accomplish this fusion of worker identity with the racial *Volk*, the Beauty of Labor office constructed new facilities that gave the factory all the comforts of home. Canteens and dining halls, restrooms and showers, community houses, swimming pools and gymnasiums, athletic fields, lawn areas and flower gardens were all designed by artists and architects to convey a healthy, community atmosphere. Early in the campaign *völkisch* symbolism was prevalent, but as war production increased simple, functional design became prominent. But this functionalism was accepted only in carefully segregated production areas. Separate Houses of Labor, serving the recreational needs of workers, were almost always built in *völkisch* styles, as were the Nazi "chapels" attached to many factories to accommodate political meetings. The landscaping of factory grounds mandated by the Beauty of Labor office, containing expanses of lawns, native trees and shrubbery, and flower gardens,functioned like that of the autobahns to integrate and relieve any remaining images of technological efficiency with the soothing, organic look of the nature.[47]

The intent of the Nazi Beauty of Labor campaign was not unlike the technocratic program of modern architects, who also realized that workers undergoing industrial rationalization had to be compensated aesthetically, in both production and leisure facilities. Both agreed that the design of factories and houses should integrate workers into a community beyond their class and avert the formation of a proletarian consciousness. But the type of community into which workers were to be integrated differed greatly. The modernists wanted to subordinate workers to a functionally differentiated, rational community, in which occupations were hierarchically graded by their skills and education in service to the efficient means. The Nazis, however, understood that many workers and petty bourgeois were threatened by the rational community, in which the better trained and educated technocrats dominated. So Hitler and his National Socialists made sure that their aesthetic efforts obscured rather than revealed these hierarchical implications of industrial rationalization. They praised factory efficiency, mechanization, and productivity, not as impositions of a hierarchy of knowledge but as cooperative efforts of a collective mass, in which each was subordinated to the entire community. Outside the factory, however, all reminders of rationalized production were obliterated in preindusrial images of this organic community. This aesthetic dissimulation made the Nazis better agents of industrial rationalization than its transparent champions, the modernists. Under this ruse, instrumental reason achieved its aims in Hitler's irrational regime.

America's Depression-Era Romance with the Streamlined Machine

In the United States capitalist rationalization of industry was too advanced to render feasible dreams of a return to a preindustrial or early-capitalist utopia, even in the face of the economic collapse of the Great Depression. The revolution of mass production had irreversibly transformed capitalism from a scatter of small-scale producers employing skilled artisans to a concentration of industrial behemoths using deskilled proletarians supervised by managers and technicians. The class basis of reaction in Europe—petty bourgeoisie, skilled artisans, rural workers—was eviscerated by industrial rationalization in America. And with these economic changes had come the cultural configuration of mass consumption to legitimate it. By the beginning of the Depression in the early 1930s, this culture of compensating consumption was so deeply ingrained in the class structure and psyche of America that it would prove exceedingly difficult to displace. After a brief struggle that challenged the Fordist system of mass production/mass consumption, the Depression-era dreams of most Americans fell back into consumer fantasies, this time projected into a future of science-fiction technology.

The first few years of the Depression did see the rise of a panoply of popular movements, many of which challenged the basic contours of Fordism. The economic collapse undermined the mass-consumption legitimation of Fordist production, exposing its naked brutality and motivating movements that sought to shift the balance of power within production. Social historian Michael Denning has argued that these movements constituted a loosely joined but ideologically united social movement called the Popular Front. Based largely in the new organizations of industrial workers, especially the Congress of Industrial Organizations (CIO), and providing the impetus behind Franklin D. Roosevelt's first New Deal programs, this tenuous alliance of class fractions offered a vision of a new moral economy, a collectively controlled economy which would temper the ravages of capitalism. The Popular Front movement, along with the New Deal programs it supported, restructured American culture during the Depression by introducing a flood of new working-class producers into the art field. New Deal relief projects for artists gave many aspiring working-class producers their first jobs, and numerous movement organizations also sponsored cultural activities that employed workers from their own ranks. This support provided working-class artists with the autonomy from the corporate-controlled consumer culture necessary to pioneer an oppositional culture based on their class habitus and class interests.[48]

This relatively autonomous Cultural Front, as Denning calls it, pioneered an aesthetic that challenged the machine aesthetic of modernism without lapsing into reactionary, *völkisch* antimodernism. One cultural response to the disillusionment with Fordist machinery was a nostalgic turn to an agrarian past for meaning and order, known as regionalism or social realism. Unlike the German *völkisch* movement, however, this American aesthetic often crossed simplistic political boundaries. The common denominator of regionalism was a realist celebration of ordinary American people and landscapes. With decidedly aniturban, anti-big-business sympathies, painters like Grant Wood and Thomas Hart Benton, writers like John Steinbeck and Carey McWilliams, and musicians like Woody Guthrie and Pete Seeger depicted common workers and small farmers realistically but heroically struggling for a better life. While this sort of regionalism could veer off into right-wing antimodernism, many regionalists were closely associated with the leftist Popular Front and offered a complex vision of modern industry and the popular classes. Although rejecting the abstraction associated with modernism, regionalists like Benton often depicted industrial scenes and technology. But inevitably intertwined with and controlling the sharp-edged machinery were the organic bodies of human workers, whose bulging muscles testified to a power not present in the inert mechanisms. Young proletarian painters working for the Federal Art Project during the Depression covered the walls of many a public building with visions of a new industrial mechanism dominated by humans. While many Americans were trying to escape from and forget the ravages of Fordist technology with the sanitized images of mass culture, this social modernism stripped off this comforting facade to reveal the real labor being done behind the scenes, labor that was dominated by capitalist technology but carried the potential to liberate itself as well as the machine.[49]

The autonomous, oppositional culture of the Popular Front was ultimately overwhelmed, however, by the corporate-sponsored culture of consumption. In opposition to New Deal programs of public employment and business regulation, corporate America launched its own program of recovery, called "streamlining" or "consumer engineering." On the assumption that the Depression was caused by consumer resistance to buying, rather than a lack of buying power, business leaders argued that prosperity would be restored by corporate efforts to make products more appealing and accommodating to consumers. Through the careful use of innovative science and technology, corporate leaders declared, business could create new, exciting goods to stimulate demand and lead America back to prosperity. Under this program, industrial artists and designers would play a new, expanded role in corporations, giving products the beautiful appearances that overcame consumer resistance and "streamlined" consumption. The aesthetic that dominated industrial design and architecture of the period was a type of modernism, celebrating science and machines. But the aesthetic of corporate streamlining was a softened, romanticized modernism without the offensive edges, an aesthetic that obscured the baleful impact of mass-production machinery and projected technology as the foundation of a science-fiction world of orderly consumption.

Heavy capitalist opposition to the Popular Front's vision of a collectively controlled economy eventually carried the day, forcing American dreams of recovery and wholeness into the corporate vision of reinvigorated individual consumption. The New Deal was pared down to a series of programs that stimulated and managed private consumption, and the new industrial unions gradually bargained away demands of workplace power for union recognition and improvements in wages and benefits. This retreat of the Popular Front starved the oppositional culture of movement and government support, forcing many new working-class cultural producers to seek employment in the mass-culture industries. There they encountered heavy managerial opposition to their attempts to express their leftist social modernism through consumer culture. Squeezed through the culture industry's imperatives to obscure the class-based miseries of the Depression and stimulate greater consumerism, the efforts of the new working-class cultural producers resulted merely in images of a classless "Americanism" that celebrated a watered down and innocuous populism.[50]

American Architecture and the Depression

The effects of these Depression-era struggles on architecture in America were not unlike those experienced in European nations. In both, the relative importance of public commissions grew quickly. In fact, in the United States the drastic decline of building in the overwhelmingly dominant private sector and the emergence of significant public-sector construction resulted in a relatively larger shift than in Europe, where the public sector had always been larger. For the first time in American history, massive public construction projects provided architects with commissions free of the exigencies of the capitalist market. This autonomy from the market did not mean, however, that American architects were now free to impose a technocratic aesthetic, as did the state-sponsored European architects in the 1920s. Although these public commissions were free of the economic demand of working-class consumers in the market, they were now subject to the political demands of a mobilized working class on the New Deal government. And workers' preferences leaned toward a populist and realist aesthetic that celebrated common people, not an abstract modernism that celebrated technocrats and their machines. Besides, the integration of most American architects into the corporate-controlled culture of mass consumption early on had undermined their taste or need for the technocratic aesthetic so popular in Europe.

Unlike literature and painting, architecture did not seem to be directly impacted by the entrance of a new wave of proletarian producers, at least not in public commissions. There was a new wave of industrial designers from working-class and petit-bourgeois backgrounds drawn into private-sector industries like automobiles, but commissions for large-scale public works were generally awarded to established architects, whose services were in plentiful supply due to the decline of private-sector construction. Further, Hitler sent a flood of European architects emigrating to the United States, most of whom had experience designing public housing. So it was not a change in architectural producers that caused these aesthetic shifts, but a change in architectural consumers. The demands on the New Deal government by an organized working class with some autonomy now to express its own aesthetic preferences out-side the market meant that architects designing public commissions would be constrained in their aesthetic choices. Consequently, technocratic modern-ism was largely absent from the public architecture of the New Deal, which revealed weaker versions of two European trends—populism and neoclassi-cism. America was distinguished from Europe during this period, however, by the ultimate overshadowing of these two styles by the private-sector aesthetic of romantic modernism.

The Popular Aesthetic in Public Housing

The 1930s saw the emergence of the first significant programs of public housing in the United States, instituted by the New Deal under pressure from work-ing-class protest. Roosevelt and his New Dealers realized that to restore the legitimating culture of mass consumption, which had been undermined by the Depression, the state would have to deliver the goods that the capitalist market could not. The most important of these goods was housing, the crucial site of consumption where employees could forget Fordist production with obfuscat-ing and entertaining products. Soaring numbers of mortgage defaults and evic-tions threatened this consumer sanctuary and created a rising tide of protest. So New Dealers poured considerable effort and public money into solving the housing problem.

Most government housing programs were structured to subsidize and stabilize the private housing market. The Home Owners' Loan Corporation launched in 1933 provided funds for refinancing mortgages in danger of default, and the Federal Housing Administration, created the next year, insured loans made by private lenders, thus lowering costs to buyers. Because both programs favored single-family homes over multifamily units, they encouraged the sub-urbanization of the white, middle-class residents who could afford to buy a home. The decentralization of urban populations was the explicit intent of some New Deal public housing programs for low-income workers. Obviously influenced by established theories that held urban concentration led to class unrest, the Greenbelt Town program built small, decentralized greenbelt or garden communities outside of population centers to entice workers out of urban slums. Three greenbelt towns were built, but all were plagued with excessive costs. More successful were the rural communities built for migrant farm workers by the Farm Security Administration to settle and stabilize this displaced agricultural population. Despite some efforts to decentralize the dangerous industrial city, however, the Depression-era American government, like the Nazi state, built most of the public housing for workers in cities. The U.S. Housing Authority funded 300 public housing projects scattered throughout the nation, but all were planned and constructed by local housing agencies packed with urban real-estate interests, ensuring that most were built in urban centers. So the overall effect of these New Deal housing programs was to encourage white, middle-class Americans to buy private homes in the suburbs and to concentrate poor and black workers in government subsidized apartments in the urban core.[51]

Whether built in urban or rural areas, however, New Deal public housing offered working-class residents at least symbolic escape from the industrial city in the aesthetics of their dwellings. Like Nazi Germany, Depression-era America experienced a revival of vernacular and rural styles, which was part of the aesthetic of regionalism or social realism. But this aesthetic was not, as in Europe, a reaction against a strong machine aesthetic. Working-class Americans had early on expressed through market purchases their preference for an aesthetic of obfuscation and entertainment, often drawing on the decoration of historical styles. However, the Depression undermined the market power of workers and created conditions like those that had given rise to modernism in Europe, namely, escalating conflict that the state sought to contain through programs of public housing. Under pressure to quickly and cheaply provide public housing to the restless American masses, housing authorities tended to use mass production in these projects. Yet, at the same time there was an awareness among government officials and architects alike that this low-cost housing for workers could not express its mass-produced origins directly in the machine aesthetic, as in Europe in the 1920s. Popular Front movements forced both to heed in public housing popular aesthetic preferences, which during the Depression were more anti-Fordist than ever. Even the American outpost for European modernism, the Museum of Modern Art in New York, was forced into this recognition by the hostile public reaction to its 1932 exhibition promoting the machine aesthetic in architecture. Elizabeth Mock of MoMA wrote in retrospect:

> There was a genuine suspicion of the romanticization of the machine which had produced these cold abstractions. Americans already suffered, if often unconsciously, from the over-mechanization of their lives, and no longer found anything romantic about it. Get up to the jangle of an alarm clock, rush through breakfast to spend an hour or two on a crowded bus or train, or driving yourself through frustrating traffic, pound a typewriter furiously all day with thirty minutes off for

a counter lunch, and you're in no mood to come home to even the most beautiful machine a habiter. Call it escapism if you will.[52]

The return to the vernacular architecture of America's past fulfilled all of the escapist demands of the overmechanized masses. Eschewing the artificiality of machine-made materials, the architecture of New Deal public housing emphasized natural materials rendered in traditional styles that seemed organically rooted in nature. In the Farm Security Administration community for agricultural workers in Chandler, Arizona (1937), for example, the row houses had the thick adobe walls, low-pitched roofs, and wide eaves of indigenous Southwest architecture. These traditional roofs and eaves served not only to functionally protect the interior from the intense sunlight, but also to symbolically express shelter from the vagaries of the outside world. Also drawing on regional styles was the defense housing built by the Federal Works Administration at Windsor Locks, Connecticut, in 1942. The unfinished redwood siding gave these small, single-family houses the rustic feel of a New England farmhouse or a mountain cabin, evoking an earlier era of petty commodity production before the advent of Fordism. The Windsor Locks project also adopted the protective aesthetic, with traditionally peaked roofs and wooden sun blinds over the windows. Privacy was also provided in this large project through the diagonal layout of houses along a triangular road pattern "to allow each a view beyond the walls of its immediate neighbors," in the words of one architectural critic. These aesthetic touches did a good job of disguising the mass-produced efficiencies of the project. Most of the houses were minuscule, space-saving boxes constructed of prefabricated roof trusses, side walls, and mechanical cores. Although every bit as small and mass-produced as

Burton D. Cairns and Vernon DeMars, Farm Security Administration apartment building, Chandler, Arizona, 1937 (Library of Congress, Prints and Photographs Division, FSA-OWI Collection, LC-USF34-036215-D)

modernist existence-minimum apartments, they did not have the latter's anonymous, packing-crate look due to the natural touches of the rustic aesthetic. The houses at Windsor Locks spoke deceptively of the autonomous frugality of the self-sufficient farmer or tradesman, not the heteronomous efficiency imposed on factory workers by niggardly capitalists.[53]

Despite attempts to create a comforting sense of rural community for low-income workers, the realities of Depression-era America were often painfully present in these housing projects. The rural community at Woodville, California, built in 1941 by the Farm Security Administration, provided an array of community services housed in buildings with a vernacular wooden aesthetic that included pitched roofs, overhanging eaves, and redwood siding. But these community facilities were grouped on the periphery of the development, not in the center, testifying to the eccentric position of the community in America's individualistic consumer culture. The individual housing units were also stratified and segregated by class. The most numerous were the mass-produced, metal Quonset huts for migrant farm workers, a kind of packing-crate architecture testifying to the rootless existence of these factory workers of the field. These proletarian huts were closest to the eccentric community facilities, which included lavatories and showers not provided in the huts. This layout made clear that only the poor in America needed the community, which was a second-rate substitute for individual goods attained in the market. The resident farmers of Woodville were housed in superior facilities—the less fortunate in row houses close to community facilities, and the more fortunate in single-family homes along suburban-like cul-de-sacs far from the eccentric community. So this New Deal "community" was really no community at all, but a collection of individuals stratified and segregated by class. Woodville testified to the fact that by 1941 corporate interests had been largely successful in channeling the collective ambitions of the popular classes back into the individual consumption of the stratified marketplace.[54]

Not merely class but racial segregation was also maintained by the public housing projects of this era. Such was the case for Carver Court (1944), a war housing project built exclusively for about one hundred black workers and their families in Coatesville, Pennsylvania. Located near a war-production foundry, which provided the hot, dangerous jobs that had always been deemed appropriate for blacks, Carver Court was designed by architects George Howe (1886–1955), Oscar Stonorov (1905–1970), and Louis Kahn (1901–74). They provided residents in this rural setting apartments and duplexes in unfinished wood siding. Although the roofs were flat, they did provide the symbolic protection of overhanging eaves. The black residents of Carver Court were probably thankful for their attractive, thoughtfully planned homes, but these did not completely obliterate the oppressive conditions in which they worked. The rigid segregation of this public housing served as a constant reminder of the separate and inferior nature of not only their jobs but their leisure lives as well.[55]

New Deal Neoclassicism in State Buildings

The second antimodern aesthetic to play a part in the drama of Depression-era America was neoclassicism. The same sort of neoclassical monumentalism that glorified the state in Nazi Germany appeared in America as well, but in attenuated form. Even here in the land of the marketplace the economic collapse had forced the state to play a larger role in the regulation of capitalism, and adopting the architectural language of the classical polis was a convenient way of legitimating this new role. So the emerging Keynesian state, like Hitler's fascist state, wrapped itself in the legitimating mantle of classical columns and architraves, farcically conjuring up the spirits of the past. But in the United States neoclassicism was modest and less militaristic, testifying to a state whose ambition was to be not the master of society but merely a helpmate of the market.

During the Depression American architects and artists began to feel the need for some form of monumentality, some architecture that represented the collective life of the people. The modernistic aesthetic that took hold in America in the 1920s symbolized a society of individualistic consumption and thus seemed inadequate for representing the new emphasis on the collective state of this period. George Nelson, managing editor of *Architectural Forum*, argued that there was emerging in America "a new concept of community…a renewed vision of society as an organism, regulated by its members in their own interest." But, he went on, American architects were unable to express this new sense of community due to their focus on "the ephemeral in architecture, the quickly obsoleted and easily removed." Elizabeth Mock of the Museum of Modern Art also saw the need in America for a monumental architecture, but one different from the Nazis. If "totalitarianism demands buildings which express the omnipotence of the state and the complete subordination of the individual," she wrote, America demands buildings "that give dignified and coherent form to that interdependence of the individual and the social group which is the very nature of our democracy." Such a democratic integration of the autonomous individual into the social group did not exist, however, in the reality of Depression-era America. The early New Deal state showed the potential to create the autonomy that individuals demanded by asserting a collective control over the heteronomous market, but by the late 1930s the strength of capitalist interests had redefined the state as merely the collective guarantor of individual consumption. Thus, the reconciliation of individual and society expressed by America's monumentality was, like that of the Nazis, a false one, an ideological attempt to assert the existence of a rapprochement not yet achieved.[56]

The aesthetic of this ideological monumentalism in America, as in Nazi Germany, was neoclassicism, for classical civilization represented in the West the ideal community, one with a perfect harmony between individual and society. The New Deal adopted for its public buildings a stripped down, simplified neoclassicism similar to that found in Germany and other European countries. During the 1930s the Supreme Court Building, designed by architect Cass Gilbert, and the Jefferson Memorial and the National Gallery of Art, both designed by John Russell Pope (1874–1937), were all built in Washington D.C. in this style. Although classicism had long held sway in the nation's capital, these Depression-era structures were more restrained and less decorative than earlier governmental buildings. The emphasis was on order and balance, displaying the power and stability of the state. Even more restrained was the national airport of Washington D.C., built in 1940 by the Public Works Administration and designed by architect Howard Cheney. The convex glass facade was classical in its divisions (raised podium, colonnade, and cornice)

Howard Cheney, National Airport, Arlington County, Virginia, 1940
(Library of Congress, Prints and Photographs Division, Theodor Horydczak
Collection, LC-H8-A05-002)

but stripped of all decoration. The columns that stood in front of the glass were reduced to simple cylinders, with no capitals, bases, or fluting. Nazi neoclassicism was similarly simplified and undecorated, but America's version of this style was distinguished by its modest scale. Absent was the intent to intimidate and overwhelm the individual with the overarching power and grandeur of the state. American neoclassicism symbolized a modern state in which efficiency and order in the service of the citizenry was the ultimate goal. But its vaguely classical precedents also testified to the historical stability and traditional legitimacy of a Keynesian state that was being forged in the crucible of social struggles.[57]

Romantic Modernism: The Aesthetic of Private-Sector Consumerism
Both populist public housing and neoclassical state buildings took a back seat in America, however, to the powerful aesthetic of romantic modernism propagated in the private sector by Fordist corporations. Although America's faith in mass production was shaken by the Depression, the religion of mass consumption proved amazingly resilient. Even as many challenged Fordist production and pressured government to regulate the market, most Americans still looked to privatized consumption to escape the ravages of the economy. As Robert and Helen Lynd noted in their Depression-era study, *Middletown in Transition*, America was still "a culture in which private business tempts the population in its every waking minute with adroitly phrased invitations to apply the solvent remedy of more and newer possessions and socially distinguishing goods and comforts to all the ills the flesh is heir to—to loneliness, insecurity, deferred hope, and frustration." No consumer good inspired more reverent devotion during the Depression than the automobile, which, the Lynds noted, had become such an important symbol of success that even workers on relief refused to sell their cars. The Muncie, Indiana, workers that the Lynds studied epitomized the attitudes with which corporate capitalists constructed their counterattack on the Popular Front movements and New Deal programs. If Fordist machines were reviled but their products still revered as symbols of freedom, then recapturing public approval and stimulating consumption required disassociating consumer goods from the mass-production process that begat them. This could be accomplished only if these goods carried no aesthetic reminders of the mechanical heteronomy of production but spoke only of the human autonomy of consumption. This mass amnesia, this superficial humanization of machine-made products, was captured under the spell-binding label of streamlining.[58]

This polysemous word described a complex program for economic recovery launched by corporate interests to channel popular discontent back into the path of rationalized capitalism. At the most profound level, streamlining described a philosophy attributing economic collapse to the resistance of people to buying goods. Depression could be cured only by overcoming this resistance, and speeding up or streamlining the consumption process. This required, business advocates argued, more planned, scientific efforts at finding and creating consumers, or "consumer engineering," which entailed creating new needs where none had existed before and rendering still useful products obsolete so new ones would be bought to replace them. Roy Sheldon and Egmont Arens, two advocates of consumer engineering, argued that the creation of consumers was best left to corporations, not the government, for it was "a problem in human engineering which political muddling will not solve."[59]

Product design was an integral part of this corporate program of streamlining consumption. Mass-production corporations became convinced that consumer resistance to buying could be overcome mainly by giving their products a more organic or streamlined look. During the Depression the American public's imagination was captured by the appearance of high-speed transportation machines like airplanes, dirigibles, ocean liners, and trains. Americans had always associated freedom with mobility, so the invention of such rapid means of mobility during this period seemed to offer an almost magical way to transcend Depression-era problems. These machines captivated Americans not merely because of their function but also because of their aerodynamic design. To overcome the forces of resistance at high speeds, engineers gave these machines rounded, curvilinear shapes, which stood in stark contrast to the rectilinearity of the early machines that inspired the modernists. For many people, such soft, rounded forms carried connotations not only of technological progress and transcendent speed but also of order and naturalism.

The American modernistic style of the 1920s had obscured some aspects of the mass-production factory, but it still bore traces of machine-made fragmentation and repetition. By comparison, the sleek, unified shells of machines like the DC-3 airplane and the *City of Salina* locomotive seemed orderly and simple, not complex and chaotic. As American designer Paul Frankl stated: "Simple lines…tend to cover up the complexity of the machine age. If they do not do this, they at least divert our attention and allow us to feel ourselves master of the machine." Streamlined designs conveyed this wishful dominion of humanity over the mass-produced machine by covering over inhuman fragmentation with the soft, organic look of the human body. Streamlining was above all an aesthetic of dissociation, a radical forgetting of the pain of mechanical production by an immersion in the ecstasy of human consumption.[60]

The corporate program of streamlining thus promised to speed up consumption by offering consumers a mass of new goods that were not only technologically sophisticated but also humanized and organicized with the streamlined look of planes and ships. These connotations of streamlined shapes beyond mere function caused them to spill over to immobile consumer goods like pencil sharpeners, refrigerators, and washing machines. The demand for such dissimulating products created an explosive growth of the profession of industrial design during the Depression. Mass manufacturers found it much cheaper to compete against rivals by changing the design of their products than by engineering new products of improved function. So while the ranks of productive professions in industry stagnated, industrial designers proliferated rapidly beyond their minuscule numbers of the 1920s. While some opened independent firms, many more were employed directly by Fordist corporations, which created permanent staffs of industrial designers. The rapid expansion of this field of commercial art created, like the expansion of government support for the fine arts during this period, opportunities for designers from petty bourgeois and working-class backgrounds. Many who would later achieve great fame, like Norman Bel Geddes, Harley Earl, and Walter Dorwin Teague (1883–1960), came from such humble beginnings, often entering the profession not through formal training but through practical experience in mass-entertainment industries like motion pictures and popular theater. These designers brought with them from the popular classes the idea of culture as diversion and escape from the mundane, rationalized work world, thus deepening an aesthetic trend that emerged in the 1920s. Harley Earl, the pioneer of American automobile styling, stated his goal as "design[ing] a car so that every time you get into it, it's a relief—you have a little vacation for a while."[61]

The American automobile industry, especially Earl's employer, General Motors, led mass-production corporations in this headlong rush toward streamlining. The 1920s had already seen auto styling move away from rigid rectilinearity toward more sleek and rounded shapes. The 1930s turned this trend into a stampede. Streamlining excitement infected the industry, and by the end of the decade nary a straight line or an exposed mechanism could be seen among the latest models. Windshields, fenders, and radiators were tilted back and rounded, and previously exposed structural and mechanical parts like frame rails and springs were carefully concealed under an increasingly unified and seamless body flowing uninterruptedly from hood ornament to rear bumper. Visual testimony that these cars were assembled from parts produced separately by unskilled workers was consciously suppressed, as the sleek, streamlined body approximated the unity of an organic object molded by the forces of nature. Although there were functional advantages to streamlined autos, like increased fuel efficiency, the fate of one car revealed that this trend was driven more by ideology than engineering. The 1934 Chrysler Airflow was a technologically advanced car streamlined by engineers in scientific wind-tunnel tests. But despite its enhanced performance, the car sold poorly because of its unfamiliar shape. Much more successful in the decade were the cars of General Motors and Ford, which wrapped old technology in sleekly rounded bodies that symbolized the excitement of speed and progress while obscuring the technological realities of its achievement.[62]

The ideology of streamlining also seized architecture during the Depression, especially in private-sector construction, where Fordist corporations searched for visual testimony to their claim to be creating a technologically advanced consumer utopia. Heavily influenced by the aesthetic changes in the American automobile, architects and industrial designers began to attach the streamlined idiom of speed, organicism, and technological progress to private houses as well as commercial buildings. While populist public housing promised a return to a simpler agrarian past and government neoclassicism

Lincoln Zephyr, with
Burlington Zephyr
locomotive, 1936
(From the collections
of The Henry Ford,
P.188.66381)

offered reassuring tradition and order, buildings in the streamline moderne style, as it was called, symbolized a modern society of scientifically engineered machines that helped consumers capture the virtues of a decentralized, preindustrial past. Hence, the best terminology for this style may be romantic modernism, for it spoke of a backward-looking progress, use of advanced technology to create a romantic past. While romantic modernism played a small part in Nazism, mainly in the design of cars and autobahns, in the United States it was the predominant aesthetic in architecture, overwhelming populist and neoclassical visions with its ideology of a corporate-controlled consumer utopia.

In American architecture there were visionary engineers who sought to streamline or make more efficient the actual technology of home construction and operation. Yet they had little impact on actual technology, but were utilized largely as alibis for the aesthetic changes that architects embraced. This is made clear by the career of technological visionary Richard Buckminster Fuller (1895–1983). A self-taught technician and engineer, Fuller espoused the technocratic idea that efficiently produced and consumed technology alone could solve problems by streamlining society, without the intervention of superfluous politics. Yet Fuller's technocratic vision in Depression-era America departed from that of the European modernists of the 1920s. The new objectivity of European technocrats was a sober vision of scarcity and limits, while Fuller's streamlined aesthetic offered a scientifically engineered abundance without limits. Although both advocated mass-produced housing, Fuller's efficient housing spoke not of a niggardly economy of production but an expansive economy of ever-growing consumption that corresponded to the corporate vision of consumer engineering.[63]

Fuller's first scheme for mass-produced housing was advanced in 1928, but attracted widespread attention only after the crash of 1929. Originally dubbed the 4D house and later renamed the Dymaxion House, this all-metal structure was hexagonal in plan and consisted of two hollow decks suspended by cables from a central mast containing all necessary services. Between the metal decks were located the living spaces, which were enclosed around the perimeter by walls of vacuum-pane glass. Protecting the entire structure was an aluminum "hood" or roof streamlined to lower the wind resistance of the suspended house. Fuller designed the Dymaxion House to be mass-produced from interchangeable parts, like autos, and to be a self-contained, autonomous unit. Feeding on the growing antiurban sentiment of the Depression and holding out the promise of population decentralization, Fuller bragged that the

R. Buckminster Fuller,
Dymaxion House
drawing, 1928
(Courtesy The Estate of
R. Buckminster Fuller)

Dymaxion House would not be "tied down to city sewage system, the coal or oil company." The complete units could be transported by dirigible and installed anywhere in the world, thus "freeing their users from shackles to any one locality, ergo, making possible world citizenry." Fuller also proposed that these houses be continually upgraded in a program of "progressive obsolescence" modeled on the auto industry.[64]

This streamlined vision of throw-away houses in an infinitely expanding economy sent America's capitalist class into paroxysms of elation and received enthusiastic praise in the popular and business presses. But Fuller could not interest any company in actual production, largely because the necessary technology and materials for the house did not yet exist. If the reality of production was daunting, the image of Fuller's streamlined house was infectious. In 1929 Marshall Field's department store asked Fuller to display and lecture about his Dymaxion model in conjunction with a promotion for their modern furniture. So Fuller, the innovative engineer, was reduced to a huckster for furniture, or, more broadly, for an ideological utopia of technological abundance engineered by corporate America.[65]

Fuller went on to develop other Dymaxion houses whose radical innovations were too quirky to win wide support, but he did inspire architects and designers to speculate about a brave new world and corporations to incorporate these fantasies into their programs of streamlined consumerism. For example, for the 1933 Chicago World's Fair architect George Fred Keck (1895–1980) designed a House of Tomorrow similar to the Dymaxion to serve as a promotional platform for the products of a plethora of corporations manufacturing building supplies. The twelve-sided house was prefabricated and constructed of a steel frame and central utility core. Like Fuller's model, it also hid these structural elements inside the smooth perimeter glass wall. Although the house was not mobile in the literal sense, metaphorically its smooth forms spoke the language of speed. Also weighing in with a corporate-sponsored vision of streamlined, futuristic housing was industrial designer Norman Bel Geddes, whose initial efforts seemed motivated by a genuine concern to solve the housing shortage. In 1939 he began a project to develop mass-produced, prefabricated housing under the sponsorship of the Housing Corporation of America. But when this corporation collapsed and the Revere Copper and Brass Company picked up sponsorship, Bel Geddes's plan became just another corporate promotion of a brave new technological future. "Americans want more copper in their home, for more copper means better living," proclaimed a 1941 Revere ad which pictured a group of Bel Geddes's streamlined houses that made extensive use of copper sheet. Once again American corporations were more interested in the superficial images of a streamlined future than pioneering the underlying technology to produce it, and Bel Geddes's socially concerned architecture languished in a sea of cynical corporate promotions.[66]

Norman Bel Geddes and others like him ultimately offered only an orderly, soothing image of the future, a modernism with the edges rounded off. These romantic modernists countered the European modernists' vision of the fragmentation and scarcity of the machine age with a holistic image of technological abundance bent to the organic demands of humanity. Although he was not an architect, the stage-designer-turned-industrial-designer Bel Geddes heavily influenced this trend in the early 1930s with his influential *Horizons* book. Influenced by the German expressionist architect Erich Mendelsohn (1887–1953), Bel Geddes's widely publicized architectural designs combined the unadorned shapes of European modernism with the dynamic movement of the American modernistic. At first glance his designs, such as the house published in *Ladies' Home Journal* in 1931, looked like the epitome of European modernism, with flat roofs, pipe railings, stucco walls, and ribbon windows.

But a closer inspection revealed features anathema to purists like Le Corbusier and Mies. First, the exterior volumes were uninterrupted shells, revealing no signs of supporting structures. Second, there was a predilection for the cantilever, the unsupported overhang that defied gravity. Finally, there were attention-grabbing rounded volumes that relieved rectilinearity with a soft, organic look. These elements quickly infiltrated the work of real architects, in both domestic houses and commercial buildings. Typical of the former was the Richard Mandel house of 1934. Designed by Edward Durell Stone (1902–1978), it was Bel-Geddes-like with its cantilevers and rounded dining room dominating the street facade. Although the latter had a ribbon window extending its entire circumference, the greatest part was filled not with transparent glass, as was the modernist practice, but with translucent glass block, signaling an increased concern for inward-turning privacy.[67]

The streamline moderne style was more prominent, however, in commercial architecture, in which corporate America sought to project an image of technological progress with a human face. Typical was the Greyhound Bus terminal in Washington D.C. (1938), one of several designed by W. S. Arrasmith (1898–1965). There was hardly a square corner on the two-story facade, where the walls of the two symmetrical wings met in a recessed entrance covered by a cantilevered, elliptical marquee. The facia of the marquee was covered with three closely spaced strips of polished aluminum, known as "speed stripes," which would become a cliché of the style. And crowning the composition above the entrance was a tower from which protruded a rounded fin carrying the bus company's name and a chrome greyhound logo. An even more elaborate and hackneyed corporate expression of the style was the Coca-Cola plant and office in Los Angeles (1936), remodeled by Robert Derrah (1895–1946). The architect surrounded the four existing buildings at the site with a high, smooth perimeter wall that curved around the street corner. Then he poked portholes and bulkhead doors in the wall, hung a promenade deck with pipe railing off the side, placed a bridge on the top with a mast/flagpole, and voilà!—a Coca-Cola ocean liner that borrowed the speed and health connotations of sailing for the peddlers of the sugary confection. Like most streamlined architecture, Derrah's design was mainly a facade, applied to the public areas of a commercial building to impress upon the consuming public an image not only of technological speed and efficiency but also of escape from the mundane scarcities of the Depression.[68]

These connotations of escape into the future made the streamline moderne style almost imperative for the entertainment industry during this period.

Robert Derrah, Coca-Cola plant and office, Los Angeles, 1936
(Courtesy you-are-here.com)

With Hollywood films offering Americans a steady diet of escapist confections with which to obliterate the realities of the Depression, it is not surprising that the industry turned to streamlining to similarly cover over the ugliness of their own mass-production methods. Such was the case with the NBC Studio Building in Los Angeles, designed by the Austin Company and completed in 1938. The focus of the composition was a rounded portico that turned the street corner and connected the two wings of the building. To the left was the office wing of three stories, unified horizontally by ribbon windows and a terrace atop the second floor, along which ran the ubiquitous speed stripes in stainless steel. To the right was the studio wing, composed of three blind, rounded boxes separated by set-back, curving entrances of translucent glass-block walls. The latter had the admirable quality of appearing open while simultaneously obscuring from public view the work of cultural production transpiring within. Also pleasantly streamlined was the new complex for Walt Disney Studios, whose animated films provided Americans with superficial fun with which to withstand deprivation. Kem Weber (1889–1963), a German émigré, designed the Burbank buildings in long, low, flat-roofed, ribbon-windowed volumes, with no structural supports interrupting their smooth surfaces.[69]

Southern California was also the home of the decade's most important development in domestic architecture, Richard Neutra's (1892–1970) brand of romantic modernism. During the 1930s this Vienna-born émigré created in and around Los Angeles an architecture that blended the rigor and discipline of European modernism with the romance of Wright's organicism. Neutra's art was more complex than the simplistic surfaces of streamline moderne, but he was driven by the same impulse to humanize the machine, to render a mass-produced society somehow compatible with the "psychosomatic organism," as he put it. Neutra's romantic modernism did not degenerate into commercial hucksterism, but it did help to create the hermetically sealed, inward-turning spaces of consumerism so important for the postwar suburbs.[70]

As an architecture student in Vienna, Neutra learned the modernist enthusiasm for the machine aesthetic and mass-production, but it was tempered by the countervailing influence of organicism. He worked for two years in the office of Erich Mendelsohn, the expressionist architect, and was impressed by the work of Frank Lloyd Wright. This combination of influences seemed to motivate Neutra's immigration in 1923 to the United States, the land of Wright's architecture and Henry Ford's mass production. After working in Wright's office for a short period, the young émigré moved to Los Angeles, where he quickly pioneered a language of domestic architecture that combined a technological modernity with a sense of freedom and health. The first expression of this language was the Lovell Health house of 1929. Built for the naturopathic doctor and exercise advocate, Philip Lovell, the Health house was ostensibly modernist, with its flat roofs, ribbon windows, and white concrete. And it paid superficial obeisance to the modernist god of mass production, using Model T headlights as lighting fixtures on the house's main stairway. But the house's real deity was individual consumption, not mass production, and to praise it all evidence of the mass-produced steel framework so dear to modernism was concealed beneath a unified skin of glass and concrete. The autos on which this house was modeled were the streamliners that were just emerging, those deceptively unified and organic vehicles that hid all features of their mass production beneath an obscuring skin that spoke of the speed and freedom of consumption.[71]

In the 1930s Neutra developed this obscuring skin aesthetic, influenced by the American trend of streamlined consumerism. Although he seldom used the curvilinear forms found in the work of Bel Geddes and others, his houses did increasingly become hermetic shells, sealed off from the public realm of production and turned inward toward a private world of consumption open only to the recuperative charms of nature. Two expressions of this evolving skin aesthetic were the Beard and Von Sternberg Houses of 1935 and 1936, respectively, both of which experimented with mass-produced metal elements. In the Beard House Neutra used corrugated sheet-metal flooring to construct hollow walls, through which hot and cold air was circulated to control temperatures. The Von Sternberg House was constructed of steel panels painted silver-gray to

Richard Neutra, Beard House, Altadena, California, 1935 (Richard Joseph Neutra Papers, Collection 1179, Department of Special Collections, Charles E. Young Research Library, University of California, Los Angeles)

give them a glimmering, airplane look. There was extensive use of glass in both houses, but it was set flush with the exterior walls to form a smooth, reflective skin broken only by raised joints. The steel columns which bore the weight of the roof across the glass sections were disguised by sheet-metal mullions. And both houses varied the skin to insulate the inner paradise of private consumption from the external world of Depression-era production. Large areas of glass in back faced views of unspoiled California landscape, while blind metal walls were turned to the street and entrances. In the later 1930s Neutra increasingly replaced his expensive metal panels with cheaper wooden ones. But he used the wood just like the metal, creating a continuous skin that concealed all elements of supporting structure. Neutra also used the larger sheets of glass made possible by improved production methods as a transparent skin, creating huge walls of undivided glass that revealed no supporting frame. These glass walls were used mainly in the private, rear portions of the houses, while more public entrances and facades constituted a protective skin of opaque materials like wood, brick, or stone.[72]

Another architect who offered during this period a vision of an individualistic and insular nation of consumers withdrawn from the abuses of machine production was Frank Lloyd Wright. The Depression of the 1930s reaffirmed and deepened Wright's belief in an organic architecture that was built with the benefits of mass production but refused to let the machine dictate aesthetic

Frank Lloyd Wright,
Johnson Wax Building,
Racine, Wisconsin, 1939
(Library of Congress, Prints
and Photographs Division,
Historic American Buildings
Survey, HABS, WIS, 51-RACI,
5-22)

form. His vision, not unlike Hitler's, was of a society using modern technology to return humanity to a premodern world of decentralized rural settlements, a petty-bourgeois paradise in which self-sufficient individuality and private property insulated all from the abuses of the Fordist capitalism on which it was based. Wright's version of romantic modernism was well expressed in his built projects of the 1930s, especially the Johnson Wax Building and the Kaufmann House (also known as Fallingwater). The former, completed in 1939, was located in the industrial city of Racine, Wisconsin, but only over the architect's strenuous objections. In his typical antiurban fashion, Wright tried to persuade Herbert Johnson, president of the Johnson Wax Company, to locate the new corporate headquarters in the suburbs, not in his hometown of Racine. Wright lost the battle for location, and apparently decided that if he could not take the building into his beloved Wisconsin countryside, then he would bring the countryside into the building and seal it in an organic shell that turned its back on the city. The exterior of the Johnson Wax Building was a windowless barrier of low, horizontal walls, with light admitted through a cornice line of translucent glass tubing. And in keeping with his own philosophy of organic architecture, as well as the streamline moderne style of the 1930s, the exterior lines of the building were smoothly rounded, revealing, in Wright's words, the "new sense of unity and continuity" more characteristic of living things than machine-made objects.[73]

Most of Wright's efforts to bring nature into the building were, however, located inside this hermetic shell. Having sealed the interior off from the offending sights of the city outside, the architect created within it an organic sanctuary that spoke of a glade in a forest, not an office building. The undivided central space was forested by a stand of slender concrete columns that rose thirty feet and then sprouted circular "lily pads" to support the roof. To create a "sky" between his concrete treetops, Wright filled the remaining ceiling with skylights of glass tubing, which admitted warm, diffused light. As on the exterior, the interior walls curved smoothly around corners and blended seamlessly into the ceiling through the cornice line of glass tubing. Finally, to seal the effect the architect designed all the office furniture in streamlined, organic forms. In the Johnson Wax Building Wright thus used modern methods to create within the industrial city an organic refuge, which, in the words of one design historian, "provided psychic insulation from the sight of bread lines, riots and the streets of Hooverville."[74]

Perhaps a better expression of Wright's romantic modernism of this period, however, arose in the countryside, where he built the Kaufmann House or Fallingwater as a getaway for the head of a Pittsburgh department store. In a dramatic setting dominated by a waterfall, Wright could let nature speak its own organic language, and merely merge the building into the site, as he had done in his Prairie style houses. Like the latter, the Kaufmann House had long, low, horizontal lines and open spaces that brought the outdoors indoors. And the structure was literally anchored in a rocky ledge just above the falls. But the Kaufmann House also departed from the Prairie style in a modernist direction. The horizontal planes of the balconies did not nestle into the landscape but were suspended in space above it, like a Corbusian cube. And they were composed not of natural stone or brick, but of machine-made concrete, finished smoothly and precisely. But unlike the totally rationalized architecture of Le Corbusier or Mies, Wright's variegated structure blended together natural and mechanical elements, thus attaining a more natural life through the means of the machine. The Kaufmann House was the microcosmic statement of a bold macroscopic scheme that Wright formulated during the Depression, a seemingly contradictory vision of a decentralized, rural utopia achieved through modern machinery.[75]

Wright had always been decidedly antiurban, preferring to live and build in the suburbs or countryside. But the onset of the Great Depression deepened his antiurbanism into a rigid ideology that assigned all of America's problems to the overgrown city. This intensifying ideology combined with the idle time forced on Wright by the Depression to produce his Broadacre City project, huge models of a decentralized, utopian "city" that used advanced technology to return Americans to the soil where they belonged. The project was influenced by the broader currents of antiurban populism of this period, sharing with these the validation of common people and the idea that decentralization could solve social problems. Yet, parts of the Broadacre City plan had more in common with the ideology of corporate streamlining than populism. It shared streamlining's idealization of modern consumer technology, especially the automobile, as the means of achieving this rural utopia. And while populism saw solutions coming through the democratic power of the masses, Wright's utopia was decidedly elitist, placing power in the hands of technocratic "geniuses" with education and vision, not the "mob" of uninformed humanity. These traits made his vision compatible with the corporate vision of a stream-lined society of privatized consumption that compensated workers in rationalized factories and bureaucracies for their degraded work.

Wright detailed the Broadacre City plan in his 1932 book, *The Disappearing City*. Here he argued that the concentration of people in the city created three forms of exploitation: rent for land, appropriated by landlords; rent for money (interest), appropriated by "moneylords"; and rent for the machine (profit), appropriated by the "machine lords." The most important was rent for land, because concentrated land ownership forced most people not only to pay to live on it but also to work for industrialists, since they had no land on which to support themselves. Wright's solution to all forms of exploitation was break-ing the monopoly of urban land ownership by distributing land freely to individuals in the countryside. In his Broadacre City each resident family would be given no less than one acre of land on which to build its own house and grow its own food. This scheme would not undermine capitalism as such, Wright argued, but merely America's "plutocratic capitalism," replacing it with "true capitalism, which is based on true individuality."[76]

Broadacre City was thus an attempt to turn the clock back to petty com-modity production, an early form of capitalism dominated by the self-employed petty bourgeoisie. But Wright sought to use modern technology to return to this economic past. The new technologies of production, transportation, and communication, he wrote, provided "the means to take all the real advantages

of centralization known as the big city into the regional field we call the countryside and unite them with the features of the ground in that union we call
modern architecture in that native creation we call the beauty of the country."
Because Wright's rural utopia was built on modern technology, its politics were
different from other forms of American populism. He sought a social base for
his plan in a coalition of intellectuals and workers, incorporating both into a
unified "artifex" defined much like Saint-Simon's all encompassing "producer
class," except that capitalists were excluded. But within this class of producers,
Wright privileged the laborers of the mind. The technocratic "geniuses" who
conceived and supervised the machines would govern Broadacre City for the
simple farmers and mechanics.[77]

Of all the machines created by the technocratic class of artifex, Wright, like
Hitler, saw the car as central to the creation of his decentralized petty-bourgeois
utopia: "The great hard-road systems of our country beckon erstwhile tenants
of the cubicle to freedom where his motor may stand not only by his gate but
wherever he goes, while he has access to everything he needs in order to live
a useful and happy family life on his own ground." Freedom was for Wright,
like so many Americans, synonymous with mobility, the ability to individually
change one's geographic location. The mass production of cars and roads thus
created a democracy of movement, allowing all to escape the exploitation of
the city to the abundant land in the countryside. Wright's Broadacre City was
thus at base an auto-utopia, in which the decentralized individuals would be
connected only by the arteries of the highway system.[78]

Wright admitted that the machines on which he would base his utopia had
been misused and misdesigned, creating the ugliness of modern architecture
and its city. He argued, however, that in the hands of intelligent designers the
machine could be rendered beautiful, merged with the natural beauty of the
landscape in organic architecture. Wright spent much of *The Disappearing City*
describing ways to render roads "organic," naturally beautiful. A year before
Hitler launched the autobahn program in Germany, he called for an expanded
highway system that would be not only safer and faster but more beautiful:
"Imagine spacious landscaped highways, grade crossings eliminated, 'bypassing' living areas, devoid of the already archaic telegraph and telephone poles
and wires and free of blaring bill boards and obsolete construction. Imagine
these great highways, safe in width and grade, bright with wayside flowers,
cool with shade trees.... Sweeping grades, banked turns, well considered cuts
and fills healed by good planting of indigenous growth have supreme beauty."
Wright, like Hitler, knew that to create a rural idyll with machines, all the

aesthetic markers of the industrial mechanism had to be carefully concealed under an organic veneer of nature. Thus, he wrote that "the complexity of crude utilitarian construction" that "did violence to the landscape" in an earlier era of industrialism must now be "swept away out of sight."[79]

Wright's organic architecture covered the ugliness of a rationalized society on buildings as well as roads. The Broadacre City scheme called for the construction of homes from factory-made, standardized units. But Wright insisted, against the modernists, that mass-produced homes need not bear the look of factory standardization. "Why try to make buildings as hard as machines," he exhorted, for when machines were guided by creative imagination, mass production was compatible with "infinite variety of form and scheme." Mass-produced parts could be assembled in different configurations, allowing residents not only to blend their house into its particular landscape but also to customize it to their individual preferences. Wright sought to provisionally implement this vision of low-cost organic architecture during the 1930s in his series of Usonian houses, single-family homes designed for mass production and selling for under $5000. The Usonian houses combined the long and low lines of the Prairie houses with the flat roof and overlapping planes of the Kaufmann House. The main walls were constructed of prefabricated, horizontal wood siding, but the vertical planes such as the chimneys were often of brick. Like Neutra's houses of this period, the Usonian houses had street facades that were generally windowless and uninviting, while the rear was opened to the landscape with expansive glass areas. So in Wright's free, democratic community of Broadacre, citizens would turn their backs on their neighbors and commune only with the natural landscape, their own individual acre of land.[80]

Broadacre City was a utopia of spatial consumption, a radical alteration of the distribution of human domiciles across the landscape that not only left alone the relations of production but actually supported them through obscuring their human and natural consequences. Although Wright wrote in *The Disappearing City* of liberating workers from the exploitation of urban rent-takers, he offered a scheme only for decentralizing exploitation, not ending it. Realizing that workers could not make a living farming one acre of land, Wright called for urban factories to be broken into small units and scattered across the countryside close to workers' rural residences. He believed that combining subsistence farming with wage labor would turn workers into truly free individuals: "Society would soon have an individual for a citizen instead of a herd-struck moron." It is difficult to understand how the worker would be more free working the same Fordist job in a decentralized factory, until one realizes that Wright's conception of freedom was solely interior, within the private realm of consumption, and had nothing to do with the social realm of production. "At home," Wright wrote, "he is lord of a free spacious interior life." But only at home. Wright's ultimate aim in Broadacre City was not the elimination of exploitation but the defusion of its consequences—the class consciousness and united actions of all those herd-struck proletarian morons. In this utopia of consumption, workers would work in dispersed factories that prevented class coordination and return to individualized homes of organic beauty that compensated for their rationalized work.[81]

With Wright, the corporate advocates of streamlined consumerism in America realized that using the machine to create a placating realm of privatized consumption required a substantial role for the state beyond Keynesian programs of demand management. The state would also have to provide the infrastructure of private consumption, which corporations found unprofitable to produce. To sell streamlined automobiles there had to be roads and bridges to drive on; to sell radios and refrigerators there had to be electricity to power them. Machines of private consumption required machines of public works to fuel them. Further, public works construction during the Depression could also generate jobs and income for the unemployed, transforming them into consumers. So the state was a vital partner in the technological progress that corporations promised would deliver consumers from economic disaster.

The state's public works projects during the Depression were constrained by the same aesthetic considerations that generated the romantic modernism of the private sector. These collective machines had to be constructed in a way that did not arouse the public's fear of the mass-production machines it blamed for the Depression. Like streamlined cars and refrigerators, the dams, bridges, and roads built by the Works Progress Administration and Tennessee Valley Authority during the 1930s and 1940s sought to cover over the frightening complexity and standardization of the machine age by evoking images of order, nature, and simplicity. But unlike the individual consumer products of the marketplace, these public works had a grand scale that captured the scope and profundity of the new civilization of consumption being constructed. They reified and monumentalized the collective power of this society of individual consumers. While Nazi monumentalism elevated the state and party to collective ideals, American monumentalism elevated technology to the ultimate expression of collective power. This was a romantic monumentalism of the modern machine, which promised that technology would move society back to a more orderly and simple life with nature.

Perhaps the highest expressions of this monumental romantic modernism were the hydroelectric dams built during this period. These projects epitomized the New Deal promise that the collective planning and efforts of humans could not only tame technology but also employ it in harmony with nature. The greatest of these dams was the Hoover (or Boulder) Dam on the Colorado River, built specifically to create jobs during the Depression. Completed in 1935, the huge construction project quickly captured the public's imagination. Concrete was poured on a scale hitherto unknown, and its nature and function created many of the aesthetic qualities of this and other dams. The streamlined, curving spillways of the Hoover Dam resulted from the plastic qualities of concrete, which allowed it to be molded into a monolithic sculpture that both conformed to hydraulic laws and also hid the mechanical grid of structural steel deep within it. The dam blended so smoothly into the curves of the canyon walls that it seemed more like a natural part of the landscape than an imposed machine. But the streamlined appearance of the Hoover and other Depression-era dams was also the result of conscious design. The federal government realized, in the words of TVA head architect Roland Wank (1898–1970), that these public works "express in steel, concrete, and glass the aspirations and spirit of a whole nation," and hired architects to capture the correct spirit. Los Angeles architect Gordon Kaufmann (1888–1949), known for his work in modernistic style, added the aesthetic touches to the Hoover Dam. On the main structure he accentuated the curving streamlines of the spillway, but his towers at the dam's crest were rather angular, in the old setback style of modernistic skyscrapers. Within the powerhouse, which was open to the public, the electric turbines were dressed up in gleaming red casings with stainless-steel trim, but at top the exposed mechanism and turbine shafts lent the powerhouse the look of mechanical complexity.[82]

A more advanced development of this aesthetic of monumental romantic modernism was found in the dams of the Tennessee Valley Authority, designed later in the decade by Wank. Like Neutra and Bel Geddes, Wank was influenced by the curvilinear expressionism of Erich Mendelsohn, and seemed aware that the image of mechanical fragmentation and complexity could overwhelm the public and awaken reservations. In his TVA designs Wank was careful to present the public with orderly, organic images that concealed the mechanical complexity of hydroelectric generation. The exteriors of his powerhouses conveyed a sense of power though their appearance as rectilinear, monolithic blocks, but his interior designs for public areas sought to impress spectators with images of friendly efficiency and order. The Visitors Lobby at the Pickwick Landing

Dam, completed 1938, was a careful study in romantic modernism. The gleaming aluminum doors, tubular furniture, and smooth, undecorated walls gave the impression of an efficient machine, but the curved corners and ceiling softened and humanized this machine. Even the control room, whose profusion of dials, levers, and buttons was visible to visitors through large glass windows, was so neat and spacious that it gave the appearance of easily governed simplicity.

The aesthetic tour de force of Wank's Pickwick Dam, however, was the powerhouse interior. In contrast to the electric turbines of Hoover Dam, with their fragmented, mechanical aesthetic, these machines were totally enclosed by sleek metal shells, making them pure geometric monoliths. The Pickwick turbines must have been much more difficult to repair and maintain, for workers had to remove sections of the casing to access the mechanicals. But this inconvenience surely was considered a small price to pay for the overpowering spectacle created by the streamlining. The sheer scale of the gargantuan engines neatly arranged in a row conveyed the great power at the service of the collective good represented by these public works. But their smooth simplicity also gave spectators a sense of human control over the machine, sufficient to ensure an orderly progress of the nation toward a consumer utopia.[83]

The other great public works projects of the decade to embody this romantic-modernist promise of a consumer utopia on a monumental scale were the roads and bridges. The idea of building public roads that evidenced a

Roland Wank, Pickwick Landing Dam, generator hall, 1938 (Library of Congress, Prints and Photographs Division, FSA-OWI Collection, LC-USW33-015669-ZC)

peaceful coexistence with nature rather than mechanical dominance emerged in the United States in the 1920s with the parkway concept. As the upper and middle classes began to flee the mechanical city for the bucolic suburbs, there arose pressure for roads that maintained the suburb's respect for nature as an insulation from urban defilement. Hence, the idea of the parkway emerged, a road surrounded by a natural landscape that created for drivers a pleasant, non-mechanical experience, just like Hitler's autobahns. The model for the modern parkway was the Bronx River Parkway, designed by Gilmore D. Clarke (1892–1982) and completed in 1923. Avoiding straightaways, the road curved back and forth beside the Bronx River. The carefully landscaped parkland along the roadsides, which were devoid of billboards and businesses, treated drivers to a changing spectacle of organic serenity as they hurtled back and forth to bureaucratic jobs in New York. The 1930s saw a proliferation of such parkways, which were a collective metaphor for the program of consumer engineering that grew stronger as the decade progressed. As architectural historian Sigfried Giedion wrote, such roads gave drivers "the freedom of uninterrupted forward motion, without the inhuman pressure of endlessly straight lines pushing one on to dangerous speeds." The parkway created the experience of machine-driven progress, but a leisurely, self-paced progress that allowed the driver to forget those endlessly straight assembly lines in Fordist factories pushing people on at dangerous production speeds.[84]

All these disparate elements of the corporate program of streamlined consumerism and its aesthetic of romantic modernism came together in 1939 in one monumental spectacle that riveted the public's attention and anticipated the landscape of postwar Fordism. The New York World's Fair, with its theme of "Building the World of Tomorrow," continued the tradition of industrial exposition as corporate propaganda, with displays dominated by companies glorifying their wares and courting public opinion. But the epochal events of this Depression decade converged to make this fair a unique and prescient image of America on the threshold of war. The 1930s had seen the greatest challenges to unadulterated capitalism and corporate power since the republic's birth, and most of these had converged in the New Deal political coalition. Most of the large corporations represented at the fair took the opportunity to incorporate anti-New Deal messages into their exhibits and trumpet the importance of free enterprise. Walter Dorwin Teague, who sat on the board of design for the fair, argued that the event provided manufacturers "an opportunity to state the case for the democratic system of individual enterprise" at a time when other countries were turning toward collectivism.[85]

To persuade fair-goers that corporate initiative, not government regulation, would secure a prosperous future for America, corporations depicted themselves in exhibits as pioneers in the science and technology that would solve all social problems. Of course, the technological ideology, which privileged the technical means over the human ends, had been prominent in America for decades. But unique to the Depression was the fair's "streamlined" version of this ideology, which focused on the technologies of consumption, not production. As late as the 1933 Century of Progress exhibition in Chicago, manufacturers had proudly displayed their production technologies to the public, often using the angular and fragmented modernistic style. General Motors exhibited there an abbreviated version of a working assembly line, while Ford displayed a modernist photomural of auto production in a gear-shaped exhibit building. The New York fair, by contrast, embodied the new streamlined aesthetic of romantic modernism, with its celebration of consumption technologies that obscured the now threatening machines of production. America's greatest industrial designers built corporate exhibits that trumpeted a world of streamlined technologies that issued forth from the black boxes of corporations, without a hint of the work that went on inside. Both Ford and Chrysler included depictions of production, but only in the highly abstract medium of animation. Ford's "Cycle of Production" exhibit consisted of a tiered turntable depicting eighty-seven steps in the production process. Each was illustrated with a display of carved, moving figures in an amusing vignette that humanized production. The Chrysler Corporation also used diverting animation to depict production in its film entitled *In Tune with Tomorrow*, in which personified Plymouth parts sang and danced as they cheerily assembled themselves into a car.[86]

More characteristic of corporate exhibits at the fair, however, were those that totally ignored the production of goods and focused exclusively on their consumption in a futuristic utopia of technology. Many were housed in buildings designed in the sleek streamline moderne style, like Norman Bel Geddes's General Motors building and Walter Dorwin Teague's Ford building. Even grander architectural visions of the future were contained *within* these buildings, especially Henry Dreyfuss's (1904–72) Democracity exhibit and Norman Bel Geddes's Futurama for General Motors. The former was the fair's theme exhibit, housed in the centrally located Perisphere. Spectators entered the globe through elevated walkways that led onto balconies overlooking the central diorama, a scale model city of 2039. Democracity contained a central hub, Centerton, which housed business, cultural, and leisure activities in low buildings separated by green spaces. Outside the perimeter highway that enclosed Centerton was a greenbelt of parks and farmland that contained twenty-five satellite towns with industries and housing for workers and managers. This suburbanization of the working class alongside the middle and upper classes was portrayed here, as in Wright's Broadacre City, as overcoming divisions and creating social unity. This was also the theme of the dramatic presentation accompanying the diorama. As the lights dimmed to simulate dusk in Democracity, projected images of separate groups of people appeared at the edges of the dome, marching and singing the fair's theme song. The marchers, representing the various occupational groups of modern society, converged at the center into a cooperative mass of humanity, singing:

> We're the rising tide coming from far and wide
> Marching side by side on our way,
> For a brave new world,
> Tomorrow's world,
> That we shall build today.[87]

The apogee of the corporate program of consumer streamlining, however, revealing both its captivating conceits and its contradictions, was the General Motors Futurama exhibit, designed by streamlining's dean of design, Norman Bel Geddes. Bel Geddes created a huge, meticulous diorama of a city of 1960 that propagandized not only for a general future of fantastic consumerism, but also for the specific technology on which General Motors' sales depended, a national system of superhighways. The Futurama was itself a careful work of consumer engineering, creating in people the desire to consume by the obsessive manipulation of their attention and vision. Visitors entered into a lobby containing a large map of the nation's existing highway system. A recorded commentary projected awful traffic congestion by 1960 if the system went unaltered. The map then changed configuration to reveal a future system of highways that would reduce congestion and usher in a frictionless society. In his 1940 book based on the Futurama vision, *Magic Motorways*, Bel Geddes argued that "freedom of movement" over great superhighways would not only relieve congestion and unify the nation but also decentralize squalid industrial cities, allowing all people to live in "a world of light, fresh air, open parks, easy movement." The city would still remain the site of production, "a working entity," but the countryside would be the site of residence and consumption, "a living entity."[88]

Norman Bel Geddes, Futurama exhibit, New York World's Fair, 1939

(Photograph © the Estate of Margaret Bourke-White/Norman Bel Geddes Collection, Harry Ransom Humanities Research Center, The University of Texas at Austin)

It was such a utopia of carefully segregated consumption and production, connected by superhighways, that Bel Geddes's Futurama for GM displayed. Exiting the Map Lobby, visitors went on to the main exhibit, a diorama covering 35,738 square feet and visualizing this future of streamlined consumerism. They sat in plush seats that moved along a conveyor belt for a fifteen-minute simulated airplane ride over the America of 1960, in which every aspect of their attention was controlled. Each chair contained a speaker playing a recorded commentary, and rotated to focus attention on specific details. Visitors saw in this world of tomorrow a landscape unified by a massive, futuristic highway system of fourteen lanes, on which cars' speed and path of travel were supposedly controlled automatically by radio beams. The trip began in the countryside, where futuristic barns, hydroelectric dams, and orchards of trees under glass gave the impression that science had transformed rural life. But the most important innovation seemed to be the highway itself, on which, the commentary pointed out, streamlined trucks carried farm products to lucrative urban markets. The spectators followed the highway toward a great city, passing along the way amusement parks and industrial towns that were relegated to the suburbs. The climax of the ride was the City of 1960, whose curving, streamlined skyscrapers were visible from a great distance. Here huge swaths of the city fabric had been gouged out to accommodate massive roads that separated pedestrians, express traffic, and local traffic. The rest of the city consisted of generously spaced, quarter-mile-high skyscrapers, interspersed with parks and lower buildings. The last stop on the motorized tour was a close-up of one intersection in the shopping district, after which visitors exited the Futurama to find themselves, magically, in a full-scale reproduction of the same intersection, complete with store windows full of goods and streets full of 1939 GM cars.[89]

In General Motors' vision of the future there was little evidence of work or production; this was a utopia of consumption, in which the citizens were constituted solely as a buyers of goods. The highway system here was not only the conduit of commerce but also the theater of consumption, a continuous screen along which consumers were passively conveyed to view the march of goods offered by corporations. Ironically, the process of consumption that was supposed to give Americans freedom and escape from the conveyor lines that manufactured goods revealed itself here to be merely another heteronomous conveyor line, but one that manufactured consumers. And there was another unspoken contradiction that underlay the exhibit. For all the anti-government and pro-free-enterprise messages explicitly incorporated by GM executives, their real purpose was to persuade Americans to support a massive, government-financed highway system. Their streamlined vision of a society of mass consumption necessitated state intervention not only to underwrite consumer demand but also to construct the public infrastructure of private consumption.[90]

Both Democracity and the Futurama epitomized the corporate program of streamlined consumerism and the romantic-modernist aesthetic that supported it. This vision of America as a consumer paradise was based on a spatial rearrangement of the built environment, from the macro siting of towns to the micro contours of cars and buildings. Both displays promised a future in which work would be confined to cities and industrial satellites and "living" would be carefully segregated in suburbs and the countryside, where rationalized work could be forgotten in homes that aesthetically reconciled the machine with nature. When the New York World's Fair was built, America was on the verge of war with Nazi Germany, but the two nations' aesthetic visions of their landscapes were remarkably similar. The build-up to war and actual hostilities dominated most of the 1940s and postponed the realization of this new landscape in America. But the promise of this consumer utopia was kept in the forefront of the American psyche by government and corporate officials, who reminded people that the freedom to consume was really what the war was about. After the war American architects and designers, in cooperation with corporations and the state, went to work feverishly to turn the nation into a collection of Futuramas and Democracities, and largely succeeded. The transformation of America's erstwhile enemies took longer, but was ultimately accomplished as well.

1. Gallup poll cited in Warren Susman, *Culture as History: The Transformation of American Society in the Twentieth Century* (New York: Pantheon, 1984), 218; Mary Nolan, *Visions of Modernity* (New York: Oxford University Press, 1994), 231–32. On the commonality of populist political rhetoric during the Depression, see Michael Denning, *The Cultural Front: The Laboring of American Culture in the Twentieth Century* (London: Verso, 1996), 126–33.

2. The quote is from Barbara M. Lane, *Architecture and Politics in Germany, 1918–1945* (Cambridge, MA: Harvard University Press, 1985), 139. See also Manfredo Tafuri and Francesco Dal Co, *Modern Architecture* (New York: Harry Abrams, 1979), 295–97; Robert R. Taylor, *The Word in Stone: The Role of Architecture in National Socialist Ideology* (Berkeley: University of California Press, 1974), 1–7, 55–63. 103–19.

3. Sigfried Giedion, *Space, Time and Architecture*, 5th ed., rev. and enl. (Cambridge, MA: Harvard University Press, 1967), 872, see also 695.

4. Paul David Pearson, *Alvar Aalto and the International Style* (New York: Whitney Library of Design, 1978), 12–70; Werner M. Moser, "A Survey of the Work of Alvar Aalto," in Alvar Aalto, *Synopsis* (Basel: Birkhäuser Verlag, 1970), 183–84.

5. Pearson, *Alvar Aalto*, 84–93, 149, 230 n.1; Giedion, *Space*, 629–32, 640.

6. Aalto, *Synopsis*, 15, 19, 20, 16.

7. Pearson, *Alvar Aalto*, 168–75; Kenneth Frampton, *Modern Architecture: A Critical History*, 3rd ed. (London: Thames and Hudson, 1992), 199–200; Giedion, *Space*, 645–48.

8. *Pravda* quoted in Jean Jenger, *Le Corbusier: Architect, Painter, Poet* (New York: Harry Abrams, 1996), 61; Frampton, *Modern Architecture*, 177, 213–14; Lars Olof Larsson, "Classicism in the Architecture of the Twentieth Century," in *Albert Speer: Architecture, 1932–1942*, ed. Leon Krier (Brussels: Archive D'Architecture Moderne, 1985), 239–41.

9. Peter Blake, *The Master Builders* (New York: Norton, 1976), 87–89; Frampton, *Modern Architecture*, 184, 224–26.

10. Blake, *Master Builders*, 84–87; Giedion, *Space*, 539–40; Jenger, *Le Corbusier*, 70–71; Le Corbusier, *The Radiant City* (New York: Orion Press, 1967), 32; Gerald Silk, "The Automobile in Art," in *Automobile and Culture*, ed. Gerald Silk (New York and Los Angeles: Harry Abrams and The Museum of Contemporary Art, 1984), 88–89.

11. Jenger, *Le Corbusier*, 74–75; Lane, *Architecture and Politics*, 181–82; Franz Schulze, *Mies van der Rohe: A Critical Biography* (Chicago: University of Chicago Press, 1985), 185–201; Philip Johnson, "Architecture in the Third Reich," in *Writings* (New York: Oxford University Press, 1979), 54; Franco Borsi, *The Monumental Era: European Architecture and Design, 1929–1939* (New York: Rizzoli, 1987), 112.

12. Elaine C. Hochman, *Architects of Fortune: Mies van der Rohe and the Third Reich* (New York: Fromm International, 1990); Frampton, *Modern Architecture*, 203–9, 214–15.

13. Lane, *Architecture and Politics*, 148–67.

14. Rosenberg quoted in Larsson, "Classicism," 239; Hitler quoted in Taylor, *Word in Stone*, 35, see also 118. See also Hochman, *Architects of Fortune*, 175–84.

15. On Nazi support among the working class, see Michael Mann, "Sources of Variation in Working-Class Movements in Twentieth-Century Europe," *New Left Review* 1st ser., no. 212 (July/August 1995): 38–49. On the growth of the German Communist Party, see Eric Hobsbawm, *The Age of Extremes: A History of the World, 1914–1991,* (New York: Vintage, 1996), 93–94.

16. Speer and Wagener quoted in Albert Speer, "Hitler and the Romantic Illusion," *Spectator*, March 31, 1979, 15. See also Leon Krier, "An Architecture of Desire," in *Albert Speer: Architecture, 1932–1942*, ed. Leon Krier (Brussels: Archive D'Architecture Moderne, 1985), 221.

17. Albert Speer, "Forward," in *Albert Speer: Architecture, 1932–1942*, ed. Leon Krier (Brussels: Archive D'Architecture Moderne, 1985), 213. For a theory of the autonomy of the state, see Karl Marx, *The Eighteenth Brumaire of Louis Bonaparte*, in Karl Marx and Frederick Engels, *Collected Works*, vol. 11 (New York: International Publishers, 1979), 181–97. On Nazi criticism of art determined by political opportunism, see Hochman, *Architects of Fortune*, 73–82.

18. For a similar assessment of Nazi architecture, see Taylor, *Word in Stone*, 54.

19. Lane, *Architecture and Politics*, 170–86; Taylor, *Word in Stone*, 52–56, 63, 121; Tafuri and Dal Co, *Modern Architecture*, 297–302; Borsi, *Monumental Era*, 12.

20. Quotes are from Lane, *Architecture and Politics*, 205–6; and Taylor, *Word in Stone*, 229–30.

21. Lane, *Architecture and Politics*, 206–7; Taylor, *Word in Stone*, 233–34.

22. Martin Heidegger, "Art in Space," 121; Heidegger, "Building, Dwelling, Thinking," 108–9, both in *Rethinking Architecture: A Reader in Cultural Theory*, ed. Neil Leach (London: Routledge, 1997). On Heidegger's phenomenology of space, see also Kenneth Frampton, *Studies in Tectonic Culture*

(Cambridge, MA: MIT Press, 1995), 21–24; Christian Norberg-Schulz, "Heidegger's Thinking on Architecture," in *Theorizing a New Agenda for Architecture: An Anthology of Architectural Theory, 1965–1995*, ed. Kate Nesbitt (New York: Princeton Architectural Press, 1996), 430–39.

23. Theodor Adorno, *Minima Moralia* (London: Verso, 1974), 38–39.

24. Taylor, *Word in Stone*, 11–12, 31–45, 57–58. The quote is on 33; Tafuri and Dal Co, *Modern Architecture*, 302.

25. Lane, *Architecture and Politics*, 190–91, 212–13; Speer, "Hitler," 15.

26. Taylor, *Word in Stone*, 145–46. The quote is on 146.

27. Ibid., 182–83. The quote is on 133.

28. Ibid., 130–40. The quote is on 140; Krier, *Albert Speer*, 111, 125–57.

29. The quote is from Speer, "Hitler," 16; Taylor, *Word in Stone*, 26, 138–40.

30. Taylor, *Word in Stone*, 12, 32–34, 54, 157.

31. Krier, *Albert Speer*, 75–82.

32. Krier, "Architecture of Desire," 225; Taylor, *Word in Stone*, 36, 160.

33. Krier, "Architecture of Desire," 225; Taylor, *Word in Stone*, 86–87.

34. Krier, *Albert Speer*, 165–75; Taylor, *Word in Stone*, 170–73. The quote is on 170.

35. Taylor, *Word in Stone*, 85.

36. Krier, *Albert Speer*, 45–122; Taylor, *Word in Stone*, 251–55; Tafuri and Dal Co, *Modern Architecture*, 302. On fascism as an attempt to escape from individuality into a primordial, irrational collective, see Erich Fromm, *Escape from Freedom* (New York: Avon, 1965); Theodor Adorno, *Philosophy of Modern Music* (New York: Continuum, 1994), 143–48, 159.

37. Fromm, *Escape from Freedom*, 262–64; Adorno, *Philosophy*, 168.

38. The Hitler quotes are from James J. Flink, *The Automobile Age* (Cambridge, MA: MIT Press, 1988), 262, 264. See also Wolfgang Sachs, *For the Love of the Automobile* (Berkeley: University of California Press, 1992), 50–55.

39. Flink, *Automobile Age*, 263–66; Sachs, *Love of Automobile*, 59–61.

40. Sachs, *Love of Automobile*, 61.

41. Flink, *Automobile Age*, 236–37, 264–68.

42. Sachs, *Love of Automobile*, 48; James D. Shand, "The Reichsautobahn: Symbol for the Third Reich," *Journal of Contemporary History* 19 (1984): 189–93.

43. Sachs, *Love of Automobile*, 55; Edward Dimendberg, "The Will to Motorization: Cinema, Highways, and Modernity," *October* 73 (Summer 1995): 104–15.

44. Taylor, *Word in Stone*, 199–204.

45. Anson G. Rabinbach, "The Aesthetics of Production in the Third Reich," *Journal of Contemporary History* 11 (1976); Taylor, *Word in Stone*, 197–98, 244–45.

46. Rabinbach, "Aesthetics of Production," 43, 51.

47. Ibid.; Taylor, *Word in Stone*, 243–45.

48. Denning, *Cultural Front*, 31–159.

49. Erika Doss, "The Art of Cultural Politics: From Regionalism to Abstract Expressionism," in *Recasting America: Culture and Politics in the Age of Cold War*, ed. Lary May (Chicago: University of Chicago Press, 1989), 195–220; Richard Guy Wilson, Dianne H. Pilgrim, and Dickran Tashjian, *The Machine Age in America, 1918–1941* (New York: Harry Abrams, 1986), 235–43; Denning, *Cultural Front*, 115–59.

50. Denning, *Cultural Front*, 83–86, 151–53.

51. Kenneth T. Jackson, *Crabgrass Frontier: The Suburbanization of the United States* (New York: Oxford University Press, 1985), 190–230; Baker Brownell and Frank Lloyd Wright, *Architecture and Modern Life* (New York: Harper and Brothers, 1937), 168–92; Frampton, *Modern Architecture*, 238–39.

52. Elizabeth Mock, *Built in the USA: 1932–1944* (New York: Museum of Modern Art, 1944), 13.

53. Mock, *Built in USA*, 58–59, 62–65. The quote is on 64.

54. Ibid., 60–61.

55. Ibid., 66–67.

56. George Nelson, "Stylistic Trends in Contemporary Architecture," in *New Architecture and City Planning*, ed. Paul Zucker (New York: Philosophical Library, 1944), 575; Mock, *Built in USA*, 25.

57. Wilson et al., *Machine Age*, 180–83; Larsson, "Classicism in Architecture," 243–44.

58. Robert S. Lynd and Helen Merrell Lynd, *Middletown in Transition* (New York: Harcourt, Brace and Co., 1937), 46, 265.

59. Roy Sheldon and Egmont Arens, *Consumer Engineering* (New York: Arno Press, 1976), 19.

60. Jeffrey L. Meikle, *Twentieth Century Limited: Industrial Design in America, 1925–1939* (Philadelphia: Temple University Press, 1979). The Frankl quote is on 153.

61. The Harley Earl quote is in Alfred P. Sloan, Jr., *My Years with General Motors* (Garden City, NY: Anchor Books, 1972), 324; Meikle, *Twentieth Century Limited*, 39–67.

62. David Gartman, *Auto Opium: A Social History of American Automobile Design* (London: Routledge, 1994), 100–35.

63. Robert Marks and R. Buckminster Fuller, *The Dymaxion World of Buckminster Fuller* (Garden City, NY: Anchor Books, 1973), 9; R. Buckminster Fuller, *Nine Chains to the Moon*, excerpted in *Culture and Commitment, 1929–1945*, ed. Warren I. Susman (New York: George Braziller, 1973), 262–63.

64. Marks and Fuller, *Dymaxion*, 83, 20.

65. Ibid., 20–23.

66. Wilson et al., *Machine Age*, 192–95, *Time* ad reproduced on 194; Meikle, *Twentieth Century Limited*, 132–33; Norman Bel Geddes, *Horizons* (New York: Dover, 1977). The quote is on 3.

67. Wilson et al., *Machine Age*, 174; Meikle, *Twentieth Century Limited*, 48–55.

68. Wilson et al., *Machine Age*, 176–78; Meikle, *Twentieth Century Limited*, 172–74.

69. Wilson et al., *Machine Age*, 182–83; Beth Dunlop, *Building a Dream: The Art of Disney Architecture* (New York: Harry Abrams, 1996), 18–22.

70. The Neutra quote is in Esther McCoy, *Richard Neutra* (New York: George Braziller, 1960), 8.

71. Ibid., 8–12; Thomas S. Hines, *Richard Neutra and the Search for Modern Architecture* (New York: Oxford University Press, 1982), 3–91; Thomas S. Hines, "Designing for the Motor Age: Richard Neutra and the Automobile," *Oppositions* 21 (Summer 1980): 34–51.

72. Hines, *Richard Neutra*, 119–38; McCoy, *Richard Neutra*, 15–17.

73. The Wright quote is in Brownell and Wright, *Architecture*, 146.

74. Donald J. Bush, *The Streamlined Decade* (New York: George Braziller, 1975), 152. See also Giedion, *Space*, 422–24; Blake, *Master Builders*, 381–84; Frampton, *Studies* 117.

75. Blake, *Master Builders*, 380–81; Frampton, *Modern Architecture*, 189.

76. Frank Lloyd Wright, *The Disappearing City* (New York: William Farquhar Payson, 1932), 4–8; the quote is in Frank Lloyd Wright, *The Living City*, (New York: Bramhall House, 1958), 46. Wright's *Living City* is an expanded rewrite of his earlier *Disappearing City*.

77. Wright, *Disappearing City*, 10–11. The quote is on 27–28.

78. Wright, *Living City*, 122.

79. Wright, *Disappearing City*, 44, 49, 52.

80. The quote is in ibid., 34. See also Blake, *Master Builders*, 387–89; Frampton, *Modern Architecture*, 190–91; Wilson et al., *Machine Age*, 195–96.

81. Wright, *Disappearing City*, 62, 83. See also Frampton, *Modern Architecture*, 190–91.

82. The Wank quote is in Roland A. Wank, "The Architecture of Inland Waterways," in *New Architecture and City Planning*, ed. Paul Zucker (New York: Philosophical Library, 1944), 449. See also Wilson et al., *Machine Age*, 111–15, 120.

83. Wilson et al., *Machine Age*, 117–23; Meikle, *Twentieth Century Limited*, 176–77.

84. Giedion, *Space*, 824–25. The quote is in on 825. See also Wilson et al., *Machine Age*, 93–102.

85. The Teague quote is in Meikle, *Twentieth Century Limited*, 197.

86. Roland Marchand, "Designers Go to the Fair, I," in *Design History: An Anthology*, ed. Dennis P. Doordan (Cambridge, MA: MIT Press, 1995), 89–100; Folke T. Kihlstedt, "Utopia Realized: The World's Fairs of the 1930s," in *Imagining Tomorrow: History, Technology, and The American Future*, ed. Joseph J. Corn (Cambridge, MA: MIT Press, 1986), 97–114.

87. Song quoted in Kihlstedt, "Utopia Realized," 104. See also Meikle, *Twentieth Century Limited*, 190–95; Rem Koolhaas, *Delirious New York* (New York: Monacelli, 1994), 284–85.

88. Roland Marchand, "The Designers Go to the Fair, II," in *Design History: An Anthology*, ed. Dennis P. Doordan (Cambridge, MA: MIT Press, 1995), 108–21; Norman Bel Geddes, *Magic Motorways* (New York: Random House, 1940), 269, 209.

89. Marchand, "Designers Go to the Fair, II," 111–115; Meikle, *Twentieth Century Limited*, 199–208.

90. Marchand, "Designers Go to the Fair, II," 115; Dimendberg, "Will to Motorization," 121–25.

4

Efficiency and Fantasy:
The Bifurcated Architecture of
Postwar Technocracy

A WALK IN THE DOWNTOWN business district of any major American major city in the late 1950s would have convinced any architecturally knowledgeable citizen that, regardless of the outcome of the previous decade's military hostilities, the war over architectural aesthetics had been won by the European modernists. Most of the new office skyscrapers built after the Second World War as monuments to American corporations' new power and wealth were rectilinear, glass-and-steel slabs of the type anticipated by the machine aesthetic of the 1920s. Particularly dominant in America's urban skylines was the severely objective vision of this style pioneered by Mies van der Rohe and epitomized in his Seagram Building in New York. Completed in 1958, this prismatic slab of bronze-sheathed steel and brown glass showed the entire world how to build a sedate but elegant headquarters that testified to the rationality and efficiency of the modern corporation and its technocratic elite. Although American business districts were contaminated by historical and modernistic buildings of the prewar era, they still bore a remarkable resemblance to Le Corbusier's Radiant City vision of the 1930s, especially when urban renewal projects plowed through these centers with elevated expressways for high-speed traffic.

At the other end of these expressways, however, the 1950s saw developments that contradicted Le Corbusier's technocratic vision of the city and drew the ire of the modernists who held sway downtown. There were found the burgeoning suburbs, the residential destination of much of the technocratic elite and white-collar proletariat that streamed out of urban skyscrapers and into their cars every evening. Le Corbusier's Radiant City anticipated the suburbanization of industry and its workers, but he housed them in modernist apartment slabs. The American suburbs, by contrast, exploded with expanses of single-family houses, which, though often standardized and mass-produced, were seldom objective machines for living in. Developers knowledgeable about America's consumer culture carefully covered over telltale signs of mass-produced similarity with a veneer of individuality and historic symbols of domesticity. So the suburbs sprouted row upon row of faux New England cottages and Western ranch houses that resembled the reassuring populism of the 1930s. Following the dictates of the government-subsidized housing market, the aesthetics of the suburbs completed the separation and insulation of consumption from work. It seems Americans could tolerate a standardized bureaucratic job in a standardized office slab as long as they could escape after work to a suburban idyll of America's preindustrial past. Making possible the quick passage from rationalized work to compensating consumption was the mass-produced automobile, whose general techniques of deception were widely emulated in suburban housing, although its specific symbolism was of a technological future, not the preindustrial past.

Blending these cultural escapes to the future and the past was the amusement architecture of the suburbs. To provide suburbanized Americans with public spaces and entertainment outside their developers' boxes, there arose new consumer attractions epitomized by Disneyland. Opening in 1955 on the suburban fringe of Los Angeles, Walt Disney's theme park pioneered an architecture of false urbanism that provided the collective concentration of people that suburbia lacked. The architecture of Disneyland and similar amusements provided suburbanites a sense of belongingness by constituting them as citizens of an accommodating community of consumers that possessed both a heroic past and a promising future.

In the 1950s, the American landscape thus contained two architectures—an architecture of corporate efficiency and an architecture of consumer fantasy. These contradictory aesthetics could be held simultaneously in the American psyche without clashing because they were spatially and temporally segregated. Work occurred in the city during business hours, while consumption transpired in the suburbs in the evenings and weekends. Thus separated from visual confrontation, the two realms conspired to legitimate one another. The efficiency of Fordist work produced the proliferating products of fantastic consumption, while the ever-escalating levels of consumption provided everyone with bureaucratized work.

Although the United States dominated architecture in the 1950s, Europeans gave rise to an important countertrend that would ultimately influence America. European cities also had modernist office slabs downtown and suburban housing in populist and historical styles. Yet, there emerged among younger architects in Europe an aesthetic that protested both the rationality of modernism and the prettiness of populism. Known as new brutalism, this aesthetic exposed the crude, primitive side of machine civilization and set the stage for the explosion of aesthetic and political protests of the 1960s.

—

The Triumph of Technocracy, or Fordism Comes to Fruition

The bifurcation of architectural styles in the postwar world was an ideological reflex to the epochal transformation of capitalism in this period, instigated mainly in America. Fordist capitalism had foundered with the underconsumption crisis of the 1930s, causing it to experiment with collectivist measures of market regulation that were deepened during the war. Yet, on the eve of the peace there was no consensus on the shape the postwar economy should take. Forces on the left, especially the new industrial unions, envisioned continued government intervention in production and consumption, and launched a massive strike wave late in 1945 to press their case. Corporate America was just as adamant that government's wartime power over production be eliminated and planning the postwar economy be left to it. The system of postwar regulation that emerged from this struggle would finally complete Fordism by stabilizing mass consumption sufficiently to match mass production.

By 1950 the regulatory framework was in place, much of it enshrined in the epochal 1950 contract between the United Auto Workers and General Motors. Labor conceded to management the prerogative to control production and pricing, while corporations recognized and bargained with unions to ensure workers a stable and rising standard of living. And both parties endorsed broad government measures to stabilize aggregate demand. All sides recognized the need for planning the economy, but responsibility for it was divided. Government planning was confined to Keynesian demand management, while corporations were granted the exclusive right to plan production. This regulatory system led to an explosion of prosperity, releasing the full potential of Fordist mass production for the first time in its history.[1]

To fulfill their promise to plan and stabilize production, capitalists needed a new kind of corporation, one insulated from the uncertainties of competition. From the beginning Fordist mass production had exerted pressure on producers to eliminate market uncertainties, due to its inflexible technology and the long period between production and consumption. But several developments enhanced the abilities of corporations of the 1950s to plan production. The Depression had eliminated small competitors and concentrated capital, while at the same time forcing corporations to manage demand through advertising and product design. The large, oligopolistic corporations dominating the American market in the 1950s had both the market power and revenues to control the production and demand for their products, especially with the government managing aggregate demand. Thus, rational, rule-governed corporate planning, not ruthless competition, became the watchword for business in the postwar era.

The new, planned corporation swept into power a new corporate elite whose methods and rationale would provide the basis for one half of the bifurcated architecture of the period. The rule-governed, predictable corporation required for its leadership not the visionary entrepreneur or profit-driven capitalist, but the educated technician, whose imperatives were collective knowledge, not individual insight; predictable returns, not personal enrichment. From the beginning Fordist mass production required a technical stratum of educated workers to manage its operations, but until the postwar era the upper reaches of corporate power were still dominated by capitalists and entrepreneurs. By the 1950s, however, the latter's power was waning, and they were replaced by legions of anonymous managers trained in business and engineering schools. Recording this shift in corporate power, John Kenneth Galbraith's *New Industrial State* introduced the term technostructure to refer to all the personnel in control of the technical knowledge and processes of production. Their control of the corporation, he argued, was collective, not individual, and their goals were much more social and selfless than those of the old entrepreneurs and capitalists.[2]

For Galbraith, America's postwar corporations fulfilled the historic dream of technocracy, placing a new class of neutral, educated professionals at the center of decision-making. C. Wright Mills, by contrast, argued that this change created merely a new power elite, a group of self-interested managers who were the most active part of the class of property-holding capitalists.[3] But even Mills did not deny that a real shift had occurred from the direct rule of individual capitalists to their indirect rule through coordinated bureaucracies of educated managers and professionals. This shift effected a palpable change in the ideological justification of corporate power and the technocratic class. When capitalists controlled corporations directly and incorporated professionals into their rule, both classes were legitimated by the ideology of the market— their profits and salaries were seen as equitable rewards for individual efforts in the market. But the justification of individual effort was undermined by the bureaucracies of cooperating professionals that now controlled and planned the corporation's market contributions. As individual effort was lost in bureaucratic anonymity, the collective knowledge of the bureaucracy itself came to legitimate power and wealth. Rationality and technology themselves became legitimations, for they seemed effective in providing for society's needs and did not carry the stigma of selfishness that tarnished the efforts of capitalists. With no personal stake in corporate profits, scientists, technicians, managers, and bureaucrats seemed to administer corporate resources with a disinterested rationality.

This is certainly how the technocratic ruling class saw and justified itself, as documented by William H. Whyte's 1956 book, *The Organization Man*. Whyte found that this class adhered to the creed of scientism, the faith that the expert in control of a neutral body of knowledge could engineer the good society, which was defined by harmony, stability, and cooperation. But if asked about the ends of this cooperation, these technicians were mute, devoid of purposes to which their knowledge should be put beyond those supplied by their own organizations. Their technocratic fetishism of means left them open to the service of any ends, and simultaneously wrapped these ends in the aura of scientific neutrality. Another central precept of these technocrats' legitimation was group conformism, or what Whyte called the "social ethic." For them, the group, not the individual, was the source of all utility, so to make a contribution the individual had to be totally integrated into the group. The highest human need was belongingness; and the highest human good, adjustment to the group. In another pivotal piece of social criticism of the era, *The Lonely Crowd*, David Riesman called the same character type "other-directed." Frustrated in their attempts to realize the traditional American character of inner-directed, autonomous individual within this bureaucratic society, mid-level technocrats as well as white-collar proletarians retreated from individuality into group integration, not unlike the Nazis. But in this postwar era the individual was annihilated not by the irrational state but by the rational corporation and consumer marketplace.[4]

Theodor Adorno provided further insight into the psychology of dependency of technocratic capitalism in his 1953 analysis of astrology columns, entitled "Stars Down to Earth." He noted that the increasing dependence of people on rational bureaucracies and technologies they did not control caused them to escape into the irrationality of astrology. The movement of the stars became a metaphor for the alienated logic of administered capitalism, whose incomprehensible and inexorable movements also affected people's lives. The only recourse open to individuals was to follow the advice of the astrologer (another kind of expert) and adjust themselves to the inevitable (the group), recruiting its forces for individual benefit. People were promised that the administered society would take care of them, "contingent upon their being 'good boys' (or girls) who behave according to given standards, but who also allow themselves, for therapeutic reasons, as it were, that range of pleasure which they need in order not to collapse under the requirements of reality, or under the impact of their own urges." These astrology columns thus revealed a schism at the heart of postwar Fordism, a yawning gap between the requirements of the corporate world of production and the domestic world of consumption. They simultaneously advised readers to subordinate themselves to the bureaucracy and work hard, and to relax and enjoy the simple pleasures of consumption. The only way that these contradictory impulses could be reconciled, Adorno argued, was by separating them in time, encouraging people to be self-denying and economically rational at work, and reserve for leisure time at home the self-indulgent pleasures of consumption. So separated, the two activities could legitimate one another: pleasure was the reward for work, while work was the guilty price paid for self-indulgence.[5]

Adorno's analysis failed to recognize, however, that spatial segregation complemented and reinforced the temporal separation of bureaucratic work and consumer pleasure. Surely the victims of rationalized work found it difficult to indulge their nonrational pleasures in urban centers containing the visual reminders of that work in rationalized, modern architecture. Given the opportunity, they chose to segregate their consumption in the suburbs, where the privacy and individuality of the detached, single-family home provided insulation from work. In the first years after the war, the Keynesian state provided millions of working Americans with their first opportunity to flee to the suburbs, laying the geographic groundwork for the aesthetic bifurcation of American architecture. Freed from the burden of entertaining consumers at leisure, the downtown homes of bureaucratic government and corporations could express in their buildings the technological rationality on which they were founded. And the suburban retreats of consumption were also at liberty to express the exuberance and affluence of Fordist mass consumption without revealing the instrumental rationality that produced the goods. The bifurcated architecture of postwar America bore witness to the rift at the very soul of America's system of technocracy.

The Architecture of American Technocracy

From its inception the modern architecture pioneered in Europe had been the ideological expression of the intellectual bourgeoisie's dream of technocratic rule. Thus, as this dream became reality in postwar America, the modernism that had been confined largely to the European avant-garde now found its way into the American mainstream. U.S. corporations, fat with war profits and unchallenged by foreign competitors, could find no better way to proclaim their triumph than by building elegantly sober, glass-and-steel monuments in the business cores of America's major cities. With consumption safely segregated in the suburbs, the stark realities of instrumental rationality could now be exposed in urban areas. Many of these monuments to rationalized mammon were designed by European modernists who had fled the disfavor of wartime regimes and staid in America afterwards to take advantage of the building boom.

To this point the American architectural profession had, with few exceptions, been hostile to the modernism of the European avant-garde. But the 1950s saw almost instantaneous conversions to the machine aesthetic, and some premier training programs were entrusted to its leaders. Walter Gropius was appointed head of Harvard's architecture department in 1937; Mies van der Rohe took over the architecture program at the Armour Institute of Technology in 1938; George Howe, an American convert to modernism, was appointed dean of architecture at Yale in 1950; and Pietro Belluschi (1899–1994) became dean of MIT's School of Architecture in 1951. The urban building boom of the 1950s saw the formation of large architectural firms that built glass-and-steel office slabs virtually indistinguishable from the unbuilt drawings of the avant-garde in the 1920s. What accounts for this sudden change in architectural aesthetics?

The answer is found not in the hearts and minds of individual architects but in their profession's position in American society. From the beginning, American architects and designers had cooperated closely with private capitalists, since they constituted the main market for architectural services in this capitalist society with a weak public sector. The rise of the postwar Keynesian state did little to change this, since it was generally content to leave most responsibility for the built environment to the private sector. The change occurred in the capitalist clients themselves. As Henry-Russell Hitchcock wrote in a 1952 publication by the Museum of Modern Art, "the old firms… are now ready to provide their clients with what are supposed to be 'modern' buildings, and the results of their subservience to a successful stylistic revaluation are not as inferior as might be expected." Corporate clients were now interested in modern buildings because, as Hitchcock wrote, they wanted "the advertising value of striking architecture." Although he was mute about *what* corporations were advertising, the answer is discovered in their technocratic transformation.[6]

The sheer size and monumentalism of the modernist headquarter buildings of corporations like Seagram, Lever Brothers, Alcoa, and Union Carbide were attempts to symbolize the size and power of these new industrial oligarchs. But the undecorated, sober facades of industrial materials reassured Americans that this power was exercised with frugality and efficiency to deliver consumers reasonably priced goods. And the stark repetition of standardized elements like beams, windows, and mullions testified to the impersonal, scientific rationality governing the entire organization. "Here rationality rules," screamed these objective skyscrapers, carefully calculated bureaucracy, operating without respect to persons, as Max Weber so aptly put it. From the exterior every floor and every office looked the same, unified in an anonymous collectivity of cooperative, rule-governed production. In short, these modernist corporate buildings testified to the emergence of corporate technocracy, standardized mass production governed by science and rationality and planned to deliver the most goods for the least cost. This is what the European avant-garde had sought to express from the beginning. Now their dream had come true.

American architects were also commissioned to design the state-financed urban renewal projects launched during the 1950s, which included government offices, public housing for the poor, and high-art venues. But these public projects had an aesthetic goal similar to corporate office headquarters—the expression of a benevolent and efficient organization that delivered the goods to the masses. There was, however, one sector of the postwar building boom from which trained architects and their technocratic aesthetic were almost completely excluded—private suburban housing. The Keynesian state tackled the severe housing shortage in the immediate postwar period not by building public housing but by subsidizing demand in the private housing market. Consequently, even blue-collar workers could now register their preferences in the housing market. They, like most Americans, demanded detached, single-family homes in the suburbs. But several factors conspired to ensure that licensed and trained American architects did not design such homes.

First and foremost, in most states licensed architects were required by law only on large buildings and public structures. This left the merchant builders in the suburbs free to hire less expensive engineers and designers, and stiff competition in this market ensured that they did so. Second, American modernists, like their European counterparts, were excluded from designing suburban housing by their economic and aesthetic convictions. They were convinced that the multifamily apartment building was the only efficient method of housing an industrial society, and that the single-family, detached suburban home was an immoral waste of land and materials. Furthermore, they knew that given a choice in the marketplace, most people would choose eclectic, pseudohistorical styles for their houses. For these reasons, few American modern architects expressed interest in designing suburban housing for the private market. Most were content to confine their efforts to urban headquarters for corporations and government, in which the look of instrumental rationality was welcome, and multifamily public housing for the poor, who had to accept whatever the state paternalistically provided them.[7]

Mies, Pioneer of Postwar Technocratic Architecture

The architect who pioneered the aesthetic of America's postwar technocracy was Mies van der Rohe. Within the space of a decade, this leader of the European avant-garde moved into the mainstream of America's market-driven architecture, becoming the darling of oligarchic corporations, urban real-estate developers, and urban-renewal bureaucrats. Some modernists were outraged at Mies's move into the technocratic establishment, but no one familiar with his aesthetic philosophy should have been surprised. Mies had made it clear from the beginning that his purpose was not to change industrial society but to aesthetically express its inexorable facts, especially its technology. In the late 1930s Mies saw that the cold facts of industrial technology had reached their zenith in the United States, which helped to motivated his migration there. It was no coincidence that of the numerous opportunities to teach, he chose a position not in a university but in a technical institute, the Armour Institute of Technology, where expression of the technical means of building was at the center of his curriculum.

Before his immigration to America, Mies had begun to develop a technological aesthetic that spiritualized industrial materials and their work of support. But his designs for glass-and-steel office buildings expressing the full grandeur of this technological rationality remained unbuilt under the scarcities of interwar Germany. Not until he had established himself in prosperous America did he have the opportunity to build on a scale that truly raised ordinary glass and steel to the level of a spiritual ideal. But as Mies's aesthetic dreams came true, they evidenced a subtle shift that reflected his attempt to accommodate the changing facts of the emerging system of technocratic capitalism. Mies's aesthetic development during the 1940s and 1950s evidenced several unmistakable tendencies. First, the nature of space in his architecture showed a slow metamorphosis. In the 1920s and 1930s, he defined a space that was open and moving, restlessly refusing to be confined. Glass walls erased the barrier between inside and outside, while other planes slid out into their surroundings almost indiscriminately. The asymmetry of Mies's early buildings also seemed to unsettle them. Throughout the 1940s and 1950s, however, he moved toward a stable and enclosed space, with the repose of axial symmetry replacing the restlessness of asymmetry. And Mies subtly transformed the glass curtain wall from a transparent non-barrier into an opaque barrier that enclosed and privatized space.

The second dimension of Mies's shift was the treatment of surface and structure. He and other early modernists exposed the structural framework of the building, idealizing not merely the mass-produced materials of which it was composed but also the work of its composition by technocratic occupations like engineers and architects. During the immediate postwar period, however, Mies moved away from the visual separation of the structural frame and the enclosing wall toward an aesthetic of a unitary skin that either incorporated the frame or obscured it from view. Increasingly the outside of Mies's buildings constituted a unitary, hermetic skin that hid the industrial materials and their work of support.

The succession of Mies's important buildings of this period, beginning with the campus of the Armour Institute (renamed Illinois Institute of Technology, or IIT) in the late 1940s and culminating with the Seagram Building in 1958, clearly testified to these changes. The buildings and layout of the IIT campus, built between 1943 and 1956, show Mies's initial tentative steps toward a new technological vocabulary. The first scheme for IIT, designed in 1939, revealed a bold move toward restful symmetry, with a central road dividing the campus into two parts containing almost identically positioned buildings. But in the final layout of 1940 Mies reverted to avant-garde asymmetry, with buildings positioned to visually move and slide past one another restlessly. The original symmetrical impulse was retained, however, in the buildings themselves, most of which were long, low, rectangular boxes with clear axes. Unified by a standard structural bay of 24 x 24 x 12 feet, these structures not only used standardized materials but also demonstrated the repose of standardized, interchangeable components. If the IIT campus was testimony to the technological rationality of the dawning postwar era, this rationality was clearly stable and orderly, not dynamic and restless.

Perhaps Mies's greatest advance at IIT, however, was his tentative integration of structure and wall. Although all buildings prominently displayed the black steel I-beams that formed the supporting framework, in most cases these beams were set flush with the glass and brick in-fill. This almost created the effect of a hermetic skin, but not quite, because the beams were always slightly recessed or slightly protruding from the wall, subtly breaking the planar surface. In some of the IIT buildings, especially the more public and ceremonial structures, Mies retreated from this emerging skin aesthetic to his avant-garde exposure of supports. For example, at Crown Hall, the crown jewel of the IIT

Mies van der Rohe, Boiler House at the Illinois Institute of Technology, Chicago, 1950 (Photograph by author)

campus and home of the architecture school, the vertical I-beams protruded prominently from the glass wall at front, and the steel trusses supporting the suspended roof soared above the building in proud display of their work. But despite this display of structure, the building had none of the asymmetry characteristic of Mies's avant-garde period. Crown Hall was the most symmetrical structure on the campus, evidencing a classical serenity of which any Beaux-Arts architect would have been proud.[8]

Mies's vacillating struggle toward a new aesthetic of technocracy was also visible in his first glass-and-steel high-rise building of the postwar period, the Lake Shore Drive Apartments (1951), a pair of twenty-six-story apartment buildings for Chicago real-estate developer Herbert Greenwald. In the glass-and-steel curtain walls of these buildings Mies was moving toward the aesthetic of a hermetic skin to enclose rather than open up space, to conceal rather than reveal structure. Building codes required him to enclose the major beams of the steel frame in concrete for fireproofing, but Mies set the steel cases of the beams flush with the glass, window mullions, and spandrels. These structural supports were visible only because their steel cases were wider than the mullions, with which they alternated in a one-three-one rhythm. But Mies was not yet ready to completely abandon structural expression, for he relieved the flatness of the Lake Shore Drive facade by welding nonstructural I-beams onto the face of the mullions and columns. Although he gave several functional excuses for these elements, their real purpose was to externally express the internalized structural supports. So Mies expressed the robust steel frame in an eviscerated

Mies van der Rohe, Crown Hall at the Illinois Institute of Technology, Chicago, 1956 (Photograph by author)

decoration, reducing to a whisper the avant-garde's once vociferous creed of structural expression. Yet, in another way these decorative I-beams running up the full height of the facade and standing out eight inches from the glass helped Mies move toward another facet of his skin aesthetic, opacity. When viewed from straight on, the facades of the towers seemed transparent—open to the sky, the lake, the city. But when viewed from an angle, the protruding I-beams obscured the glass and visually blended into an opaque plane that closed off the building. To ensure that at least one facade would be so perceived, Mies set the two rectangular towers of apartments asymmetrically in space, touching off a spinning, twisting dialectic of transparency and opacity.[9]

The culmination of Mies emerging architecture of technocracy would come, however, not in these high-rise residences for the technocratic elite but in its workplaces, the headquarters of Fordist corporations. In 1954 Mies designed his first office building for a major corporation, Joseph E. Seagram and Sons, a liquor producer that sought to symbolize its success with a significant office building on Manhattan's Park Avenue. Phyllis Lambert, the daughter of the corporation's president, took responsibility for finding a prestigious architect and turned for advice to Philip Johnson of the Museum of Modern Art, who carefully steered her toward Mies and ended up collaborating on the building. In the generosity of the liquor salesman Mies found the lavish budget and freedom to realize his new aesthetic, producing a building that became the archetype for corporate trophy headquarters over the next decade. Abandoning all pretense of structural expression, openness, and asymmetrical movement, the Seagram Building, completed in 1958, was a stable, symmetrical composition with a hermetic skin that shut the technocratic elite off from the world. Unlike the spinning asymmetry of the Lake Shore Drive Apartments, the Seagram Building was laid out in perfect axial symmetry, and set back from Park Avenue with a wide plaza flanked by two identical pools. The entire composition was raised several feet above street level by a classically inspired podium. Compared to the surrounding buildings, which crowded close to the street to grab the attention of pedestrians and motorists, the Seagram Building seemed serene, separated from the urban bustle by the wide expanse of the calm plaza.

Here Mies also made the most direct statement of his skin aesthetic. At first glance the Seagram Building seemed almost identical to the Lake Shore Drive Apartments, with its glass-and-steel curtain wall and welded-on I-beam decorations. But unlike the Lake Shore Drive, where the concrete-encased I-beams were set flush with the glass and mullions, at Seagram the entire steel frame was set behind the glass curtain wall and hidden from view. Consequently, there were no wide columns visible on the facade to break up the march of thin mullions across each floor. Although the same decorative I-beams were welded to each mullion, the effect at Seagram was a depthless membrane composed of

Mies van der Rohe and Philip Johnson, Seagram Building, New York, 1958 (Mary Ann Sullivan, Bluffton University)

identical cells. Enforcing this new aesthetic of insularity were the colors of the building—bronze-sheathed mullions and spandrels, and brown-tinted glass. The brutal contrast at Lake Shore Drive between transparent glass and black steel was replaced by a monochrome sheathing of brown which made it difficult to detect floor divisions. From the outside there was no indication of the actual work here, either the building's work to counter gravity or the human work to produce products. The organized skin of identical cells was testimony to the superficial rationality of bureaucracy, without any sign of the actual process of mass production once celebrated by Mies and other modernists.[10]

Mies's aesthetic shift from moving, open space defined by structural supports to stable space enclosed by a hermetic skin reflected the emergence of the system of regulated postwar Fordism. Both interwar and postwar modernism expressed the rationality of Fordism, the planned, efficient nature of a system based on the technical expertise of the professional-managerial class. But interwar, avant-garde modernism idealized the destabilizing rationality of mass production, while postwar modernism expressed the stable rationality that balanced mass production with mass consumption. Mies's earlier aesthetic testified to the unrelenting movement and restructuring of labor and capital necessary to implement Fordist production in Europe. But the postwar regulation of Fordist production by both corporations and state stabilized mass production by ensuring a predictable, broad level of consumer demand. Corporations building monuments to themselves sought to express and take responsibility for this stability in buildings like Mies's symmetrical, classically proportioned Seagram Building, which quietly proclaimed itself as the home of a rational force in America. Mies's aesthetic of technocracy could make even a liquor company appear to be the epitome of sobriety and rationality.

Unlike avant-garde modernism, this aesthetic obscured rather than revealed the technology on which Fordism rested, hiding it behind a curtain wall that contained merely the superficial forms of mass production. This technological obfuscation is explained by several factors. First, the actual process of mass production once celebrated by avant-garde modernism was fading from the American consciousness because the factories containing it were decentralized after the war, moved from urban locations to sprawling suburban sites. The highly visible corporate headquarters in urban areas housed not blue-collar production workers but while-collar bureaucrats, who attached symbolic significance to the physical products through accounting, design, engineering, advertising, and sales. Mies's office slabs testified to the abstract, symbolic rationality of this technocratic elite, purified of any reminders of the ugly material reality of physical production. This architecture of technocracy displayed corporations as the rational *providers* of consumer goods, not their *producers*. Second, corporate elites knew that most Americans did not want to be reminded of the price they paid for expanding consumer abundance—the intensified process of stultifying mass production. Most workers had moved to the suburbs to escape the reminders of this production process through consumption in privatized homes. So Mies gave corporations what they needed, and what most Americans wanted—hermetic skins of buildings obscuring any technological reminders of the dirty work necessary to produce consumer goods. Mies's buildings were testimony to the superficial bureaucratic rationality of stabilized postwar Fordism, which ultimately was limited by and rested upon the irrationality of the marketplace.

The glass-and-steel, curtain-walled skyscraper that Mies formulated in the 1950s was an architecture of bureaucracy in another sense as well. It not only symbolized bureaucratic Fordism but also facilitated the bureaucratization of architecture itself. The aesthetic model that Mies pioneered for the post-war office building encouraged the formation of large architectural firms with a hierarchical division of labor that turned out standardized, mass-produced buildings at minimum cost. Ironically, Mies's own firm was rather small, and his buildings were often expensive and luxurious. The Seagram Building, for example, contained costly materials like travertine, terrazzo, and bronze-anodized steel, and was probably the most expensive skyscraper per square foot built up to that time. Yet, stripped of these luxurious appointments, Mies's basic glass-and-steel skyscraper could be built more cheaply than the traditional tall building sheathed in stone. The cost-conscious developer who commissioned the Lake Shore Drive Apartments calculated that the final cost per square foot was $10.38, lower than most comparable residential complexes of the day. The repetition of standardized elements kept design, material, and construction costs down. As James Ingo Freed (1930–2005), an architect in Mies's office, stated, "Mies unwittingly made it possible in the long run to build in a shoddier way."[11]

Further, since Mies applied the same standardized architectural solution to every program, his aesthetic facilitated the bureaucratization of architectural firms. The standardized parts of the plan could be divided between and designed by hundreds of architectural specialists in a firm, and then assembled into a building by a few partners at the top, in assembly-line manner. Given the large demand for corporate headquarters and speculative office buildings during the 1950s, large, bureaucratic architectural firms could be sustained. The

model for such firms was Skidmore, Owings & Merrill, which was responsible
for dozens of Mies-inspired buildings during the period. So Mies's architecture
of bureaucracy and technocracy spread like a plague over the urban landscape
of America. Corporations lined up for their copy of the rational, sober, curtain-walled trophy building. And so did the institutions of the Keynesian state,
which were also anxious to testify to their power and technocratic rationality.
During the 1950s government agencies began a massive program of destruc-
tion/construction in major cities, known as "urban renewal," and modern
architecture became its major accomplice.[12]

Modern architects like Le Corbusier had long dreamed of the state-sponsored razing of the historic centers of major cities and their reconstruction
into strictly segregated and rationalized zones of function. By the late 1950s
America's cities had begun to resemble his Radiant City model developed in
the 1930s. This resulted, however, not from a comprehensive state plan but
from a coincidence of decisions by different segments of the technocratic elite.
In the postwar period, major corporations increasingly located production in
suburban sites, while millions of working-class families also moved to new,
inexpensive housing developments in the suburbs. These relocations left urban
cores dominated by smaller industrial concerns and retail stores, government
agencies, corporate headquarters, and poor and minority workers. Downtown
real estate consequently suffered a devaluation, which mobilized its owners to
pressure the state to take action to revalue their assets. When an infusion of
federal money became available in 1954, downtown interests teamed up with
local state agencies to reshape urban cores for their interests. Their goals were
to attract and keep middle- and upper-class consumers while removing the
poor. These urban redevelopers' attempt to empty out large tracts of urban
real estate for commercial development coincided with modern architects'
long-held dreams of razing city centers and building from scratch. In fact, the
acknowledged model for much of America's postwar urban renewal was Le
Corbusier's unrealized plan for the bombed-out French city of Saint-Dié. His
plan exiled all industry and residences to the periphery, reserving the city center for government office slabs placed in a vast pedestrian plaza. In the United
States, however, the role of enemy bombers was played by developers' bulldozers, which razed huge swaths of land to make room for an urban consumption
machine that promised to save downtown.

Unlike the Saint-Dié model, however, most American renewal projects
were dominated not by pedestrian plazas but by roads to accommodate the
automobile, which was central to the system of postwar consumption. Urban

developers and businesses knew that to attract the prosperous suburban classes downtown, they had to provide ample access by roads, so they built expressways, acres of elevated concrete that sliced through neighborhoods and dumped thousands of cars downtown. Between these roads went up government buildings, office towers, upscale apartments, and cultural complexes, all in the Miesian style of rationalized, abstract modernism. In Pittsburgh, for example, the Golden Triangle renewal area became an ensemble of modernist skyscrapers and elevated expressways that pushed the poor out of the city center with no provision for their rehousing. In Philadelphia, the only housing to come out of the mid-1950s renewal of downtown was architect I. M. Pei's (b. 1917) luxury apartments, Society Hill Towers (1963). In the few cases where housing was provided for low-income residents, it was in modernist slabs of apartments in the middle of dreary, desolate space. Instead of the elegant glass-and-steel apartment buildings like Mies's Lake Shore Drive, public housing was provided in frugal, monotone brick with tiny windows, like the Alfred E. Smith Houses in New York (1953) and the infamous Pruitt-Igoe complex (1955) in St. Louis by modern architect Minoru Yamasaki (1912–86). Many architects, developers, and government officials hoped that the efficient, clean forms of modernist housing would bring discipline and rationality to the messy disorganization of the ghettos. But these blocks that forcibly corralled the poor on unwanted urban land did little more than remind them of their status as expendable jetsam of postwar Fordism.[13]

Despite the popularity of Mies's architecture of technocracy in private office slabs and public renewal projects, there was a limit to its proliferation, as demonstrated by one postwar polemic. In the April 1953 issue of *House Beautiful*, a magazine aimed at the expanding mass of suburban home owners, editor Elizabeth Gordon published a blistering assault on modern architecture, entitled "The Threat to the Next America." She charged that the minimalist, undecorated style being disseminated in America by European émigrés was a communist plot to undermine American freedom and institute totalitarianism. After exposing the early left-wing political sympathies of some of the modernists, Gordon singled out Mies's dictum of "less is more" as a pernicious attack on private property. "They are promoting unlivability, stripped-down emptiness, lack of storage space and therefore the lack of possessions." She concluded that if people accepted the advice of this "self-chosen elite" in matters of taste, they would be prepared to accept dictators in other areas as well.[14]

This diatribe against modern architecture as a communist plot contained no mention of all the capitalist corporations that embraced this style to symbolize their new power and rationality. Gordon was interested only in modernism in the private residence, and Mies's buildings were a special focus. She charged that all the glass in the Lake Shore Drive Apartments made them too hot in summer and too cold in winter. And Mies's one-room, rectangular house of glass and steel for Edith Farnsworth was also attacked as impractical for family living. Thus, the real object of Gordon's ire was the infiltration of cold, technocratic reason into "the heart of our society—the home."[15] Technocratic corporations had already created a work world of regimentation and total control, but she was drawing the line against this rationality at the private house and the goods consumed therein. In the individuality and variety of these possessions lay the legitimation for bureaucratic work in Fordist corporations. Americans were constantly reminded during these Cold War days that what distinguished their society from communism was the freedom to choose from a variety of goods to express their individuality. To give away this "freedom" to an aesthetic elite would undermine the alibi for technocracy and make pale the differences between Cold War contestants. So the underlying resentment among many Americans against technocratic capitalism was diverted into the realm of aesthetics. The economic (corporate) fraction of the new class of technocrats was too powerful to attack, so a substitute target was found in the less powerful cultural fraction of artists and designers. They could be pilloried with impunity, for their power extended only as far as the urban institutions of high culture and ended at the mass culture of the suburbs.

Meeting the Suburbs Halfway: The Rise of Expressive Modernism
There began to emerge during the 1950s a branch of modern architecture that sought a rapprochement with the segregated aesthetic of consumption holding sway in the suburbs. This aesthetic appeared in the buildings of Fordist institutions that were moving from the urban core to suburban sites. Some were buildings for corporate branch operations, while others were for the suburbanized cultural institutions of Fordism, like universities and churches. For such institutions the totally silent, reified modernism of Mies's corporate headquarters was inappropriate. In the suburbs, where people lived in isolation from the rationality of downtown technocracy, people demanded visual expression of the human ends of life—happiness, entertainment, togetherness. Fordist institutions in the suburbs had to transform the mute modernist box into a lively package that spoke of their purposes, not merely their rationalized means.[16]

Two pioneers of this package architecture or expressive modernism were Philip Johnson and Eero Saarinen (1910–61). By the time Johnson collaborated with Mies on the Seagram Building, he was already breaking away from the strict modernist creed, as was evident in 1949 when he designed his famous glass house. While Mies was still exposing the structural frame, Johnson set the steel columns of his house flush with the glass walls, creating a unified and hermetic skin. By the time Mies perfected the glass curtain wall, Johnson had moved on to manipulate the surfaces of his sealed packages to create interest and difference. In the Wiley House of 1953, Johnson created a dramatic surface effect by playing the transparency of the glass walls of the upper floors against the opacity of the masonry base. In Johnson's Kneses Tifereth Israel Synagogue (1956), the surfaces were even more decorative, with the white walls of the main facade punctured with a staggered pattern of narrow, dark slits.[17]

Johnson's manipulations of the surface of the modernist box paled, however, in comparison to the eye-popping packages designed by Saarinen for the suburban outposts of technocracy. In his hands, the entire building was sculpted into an abstract expression of technological futurism. Son of Finnish architect Eliel Saarinen (1873–1950), Eero immigrated to America with his family and taught in his father's Cranbrook Academy of Art, located in Bloomfield Hills, a suburb of Detroit. He also apprenticed in the late 1930s with the dean of streamlining, Norman Bel Geddes, and did extensive design work on the exterior of the building housing GM's Futurama exhibit. From his master Saarinen learned

Philip Johnson, Glass House, New Canaan, Connecticut, 1949 (Photograph Richard Payne)

to express the excitement of technology without revealing its threatening het-eronomy. But in his hands such technological excitement transcended Bel Geddes's cool Depression-era promises to culminate in hot paroxysms of fulfill-ment. In 1948 he received his first major commission, the design of the General Motors Technical Center in Warren, Michigan. GM Styling head Harley Earl convinced his boss, Alfred Sloan, to build a new suburban center to house the corporation's styling, research, and engineering staffs. Earl wanted for the Tech Center an architect of stature, who could design, in his words, "an ultra-modern monument to General Motors' faith in tomorrow." Saarinen gave GM just such a symbol of technological leadership that obscured the unchanging reality of standardized mass production beneath a slick, exciting surface. Completed in 1956, the 320-acre campus of the GM Technical Center was covered with build-ings that critics argued were modeled on Mies's IIT campus. They were all long, low, rectangular structures based on a standardized module and built with glass and steel facades and brick end-walls. But a closer inspection revealed marked differences from Mies's IIT aesthetic and an anticipation of his later curtain wall. While Mies exposed the structural steel beams in IIT facades, Saarinen revealed no structural elements but gave his buildings slick skins composed of glass, aluminum, and enameled panels. On the Styling Building, for example, the steel beams of the frame were placed behind the obscuring curtain walls, which were composed of glass and enameled panels divided by uniformly thin window mullions that protruded ever so slightly beyond the surface. Structural elements were visible only on the backs of buildings, especially the shop areas. So the fronts of the buildings presented the purified, ethereal face of technocratic Fordism, which covered the dirty reality of work done in the pro-duction shops.[18]

Unlike Mies, however, Saarinen was not content merely to obscure the reality of mass production behind sober skins of pure reason, but went on to provide expressive symbols of the excitement of technology in a style reminis-cent of Bel Geddes's streamlining. The entire Tech Center was dominated by a 132-foot stainless-steel water tower at the far end of the twenty-two-acre reflec-tion pool. Soaring above the buildings, the gleaming spherical tower mounted on a tripod of steel columns looked vaguely like something out of Buck Rogers. Equally eye-catching and expressive of some technological demiurge was the stainless-steel dome of the Styling Auditorium, which loomed above the recti-linear Styling Building like some hovering spacecraft.[19]

As the 1950s progressed, Saarinen continued to obscure the real technol-ogy of his buildings, but the abstract expression of technology migrated from

Eero Saarinen, General Motors Technical Center, Warren, Michigan, 1956
(Photograph Ezra Stoller © Esto/Eero Saarinen Collection, Manuscripts and
Archives, Yale University Library)

incidental details like water towers onto the surface of the skin itself, which
he sculpted into wild packages that testified to the program and image of the
client. Like his patron Harley Earl and unlike most other modern architects
of the decade, Saarinen had his finger on the pulse of the delirious consumer
marketplace. Two of his more memorable expressionist adventures were
the Trans World Airlines Terminal at John F. Kennedy International Airport
(1962) and the Ingalls Hockey Rink at Yale University (1958), both of which
repeated the Saarinen formula of a monumental and unique shape backed by
a bravado display of pseudostructure. At the TWA Terminal he sought, in his
words, to create a distinctive building for the corporation that would "express
the drama and specialness and excitement of travel." This he did with a concrete shell in the shape of an eagle with two uplifted and cantilevered wings.
The buildings' symbolism was so obvious that it became almost a corporate
logo. A bit less commercial and figurative but no less dramatic in its technological expressionism was the Ingalls Hockey Rink at Yale. The composition was
dominated by a huge, high-arched concrete beam whose curve was reversed to
kick up on either end. The beam spanned the length of the rink and provided
the support from which the wooden roof was hung, like a tent over a ridge-
pole. Although the swooping roof captured the smooth excitement of a hockey
game, the robust look of the concrete beam was all pretense, for it was wob-
bly and required guying for lateral stability. The rink epitomized this branch
of modernism that moved away from severe rationality downtown toward the

Eero Saarinen, TWA Terminal at Kennedy International Airport,
New York, 1962 (Mary Ann Sullivan, Bluffton University)

consumer excitement of the suburbs. In this aesthetic the drama and expression of the surface was beginning to overtake the instrumental logic of the structure. The precarious balance between the two was tipped toward the former the further one moved toward the suburbs.[20]

Entertainment Architecture in the Suburbs

As the masses of technocrats and white-collar proletarians poured out of modernist urban centers on concrete arteries to the suburbs, they were prepared for the transition from work to leisure by a gradual transformation of the landscape. As the glass-and-steel office slabs faded in their rear-view mirrors, they were treated to a variety of attention-grabbing symbols in the approach strips of roadside shops and businesses. Then, just as the rows of mass-produced suburban houses were becoming visible, the strips of road-hugging businesses gave way to larger shopping centers set back from the road. Scattered sparsely among these centers and set back further were the shopping malls, which turned blank walls to the road to protect the consumer feast within. Finally, after negotiating off-ramps and a stretch of surface road, commuters came to the green serenity of the suburban housing tracts, composed of row upon row of detached houses protected by a green moat of lawn and tricked out in a variety of historical styles. This was the small-scale, human world of meaning and symbolism that made working in that bureaucratic cell downtown worthwhile.

The blue- and white-collar workers of postwar America were forced to acquiesce to the modernist aesthetic in their places of work. But when given the opportunity to escape the urban signs of instrumental rationality, the victims of technocracy fled quickly in their cars to the suburbs and created a life of consumption that provided the aesthetic opposite of but social complement to Fordist production. The entertainment aesthetic cultivated in suburban homes, businesses, and amusements provided the superficial sense of rootedness and classlessness that soothed the work-inflicted wounds of rootlessness and class degradation.

Mass Suburbia: The Home of Classless Consumerism

The opportunity for the working-class exodus to the suburbs was provided by the postwar Keynesian state's subsidy and stabilization of consumer demand. During the war both government and corporations legitimated the sacrifices of Americans with promises that wartime technology would generate peacetime consumer goods for all, especially modern housing. As the war wound down, the federal government feared that a failure to deliver on these promises would strengthen the socialist left that had grown during the Depression. These fears of postwar unrest were validated in 1945, when industrial workers launched the biggest strike wave in American history, demanding price controls, pay increases, and constraints on corporate power. In response, corporate managers engineered the labor-capital accord that traded increased consumption for retained power, and the federal government subsidized the most important consumer market, housing.[21]

Following the precedent of the New Deal, postwar support for housing came in the form of government subsidies to the private sector—loans to large developers, mortgage guarantees to lending institutions, and mortgage subsidies to individual consumers. Also like New Deal programs, the postwar support of the housing market favored detached, single-family suburban homes. The Federal Housing Administration produced bulletins for lending institutions and construction companies recommending as the favored design a single-family, one-and-a-half story Cape Cod or bungalow. Some scholars have argued that these housing programs were passed with the intent of controlling unruly workers by making them property owners, thus securing their support for capitalism.[22] This may have been an effect of postwar housing policies, but it is doubtful that home ownership was imposed on workers unilaterally by capitalist interests. The desire among the working class for single-family, suburban homes had been established as far back as the 1920s and was shaped not by manipulating capitalists and reformers but by the structure of Fordist labor. The loss of individual freedom in this increasingly fragmented and collectivized process of production led many to seek compensation in a private home that they owned, free from the prying intrusions of landlords and forced propinquity of neighbors. And like other classes, workers preferred a suburban location for their homes, far away from the urban reminders of Fordist work, where they could cultivate a compensatory life of consumption. So these postwar federal government housing programs were not simply following the dictates of capitalist interests in either accumulation or legitimation, but also yielding to the desires of working-class consumers themselves.

The development that pioneered and epitomized postwar suburban housing for the working class was Levittown, the sprawling community of low-cost, single-family homes built on Long Island, New York, by Abraham Levitt and Sons. Containing 17,400 houses built over several stages, Levittown was the largest housing development ever put up by a single builder. During the war the Levitt company constructed emergency housing for thousands of war workers in Norfolk and Portsmouth, Virginia, pioneering mass-production methods in the process. Levittown further developed these methods, Taylorizing and speeding up construction to an almost assembly-line process. After the land was bulldozed of vegetation, standardized lots were marked out and almost identical packets of standardized, preassembled materials were delivered to each. Then crews specialized in one of the twenty-seven steps of construction alternately worked on a house, moving down to the next house in the row upon completion. Unlike Ford, Levitt could not control the pace of work with an assembly line of houses moving past workers, so he stimulated a fast pace with piecework. Circumventing union rules, he hired workers as subcontractors and paid them by the number of units completed. At the peak of production in 1948 more than thirty houses were built each day, allowing the company to sell them for $7500 and to market them mainly to blue-collar and lower-level white-collar workers with modest incomes.[23]

Levittown provided other companies with a model of privately built, publicly subsidized, low-cost, mass-produced housing for American workers. It also provided an ideal type of what was wrong with suburban housing to a growing chorus of critics, most of whom were members of the intellectual bourgeoisie, especially modern architects. They saw these sprawling tracts of low-cost housing on the edges of America's cities as inevitably connected to the emergence of a mass society without diversity and distinctions. This homogeneity was said to be visible in the physical landscape itself. As European-born architect Peter Blake (1920–2006) wrote: "Our suburbs are interminable wastelands clotted with millions of monotonous little houses on monotonous little lots and crisscrossed by highways lined with billboards, jazzed-up diners, used-car lots, drive-in movies, beflagged gas stations, and garish motels." This aesthetic similarity was said to either indicate or create the social homogeneity of the people living there, who constituted one big mass of "middle-class" families consuming the same standardized goods. But while suburbanites were said to slavishly follow the dictates of the mass market to "keep up with the Joneses," they were also said to be devoid of a sense of community, because they lacked public space and buildings. Modernist planners also argued that the homogeneous rows of detached houses were too close together and too poorly designed to deliver the promised privacy and escape from the conformity of mass culture. And what was to blame for this plague upon the landscape? Blake blamed suburbia on the profit motive of the real-estate industry, while planner Serge Chermayeff (1900–1996) saw cheap cars and mass production as the real culprit.[24]

These simplistic charges against postwar suburban developments were themselves criticized by populist defenders of suburbia, who saw this type of housing as an expression of the legitimate desires of the working class. Herbert Gans and Bennett Berger in particular carried out sociological studies that took issue with the charge that suburbia was homogenizing America into one middle-class mass. In his study of the Levittown development in Pennsylvania, Gans argued that within particular suburbs residents were of similar income and age, largely due to self-selection on the basis of housing cost and type. But beneath the superficial similarities of income, age, and family situation, Gans found enduring differences of class. Working-class residents did not become "middle class" simply by moving to the suburbs but retained their working-class culture, which often led to clashes with their lower-middle and upper-middle class neighbors. Berger came to the same conclusion in his study of a predominantly working-class suburb. Gans conceded that conformity did prevail, but it was driven not by status striving but by a desire to blend into the community. He also found that although his Levittowners cared little about national issues, there was no lack of involvement in the local community. Finally, the residents did not mind the aesthetic similarity of their houses, and many were already undertaking alterations to individualize them.

Both Berger and Gans argued that criticism of the new working-class suburbs was coming mainly from the upper-middle class. Berger opined that the distinctive status of this class was being threatened now that the working class was attaining the consumer trappings of its lifestyle, including the single-family home in the suburbs. Gans, by contrast, argued that this was not a case of status competition based on similar values but the clash of distinctive class cultures. Those criticizing the comfortable dullness of the mass-produced suburbs were upper-middle-class cosmopolitans, who ethnocentrically judged the lower classes by their own values of urbanity, cultural diversity, and aesthetic pleasure. Working-class people, he argued, had every right to pursue their own preferences for a quiet, family-centered life in affordable dwellings free from the crowded city and prying landlords.[25]

Both sociologists were partially right about critics. Berger's explanation seems true of the economic-bourgeois critics, who had legitimated their social position largely by luxurious material possessions, especially the suburban home. Crafted in historic styles or Wright's organic aesthetic, the suburban homes of the prosperous testified to distance from economic necessity. When suburban developments for the working masses proliferated after the Second World War, the cheap copies of its homes undermined the distinction of this bourgeois fraction's culture of luxury. Gans's explanation of this criticism as based in a "cosmopolitan" upper-middle-class culture seems true of the cultural or intellectual fraction of the bourgeoisie, whose culture of aristocratic asceticism was affronted by the cheap luxury of these mass-produced suburbs. But why did modern architects of this class fraction, who had long advocated mass-produced housing for workers, suddenly sour on the reality of mass-produced housing in the suburbs? Because they were excluded from its design. In prewar Europe, modernists were successful in designing worker housing because it was state-delivered and did not have to meet the dictates of consumers. In postwar America, however, the state merely subsidized the private housing market, subjecting the for-profit industry to the demands of working Americans. And they demanded two criteria that effectively eliminated modernists from the market—single-family, detached houses and decorative insulation from reminders of rationalized work. When given a choice, most Americans rejected reminders of the forced collectivism of their work in apartment buildings, and sought to create a compensating realm of privacy in detached houses. Gans found that one of the most frequent reasons workers gave for moving to Levittown was to escape from the prying closeness of unchosen neighbors in urban apartments. Another reason Levittowners rejected high-density housing, according to Gans, was that "they do not accept the business efficiency concept and the upper middle class, antisuburban esthetic" based on it. That is, the celebration of work efficiency in undecorated, standardized forms was simply unacceptable to working Americans, thus effectively excluding modernists from the market.[26]

The populist defenders of the lower-class suburbs were correct to attribute much of the vitriol and hyperbole of their critics to bourgeois resentment of the American working class. Yet, there was still a truth in this criticism that the populists ignored—America was becoming a mass society as the result of the explosion of mass-produced consumer goods. Gans and Berger found underneath the superficial sameness of America's consumer culture the persistence of real class differences in income, power, and attitudes. But they ignored or downplayed the ideological effects of the similarities of mass consumerism. After noting, for example, that suburbanized workers retained their previous attitudes toward social mobility, organizational participation, and politics, Berger wrote that "it would be difficult to overestimate the intensity with which they feel that they are better off" and the extent to which they experienced the "exhilaration of arrival." The purchase of a suburban home so increased these workers' respectability and stake in mainstream America that almost as many identified themselves as "middle class" or "average" (47 percent) as identified themselves as "working class" (48 percent). The culture of mass consumption did not eradicate class differences, but it certainly made them less visible. Gans came to a similar conclusion about his Levittowners, writing: "no clearly visible class structure had evolved in the first three years of Levittown's existence.... Without knowledge about people's income, with the absence of very poor and very rich neighbors, and with the ever present fact that everyone lived in virtually the same house, it was difficult [to make traditional class distinctions]." People had little knowledge of their neighbors' income or occupation because, in this bedroom community focused on consumption, others' work lives were largely invisible. So the aesthetic similarity of goods in America's mass material culture, as well as the segregation of this consumer realm from work, helped to obscure continuing class differences and make it seem that all were part of a classless mass society. And to help maintain this comforting illusion of class-lessness Levittowners enforced on one another a relatively leveled standard of consumption, especially in those goods visible from the exterior, so all blended seamlessly into the community. Those residents displaying above average afflu-ence were ridiculed as showy and ostentatious.[27]

Automobiles and Technological Futurism

A fundamental part of this ideology of classlessness was the aesthetics of the mass-produced goods that were the foundation of the suburban realm of consumption. This illusion could not have been sustained had the goods carried symbolic reminders of the hierarchical and heteronomous labor processes that produced them. To be acceptable to consumers seeking refuge from technocracy and its urban aesthetic of modernism, consumer goods had to cover over the marks of mass production. This process began in the 1920s and 1930s, but the explosion of consumerism in the 1950s brought this aesthetic of obfuscation and diversion to new heights.

The consumer goods in this decade expressed exuberance, the sheer joy of so many people having so much. Product design captured Americans' confidence in technological progress by fetishizing the latest machines, but manufacturers also understood that consumers did not want to be overwhelmed by mechanical complexities. So, extending the trend started in the 1930s, they covered over all mechanicals with neat shells reminiscent of the jet planes of the period. Then manufacturers manipulated the colors and contours of the shell to convince consumers of the wonderful progress and variety of their unchanging, standardized goods. At the same time that Americans craved the symbols of technological progress, however, they also sought the reassuring stability of the past. Millions of blue-collar workers were leaving the ties of extended family and ethnicity behind in urban tenements and moving their nuclear families to the suburbs. Millions of white-collar organization men were moving frequently to take advantage of promotion opportunities. All this movement induced an uneasiness about affluence that was alleviated by symbols of a stable, shared past. In order to rush ahead into the brave new world, Americans needed a reassuring tradition, which they sought in historical design. Thus, the aesthetic of suburban entertainment was itself internally bifurcated, offering in different consumer goods either the excitement of progress or the stability of history.[28]

The leader in the aesthetic of technological progress was the automobile industry.[29] Postwar prosperity exacerbated the exigencies that led the industry to pioneer the profession of industrial design back in the 1920s. The introduction during the 1950s of automated production lines made mass-production technology more expensive and inflexible, increasing pressures on automakers to increase economies of scale and avoid costly technological innovations. But how could manufacturers persuade consumers in an increasingly saturated market to trade in their old models for new ones if they did not introduce technological improvements? The answer lay in changing the superficial aesthetics to give cars the look of constant change and progress. While mass-produced mechanicals staid stubbornly unchanged year after year, the body and its decorative accessories presented a changing kaleidoscope of differences to cover mechanical sameness. Totally new body shells were introduced every three years. In the two intervening model years the old shell was given a "face-lift" by the addition of new accessories like taillights, chrome strips, and fenders. This shell game of the annual model change was effective largely because this postwar period also saw the complete obfuscation of mechanical parts by the all-encompassing envelope body, completing a trend begun by the streamlining of the 1930s.

The same aesthetic tricks were used to give consumers the look of individuality and difference that they craved as a palliative for standardized work. Each corporation offered consumers a full line of models graded by price, but to save production costs the different models shared basic mechanical parts and often the same body shell. Stylists made the models look different by tacking on differentiating incidentals like bumpers, grilles, trim, and fenders. During the 1950s both the need for manufacturers to differentiate their products and the need of consumers to express their new-found prosperity pushed these preexisting policies to extremes. By mid-decade, the three-year cycle of major body changes had been shortened to two, and the yearly face-lifts had turned into major surgery.

The decoration that adorned the obscuring shells of 1950s cars exemplified the side of the suburban entertainment aesthetic that catered to the demand for technological progress. The look of these automobiles bore a direct resemblance to the architecture of expressive modernism pioneered by Philip Johnson and Eero Saarinen, especially the latter. In both there was an initial impulse to obscure all functioning technology behind a seamless package, followed by an attempt to mold that package into an expressive symbol of technological progress. It was not by chance that the inventor of this expressive-modernist aesthetic in automobiles, Harley Earl, insisted that Saarinen design the GM Tech Center that housed his styling studios. They spoke the same design language, but with different accents. While Saarinen's expression of technology was sufficiently abstract to qualify as high art, Earl's literal symbolism appealed mainly to the masses and drew the ire of modernists. Earl's preferred source for popular symbolism of technological excitement in this era was the airplane, a perennial metaphor for escape and a machine at the cutting edge of transportation technology. Earl borrowed the airplane's progress and escape by hanging on his earthbound vehicles literal references to aeronautics like the tail fin, which originated on the 1948 Cadillac as a copy of the twin vertical stabilizers on the P-38 fighter plane. In some respects this expressive modernism of the 1950s was an extension of the romantic modernism of the 1930s and 1940s, for both obscured the disturbing mechanics of Fordist production behind smooth shells implying motion. But the exuberant and often discordant symbolism of 1950s automobiles went beyond the sedately streamlined shells of the Depression era to offer a uniquely celebratory aesthetic of expanding consumerism.

The modern architects and designers who were so successful in implanting their sober aesthetic downtown were highly critical of these automobiles that provided the model for so much suburban design. Some, reaffirming their allegiance to efficiency, criticized the wastefulness of these huge and uselessly decorated cars. But it is clear from a symposium on automobile design held at the Museum of Modern Art that aesthetics, not efficiency, was what bothered modernists most about postwar cars. There Philip Johnson stated that from a functional standpoint his 1950 Buick was "the most wonderful car in the world," but he also called it "the ugliest object I have ever owned," largely because of the superfluous chrome decoration. His friends, Johnson continued, drove little imported sports cars like MGs, which had little power but looked good. Another MoMA panelist clarified that the Buick and Cadillac had "a certain nouveau riche glitter," while the MG roadster was an example of "honesty" in design and "economy of line. There is no pretentiousness, no excess decorative baggage." This critique of mass-produced cars, like that of mass-produced suburbs, was based on the peculiar aesthetic of the cultural bourgeoisie of America, especially that part catering to a limited market of production, like the modernists. Against the economic bourgeoisie's values of comfort, ostentation, and luxury, which the working masses now emulated in their automobiles and homes, these intellectuals asserted their values of structural honesty and functionality, the marks of a class long on intellect and short on money. As with the design of suburban houses, they also resented the fact that they

Cadillac Series 62, 1948 (Detroit Public Library, National Automotive History Collection)

Louis Armet and Eldon Davis, Norm's Restaurant, Los Angeles, 1957 (Courtesy you-are-here.com)

were not employed in the auto market, where corporate designers catered to the tastes of the masses.[30]

The same aesthetic of expressive modernism displayed on the automobiles carrying commuters to suburban escapes also infiltrated the commercial architecture that they encountered along the way. While commercial structures in the central business district often followed the architecture of neighboring buildings, roadside businesses outside the city had to conform to fewer legal and aesthetic standards and found more room to innovate. Already by the 1920s, roadside commercial architecture had begun to fuse building and advertising, attracting the attention of consumers in cars by expanding the scale and ostentation of signs until they engulfed the entire structure. But it was the postwar expansion of consumerism and suburbanization that touched off an explosion of building-as-sign architecture. More businesses moved to the suburbs, and they attracted the attention of commuters moving at escalating velocities on new highways with an escalating vocabulary of brash, transparent symbolism of the kind that Harley Earl loaded onto his cars. Like the era's autos, these commercial structures were mass-produced from standardized materials, but they sought to stand out visually along the commercial strip with eye-grabbing appliqué and cheap structural variations. The most suitable vocabulary for such superficial distinction was expressive modernism, which dramatically exaggerated the technology of building to iconic proportions. So small shops, diners, and drive-ins sprouted raked roofs with large cantilevers, undulating canopies, and faux suspended roofs with exaggerated supports. Other symbols of technological progress were used as appliqué. Irregular amoeboid shapes borrowed from the biological sciences appeared on signs and buildings, as did orbital shapes and satellite symbols after the Sputnik launch in 1957, reflecting a superficial public faith in unlimited technological progress in this age of expanding consumerism.[31]

The Mass-Produced Historicism of Suburban Homes

Complementing this aesthetic of technological expressionism in cars and commercial architecture was an emphasis on tradition and historicism in mass-produced housing tracts. The wildly expressive modernism of the transportation machines that carried commuters to suburbia and the retail machines that lined the route seemed for most Americans an appropriate symbol of the progress and movement of the age. But once they reached their suburban retreats of consumption, the "middle-class" masses sought to balance the excitement of new technology with the stability of historical traditions. Just beneath the superficial exuberance of the American psyche could be found a creeping insecurity about the new affluence and its implications. Although Herbert Gans's Levittowners reported that they were generally not bored, lonely, or isolated in their new neighborhoods, Lee Rainwater's in-depth interviews with working-class housewives revealed underlying feelings of boredom, insecurity, and uncertainty about a future beyond their control. This sense of imminent danger lurking under the surface of suburbia could also be seen in the film noir genre of the period, especially the work of Alfred Hitchcock, in which insecurity, decay, and terror were exposed behind the facades of middle-class respectability. The constant tension of Cold War confrontation also added to the decade's undercurrent of uneasiness. There even seemed to be questions about the origins and worth of America's consumer culture. In his best-selling *Hidden Persuaders* of 1957, Vance Packard convinced millions of Americans that their desire for ever-improving goods was manufactured by the surreptitious manipulations of merchandisers and advertisers using psychology to turn consumers' deepest needs against them.[32]

It is not surprising, then, that in their homes the consuming masses sought to alleviate doubts and insecurities with the comforting signs of a stable past. Rainwater found that the major aim of his working-class wives was to create a stable world among these insecurities, and the suburban home was the site of this world. The ownership of a single-family home connoted for them the freedom of private property, in contrast to the domination by landlords in rented apartments. Historical styles harking back to America's early period of petty commodity production helped to symbolize this sense of freedom and the individualism of property ownership. As architect Denise Scott Brown (b. 1931) pointed out, for most Americans of this period the ideals of home and domesticity were closely associated with rural areas and small towns, not the city. As urban America became the site of technocracy and a modern architecture that symbolized it, Americans fleeing to the suburbs wanted none of these symbols in their homes.[33]

The historical styles of an early America of small property and rugged individualism provided insecure Americans the compensating sense of freedom and security they craved. The most popular suburban style in the early postwar period was the Cape Cod cottage, which was the sole style of the Levitt company's first phase of development on Long Island. Called "Island Trees," this phase was built in 1947 as rental housing for homecoming veterans. Drawing on the ideas of Progressive reformers early in the century, Abraham Levitt saw this boxlike bungalow design as simple and efficient. It conveyed the individualism of agrarian life, while simultaneously asserting a community through conformity to established aesthetic standards. On the exterior, these houses had all the symbols of security and protection. The steeply pitched roof connoted shelter from the elements; the front windows were protected with small shutters; and the front entrance was shielded with short sections of pickets, split rails, or lattice-work. But probably most effective in conveying the insulated remove of these houses from urban dangers were the large, 6,000-square-foot lots. This land not only reinforced the rural ideal and let the male home owner play at yeoman farmer. It also allowed a large front lawn that provided a green moat of protection from the dangers of the street. Inside these small Cape Cod cottages there were also obvious symbols of America's comforting past, like exposed ceiling beams in the living room and pine wainscoting with stamped-out candle reliefs on the stairs and in the kitchen.[34]

Not just the aesthetics but also the spaces of these 750-square-foot Cape Cod homes of Levittown reflected the insular ideals of the postwar consumer paradise. Although the houses were designed and sited to be secluded from neighbors, within there was little privacy for individual family members but an almost enforced togetherness. The two small bedrooms allowed only the separation of adults from children. The small kitchen provided a separate space for the woman, but there was no separate male space, not even in a garage or carport, which were nonexistent. These new suburban families of working-class background were expected to conform to the emerging model of domesticity—the family as a consumption unit that relaxed and had fun together.[35]

Alfred Levitt, drawing of Model 4 Cape Cod house of Levittown, 1947 (Nassau County Museum)

Although these early bungalows attempted to address the symbolic and practical needs of working-class Americans, they promised more than they delivered. The meager, cramped spaces bore the stigmatizing mark of factory efficiency and stifled the expansive attitude required by consumerism. The aesthetics of these Cape Cods also seemed offensive, for their boxiness made them *look* like efficient containers for storing people, not exciting sites of consumption. Evidence of these deficiencies was given by the changes that Levitt was forced to make in the houses of the second phase of Levittown. Due to severe housing shortages, the company had no trouble renting the small, boxy Cape Cods of the first phase. But by 1948 the construction boom was softening the housing market, and federal legislation was making ownership easier for low-income Americans. When Levitt decided to sell off the rental houses, he had difficulty because the Cape Cod model was less desirable to choosy buyers. So for the second phase he offered a new model, the ranch house or, as Levitt called it, the Forty-Niner. This model also evoked a past of rugged individualism, but not the colonial past of Eastern scarcity and efficiency. It was reminiscent of a past of Western expansion and windfall abundance. The ranch house was fifty square feet larger than the Cape Cod, but it looked even larger due to aesthetic tricks of the type pioneered by the auto industry. Like the Cape Cod, the new model was almost square in plan, but clever decoration hid this boxiness by stressing the horizontal dimension. Instead of double-hung vertical windows, the Forty-Niner had horizontal sliding windows, and asbestos shingles across the lower half of the front wall also emphasized a horizontal line and broke up the height. And unlike the Cape Cod, the ranch house had deep, sheltering eaves, like Frank Lloyd Wright's Prairie style homes. In fact,

Alfred Levitt (1912–1966), who designed all the houses for the firm, claimed that Wright had inspired this design.

Also similar to Wright's architecture was the Forty-Niner's attempt to incorporate nature into the home to counter the mechanical look of the city and serve as a restorative palliative. Two of the main reasons that male Levittowners gave to Gans for moving to the suburbs were to attain "the peace and quiet of the country after the day's work" and "outdoor living." The ranch house facilitated these by shifting the living room from the street-facing front wall to the private back wall, where pastoral vistas of the back yard were available through an 8-by-16-foot picture window. The back yard was also made more accessible by moving the second door from the side to the rear of the house, opening into the living room. Finally, Levitt gave the entire second phase a more rural look with an altered street layout. While the streets of Levittown's first phase barely departed from an urban grid, the streets of the second phase were strongly curved and had cul-de-sacs, assuring a rural look as well as greater privacy. In the 1930s and 1940s Wright and Richard Neutra had introduced these ranch elements in the affluent suburbs. In the 1950s they were incorporated into millions of low-cost suburban developers' boxes to capture a carefree, outdoor style of living associated with California.[36]

The interiors of Levitt's ranch houses were also altered to reflect the ideal of expansive, family consumerism. The kitchen in the Cape Cod was a walled-off space along the front wall, completely separated from the living room. In the ranch house, however, the kitchen became part of a large, open living space that was divided only by a hearth, which symbolized family togetherness. No longer conceived, as in modernist ideology, as a factory-like setting for efficient production, the kitchen now became another family room in the tradition of working-class Americans. Thus this room, like others in the suburban home, was decorated with an eye to nonutilitarian beauty, and became adorned with decorative linoleum, pastel appliances, brick walls, and natural-wood cabinets.[37]

In order to fulfill the consumer dreams of togetherness, individualism, and security, however, these suburban houses had first to obscure their origins in the system of mass production from which their owners were escaping. They were, after all, built to standardized plans from standardized components by semiskilled labor and, consequently, tended to look like homogeneous Model Ts lined up along the assembly lines of suburban lanes. It did not matter that they looked like Cape Cod cottages or Western ranch houses; if they looked like the *same* rural dream of individualism, the spell was broken by the monotonous drumbeat of mass production. Sensitive to critics' accusations of standardization and to consumers' demands for individuality, big suburban developers borrowed the aesthetic tricks of the auto industry to make their standardized models look different through inexpensive adornment. In Levittown's first phase, for example, the same Cape Cod floor plan came in five models that differed mainly in the facades. The front door was placed in one of two positions, while front windows varied in number and size. The models also differed in siding, with three using classic clapboards, while the other two had wooden shingles. Roofs also varied to break up the monotony. Two models had planes offset several inches, either on the front or rear elevation, and one had a deep eve over the facade. These tricks, along with different colors, made the standardized floor plan look distinctive with little additional cost. The same type of variations in the five ranch house models also added cheap variety to this new floor plan.[38]

These aesthetic tricks did not, however, fool the intellectual critics of the working-class suburbs, who railed against the physical homogeneity of their landscape. So developers added more floor plans and mixed them up on the same street to break up the homogeneity. Thus, in his third Levittown, built in Willingboro, New Jersey, William Levitt offered three house types: a four-bedroom Cape Cod, a three-bedroom ranch house, and a three- or four-bedroom colonial. Each type was available in two superficially differentiated elevations. Highly varied external color schemes further increased diversity, ensuring 150 house variations in this sprawling subdivision. Consequently, Gans's interviews with these Levittowners revealed that, although they preferred aesthetic diversity, they had no objections to the appearance of their houses. There were, however, two other factors that mitigated resident's objections of homogeneity. First, many Levittowners saw their homes as temporary stops on a ladder of residential mobility, and hoped to eventually move up to a custom-built home in an upscale suburb. Second, many suburbanites, including Levittowners, undertook alterations to counter lingering traces of homogeneity, just like the working-class residents in Le Corbusier's Pessac housing project. Like those at Pessac, many Levittown alterations were made on the interior to achieve individuality and customize the living spaces. In these alterations Levittowners and other new suburbanites felt free to express themselves with few restraints. Exterior alterations, however, were more restrained, for their greater visibility compelled residents to maintain the visual harmony of the community and not to distinguish themselves too much. So the dialectic of individuality and collectivity was played out in the mundane architecture of suburbia. In their suburban interiority, residents were free to do as they pleased. Yet, to stand out too distinctly on the exterior was an unwelcome reminder of continued class inequalities. It was un-American, and carried the risk of marking one as a status striver or, worse, a subversive. Even in the sphere of consumption there were limits to the individuality that the administered society of technocratic capitalism could tolerate.[39]

The Ersatz Urbanism of Amusement Architecture

In the suburbs there was a bifurcation of consumer aesthetics. In automobiles and the commercial establishments oriented to the road, an expressive modernism pointed to a technological future, while in suburban homes a restrained historicism looked to America's rural past for stability. Yet there was a zone of suburban architecture that mediated this schism between past and future, jamming the two together in a juxtaposed space, as if propinquity could resolve this American ambivalence. This was the zone of amusement, a place set aside within the suburban fringes for the public celebration of consumer culture. Beyond the introverted walls of tract houses, suburbia offered few public places where people could congregate to feel the transporting press of the collective. In urban areas the street provided for this need, but it also carried the dangers of class and ethnic diversity, as well as the enforced intercourse reminiscent of the workplace, both of which drove Americans to suburbia. Could Americans have a place of public intercourse to collectively fulfill their dreams that was also protected from the disturbing diversity and estrangement of city crowds? The answer was found in the insulated urbanism of amusement parks and resorts, privatized places of purchased fantasy posing as the public sphere of free intercourse.

No place better captured the amusement architecture of ersatz urbanism in the 1950s than Disneyland. Walt Disney, head of his own film studio that produced cartoons, conceived of this amusement park in 1953 as a materialization of his celluloid fantasies. It must be, he argued, "a world of people past and present seen through the eyes of my imagination, a place of warmth and nostalgia, of illusion and color and delight." So Disney put his animators to work creating a real-life cartoon, in which every space and building was created first and foremost for its visual effect. When Disneyland opened in the Los Angeles suburb of Anaheim on July 17, 1955, his cartoonists had created a fantastic simulation not only of America's imagined past but also its wishful future. The dedication plaque unveiled at the ceremonies that day read: "Here you leave today and enter the world of yesterday, tomorrow and fantasy."[40]

Most of Disneyland created a nostalgic and sanitized simulation of America's past, focused around the recreation of small-town America in an area known as Main Street, U.S.A. Here Disney gave visitors a safe, organized, auto-free urbanism to compensate them for the fragmented and monotonous spaces of both modernist downtown and historicist suburbia. The entire park was clearly organized and easily readable, for Disney dictated that "Disneyland is going to be a place where you can't get lost or tired unless you want to." It was easy for people to become disoriented in both the fragmented and disorganized spaces of downtown and the homogeneous and dispersed suburbs. On Main Street, Disney avoided both types of confusion with a well-organized layout of space that borrowed heavily from the Beaux-Arts school of architecture. Visitors entered the park through Town Square, which was surrounded by public buildings like the city hall and firehouse. The entire area was designed in a sentimentalized Victorian style, but the public buildings of the square were clearly differentiated from the private shops along Main Street by their larger scale and civic symbolism. From Town Square, the organization of Disneyland followed a clear axial symmetry. Main Street terminated in a traffic circle, from which roads radiated to the rest of the lands. And just beyond the circle stood the focal point of the composition, the Sleeping Beauty Castle, with its faux monumental scale that made it visible from anywhere in the park.

Disneyland gave its eager consumers not merely an organized landscape of the past, but also a seemingly safe and civil one. This was an autoless land, where pedestrians were free from the noisy menace of dream machines. Disney's land was also free of the "dangerous" classes and races, because fees for entrance and individual rides effectively excluded the lower classes, as did the fact that getting to its suburban location required a car. But once inside, these exclusionary devices were forgotten, and "middle-class" Americans could delude themselves that they lived in a classless society. Also making the park less alienating than either city or suburb was the manipulation of scale through architectural illusions. Disney was obsessed with the authenticity of his buildings, but only in appearance. Every scene was designed to appear right to consumers who had grown up at the movies and expected reality to look like a cinematic fantasy. The Disney animators who designed the park gave it the palpable feel of the two-dimensional movie screen. Thus, in Main Street buildings the first story was full scale, but the floors above were smaller, producing an architectural foreshortening effect. The same was true of the park's centerpiece, the Sleeping Beauty Castle, which appeared taller than it really was because the bricks in the upper courses were thinner than those below.

These devices gave the buildings a more human scale, making them look big without intimidating viewers with the grand monumentality of the city's skyscrapers.

In addition to this orderly vision of a recent, small-town past, Disney also created images of more exotic pasts. Early amusement parks like those on Coney Island offered working-class visitors transportation to exotic places that included elements of danger and sensuality, but Disney offered the sub-urbanized masses of working Americans a sanitized history, in which fun and adventure were accompanied by careful control. So the Wild West boomtown of Frontierland was not very wild at all. Even the saloon girls were washed and well-mannered, and there were no miners or timberjacks to reveal the proletar-ian side of what Disney portrayed as a petty bourgeois utopia. And the nine-teenth-century town on the Mississippi, complete with a sternwheeler named *Mark Twain*, was curiously free of slaves. In Tomorrowland, the future was also sanitized and controlled, and focused on transportation technology. One could ride a monorail train, rocket ships, submarines, and miniature automobiles. But the rockets and submarines carried no hints of the nuclear weapons race in which they were central, and the "Autopia" simulated a drive along an idyllic parkway, without a hint of the increasingly crowded and polluted freeways that lay just beyond the park's gates.

Perhaps most appalling about Disney's entertainment architecture was the way it turned history, the succession of time, into an expanse of incommen-surate spaces differentiated for consumption. American history was presented not as a succession of human efforts but a series of discrete locations, identi-fied with visual symbolism derived from the movies. The purpose of these his-torical places was not to understand but to entertain, to stop the flow of time and hold consumers within a simultaneity of differentiated experiences that distracted them from the creeping homogenization of postwar Fordism. This homogenization lurked just beneath the surface at Disneyland, for all attrac-tions were variations on a few basic rides—roller-coaster, merry-go-round, boats. It was only the architectural design of the containers that made the Matterhorn bobsled ride look different from Big Thunder Mountain Railroad. Disneyland transferred the regimentation and rationalization of the Fordist workplace to the world of leisure, processing fun-seekers with just as much efficiency and standardization as autos on an assembly line. Yet, architectural illusion transformed rationalized movement into entertainment, and a private corporation selling individual entertainment into a public place that satisfied longings for community.[41]

The same can be said for the other great venue of amusement architecture in postwar America, the resorts of Miami, Florida. Although this world did not purport to transport consumers to exotic lands and historical times, the architecture had these same fantastic effects, even though the entertainment was quite standardized. As at Disneyland, many of the resort hotels were designed as movie sets, so ordinary Americans could star in their own movies. The man single-handedly responsible for realizing in material architecture this other world of cinematic amusement was Morris Lapidus (1902–2001).

Unlike Disney, Lapidus was a trained and licensed architect, but like the cartoonist his visual sensibilities were theatrical, crafted with an eye to dramatic effect, not material accommodation. Growing up in the tenements of the Bronx, New York, the son of a poor Jewish coppersmith, Lapidus first aspired to become an actor, for as he stated, in the theater he "found refuge in a world of dreams, of romance, of love and hate, a world that had nothing in common with the everyday world I lived in, a world from which I wanted to flee." Failing to distinguish himself as an actor, Lapidus began to design theatrical sets and resolved to become a scenic artist. He attended the Columbia School of Architecture in the 1920s, and unable to get a job as a set designer after graduation, Lapidus was hired as a designer by a contractor building retail stores in Chicago. For this work he ignored his Beaux-Arts training and employed the streamline moderne style of the Depression decade. But Lapidus also brought a theatrical flair to his stores, creating spaces that lifted shopping out of the mundane and elevated it to the plane of high drama. With dramatic lighting the architect gave dull products the sheen of irresistibility, and with curving walls and counters he kept consumers circulating past the merchandise. Lapidus also left no surface undecorated but covered every inch with often meaningless ornament: "I offered the customers something to look at," he explained.[42]

Lapidus's success in creating consumer dramas that stimulated sales brought real estate developers to his door in the 1950s. The postwar boom began to enrich many Americans from working-class and petty-bourgeois backgrounds, who now had the money to escape from their business lives on expensive vacations but lacked the cultural capital to consume the sophisticated touring of the established bourgeoisie. Some developers sought to provide this arriviste class with exotic escapes that had the aura of European sophistication without the depth and difference that came with actual international travel. Miami, Florida, became the privileged site of such simulated extravagance; and Morris Lapidus, its privileged architect. In a remarkably successful series of hotels in Miami, Lapidus did for the resort hotel what Disney did for the amusement park—turned a set of simple, mass-produced accommodations into a series of dramatic movie sets that provided escape from routine lives. As Lapidus stated his design philosophy: "What a resort hotel sold was a feeling of relaxed luxury and a freedom from the everyday humdrum existence that the guests were trying to escape....People wanted fun, excitement, and all of it against a background that was colorful, unexpected, in short, the visual excitement that made people want to buy—in this case, to buy the tropic luxury of a wonderful vacation of fun in the sun."[43]

Lapidus, who was also from a working-class background, knew that modern architecture could not give the nouveau riche the escape they longed for: "If the modernist stops at the skeletal stage, 99 percent of the human race is going to be unhappy. You can't create a steel-and-glass grid and expect people to be happy." In reality, the wings of guest rooms in his Miami hotels were fairly drab, modernist blocks that economized on costs. But Lapidus concentrated his attention on the public rooms of the hotels, where he countered this bare-bones modernism with a vocabulary of Hollywood-set luxury and overabundance for which he became famous. Many of the details of his designs were dictated by his developer clients, whom Lapidus described as "men who usually have come up the financial ladder the hard way and at an accelerated pace." Since they were also from lower-class backgrounds, their tastes were similar to those of their consumers. Thus, for example, developer Ben Novak insisted that the interior of the Fontainebleau Hotel (1954) be done in French Provincial, although he had only the vaguest idea of what the style entailed. So Ladipus avoided the stylistic details and captured merely the spirit of French elegance with a few references and stylized quotations. As he admitted, he gave consumers a movie-set cliché of French Provincial, for movies provided their only acquaintance with high style. In his next hotel, the Eden Roc (1956), developer Harry Mufson, who made his money selling tires, declared: "My guests... don't go for that modern jazz. I want antiques and crystal and marble and fancy woods." Lapidus gave him a vaguely Italianate style. For the Americana Hotel (1957), Lapidus cast his guests in a tropical adventure movie among exotic pre-Columbian ruins. The lobby contained a miniature rain forest of exotic plants inside a glass terrarium open to the sky. The rest of the lobby was decorated in columns with Aztec-like carvings and a screen painted with Mayan-like motifs.[44]

The purpose of this stage-set architecture was to turn guests from mere spectators into the stars of their own cinematic fantasies. As Lapidus stated:

Morris Lapidus, Eden Roc Hotel, lobby, Miami, 1956 (Reprinted from
Morris Lapidus, *An Architecture of Joy*. Miami: E. A. Seeman, 1979, 165)

"I was selling them the idea that, for a short time that they were guests, they
were really royalty—they were on stage." He created spaces in which ordinary Americans could make dramatic, movie-star entrances. Lapidus usually
brought guests down a long, elevated drive to the hotel's grand entrance, where
they were ushered by a doorman in livery into an entrance hall for a long procession. Finally, they arrived in the main lobby, where a grand, sweeping staircase that led nowhere provided a backdrop to their entrance. In these dramatic
and exotic surroundings, successful automobile dealers, tire salesmen, and
insurance agents could escape not only the humdrum world of business but
also the dispersed anonymity of the suburbs. Unlike the individualized consumption of the suburbs, this was a public space, where one could see and be
seen by others. Yet, like Disneyland, Lapidus's Miami movie sets were mere
simulations of public space, social settings surrounded by steep walls of admission price. This was a privatized and commodified public world, whose streets
and promenades were safely sealed from the intrusive ugliness of the costs of
the postwar Fordist system.[45]

Critical Countercurrents in European Architecture

In the American homeland of Fordism, architecture became geographically and
aesthetically bifurcated to accommodate the system's contradictory components. In the urban homes of technocratic corporations, buildings and spaces
were reconfigured to symbolize the efficient machines and bureaucracies of

Fordist production. In the suburban spaces of consumption, however, homes and amusement spaces countered present efficiency with past symbols of stability and future promises of abundance. The aesthetics of postwar European architecture were different, however. Although variants of both modernism and consumer populism could be found, neither was as strong as in America. The evisceration of the poles of postwar European architecture left a space for a new aesthetic that rejected both modernism and consumerism to expose the costs of mass production and mass consumption.

The postwar decade saw most of Europe swept rapidly into the powerful current of Fordism generated by the United States, which was now unarguably the capitalist world's dominant power. The installment of Fordism in Europe was the result of a conscious political strategy undertaken by America to consolidate an advantage in the new international hostilities, the Cold War with the Soviet Union. As after the First World War, Europe was again a collection of hungry and desperate peoples, ready to listen to appeals for social revolution. But now there was a national agent of revolution to the east, and a dominant capitalist power in America determined to contain its influence. European communist parties emerged from the war stronger than at any time in the past and threatened to extend the zone of Soviet control. By 1947 there were dangers of communist electoral victories in both France and Italy. To quell the winds of discontent filling revolutionary sails the United States launched in this year the Marshall Plan, whose direct grants of aid allowed Europeans to import American production technology. Along with Fordist machines also came labor-management "missions" advising Europeans on the construction American-style labor relations that stabilized production relations and consumer demand. Leading the rise of Fordism in Europe was the auto industry, in which industrial giants like Renault in France and Fiat in Italy became symbolic not only of new mass-production techniques but also the new working class. The Fordist rationalization of industry in Europe differed from the American model, however, in being more rapid and more state-led. As the primary agents of rationalization, European governments intervened more heavily in their economies, even to the point of nationalizing key industries. And they also took greater responsibility for delivering the goods of mass consumption to consumers, creating welfare states much larger than that in the United States.[46]

One result of this forced importation of Fordism was a class structure that increasingly resembled that of America. The consolidation of oligopolistic industries necessitated by Fordism spelled the decline of the traditional petty bourgeoisie and a transformation of the bourgeois class of industrialists. As in the United States, European Fordism shifted control of industries from individual entrepreneurs and owners to an educated technocratic class, know in France as the *jeune cadre*. Further, due to the program of mass consumption underwritten by state management, the working class in Europe began to lose its specific class identity and became incorporated into a broad middle stratum defined by consumer goods. But due to the different character of European Fordism, the distribution of these classes over space diverged from the American model. In the United States the technocratic middle class and more prosperous workers decamped to the suburbs, leaving behind in cities the poorest workers. In Europe, however, the poorest workers were moved to the suburbs along with the prosperous ones, leaving cities to be rebuilt as centers for the technocratic cadres, who both lived and worked downtown. This was the consequence of the more state-driven housing sector in Europe, which also influenced the architecture of the European postwar transition to Fordism.[47]

The main construction activity in Europe after the war was in residential housing to address the severe shortages brought on by wartime destruction and delayed construction. The vast majority of this construction was undertaken by state agencies, so most European architects during this period were employed in the public sector. Similar circumstances of war-created housing shortages, public construction programs, and government-employed architects had produced the great flowering of modern architecture in the housing estates built after the First World War in Europe. But the post-Second-World-War political conjuncture prevented a second bloom of modernist housing. While Central European, especially German, politics of the 1920s were characterized by a gradual shift to the right and a demobilization of the working class, the mobilization of the working masses of Europe after the Second World War turned politics to the left, sweeping into power social-democratic governments with a political mandate to construct welfare states that planned production and underwrote consumption. It was through these receptive governments, backed by Americans who feared Communist influence, that European workers registered their aesthetic preferences in housing, not through the private marketplace. Due to these political pressures, even architects with modernist sympathies were compelled to bow to the tastes of the masses. Although the aesthetic that emerged from this European conjuncture was unique, it bore similarities to the suburban historicism created by market pressures in the United States.

Like America's market-delivered postwar housing for workers, Europe's state-built worker housing was predominantly in the suburbs. Following long-standing modernist models of urban planning, postwar governments sought to move industries and their workers to the urban periphery, both to contain the postwar migration to cities and to "sanitize" urban areas. There is also evidence that European workers, like American ones, preferred suburban housing. Unlike in America, however, this suburban worker housing in Europe was in multifamily apartment buildings, not single-family homes. Since most of these apartment blocks were designed by trained architects, they were aesthetically unified and more restrained than America's merchant-built collections of historical clichés. Further, material shortages and a somber mentality prevented the exuberant overabundance that drove America's entertainment architecture. And even though European architects were following political instructions to communicate directly to the people, they were nonetheless insulated from their direct market demand by their state employers. Yet, the residential housing aesthetic of both America and Europe were backward-looking, focused on an idealized national past, not a projected technological future.

This trend toward a more humanized and antitechnological architecture that drew on vernacular styles was known by different names in different countries. Although it was related to both American populism and the Nazi *völkisch* aesthetic of the 1930s and 1940s, neither country was acknowledged as an influence for political reasons. Neither Nazi totalitarianism nor American laissez-faire capitalism matched the welfare-state capitalism that Europeans sought to construct. Most European architects looked to the politically legitimate aesthetics of the established welfare states of Sweden and Switzerland, which had pioneered in the 1930s and 1940s a style known as new empiricism. Drawing upon the existing architecture among the people, as opposed to the principles of experts, this style was characterized by vernacular features like pitched roofs, brick walls, window boxes, pretty paintwork, woodwork details, and picturesque siting. As one British architect described the philosophy behind a Swiss hospital in this style, "efforts are made through detail, interesting surface patterning, landscaping to meet the legitimate demands for richness, intricacy, dignity, which were often left unsatisfied by the over-schematic and blatant solutions in earlier phases of modern architecture." Such efforts were also visible in government-built apartment towers designed by architects Sven Backström (1903–1992) and Leif Reinius (1907–1995) and built in Stockholm in 1945. Although each tower was comprised of eight to ten stories and constructed of reinforced concrete, the detailing was more reminiscent of a mountain cottage or chalet. To break up the flat planes celebrated by modernists, the buildings had facades with numerous small facets. Although the roofs were flat, there were pleasantly sloped and protruding eaves at the cornice lines that simulated a pitched roof. Countering the factory-like, metal-framed ribbon windows of modernism were the small, square, wood-framed windows on these buildings, which spoke of the separation of individual rooms and apartments. Such details camouflaged the anonymity of large-scale apartment living with the local dialects of individual domesticity.[48]

Several European countries seeking to replicate the popular success of these welfare states similarly dressed public housing in the vernacular costumes of the past. British architects seemed particularly enamored of new empiricism in the immediate postwar period, when the new Labor government headed by Clement Attlee was committed to constructing a welfare state to serve popular needs. Yet, their adaptation of this aesthetic was given a British inflection and known as the New Humanism or people's detailing. This aesthetic incorporated much of the symbolism of new empiricism, but it also drew on the anti-industrial vocabulary of the Arts and Crafts movement. British critic Reyner Banham attributed the revival of these nineteenth-century details to the nostalgic longing for a return to a stable and identifiably British way of life after the trauma of the industrialized world war. In Italy the postwar regime also sought to appeal

Sven Blackström and Leif
Reinius, Apartment block,
Stockholm, 1945 (Reprinted
from Sigfried Giedion, ed., A
Decade of New Architecture.
Zurich: Editions Girsberger,
1951, 104)

to the poorer classes, and its architects produced a variant of new empiricism known as neo-realism, which extolled the naturalism of the peasant world by using artisanal techniques and natural building materials. For example, the INA-Casa housing blocks of the Tiburtino district of Rome, designed by Mario Ridolfi (1904–1984) and Ludovico Quaroni (1911–1987), used wrought iron and Roman-style brick vaults to evoke a past of rural purity.[49]

As economic recovery took hold in Europe in the 1950s, these countries also began to build in urban areas modernist office buildings in Mies's style to testify to the power and rationality of European technocracy. Yet, the delay in this reemergence of modernism created the space for an architecture of opposition that rejected both insular modernism and nostalgic humanism. Many younger architects in Europe, especially Britain, sought a popular aesthetic, but one more forward-looking and modern. At the same time they demanded an aesthetic that exposed the often brutal reality of modern technology revealed by the war and did not gloss over these unpleasant facts with slick facades of rationality and abundance. Such an aesthetic emerged mainly among young British architects, but they drew their inspiration from Le Corbusier, the venerable old pioneer of modernism who was moving away from the technology-venerating aesthetic of his youth toward a brutally primitive confrontation of humanity and machine.

Le Corbusier's Brutal Humanism

In his small-scale projects of the 1930s, Le Corbusier had developed a more organic and human architecture, embracing a vernacular not of pretty craftsmanship but of crude methods and materials. It was not until 1950, however, that Le Corbusier published the philosophy behind this developing aesthetic in a book entitled *The Modulor*. Here he offered a new humanism, an architecture built to the measure not of machines and their forms but of human beings and their bodies. Primitive people, he argued, built to the measure of the human body, but beginning with the Renaissance the rational spirit introduced into architecture "a measure devoid of personality and passion,... indifferent to the stature of man." Le Corbusier proposed to reassert the priority of humanity by governing building by a set of measurements based on the major intervals of a human with an upraised arm. Such measurements, he declared, would bring unlimited variety to mass-produced products and alleviate the "dislocation and perversion of architecture."[50]

Le Corbusier's attempt to humanize postwar architecture was altogether different from the humanism of American suburbs or European housing blocks.

In both of these, handcrafted ornament from a proximate past was applied to obscure standardization and make occupants feel at home in Fordism. Le Corbusier's humanism also sought to leave a human imprint on architecture—not to reconcile people with a mechanical society, however, but to bring the two into confrontation. To do so he drew on primordial methods and materials—coarse brickwork, rubble stone walls, unfinished concrete imprinted with the wood grain of the pouring forms. The human hand was present here, but its marks were left on buildings that were modern in their rectilinearity, asymmetry, and lack of decoration. What Le Corbusier revealed in these brutal buildings was the crude hand of humanity distorted by the instrumental reason of the machine. Here is a civilization, he seemed to say, whose rational techniques deliver humanity back to its brutal beginnings, just as the amoral machinery of bureaucracy and mass production had recently created the most murderously barbaric war in history. Le Corbusier's cry of humanistic protest against the barbarism of modernity was realized in a series of remarkably unreconciled structures after the war.

The earliest indication of this emerging postwar aesthetic was Le Corbusier's apartment block known as Unité d'Habitation, completed in 1952 on the outskirts of Marseilles under commission by the French Ministry for Reconstruction. This block of 337 dwellings marked a new departure not merely in aesthetics but also in conceptions of society and humanity. Unlike his earlier housing blocks, which were proportioned to mass-produced building materials, the Unité molded materials to human proportions, producing spaces that, although sparing, seemed particularly accommodating to inhabitants. Also indicative of Le Corbusier's new humanism was the concern for segregating the individual from society. Like most housing projects, the Unité provided residents with centralized communal services (laundry, school, nursery), but here they were spatially confined to separate floors, away from apartments. And instead of forcing individuals into the sight of the community with transparent curtain walls, Le Corbusier marked off each individual apartment with a deep *brise-soleil*, screening residents not only from the sun but also from the sight of the society outside. The resulting cellular morphology of the facade revealed the building to be not a collective of workers forced together by machine production but an agglomeration of individuals living in a tense community.[51]

The Unité's most influential feature, however, was the treatment of the building's reinforced concrete. In the 1920s and 1930s modern architects conceived concrete as a precise, industrial material, pouring it in rectilinear forms

Le Corbusier, Unité d'Habitation, Marseilles, 1952 (Photograph Lucien Hervé, reprinted from *The New Brutalism*. New York: Reinhold Publishing Group, 1966, 22)

and finishing it to smooth, machinelike surfaces. At Unité Le Corbusier broke with this practice and treated concrete as a plastic material, crudely sculpting it into bold forms and calling the results *béton brut*, brutal concrete. He refused rectilinear forms and shaped his concrete into an sensuous, organic skeleton for the building. Although the architect lifted the building off the ground with his characteristic pilotis, these were no longer lithe, insubstantial shafts but massive ovoid legs that seemed to compress under the building's weight. On the roof the sculptural forms of the gymnasium and children's playground echoed the organic pilotis on the ground. But perhaps more shocking to most modernists than the forms of Le Corbusier's concrete was its finish, which was equally organic and brutal. Instead of finishing the concrete to a smooth surface, he left it unfinished, crudely imprinted with the wooden forms into which it was poured. The architect thus exposed the imprint of the human hand of construction on this modern material, making it more human and organic. Many of these marks were not accidental but contrived. Le Corbusier planned the planking in the forms to create a pattern of large squares whose thin components ran, alternately, horizontally and vertically, giving the concrete a woven texture that implied the hand of a weaver. But there was nothing subtle or pretty about this weaver's work; it was coarse and tortured, as if the hand struggled to bend recalcitrant materials to human use. Le Corbusier revealed here the crude work of human assembly, not in a slow process of discretionary craftsmanship but in a hurried process in which humanity clashed with machines. It was as if the architect who once so obsequiously admired Ford's assembly line had stripped the Model T of its body and revealed all the defects of its hasty construction. No wonder, then, that the defenders of Mies's obscuring modernism labeled this naked brute of a building "the monster."[52]

The Unité d'Habitation was Le Corbusier's last attempt to realize his dream of the Radiant City, an aesthetically unified and totally planned urban environment for the machine age. In his subsequent work he withdrew from the reality of the postwar metropolis, refusing to become complicit with the slick architecture of technocracy that surrendered the planning of the city to the vicissitudes of corporate capital. The incident that precipitated this withdrawal was the conflict over the United Nations Headquarters building. Although Le Corbusier initiated the design and determined its basic configuration, in 1948 John D. Rockefeller, Jr., who donated the Manhattan land for the building, got Wallace Harrison (1895–1981), an architect who helped design Rockefeller Center, appointed as chief architect. Feeling he had been cheated out of the commission, Le Corbusier henceforth refused to work for the capitalists who shaped America's postwar cities, declaring that free enterprise would never build truly humane and civilized communities. The disillusioned architect withdrew to the countryside, developing his language of primitive contradiction and fragmentation that denied the reality of the technocratic metropolis.[53]

Le Corbusier's new language of negation was best seen in two adjacent houses in the Paris suburb of Neuilly-sur-Seine and a chapel in the French countryside. In the houses, known as the Maisons Jaoul and completed in 1955, Le Corbusier returned to the archaic features of the Mediterranean vernacular he had explored in the weekend houses of the 1930s. The Maisons Jaoul were, like American suburban houses of the period, individual refuges from the madness of urban technocracy. But they were primitive, rough refuges that spoke of the regression of humanity, not its progress. Resembling cave dwellings carved out of a mountain of brick and concrete, these three-story structures were built of unfinished concrete beams and vaulted roofs, with crude brick in-fill. Also like America's suburban vernacular, these houses offered inhabitants insulation and hermetic enclosure. The numerous windows punched out of the heavy walls were small and had glass that appeared more reflective than transparent, exposing little of the interior. One British commentator, architect James Stirling (1926–1992), was shocked by this abandonment of the modernist ideal of emancipation through rationality, and wrote that the Maisons Jaoul were "built by and intended for the status quo" of the suburban housing situation. It is true that Le Corbusier was here trying to build in a humanized way that gave inhabitants a refuge from the technocratic city, but he was not seeking to reconcile them to the status quo, as did American suburban builders. The inhabitants of the Maisons Jaoul may have felt protected from the outside world, but surely they could not feel at home in their low-ceilinged, crudely tiled concrete houses. If they did not feel the primeval fear of cave dwellers for the world beyond their door, then they must have they felt like combatants hunkered down in hastily constructed bunkers against a siege waged by the machinery of technocratic Fordism. Unlike American suburban refuges, these were not places of amnestic or nostalgic delight.[54]

A remarkable religious structure that Le Corbusier completed in 1955 retreated even further from the degraded technocratic city to the primitive surrounds of the French countryside. And it also seemed to mark a retreat from a progressive belief in science and technology to a more primordial faith in natural forces. The pilgrimage chapel of Notre Dame du Haut, commissioned by the French government to replace a bombed out neo-Gothic church in Ronchamp, could not have been more different from its elaborately ornamented predecessor. Built on the crown of a hill overlooking the nearby Vosges mountains, the church was designed by Le Corbusier as an organic structure that echoed the severe landscape and seemed as old as the hills themselves. The structure was built of a concrete frame filled in with rubble walls that incorporated stone from the destroyed church. Unlike the generally rectilinear forms of the Unité or Maisons Jaoul, however, the Ronchamp Chapel had nary a straight line. The roof was a curving, hollow concrete shell that Le Corbusier claimed was inspired by a crab. And the white-washed walls were convexly curved and in some places sloped, as if frozen in the process of collapsing. Inside the small chapel the roof sagged down dangerously, and one wall tottered ominously outward, symbolizing perhaps the imminent demise of the Roman church and its replacement by some primitive belief. Indeed, there were few Christian symbols here and numerous references to archaic beliefs, such as Maltese tombs, Sardinian cult steles, prehistoric dolmens. And all surfaces, save the concrete roof imprinted with the boards of the pouring forms, were finished with an extremely coarse, white roughcast covering. Yet there was still something severely modern about the composition, from the concrete roof and

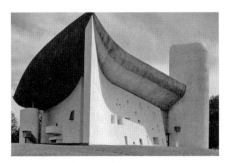

Le Corbusier, Ronchamp Chapel,
near Belfort, France, 1955
(Kavaler, Art Resource, NY/Artists
Rights Society, NY)

white walls to the irregularly arranged rectilinear windows that penetrated the sloping chapel wall and looked remarkably like a De Stijl painting. Even in this religious retreat the threatening intrusion of the modern world could not be forgotten. Here once again Le Corbusier refused to resolve the contradiction between the brutal rigidity and hardness of the postwar world of technocracy and the demands of humanity for comforting and accommodating retreats. The two stood in stark, constant opposition to one another, carrying on an uninterrupted, now hidden, now open fight, which threatened to end not in a revolutionary reconstitution of society at large, but in the common ruin of the contending forces, in a reversion to a primitive, barbaric state.[55]

Britain's New Brutalist Revolt

Le Corbusier's refusal to accommodate the prevailing postwar trends of either technocratic modernism or historical populism made his later work an exemplar for the younger architectural generation in Europe, especially Britain. Modernism had always been weak here, largely because the country did not experience the contradictory clash of rapid industrialization with an Old Regime, as did Central European countries. Britain made a slow and gradual entry into industrial capitalism in the eighteenth and nineteenth centuries, allowing it to incorporate both the economic and intellectual fractions of the bourgeoisie into an Old Regime that gradually liberalized itself from within. And unlike in Central Europe, where radical worker movements in the interwar period created the possibility of political revolution that fueled artistic hopes for cultural revolution, in Britain the working class had been incorporated into parliamentary democracy in the last decades of the nineteenth century, diffusing discontent and quashing chances of a labor insurgency. Britain did have a small group of modern architects, but they were relatively uninfluential in such a sociocultural configuration. The Second World War changed their outlook and aesthetics, however. The inflammation of popular and nationalist sentiments by war mobilization sent these modern architects in search of a peculiarly British aesthetic that appealed to the masses. After the war the rise of the Labor government solidified this trend, and these erstwhile modernists became some of the strongest advocates of the new humanism, which they incorporated in postwar public housing.[56]

This abandonment of modern architecture by its erstwhile advocates and their defense of a pretty humanism seemed intolerable to a younger generation of British architects, who formed part of an intellectual generation known as the Angry Young Men. Many had been educated in newer, less prestigious

technical schools, called Red-Brick universities after their predominant building material, which differentiated them from the traditional stone construction of Oxford and Cambridge. The expanded educational opportunities of
postwar Britain gave young people of lower-class backgrounds the qualifica-
tions to enter cultural fields. Unlike in America, however, the emerging industries of mass culture were too young to absorb many of this new generation
of the cultural bourgeoisie, so many crowded into the restricted field of culture. In architecture heightened competition for a limited number of commissions motivated the young to create new styles to distinguish themselves.
Consequently, many rejected the new humanism of their elders and sought a
style that expressed both the harsh reality of emerging mass production and
the popular joy of the new mass culture. Their attempt to blaze a third path
between a compromised modernism and a trumped-up humanism came to be
known as the new brutalism.[57]

At the forefront of this British movement were two young architects,
Alison (1928–1993) and Peter Smithson (1923–2003). In their first postwar
design project, the influential Hunstanton Secondary School (1954), the
Smithsons used the language that Mies developed at the Illinois Institute of
Technology, which countered the prettiness of Britain's new humanism. But
after this, they rejected Mies in favor of the more primitively humanistic aesthetic being developed by Le Corbusier, whose influence could be seen in their
1953 installation at the Institute of Contemporary Arts entitled "Parallel of Art
and Life." Collaborating with sculptor Eduardo Paolozzi and photographer
Nigel Henderson, the Smithsons offered a collection of coarse images culled
from newspapers, magazines, and scientific texts that defied humanistic conceptions of beauty. There were scenes of technological violence, x-rays of the
human body, and distorted masks and figurines from primitive art. Like Le
Corbusier's Unité d'Habitation, these images attempted to capture a realistic
aesthetic that testified not only to the brutality and crudeness of the postwar
era, but also to its vitality. Clarifying their aesthetic objectives, the Smithsons
wrote: "Brutalism tries to face up to a mass-production society, and drag a
rough poetry out of the confused and powerful forces which are at work."[58]

The Smithsons' attempt to simultaneously humanize modern architecture
and expose the brutality of its technology was revealed in their unbuilt 1952
design for the Golden Lane housing complex for the City of London. The
housing blocks themselves were reminiscent of Le Corbusier's Unité, but the
innovation that revealed an effort to accommodate the real life of residents was
the "street deck," a twelve-foot-wide pedestrian walk on the exterior of every

floor of apartments. This feature defied the modernist attempt to impose a privatized, bourgeois way of life upon residents of public housing and sought to accommodate the varied and vital street life of the working-class districts of London. To recreate a real communal life, however, these streets in the air had to be continuous between buildings in the project, stimulating the informal, snake-like layout of the blocks. Such informal siting could also better accommodate the existing fabric of the surrounding city, meandering around and leaving unmolested established structures and neighborhoods.

Though unbuilt, the more humanistic and contextual housing scheme of Golden Lane laid the basis for a gathering revolt of young architects across Europe against the technocratic and intrusive city planning schemes of the older modernists. By the mid-1950s young architects were challenging the rigid schemes of functional zoning laid out by the International Congress of Modern Architecture's (CIAM) Athens Charter of 1933. The Smithsons, Aldo van Eyck (1918–1999), Jacob Bakema (1914–1981), and others saw this dream of the totally rational city turn into the nightmare of technocratic urban renewal, which deprived residents of any architectural symbols of identity or place. Against the urban rationalism of modernists, they argued for a unique solution for each site that took into account the need for popular identity within the featureless expanses of autopia. By 1956 this youthful revolt had succeeded in demolishing CIAM and replacing it with a looser confederation known as Team X (ten), which implemented some of these ideas. The Smithsons' streets-in-the-air were incorporated into the Park Hill housing project of 1961, designed by Jack Lynn and Ivor Smith and built in Sheffield, England. But they did not engender the hoped-for street life, for the decks on different levels were isolated both from one another and from the surrounding streets on the ground. Working within the existing city fabric dominated by real estate and automobile interests merely created enclaves of identity, not communities.[59]

As the ethical ideals of the younger generation were drown in the cold bath of existing urban interests, the only remnant of the brutalist challenge that survived was the superficial aesthetic of surfaces, which became integrated into commercial culture. This integration was initiated by the architectural firm of James Stirling and James Gowan, which was responsible for the design of the influential Ham Common housing project in Surrey, completed in 1958. Here Stirling was admittedly influenced by Le Corbusier's Maisons Jaoul. But even though the housing project was similarly constructed of form-marked concrete beams with brick in-fill, differences were obvious. While Maisons Jaoul were casual and untidy, the Ham Common flats were neat and detailed. Brickwork was more careful, formwork on beams was less assertive, and brick and concrete were neatly segregated by thin, recessed details. Purged of the critical crudeness of Le Corbusier's original language, brutalism could now be reinserted into the technocratic city as a humanized vernacular more reminiscent of nineteenth-century English factories than primordial huts. Over the course of the late 1950s and early 1960s this tamed and unbrutish brutalism appeared in such British structures as the Gatwick Airport control tower (1957), the "Old Vic" Theater Workshops (1958), and Churchill College (1968). In the United States Brutalism's influence could be detected in the work of architects like Louis Kahn and Paul Rudolph (1918–1997), whose work was also more mannered and civilized than the original English brutalists.[60]

This taming of the critical aesthetic of brutalism was paralleled by a gradual shift in the ethical underpinnings of the movement in Britain. From the beginning brutalism was based on an unstable balance between popular needs for identity and the brutal, mass-produced means for fulfilling these. Only a crude, primitive modernism seemed to speak to popular desires in this postwar context of destruction and turmoil. But this dialectic of populism and modernism shifted as the British economy recovered from wartime destruction

Jack Lynn and Ivor Smith, Park Hill, Sheffield, England, 1961
(Photograph William Toomey/The Architectural Review, reprinted, by permission, from Reyner Banham, *The New Brutalism*. New York: Reinhold, 1966, 183)

and moved toward a Fordist system combining mass production with mass consumption. The brutalists now looked to another source for a popular but modern language—the American consumer aesthetic, which, unlike the original brutalist synthesis, obscured rather than revealed the atrocities of Fordist production. By 1955, the Smithsons were using the style of American products, especially autos, to create a more emotional and vital modernism. They were aware that for the vast majority of postwar modernists American car design was the epitome of mass culture's bad taste. But Reyner Banham (1922–88), who was associated with the Smithsons in the avant-garde Independent Group, wrote: "Unlike European architecture, U.S. car styling seemed to have tapped an inexhaustible supply of new forms and new symbols of speed and power, the sheer aesthetic inventiveness displayed by Detroit designers in the middle years of the fifties was a constant reproach to the faltering imagination of European architects and the industrial designers they appeared to admire." Banham went on to argue that American product design was not only more democratic but also more economically "functional" because it stimulated the turnover of goods to facilitate constant technological advance.[61]

In the mid-1950s the Smithsons showed traces of this new consumerist or pop aesthetic in their architecture. In 1956 they displayed their prototype House of the Future, a standardized, prefabricated structure that was to be mass produced like an automobile. The entire house was enclosed by a smooth, plastic, double-shelled box, like a car body but with no external windows. There were even autolike chromium strips on the shell's exterior to give it interest. Although rectilinear on the outside, the house's interior followed the contemporary auto aesthetic with its curving, free-form shapes that de-emphasized signs of assembly. The Smithsons' House of the Future, like Buckminster Fuller's Dymaxion House, was even planned to undergo an annual model change. This prototype anticipated the brutalists late-1950s move toward a more consumerist aesthetic, which focused on eye-catching surface treatments rather than the brutal realities of mass production.[62]

What began in British architecture as a movement to challenge both corporate modernism and residential historicism ended up reconciling the two in a high-art consumerism. This quick transformation anticipated a development that would take over twenty years in America. There in the 1960s young architects also grew disenchanted with Fordist modernism and created an alternative high architectural style that incorporated aspects of the consumer aesthetic. This style emerged from the revolt against the machine in America

and elsewhere and became known as postmodernism. But like the British brutalist movement, the initially oppositional postmodernism was absorbed into
the changing landscape of Fordist capitalism as the new language of commercial vitality.

NOTES

1. For a general account of this completed
regulatory system of Fordism, see Michel Aglietta, *A
Theory of Capitalist Regulation* (London: New Left
Books, 1979); Michael J. Piore and Charles Sabel, *The
Second Industrial Divide* (New York: Basic Books,
1984), 73–104.

2. John Kenneth Galbraith, *The New Industrial
State* (New York: New American Library, 1972).

3. C. Wright Mills, *White Collar* (New York:
Oxford University Press, 1951), 77–160.

4. William H. Whyte, *The Organization Man*
(New York: Simon and Schuster, 1956), 22–59; David
Riesman, *The Lonely Crowd*, abridged ed. (New
Haven, CT: Yale University Press, 1969).

5. Theodor W. Adorno, *The Stars Down to Earth,
and Other Essays on the Irrational in Culture*
(London: Routledge, 1994), 51–77. The quote is
on 57.

6. Henry-Russell Hitchcock and Arthur Drexler,
Built in USA: Postwar Architecture (New York:
Museum of Modern Art, 1952), 15, 17.

7. Margaret Crawford, "Can Architects Be
Socially Responsible?" in *Out of Site: A Social
Criticism of Architecture*, ed. Diane Ghirardo (Seattle:
Bay Press, 1991), 29–31. On the modernist critique of
suburbia, see Peter Blake, *God's Own Junkyard* (New
York: Holt, Rinehart, and Winston, 1964); Serge
Chermayeff and Christopher Alexander, *Community
and Privacy: Towards a New Architecture of
Humanism* (Garden City, NY: Doubleday, 1963).

8. Kenneth Frampton, *Modern Architecture: A
Critical History*, 3rd ed. (New York: Thames and
Hudson, 1992), 232–36; Kenneth Frampton, *Studies
in Tectonic Culture* (Cambridge, MA: MIT Press,
1995), 189–202; Peter Blake, *The Master Builders*
(New York: Norton, 1976), 229–41; Franz Schulze,
Mies van der Rohe: A Critical Biography (Chicago:
University of Chicago Press, 1985), 220–30, 261–64.

9. Blake, *Master Builders*, 255–62; Schulze, *Mies*,
241–45; Frampton, *Studies*, 191–93.

10. Blake *Master Builders*, 263–70; Schulze, *Mies*,
270–81; Frampton, *Studies*, 192–94.

11. Schulze, *Mies*, 244–45, 272; Frampton,
Modern Architecture, 237; Freed quoted in Barbaralee
Diamonstein, *American Architecture Now II* (New
York: Rizzoli, 1985), 93.

12. Blake, *Master Builders*, 238; Diamonstein,
American Architecture Now II, 65; Manfredo Tafuri
and Francesco Dal Co, *Modern Architecture* (New
York: Harry Abrams, 1979), 340, 366.

13. On urban renewal and modernism in the
1950s, see Tafuri and Dal Co, *Modern Architecture*,
305–10; Vincent Scully, *American Architecture and
Urbanism*, rev. ed. (New York: Henry Holt, 1988),
165–70; Blake, *Master Builders*, 113–17; Vincent
Scully, "The Threat and the Promise of Urban
Redevelopment in New Haven," *Zodiac* 17 (1967):
171–75.

14. Elizabeth Gordon, "The Threat to the Next
America," *House Beautiful* (April 1953): 126.

15. Ibid., 127.

16. On the general concept of package
architecture, see Scully, *American Architecture*,
191–93.

17. Ibid., 194–95; Frampton, *Modern Architecture*,
240–41.

18. The Earl quote is from "Setting the Style,"
General Motors Corporation, *Opportunities
Unlimited—Meeting Tomorrow's Challenge*
(published speeches delivered at the 1955 GM
Executive Conference, September 26–28, 1955) in the
Historic Files of the General Motors Design Staff,
Design Library, General Motors Technical Center,
Warren, Michigan, 192; see also Alfred P. Sloan, Jr.,
My Years with General Motors (Garden City, NY:
Anchor, 1972), 300–5.

19. Eero Saarinen, *Eero Saarinen on His Work*
(New Haven, CT: Yale University Press, 1962),
24–33.

20. Ibid., 54–67. The quote is on 60; Scully,
American Architecture, 198.

21. Barbara M. Kelly, *Expanding the American
Dream: Building and Rebuilding Levittown* (Albany:
State University of New York Press, 1993), 163–67;

Arthur M. Pulos, *The American Design Adventure, 1940–1975* (Cambridge, MA: MIT Press, 1988), 50.

22. For an example of these arguments, see David Harvey, *Consciousness and the Urban Experience* (Baltimore: Johns Hopkins University Press, 1985), 36–61.

23. Kelly, *Expanding the American Dream*; Kenneth T. Jackson, *Crabgrass Frontier: The Suburbanization of the United States* (New York: Oxford University Press, 1985), 231–38.

24. Blake, *God's Own Junkyard*, 8; Chermayeff and Alexander, *Community and Privacy*, 37–38.

25. Herbert Gans, *The Levittowners: Ways of Life and Politics in a New Suburban Community* (New York: Columbia University Press, 1982); Bennett Berger, *Working-Class Suburb: A Study of Auto Workers in Suburbia* (Berkeley: University of California Press, 1971).

26. Gans, *Levittowners*, 38, 274. The quote is on 293.

27. Berger, *Working-Class Suburb*, 80; Gans, *Levittowners*, 131–33, 154–55, 418. The quote is on 131.

28. Thomas Hine, *Populuxe* (New York: Knopf, 1982).

29. The following paragraphs on automobile design are based on David Gartman, *Auto Opium: A Social History of American Automobile Design* (London: Routledge, 1994), 136–81.

30. "The Body Beautiful," *Industrial Design* (June 1950): 112–19. The quotes are on 113, 114.

31. Chester H. Liebs, *Main Street to Miracle Mile: American Roadside Architecture* (Baltimore: John Hopkins University Press, 1995), 20–65.

32. Gans, *Levittowners*, 226–39; Lee Rainwater, Richard P. Coleman, and Gerald Handel, *Workingman's Wife: Her Personality, World and Life Style* (New York: Oceana Publications, 1959), 32–46; Vance Packard, *The Hidden Persuaders*, rev. ed. (New York: Pocket Books, 1980). On American culture during the 1950s, see also Warren Susman, "Did Success Spoil the United States? Dual Representations in Postwar America," in *Recasting America: Culture and Politics on the Age of Cold War*, ed. Lary May (Chicago: University of Chicago Press, 1989), 19–37.

33. Rainwater et al., *Workingman's Wife*, 51, 174; Denise Scott Brown, "Architectural Taste in a Pluralist Society," *Harvard Architecture Review* 1 (Spring 1980): 48.

34. Kelly, *Expanding the American Dream*, 59–65.

35. Ibid., 69–72; Clifford E. Clark, Jr., "Ranch-House Suburbia: Ideals and Realities," in *Recasting America*, ed. Lary May (Chicago: University of Chicago Press, 1989), 171–91.

36. Gans, *Levittowners*, 38; Clark, "Ranch-House Suburbia"; Kelly, *Expanding the American Dream*, 40–47, 77–86.

37. Kelly, *Expanding the American Dream*, 82–85, 91–96.

38. Ibid., 42–43, 64–65, 76; William M. Dobriner, *Class in Suburbia* (Englewood Cliffs, NJ: Prentice-Hall, 1963), 88; Hine, *Populuxe*, 50–53.

39. Gans, *Levittowners*, 7, 282, 171–72, 176–80; Kelly, *Expanding the American Dream*, 100–23.

40. Beth Dunlop, *Building a Dream: The Art of Disney Architecture* (New York: Harry Abrams, 1996), 25–41, the quotes are on 25, 41.

41. This analysis of Disneyland also draws on Mark Gottdiener, *Postmodern Semiotics: Material Culture and the Forms of Postmodern Life* (Oxford: Blackwell, 1995), 99–118; Michael Sorkin, "See You in Disneyland," in *Variations on a Theme Park: The New American City and the End of Public Space*, ed. Michael Sorkin (New York: Hill and Wang, 1992), 205–32; Sharon Zukin, *Landscapes of Power: From Detroit to Disney World* (Berkeley: University of California Press, 1991), 212–50.

42. Lapidus quoted in Morris Lapidus, *An Architecture of Joy* (Miami: E.A. Seeman, 1979), 44; Hans Iberlings, "In Pursuit of Happiness and Delight: An Interview with Morris Lapidus," in *Morris Lapidus: Architect of the American Dream*, eds. Martina Duttman and Friederike Schneider (Basel: Birkhäuser Verlag, 1992), 18.

43. Lapidus, *Architecture of Joy*, 125, 129.

44. Ibid., 174, 163.

45. Lapidus quoted in ibid, 219–20, 164. See also Martina Duttman, "Morris Lapidus: The Architect of the American Dream," in *Morris Lapidus: Architect of the American Dream*, eds. Martina Duttman and Friederike Schneider (Basel: Birkhäuser Verlag, 1992), 7.

46. Eric Hobsbawm, *The Age of Extremes* (New York: Vintage, 1996), 225–42.

47. For the effects of postwar European Fordism on classes, see Kristin Ross, *Fast Cars, Clean Bodies: Decolonization and the Reordering of French Culture* (Cambridge, MA: MIT Press, 1995); John Goldthorpe, David Lockwood, Frank Bechhofer, and Jennifer Platt, *The Affluent Worker in the Class Structure* (Cambridge, UK: Cambridge University Press, 1969).

48. Tafuri and Dal Co, *Modern Architecture*, 358; Sigfried Giedion, ed., *A Decade of New Architecture* (Zurich: Editions Girsberger, 1951), 2, 104; the quote is from *What Is Happening to Modern Architecture?* (New York: Museum of Modern Art, 1948), 17.

49. Reyner Banham, *The New Brutalism* (New York: Reinhold, 1966), 11–13; Tafuri and Dal Co, *Modern Architecture*, 310–15, 358; Frampton, *Modern Architecture*, 262–63.

50. Le Corbusier, *The Modulor* (Cambridge, MA: Harvard University Press, 1954), 20.

51. Jean Jenger, *Le Corbusier: Architect, Painter Poet* (New York: Harry Abrams, 1996), 77–81; Frampton, *Modern Architecture*, 226–27; Le Corbusier, *Modulor*, 123–46.

52. Banham, *New Brutalism*, 16 ; Sigfried Giedion, *Space, Time and Architecture*, rev. and enl. (Cambridge, MA: Harvard University Press, 1967), 544–48.

53. Peter Blake, *No Place Like Utopia* (New York: Knopf, 1993), 192–98; Blake, *Master Builders*, 125–32; Tafuri and Dal Co, *Modern Architecture*, 352.

54. Banham, *New Brutalism*, 85–87, 99–101. James Stirling is quoted on 85, 86. See also Frampton, *Modern Architecture*, 225–26.

55. Frampton, *Modern Architecture*, 228–29; Jenger, *Le Corbusier*, 82–86; Tafuri and Dal Co, *Modern Architecture*, 347.

56. Perry Anderson, "Modernity and Revolution," *New Left Review* 1st ser., no. 144 (March/April 1984): 96–113; Perry Anderson, *The Origins of Postmodernity* (London: Verso, 1998), 81–83; Alex Callinicos, *Against Postmodernism* (New York: St. Martin's, 1989), 38–48; Banham, *New Brutalism*, 11–13; Frampton, *Modern Architecture*, 262.

57. Banham, *New Brutalism*, 12–15.

58. Ibid., 19–20, 41, 61–62. The quote is on 66.

59. Ibid., 70–73; Frampton, *Modern Architecture*, 269–79; Tafuri and Dal Co, *Modern Architecture*, 373.

60. Banham, *New Brutalism*, 87–90; Frampton, *Modern Architecture*, 266–68.

61. Banham, *New Brutalism*, 45–47, 61–63. The quote is on 63. See also Banham's essays of the period, collected in his *Design By Choice* (New York: Rizzoli, 1981), esp. 90–93, 97–107.

62. Banham, *New Brutalism*, 63–67.

5

Revolt Against the Machine:
The 1960s and the Death of Modernism

CHARLES JENCKS, the critical coroner of modern architecture, informs us that although the deceased had been ill for over a decade, death came precisely at 3:32 p.m. on July 15, 1972. The coup de grâce was delivered by charges of dynamite that reduced several blocks of the Pruitt-Igoe housing project in St. Louis to an ignominious pile of rubble. This ended, Jencks has argued, not merely one modernist site of concentrated poverty and crime, but modernism's entire dream of mass-produced architecture for the masses. The brave new world envisioned by modern architecture had turned into the dystopia of urban renewal, against which the poor in Watts, Detroit, and New Haven revolted in the 1960s. There were even signs of discontent among middle-class urbanites, who during this period often banded together to save beloved historic landmarks from the juggernaut of ground-clearing renewal.

The death of modern architecture was only one event among many that portended the demise of the entire system of Fordism in the early 1970s. The crisis of Fordist mass production was epitomized by a landmark 1972 labor struggle at General Motors' Lordstown, Ohio, plant, where young workers stopped speeding assembly lines with a strike. Defying the traditional Fordist bargain, they struck not for higher wages but for greater control over their work. The demise of the international system of resource supply that fueled Fordism's auto-driven growth was symbolized by the 1973 OPEC oil embargo. Since the late 1950s Third World suppliers of raw materials for First World Fordism had been breaking free of colonialism and seeking to control their own economic destinies. But the real costs of these struggles hit home in 1973, when the Arab oil producers' embargo against the United States revealed not only the vulnerability of Fordist production to Third World independence but also the ecological limits to Fordism and the environmental folly of ever-expanding consumption. So in retrospect it is no surprise that the modern architecture that aesthetically expressed the logic of Fordism came crashing down with its economic foundation after a decade of struggles.

———

Crisis and Discontent in Fordism

The problems faced by Fordism in the 1960s were not, like those of the Great Depression, the growing pains of an immature system that had yet to create institutions to regulate mass production and consumption. This decade saw a systemic crisis resulting from basic contradictions within the mature institutions that had guaranteed postwar prosperity. The crisis emerged first in the

United States, where Fordism had reached its highest development. The initial problems came in mass consumption, where aesthetic excesses provoked a general questioning of the culture of consumerism. It was evident that something was amiss in the postwar paradise of mass consumption by 1957, the year of both the first major postwar recession and a business debacle in the founding firm of Fordism. The Ford Motor Company introduced its newest automobile model, the Edsel, to compete in the increasingly crowded market for middle-priced cars. To make the car stand out and disguise the mass-produced components shared with Ford's other models, the designers made the car look different by tacking on an outrageous orgy of chrome superfluities. But the Edsel protested its difference so loudly that its exhortations rang hollow, and consumers detected a standardized similarity to Detroit's other dream machines, which were converging toward excesses of power, size, and accessories. The abysmal sales of the Edsel seemed to say that Americans were seeing through the game of disguising standardized mass production under superficial individuality and change.[1]

That Americans were increasingly aware of the deceptions of mass-consumption was also indicated by the popularity of consumer exposés like Vance Packard's *The Hidden Persuaders* (1957) and John Keats's *The Insolent Chariots* (1958), both of which argued that corporations teamed up with depth psychologists to turn consumers' deepest desires into irresistible products. Popular resentment against merchandisers seemed to assuage the guilt that many Americans felt after a decade of consumer self-indulgence. This guilt was further focused by the 1957 launch of the Sputnik satellite by the Soviet Union. This victory in the space race by America's Cold War enemy shattered the myth of America's technological superiority and made its emphasis on superficially styled consumer goods seem self-indulgent. *Life* magazine editors scolded Americans for placing luxury before liberty. "We should each decide what we really want most in the world.... A Cadillac? A color television? Lower income taxes?—Or to live in freedom?" This discontent with what were perceived to be increasingly homogeneous and self-indulgent consumer products was also registered by an increase in imported goods during this period, especially automobiles. By 1959 European automakers had captured 10 percent of the American auto market by offering consumers small, simple cars like the Volkswagen, which conferred individuality on their owners among increasingly homogenized domestic products focused on bigness, power, and decoration.[2]

Thus, in the late 1950s the system of mass consumption was falling into disrepute, for it no longer seemed able to compensate workers for the individuality that they sacrificed in Fordist bureaucracies and factories. This crisis in mass consumption ultimately redounded on the mass-production process itself. The response of manufacturers in the early 1960s to consumer complaints about superficial diversity was to give them a growing range of products distinguished not merely in style but also in function. In the auto industry manufacturers moved away from the standardized family sedan and offered a diversity of specialized cars—compacts, muscle cars, pony cars, mid-sized sedans, personal luxury cars, sports cars. But this escalation of automotive diversity threatened product standardization, upon which rested the economies of scale of Fordist mass production. As the number of different models grew, volume per model dropped and unit costs rose. Further, the plethora of options available on each model meant variations in assembly time on lines, thus giving workers the power to slow work down. The consequence of consumer-driven diversity was thus lower profit margins. Automakers and other manufacturers suffering from the escalating costs of greater product variety sought to increase productivity by speeding up assembly lines and machines. But this traditional cost-cutting method failed, exposing further contradictions between Fordist production and consumption. Keynesian methods of demand stabilization like unemployment insurance and other social wage programs greatly reduced the cost to workers of losing their jobs. So when managers stepped up the work pace, secure and protected workers resisted, sending the rates of absenteeism, turnover, and work stoppages skyrocketing. The 1972 strike of young auto workers at GM's Lordstown plant was merely the culmination of a decade of worker discontent and refusal to accept the Fordist trade-off of alienated work for compensatory consumption.[3]

American manufacturers' attempts to quell the crisis in mass consumption by offering greater product variety not only undermined mass production but also revealed contradictions in Fordist consumption itself, especially in Americans' automotive obsession. During the 1960s auto ownership exploded, as the family sedan was replaced by specialized cars to express each family member's individuality. But when each American sought individual fulfillment in a unique car, this created unintended social consequences that prevented all from attaining it. Traffic and accidents escalated, pollution proliferated, and the countryside was devoured by development. The advance of auto-driven consumerism thus undermined the escape from cities and Fordist production that it promised. Fueled by these frustrations, the environmental movement arose to protest the destructive folly of Fordism's promise of progress as ever-expanding consumption. The problems arising from many Americans consuming too much also helped heighten awareness of the corollary problem that some were forced to consume too little. Poverty was "discovered" as the contradictory corollary of Fordism's prosperity. The regime depended on the threat of replacement by low-wage workers—mainly women and minorities—to drive down wages and drive up the work intensity of privileged workers in Fordist industry. These excluded workers began to rebel, especially blacks, whose displacement by urban renewal was the spark that ignited decades of grievances. Ghettoes across the country exploded into flames, and the state's attempt to buy off this revolt through public programs only increased the fiscal burden on the faltering production system.[4]

Also raising the costs of maintaining the Fordist system were revolts in Third World countries, whose raw materials were the foundation for mass production and consumption. The 1960s saw a rising tide of dissent against U.S.-backed regimes that ensured access to the resources of these countries. Consequently, Third World bargaining power rose, and with it the prices of their raw-material exports. Also rising in conjuncture with rebellion in the periphery were the costs of First World military dominance, which strained an already lagging economy.[5]

Making common cause with both inner-city and Third World rebels were many of America's privileged suburban youth, who were not spared the converging contradictions of the decade. This first generation to grow up under the full sway of Fordism saw the costs of the system so increase and its benefits so decrease that to many it hardly seemed like much of a bargain. For them the rewards of a homogenous and standardized consumer culture seemed hardly worth the sacrifices entailed by standardized Fordist work. So middle-class college youth rebelled against their degrading apprenticeship for white-collar jobs in authoritarian schools. And working-class kids who went into factories rebelled against the authoritarian assembly lines and machines of Fordism. On this generation also fell the preponderance of the human costs of the Vietnam war, one of a series of conflicts to maintain America's international dominance. To many of America's draft-age youth, a premature death in a far-off jungle seemed a steep price to pay for the freedom to choose between different types of washing machines, which Richard Nixon touted in his kitchen debate with Soviet premier Nikita Khrushchev. They also began to question the superiority of America's technology when a high-tech military could not stop the determined onslaught of poorly armed peasants. To express their growing alienation America's youth pioneered a counterculture that offered a more diverse and vibrant range of practices and products to substitute for the standardized mass culture. Often identifying with Fordism's disadvantaged victims, youth incorporated motifs from black, peasant, and indigenous cultures, implicitly asserting the superiority of technological backwardness. Fordist manufacturers incorporated bits of this counterculture into their products to enliven and individualize them. But they did so at the ideological price of undermining mass culture's idolatry of technology.[6]

The United States was not the only country to experience the contradictions of Fordism. Thanks to the Marshall Plan, most countries in Western Europe experienced in the 1950s the "economic miracle" of expanded consumption based on mass-production techniques. But by the early 1960s the initial Fordist boom had subsided, raising European doubts about the staying power of their new economies. Because Fordism was not fully developed in Europe, however, its contradictions were neither as intense nor as disruptive as in the mature American system. This made it possible for some youthful supporters of the new economy to see the cause of problems as a lag in the development and diffusion of Fordist technology. Consequently, fantasies of technological utopias survived and thrived in Europe and Japan. However, critics of Fordism also found in European societies a historical reservoir of recent alternatives to this regime, making the past just as attractive as the future as a solution to the decade's social and aesthetic problems.[7]

Crisis of Modernism in Art and Architecture

The crisis of Fordism touched off a concurrent crisis in modernism, the aesthetic expression in high culture of this regime of accumulation. Modernism had soared to aesthetic dominance of legitimate art and architecture by the early 1960s, lifted by the triumph of Fordism and its technocratic elite of engineers, experts, and managers. No longer a struggling avant-garde outside the mainstream, advocates of modernism assumed central positions in the restricted art field as artists, teachers, critics, editors, and dealers. This institutionalization of modernism was made possible by a large infusion of both government and corporate funding of the arts in the 1960s. The technocratic elites in these institutions saw modernism as compatible with the promotion and legitimation of their interests. State technocrats saw modern art as a propaganda tool in the Cold War, since it avoided the criticism of social realism and presented the progressive image of a nation of creative freedom on the cutting edge of high culture. State sponsorship of modernism also helped domestically to secure the allegiance of the cultural bourgeoisie, which not only patronized the high arts but also controlled the transmission of culture. For its part, the corporate elite saw support of the arts as a public-relations strategy to demonstrate its civic responsibility. But modern art in particular seemed to carry the connotations of innovation, individuality, and personal freedom with which corporate managers could cover the conformity and heteronomy of their own organizations. The association of modernism with the machine aesthetic and technological modernization also provided a legitimation of the instrumental reason at the heart of corporate and state technocracy.[8]

Modern art and architecture had become so inextricably intertwined with the political and economic establishment of Fordism that when Americans began to question this establishment, modernism was questioned as well. This aesthetic crisis of modernism was instigated, however, not merely by struggles in the larger social field but also by conflicts internal to the art field itself. Pierre Bourdieu's theory of cultural fields provides a basis for explaining the revolution against modernism in the 1960s. He argues that in high art there is an inherent cycle of struggle that motivates change. To distinguish themselves in the competition for symbolic profits with successful or "consecrated" artists, youthful newcomers to the field pioneer new aesthetics. If they are successful in their quest for recognition, the avant-garde succeeds to the consecrated position, only to be challenged by a younger generation of upstarts. Bourdieu argues that revolutions are more likely to occur, however, when there is a drastic increase in the volume of producers, which not only intensifies the competition for distinction but also introduces producers from different social backgrounds carrying new habitus to the field.[9]

The United States in the 1960s saw just such an influx of new producers into high art, largely as a result of the postwar explosion in higher education. Unlike the new working-class producers drawn to the field during the Depression, the aesthetic upstarts of the sixties were mainly from middle-class backgrounds, because art careers were increasingly institutionalized and demanded formal training in schools and universities. Many received education and subsequent employment in commercial arts like advertising and graphic design, but sought to break into high art by rejecting modernism and pioneering a new style based on mass culture. Thus in painting, pop art emerged among American artists like Andy Warhol, Roy Lichtenstein, and Jasper Johns. By introducing into high art both the subject matter and techniques of America's mass culture, these artists not only stood out in the fierce competition between modernists but also appealed to a broader, popular audience. Bypassing the established mediators of high art, pop art was promoted by the mass media and acquired directly by collectors, both of which immediately understood it. These upstart artists also benefited from the fact that increasing levels of education among the general populace created an expanded high-art audience, especially for styles that came down to meet rising levels of taste halfway.[10]

The success of pop art and other aesthetic challengers to modernism is not, however, explained solely by the internal dynamics of the field. As Bourdieu argues, the outcome of the internal struggles of an artistic field always depends on their correspondence with external struggles in the social class field as a whole. Pop art was successful in displacing modernism in painting because it corresponded to the larger societal questioning of the Fordist system, of which modernism was the aesthetic expression. One correspondence of the artistic and social revolt was formal, a structural homology of positions of the type Bourdieu emphasizes. Pop artists found sympathy among Fordist challengers, especially radical and countercultural youth, because both were on the periphery of their respective fields. Yet reinforcing this formal sympathy among underdogs was also a convergence of content among the challengers to power. Pop art challenged the same themes in high art that students and others challenged in the Fordist system as a whole—rationality, objectivity, technology. By bringing into the world of high art the playful, exuberant attitude of mass consumption, pop art challenged the sober rationality of modernism, and in the process discredited the mass production and technology that this style symbolized. But the uncritical elevation of a newly enlivened and individualized mass culture left pop wide open for subsequent manipulation by a transformed culture industry.[11]

A similar transformation was unfolding simultaneously in the artistic field of architecture. Peter Blake, an influential modern architect and journalist, has placed the beginning of the crisis of modern architecture in the year 1960, at which time "I, and many of my contemporaries, began to question almost everything....By 1960 or thereabouts we confronted a severe crisis of confidence and competence." This initial questioning was motivated by an embarrassment of riches. The modern architects who were aesthetic revolutionaries in the 1920s found themselves at the end of the 1950s as dominant in the field, racking up not only symbolic profits but economic profits as well. As Bourdieu argues, the economic success of the consecrated in a field invariably incites dissent, since in art cultural capital, not money, is the privileged currency. Young architects began to denounce the modernists as "sell-outs" and to reassert the inverted logic of art, in which the monetary winners become the symbolic losers. Recalling the sentiments of the 1960s, Blake declared: "The Modern Movement—once dedicated to the ideals of an egalitarian democracy—had suddenly become the symbol of American capitalism at its most exploitative." Philip Johnson, once a modernist, began to lose faith in the early 1960s as well, averted by the same discrediting stench of money. He wrote in 1962: "Another danger…is an identification with what we might call our Establishment— namely the world of business." Economic success, he declared, has "precious little to do with the Art of Building.…Soon, under the influence of the market- place, we architects begin to count our success in dollars of income."[12]

Just as in the field of painting, in architecture this cycle of generational crit- icism was exacerbated by the secular trends of the period. In both the United States and Europe there was a dramatic increase in architects stimulated by the postsecondary education boom. Between 1950 and 1970 the number of archi- tects in the United States increased by 128 percent. This overproduction of pro- fessionals was worsened by modern architecture itself, for its standardization of design and construction made it possible for a few large bureaucratic firms to supply a large proportion of the market demand for office and institutional buildings. Younger architects with new firms were thus left with little business, and many were forced to work for the big firms in subordinate positions or to rely on teaching and writing for a living. As Viennese architect Hans Hollein (b. 1934) characterized the situation: "The international style and the interna- tional scene had stagnated.…Hardly discussed were new concepts and ideas. These discussions had to be reopened and provoked. A new generation had built little or nothing and thus could not enter the debate with building."[13]

This crowding of young architects into a field where a few established mod- ernists dominated building heightened aesthetic competition and stimulated innovation. Since the young could not build on a large scale, this competition took the forms of provocative drawings, critical writings, and small commis- sions from friends and family. Robert A. M. Stern (b. 1939) stated of one rebel from the 1960s, Stanley Tigerman (b. 1930), that although he began his career as a Miesian modernist, he was forced to abandon this aesthetic in a search for distinction: "Almost all of Stanley's work has been in Chicago, which is full of the ethos of Mies and the serious, heavy-handed Germanism that went with one side of Mies's nature—Stanley had to take the most outrageous counter- position to get even a moment's hearing by the press or public." Like pop art- ists in the field of painting, Tigerman and other young architects drew on consumer culture to create a new aesthetic, for as Bourdieu argues, newcom- ers to the field are more likely than established artists to introduce influences from outside the field in their search for distinction. But these internal dynamics must be combined with the external struggles in the social field to understand *which* outside influences the young architects chose to counter modernism.[14]

These young architects were heavily influenced by the larger societal struggles of the 1960s against the contradictions of Fordism. The general questioning of instrumental rationality and technological progress impacted young architects in several ways. First, like college students in other disciplines, architecture students rebelled against an authoritarian educational structure that allowed little room for creativity or innovation. They launched major protests in Italy in 1964, France in 1968, and the United States in 1968. Second, the Vietnam War and its brutal use of advanced military technology also raised questions about modernism's idea of technological progress for the benefit of humanity. Tigerman asserted that the challenge to modernism was directly related to the struggles around Vietnam, both of which were "stunning examples of a country coming to grips with its own imperfection." Similarly, Stern wrote that most of his generation of architects rejected modernism's "mystique of power and progress" on "the night Lyndon Johnson told the nation that we could have guns and butter, war in Vietnam, peace and progress at home."[15]

The external social struggle that had the greatest impact on the internal architectural struggle against modernism, however, was that against urban renewal. Throughout the 1950s and early 1960s modern architecture was directly associated with the type of urban renewal that displaced the poor and working class for the benefit of developers and their upper-middle-class clients. When the victims of this policy began to fight back, young architects and students found an ally in their struggle against modernism. But they also had an internal reason for resenting urban renewal—it was controlled by older modernist architects who, in cooperation with their technocratic political allies, froze the young out of architectural commissions. Yale architecture historian Vincent Scully, an elder champion of the young rebels, wrote with ire in 1968 of the conspiracy between the large architectural firms and architects on urban renewal boards to deny work to creative young architects. He cited as a particularly egregious abuse of bureaucratic power the forced revision and subsequent denial of the proposals of Romaldo Giurgola (b. 1920) and Robert Venturi (b. 1925) by the Washington, D.C., Fine Arts Commission. This struggle for resources within the architectural field would have had little impact, however, had it not been for the external allies found against urban renewal among those poor and working-class people displaced by it. This seemingly unlikely alliance of young, white, upper-middle-class architecture students with older, often black, poor, and working-class people was precipitated by the fact that both were peripheral and powerless in their respective fields, and shared a common subordination to the technocratic power structure behind urban renewal.[16]

The aesthetic alternatives advanced within the architectural field to replace the discredited modernism were also influenced by the larger societal revolt against Fordism. As in the field of painting, in architecture influences from the culture of mass consumption were introduced by young architects to counter modernism. This was partially due to the middle-class habitus brought into the field by the new entrants, but also important was the explosion of diversity in consumer culture during the 1960s. When architects searched for a more exciting and diverse aesthetic to counter modernism's homogeneity, this revitalized commercial culture provided an obvious source. Also influential on young architects was the emerging environmental movement, which provided the impetus for a natural architecture more friendly to the environment. And finally, the general questioning of technological progress caused some architects to turn to the past for an architecture that revalidated history and memory.

What Went Wrong with Modernism? Diagnoses of an Architectural Illness

Throughout the 1960s and early 1970s young rebels attacked modern architecture with the kind of revolutionary polemics that had been unprecedented since its birth. Manifestos burst forth in a previously barren architectural field like spring wildflowers after a harsh winter. All denounced modernism, but for divergent and often conflicting reasons. These different diagnoses of the modernist disease also gave rise to different cures. Although the criticisms were often overlapping and interwoven, the major themes were as follows:

Modern architecture is elitist and undemocratic.
Modern architecture is meaningless and does not communicate.
Modern architecture is wasteful and destructive of nature.
Modern architecture is technologically obsolete and backward.

The Political and Social Critique: Modernism as Elitist
From the outset modernism legitimated its aesthetics with a political polemic for democracy and egalitarianism. So when modern architects and planners achieved power and wealth in the 1950s with the rest of their technocratic comrades, powerless young architects exploited the gap between their rhetoric and their realpolitik. Some of the most vehement voices raised against modernists

were replete with charges of elitism, of the undemocratic imposition of their own interests on the masses whom they claimed to champion. Young architects around the world charged that the aesthetic revolutionaries of the 1920s had become the sycophantic servants of the establishment by the 1960s. From France the Situationist International declared that "functional architecture reveals itself as a fully developed architecture of functionaries, the instrument and the microcosm of the bureaucratic *Weltanschauung*." In Italy Paolo Portoghesi argued that modern architecture had survived in the postwar world only by forming "a solid alliance with power, as a result of its identification with the productive logic of the industrial system." In Britain Charles Jencks wrote that there had been a "strange deflection of the Modern architect's *role as a social utopian*, for we will see that he has actually built for the reigning powers of an established commercial society." And in Germany Claude Schnaidt wrote that the bourgeoisie lost no time in "pressing them [modern architects] into service for the purposes of money-making. Utility quickly became synonymous with profitability. Antiacademic forms became the new decor of the ruling classes."[17]

While youthful critics took their modernist elders to task for erecting glass-and-steel corporate headquarters, most of their political and social criticism focused on modern architecture's role in urban renewal. The indictment handed down by architectural rebels charged establishment modernists with the destruction of entire neighborhoods and the forced migration of their already dispossessed residents. For young architects raised on a steady diet of modernist propaganda about democracy and the people, this seemed unconscionable. Vincent Scully wrote that urban renewal had become "a device to turn the old New Deal around in order to use the taxes of the poor to subsidize their own removal for the benefit of the real estate men, bankers, suburbanites and center city retailers." American planner Paul Davidoff claimed that even when housing for the displaced poor was built, it was generally segregated into separate "projects" far removed from the new upper-middle-class housing, and hence reinforced inequalities of class and race. Young architects also attacked the high-rise apartment blocks built for the poor in renewal projects as "vertical ghettoes" and "cemeteries of reinforced concrete" that fragmented social relations and isolated people from the vital life of the city.

The most influential critique of urban renewal in this decade came from a trio of Americans who laid the blame for this catastrophe on the class snobbery of modern architects and planners. Herbert Gans, a sociologist and urban planner at the University of Pennsylvania, initiated the critique in his 1962 book *The*

Urban Villagers. In this study of the West End, an inner-city Boston neighbor-hood, conducted just before it was demolished, Gans attacked the redevelop-ers' assumption that such areas were disorganized "slums" that were harmful to residents. He argued that although the West End was a run-down, low-income district, it was also a closely knit society of family and peer ties, and generally a good place to live. The definition of the area as a slum, Gans asserted, was the class-biased opinion of planners, politicians, and social workers, who judged this group-oriented, working-class subculture by their own upper-middle-class subculture that valued individual pursuit of occupational status. He recognized that the West Enders needed help, but argued that programs for this purpose should respect their way of life and offer opportunities to attain *their* goals. Class-bigoted urban renewal programs, however, destroyed the West End and other neighborhoods like it without ever taking into account their culturally defined needs and desires.[19]

Despite the importance of Gans's book, the most influential and far-rang-ing critique of urban renewal in the 1960s was Jane Jacobs's angry broadside in *The Death and Life of Great American Cities.* Trained as a journalist, Jacobs learned about architecture and urban issues while working for *Architectural Forum,* a stronghold for American modernists. But in her 1961 book she attacked every premise of modernist planning, arguing like Gans that urban renewal was undemocratic because it was driven by the contempt of upper-middle-class intellectuals for the needs of ordinary people. But unlike Gans, Jacobs singled out from among this group architects and planners as the real culprits. It was these intellectuals who tried to impose their own "puritanical and Utopian conceptions" on "ordinary people," and thus replace the diversity and vitality of the real city with the homogeneity of their rational utopias.[20]

In addition to attacking the undemocratic and patronizing destruction of diverse, vital neighborhoods by urban renewal, Jacobs also denounced what poor and working-class people were given in return—high-rise apartment blocks in open green parks. People want closely spaced streets packed with activity, she declared, not open and empty parks. Along such densely occupied streets crowded with a diverse mix of functions, people could socialize, create community ties, and watch their children play. Modernist housing projects, by contrast, destroyed social ties by providing only residences and open spaces, the latter of which were usually empty because there was nothing of interest to do in them. Further, the cataclysmic approach to renewal—tearing down and rebuilding entire areas—destroyed the low-rent old buildings, which provided space for new businesses that enhanced diversity. In short, Jacobs concluded, modernist housing eliminated the social, physical, and economic diversity that prevented neighborhoods from becoming slums. Interesting, diverse neighborhoods attracted "more energetic, ambitious, or affluent citizens," while dull and homogeneous modernist projects inevitably degenerated into slums.[21]

Most of Jane Jacobs's highly influential book was focused on the contributions of economic, social, and cultural diversity to the vitality of the city. Yet, she did recognize that aesthetics made an important contribution to the life-giving diversity of urban areas. City neighborhoods that had a diversity of uses, she argued, naturally gave rise to buildings with a diversity of aesthetics, which was exciting. When modernist planners tried to impose homogeneity of use on neighborhoods, they ended up imposing a boring, homogeneous aesthetic as well. Her example was Park Avenue, where the Seagram Building and other exemplars of postwar modern architecture were built. Yet, because they were all glass-and-steel office buildings, the result was a sea of aesthetic similarity in which no one could get her bearings. Aesthetic monotony thus compounded functional monotony, driving the nail in the coffin of urban vitality. Only the cultivation of real economic and social diversity created the visual difference and excitement that drew and kept people in cities. The mistake of modern architecture was to try to impose a homogeneous order on this lively aesthetic diversity. It was Jacobs's aesthetic critique that was seized by architects and honed into a weapon against modernism. The charge was once again that this school was elitist and undemocratic, but this time for imposing its *aesthetic* interests on the public. Modern architecture was criticized for denigrating the tastes of the common people, resulting in an architecture lacking in diversity and individuality.[22]

This charge of a lack of diversity was widespread in the decade. The artificial differentiation of products on which Fordism rested was wearing thin, especially in the United States. Consumers demanded greater individuality in goods, and manufacturers responded with greater real variety. Compared to this emerging diversity of consumer goods, modern architecture looked boring, especially to the young architects who had grown up in this postwar consumer culture. This critique of modernism as failing to acknowledge the popular demand for individuality was developed most fully by Denise Scott Brown (b. 1931), an architect who was a student of Herbert Gans at the University of Pennsylvania. By the mid-1960s Gans had extended his critique of class bias from urban renewal to culture in general. He argued that the United States possessed a variety of "taste cultures," sets of aesthetic values largely determined by class, that reflected legitimate needs and were equal in value. The problem, Gans proclaimed, was that the educated practitioners of high culture had declared a war on the mass culture of the lower classes in a desperate attempt to restore their own power. Against such class snobbery Gans advocated a policy of cultural pluralism, which entailed creating cultural content for every taste public.[23]

Gans's analysis of culture gave young architectural challengers like Denise Scott Brown the sociological basis to attack the modernist aesthetic of their elders. Beginning around 1968, she and her partner, Robert Venturi, elaborated a critique of modern architecture as class snobbery that culminated in their 1972 manifesto, *Learning from Las Vegas*. Here they, along with their colleague Steven Izenour, defended the aesthetics of the commercial strip, Las Vegas, and developers' suburbs, arguing that they expressed the real needs of the "middle class" majority. People liked Las Vegas and suburbia, the authors argued, and by rejecting their aesthetics modern architects "reject the very heterogeneity of our society" and are guilty of "old-fashioned class snobbery." "They build for Man rather than for men—this means to suit themselves, that is, to suit their own particular upper-middle-class values, which they assign to all mankind.… Developers build for markets rather than for Man and probably do less harm than authoritarian architects would do if they had the developers' power."[24]

For Venturi and Scott Brown, as for Gans, popular culture was synonymous with commercial culture. They depicted elitist modern architecture as forced upon people by the power of the state, while declaring commercially driven architecture as the true expression of popular needs, since it was freely chosen in the marketplace. To express the diversity and heterogeneity of a truly pluralist society, architects needed to look no further than the abundant alternatives available in consumer markets. But when referring to the taste culture reflected in mass markets, the authors of *Learning from Las Vegas* spoke of the "middle class" or the "middle-middle class," not of the "working class" or "the masses," for whom modern architecture purported to build. Although Venturi and Scott Brown did not directly address what happened to this erstwhile client of architecture, critics of modernism generally followed the popular argument that the working class had become part of the "middle class" due to its rising standard of living. So with the rest of this vast "middle class" defined by consumption, workers increasingly demanded during the1960s that their products express individuality. This demand for consumer difference destroyed the basic needs of the undifferentiated "masses," for whom modernism purported to build, and created a consumer market of diversity. As Dutch architect N. J. Habraken (b. 1928) wrote in 1961, "the average working-class family has long since ceased to exist....Even within the same income group there are many families and individuals with widely differing backgrounds, ambitions and living habits. How can mass housing deal with that?"[25]

Habraken argued that the uniform appearance of modernist mass housing violated the "stubborn desire for variety" that was also acquired by workers as their standard of living increased. The reason why workers would no longer settle for the uniformity of modern architecture was further clarified by Robert A. M. Stern: "A man working all day in a [Chevrolet] Vega plant, on the assembly line, does not want to come home to a house that looks like another form of the Vega that's parked in his yard. That explains the tremendous split between popular taste in architecture—the neo-raised ranch colonial—and what an architect imagines the house will be—let us say Philip Johnson's glass house." In other words, workers did not want to live in look-alike housing because it reminded them of the mass-produced goods they manufactured on boring assembly lines. Since at least the 1920s industrial workers had rejected products whose aesthetics were reminiscent of the uniformity of mass production. But in the 1960s and early 1970s, the demand for variety intensified with the opposition to the production process itself. It was no coincidence that Stern chose the Chevrolet Vega to illustrate these escalating problems, because the struggles at the Lordstown plant that produced it became symbolic of the youthful rejection of the indignities of the mass-production process.[26]

Many young architects during the 1960s shared this social and political critique of modernism as elitist and undemocratic, but their political solutions varied. The leftists, who were allied with the student movement and its concept of participatory democracy, proposed that public planning institutions be democratized to allow the participation of the powerless people often displaced by urban renewal. They developed an alternative to elitist urban renewal called advocacy planning, in which architects offered their professional expertise to residents of neighborhoods fighting renewal projects. The role of the advocate was to make planning a "plural process" by helping these residents develop alternative schemes for renewal that expressed their interests in saving and improving their housing stock. Advocacy planning was popular in the United States, with organized groups operating in Boston (Urban Planning Aid), San Francisco (Planners and Architects for Neighborhood Regeneration), and New York (Architects Renewal Committee in Harlem). Scott Brown became involved in an advocacy role to save the South Street section of Philadelphia from destruction to make way for an expressway. An advisor to the group fighting the expressway invited her firm, Venturi and Rauch, to help develop an alternative plan, stating "if you can like the Las Vegas Strip, we trust you not to try to neaten up South Street at the expense of its occupants." With ideas offered by the community, Scott Brown developed a counterplan, which although not fully realized did stop the expressway. Such advocacy planning became so popular with increasingly militant inner-city residents that after the urban riots the U.S. federal government's renewal agencies provided funds to community groups for devising their own renewal plans. In Britain, input from concerned neighborhood groups was institutionalized in the 1968 Town and Country Planning Act. For a brief historical moment, radical architecture students, energized by an alliance with inner-city poor, were able to thwart the renewal establishment.[27]

Yet, the right wing of the assault on modernist planning started a trend within architecture that proved more successful than the left once the fervor of the 1960s subsided. This trend originated with Jane Jacobs's book, which was such a welcome gust of fresh air that many architects did not notice that it blew unabashedly from the libertarian right. Jacobs rejected not merely the undemocratic form of urban renewal but city planning as such, championing instead the mechanisms of the free market, through which ordinary people were said to express the plurality of their real needs. In Jacobs's morality play, the bad guys responsible for the death of cities were intellectuals and the institution through which they exerted power, the state. All urban evils originated from this group, whose aim was nothing less than "the restoration of a static society, ruled—in everything that mattered—by a new aristocracy of altruistic planning experts." All interests in the private sector—bankers, developers, landlords, lenders—were exonerated of blame, and said to be the unfortunate victims of the intellectuals and their governmental enforcers: "Private investment shapes cities, but social ideas (and laws) shape private investment. First comes the image of what we want, then the machinery is adopted to turn out that image." Cities needed, Jacobs argued, fewer ideas and laws and more marketplace freedom for both consumers and businesses.[28]

Jacobs was not the only critic of modernism to attack state planning as such, and to raise the banner of laissez-faire capitalism as liberation. Scott Brown and Venturi also celebrated free markets, where people could buy what they really wanted. Scott Brown went so far as to attribute all of modern architecture's successes to the power of state bureaucracy. By contrast, when the free market dominated housing, she argued, people were able to get what they really wanted, i.e., Levittown and Las Vegas. By 1973, the British-trained architectural academic Colin Rowe declared that modernism's attempt to rationally plan cities as well as whole societies was inherently impossible because, he argued, following Karl Popper, rationality could only determine means, not ends. And to gain a consensus on the ends of planning inevitably required a coercive, totalitarian government. Summarizing this trend, Tomás Maldonado, head of Germany's premier design school, Hochschule für Gestaltung, declared in 1972 that there had arisen a worldwide rejection of planning as such, defined as any action with a concrete end or hope.[29]

This right-wing attack on social planning is explained by the struggles not only in the architectural field but also in the larger social field in the 1960s. Within architecture, modernists had risen to dominance in part by allying with technocratic politicians who controlled the urban growth machine. Being denied access to state power for their architectural struggle, some challengers sought to ally with that other concentration of power outside the field, capital. This embrace of business and the market occurred mainly in the United States, where architects and designers had traditionally been more closely integrated with private business. Here the influence that modern architecture had gained in the state after the Second World War was recent and tenuous, so it was relatively easy for some architectural challengers to fall back to this capitalist alliance to attack the field's establishment. In Europe the profession had early on developed strong ties to the more robust state, and became even further entrenched in the postwar welfare states. So there the temptation was not as strong to embrace capitalists and the market to attack the excesses of modernist elders. Upstart European architects were more likely to advocate a radically democratized process of urban and social planning, rather than toss out the baby of planning with the bath water of technocracy.

The free-market move within the architectural field must also be understood in the context of larger social struggles. During the 1960s it was easy for many youthful critics of power both within and outside of architecture to see the state and its planning as the main source of social ills. The state was the visible force behind the most violent and destructive episodes of the decade, such as the Vietnam War and urban renewal. Given its role as the rational regulator of the Fordist-Keynesian order and the public face of its technocratic ruling class, it is not surprising that the state became the focus of dissent, and that the private marketplace appeared as a refuge of political and aesthetic freedom. It was easy for youthful architects to believe that by validating the increasing diversity and individuality found in private markets, they were placing themselves firmly on the side of the people against totalitarian bureaucrats.

This right-wing attack on modern architecture, however, failed to see the tyranny lurking behind the libertarian face of the marketplace. But some left-wing architects and planners did make the connection between public renewal projects and private profits. Although Herbert Gans recognized the complicity of state politicians and bureaucrats, he argued that ultimately the system of urban renewal was shaped by capitalist interests: "This system, however, is intrinsically related to the country's economic and political structure, especially to the long-standing public policy of giving private enterprise a free hand in the profitable sectors of the housing market." Public officials felt compelled to provide incentives—that is, profits—to attract private developers, so they molded projects to their interests. The remedy suggested by Gans was not to eliminate urban planning, but to ensure it served the public interest by providing more government funding, thus insulating it from the exigencies of private profits in the marketplace.[30]

The conservatives were also mistaken in seeing the commercial architecture of Main Street and Levittown as the free expression of popular desires. They failed to recognize that the marketplace could also further aesthetic tyranny, especially for those who did not possess the money to "freely" express themselves there. The assertion of these populists that the poor preferred the "messy vitality" of their inner-city neighborhoods, for example, totally ignored the powerlessness of poor residents to shape their environs, in which most of the buildings and businesses were owned by absentee capitalists. Contrasting the "vitality" of the ghetto to the "sterility" of modernist redevelopment did not display the difference between a popular aesthetic with a bureaucratic one, but merely revealed two sides of the same market, one poor, the other affluent. Not even the affluent building market could be convincingly depicted as the true expression of popular demands. Tomás Maldonado argued, contra Venturi and Scott Brown, that Las Vegas and Levittown responded not to the needs of the people but only to the needs of casino and hotel owners and real estate speculators: "Las Vegas is not a creation *by* the people, but *for* the people....It is an environment in which men are completely devoid of innovative will and of resistance to the effects of the pseudocommunicative intoxication." For Maldonado, consumer needs were cleverly manipulated by businesses to dupe people out of their freedom as well as their dollars. Hoever, perhaps the expression of consumer needs was distorted not directly by marketplace manipulation but indirectly by workplace structure. Blocked from meeting their needs for autonomy and individuality by the authoritarian structure of Fordist work, people turned to consumer substitutes for fulfillment. So the builders of Levittown and Las Vegas gave consumers what they wanted, but what they wanted was distorted by refraction through the alienating lens of Fordist production.[31]

The Phenomenological Critique: Modernism as Meaningless
Also popular among young detractors from modernism was the related but distinct criticism that its aesthetic was devoid of meaning for a majority of people. Borrowing phenomenology's focus on subjective perception, these critics were less concerned that modern architecture was imposed on people by an unresponsive elite than with the fact that its aesthetic communicated little subjective meaning. In its attempt to be totally objective, expressing merely the functional and technical requirements of building, modernism stripped architecture of meaning; it had no story to tell. As German critic Heinrich Klotz stated: "As soon as the geometry of modern architecture was deprived of any fictional aspect and only the pure objectivity of functionalism was left, the 'white bodies under light' revealed the meaninglessness of bare facts."[32]

The charge that modernism had no symbolic or communicative content was not, however, precisely true. Modern architecture was never just a technique without an aesthetic; it was the aesthetic of technique. On top of the technical requirements of building, modernism possessed a symbolic layer that told the story of technological progress and its salvation of mankind. If by the 1960s modernism was seen as meaningless, it was because this message had lost its promise. Charles Jencks wrote that many architects abandoned modernism because of "its obvious inability to deal with or pose general questions of architectural meaning: what was architecture 'to be about,' especially now that the Modernist beliefs in progressivist technology and the Machine Aesthetic were seen to be so naive (or boring)?" The environmental movement and consciousness of the 1960s helped to undermine the faith in technology, revealing that new technologies like nuclear energy often threatened nature and humanity. The student and consumer movements also contributed, questioning not only the quality of consumer products but also the technology of mass production itself. In the broadest sense, the movements of the decade began to question the primacy of technological means over human ends. They demanded that humanity and nature be seen as ends in themselves, not merely as means of achieving an objective, material progress outside and above them.[33]

Phemenological criticism was not merely a rejection of the story of technological progress that modern architecture told, but also a lament about the stories it did not tell, stories that people wanted and needed. Thus it overlapped with the populist criticism of Scott Brown and Gans, who argued that modernism imposed an elitist code of meaning on all. But while the populists' critique was underwritten by an empirical pluralism—different subcultures wanted different things—phenomenological critics grounded their arguments in an idealist universalism, asserting that certain universal meanings found in the mind were shared by all. This phenomenological critique borrowed heavily from the philosophy of Martin Heidegger, whose Nazi past had been carefully forgotten by the 1960s. The Norwegian architectural theorist Christian Norberg-Schulz was most responsible for developing his thought for architecture. He argued that modern architecture's focus on the technical functions of building created an abstract, objective "space" in which humans could not "dwell," or lead an authentic existence: "Meaning is the fundamental human need," he proclaimed, and humans could dwell in a meaningful way only in a "place," which provided a sense of orientation and identification. He continues: "To gain an existential foothold man has to be able to *orientate* himself; he has to know where he is. But he also has to identify himself with the environment, that is, he has to know *how* he is in a certain place." A place created identity by focusing or gathering up the natural surroundings and bringing them close to humans in an enclosure. Thus, the true purpose of the art of building was not to make a functional shelter but to build an existential home for humans in the environment.[34]

The phenomenological criticism of modern architecture was advanced not only by the rediscovery of Heidegger's philosophy but also by empirical studies like Kevin Lynch's *The Image of the City*, a 1960 book on the perception of city structures. Lynch declared that cities were not mere places to live but works of art and, as such, should be adapted "to the perceptual pattern and symbolic process of the human being." His interviews with residents of Boston, Los Angeles, and Jersey City, New Jersey, revealed that they did not identify with or feel oriented in their cities, because major landmarks and distinct districts were missing in the amorphous sprawl of postwar urban areas. This was especially true of Los Angeles, where development and redevelopment occurred so rapidly that there were few enduring physical elements in which people could invest identity and memory. Such rapid changes in the physical landscape, Lynch declared, often left "scars" on the mental images of the city, rendering people lost and disoriented in their own homes.[35]

Even though the phenomenological critique was based on a universal idealism, it did not deny the importance of history and social change. Even a

Heideggerian like Norberg-Schulz argued that the real essence of a place might only be realized by human action over time, by a sort of "self-realization." Lynch also spoke of the need for the city's image to symbolize the passage of time by contrasting the old with the new. The importance of the city as a symbol of history and the repository of memory was developed most fully, however, by the Italian neoliberty movement of the postwar period. Italy was the European country least influenced by the postwar rush to functionalism. The vast majority of its building industry remained in private hands and was dominated by small-scale craft builders, who stressed the historical symbols of craftsmanship. Further, by the late 1950s Italians were beginning to chafe under the constraints of the bureaucracies that had engineered postwar prosperity, giving rise to the neoliberty movement, which countered the modernist architecture of bureaucracy with a renewed emphasis on historical meaning.[36]

The founding manifesto of this Italian historicist revival was Aldo Rossi's (1931–97) *The Architecture of the City* of 1966, in which the author sought to refute the modernist idea of the city as machine. For Rossi, the city was an end in itself, the material embodiment of human activities and events that testified to the attitudes and values of the generations: "The city [is] seen as a material artifact, a man-made object built over time and retaining the traces of time.... The city itself is the collective memory of its people, and like memory it is associated with objects and places." But Rossi also believed that the meaning and order of urban forms came from certain aesthetic constants within the flux of time, which he called types. Although these architectural types might emerge in particular times and places, their principles transcended history and testified to certain unconscious human needs. Rossi's architectural types were not mere styles, nor were they functional categories of buildings. Rather, they were forms of buildings that transcended function and style, allowing their adaptation to historically specific styles and functions without losing their meaning. Types like the block with an arcade, the church with a central plan, and the house with a loggia had existed since antiquity, yet were adapted to the needs of each historical period and its styles, techniques, and functions. Such types were the architect's basic elements, which could be used to create an urban scene that not merely "worked" but also evoked deep memories and associations. In such cities, Rossi argued, people could feel truly centered, at home not only with nature but with the ages of humanity.[37]

This historicist impulse represented by Rossi manifested itself during this period not only in the development of a new historical aesthetic, but also in a validation of existing historical architecture. In reaction to the modernist obsession with building the city of the future, some turned to the task of pre-serving the city of the past, launching the preservationist movement. These activists battled modernist urban renewal on the aesthetic grounds that it tore down historical buildings and landmarks that constituted the city's heri-tage. Upper-middle-class, urban professionals launched well-organized move-ments to save from the developers' bulldozers architectural treasures like New York's Penn Station and New Haven's Beaux-Arts Post Office. And other groups worked just as diligently to save rather ordinary old townhouses, row houses, and apartment buildings. These groups were less interested in saving the social diversity of the city by protecting black and working-class neighbor-hoods, than in saving the aesthetic diversity of the urban landscape for their own enjoyment. As Gans argued in *The Levittowners*, it is a propensity specific to the "cosmopolitan upper-middle-class" to seek in its environment visual interest and aesthetic pleasure. Similarly, within Pierre Bourdieu's theory these preservationists could be seen as members of the cultural bourgeoisie seeking to culturally distinguish themselves in a housing market in which the working class had devalued the suburban house as a status symbol. But Bourdieu's the-ory does not explain why this search for distinction took this historicist path, or why such styles were also valued among other classes. The broad appeal of this movement is attributable to a shared rejection of technology and bureau-cracy and the modern architecture that celebrated these. Further, preservation of historical buildings also seemed less wasteful of resources and less disruptive of the environment, themes that also emerged as a major critique of modern-ism during the decade.[38]

The Environmental Critique: Modernism as Wasteful

The environmental movement was an increasingly influential critic of mod-ern architecture as the 1960s progressed. Two decades of experience with modernist buildings and urban planning, combined with a rising conscious-ness of environmental limits, led many to conclude that modernism was inherently wasteful of human and natural resources. This critique was perhaps the most ironic, for efficiency had been the main justification for early modern architecture. The interwar avant-garde argued that only standardized indus-trial materials assembled by unskilled workers could meet society's housing needs rapidly and cheaply. Early modernists focused not only on efficiency of construction but on efficiency of use as well, stripping buildings down to their bare functions and providing minimal accommodations for these. But these early arguments for the efficiency of modern architecture were focused almost exclusively on saving labor, not materials. Mass-production methods were said to be quicker than craft production, and to allow builders to use the more plentiful supply of unskilled workers for construction. Natural materials requiring craftsmen were replaced by industrial materials because these required only unskilled workers for their assembly. It never occurred to functionalists that these industrial materials should be economized due to scarcities.

Yet, it was limits to material resources and the pollution associated with their extraction and use that drove the environmental movement in the 1960s and early 1970s. Measured by this new standard of efficiency, modern architecture was deficient. The most insightful environmental critic of modern architecture was Peter Blake, a former true believer who fell from the modernist fold in the 1960s. In a series of articles begun in 1974 and subsequently published as a book, he first attacked modernism's adaptation of the auto industry's policy of planned obsolescence. In their fetish for the new, modern architects produced throw-away buildings with short life spans geared to accelerated depreciation allowances. Their cheap materials did not withstand even the slightest indignities of weather or age. Stucco and poured-in-place concrete cracked and stained, flat roofs leaked and collapsed, metal panels bowed, plastics cracked, and sealants bled. Because traditional materials such as stone, brick, and wood lasted hundreds of years, it was less wasteful and cheaper in the long run to build with them and use craft methods. Further, instead of tearing down the old to make way for new buildings, Blake declared that it was less costly to refurbish old buildings for new uses.[39]

Modern architecture wasted resources not only in initial construction, Blake argued, but also in daily use. This was especially true of glass-and-steel skyscrapers, whose plate-glass curtain walls caused tremendous heat loss and gain and caused power bills to soar. Further, to absorb wind loads, tall glass buildings had to be cross-braced between columns and anchored with foundations so deep that they endangered neighboring buildings. Blake also attacked modernist city planning, declaring the Radiant City to be in fact the Wasteful City and the Environmentally Destructive City. The decentralized and functionally zoned cities planned by modernists were absolutely dependent on the automobile and its ever-expanding road and parking surfaces, all of which wasted resources and destroyed the environment. Such cities wasted resources not only in transportation but also in underutilization, for many specialized areas like downtown office districts stood idle for large portions of the average day and week.[40]

273

Finally, Blake attacked the modernist faith in mass-production methods and materials. With the authority of a practicing architect, he declared that buildings assembled from prefabricated materials invariably cost more than conventionally built structures, because economic and political fragmentation prevented the standardization of materials. Capitalist supplier firms competed for market share by designing unique products with incompatible dimensions, while local officials adopted varying building codes adapted to their meteorological and political climates. Finally, consumers also undermined standardization by their preference for variety. Just as they resisted Ford's standardized, black Model T, consumers resisted standardized housing in an attempt to express individuality. And all these barriers to standardized, mass-produced buildings were compounded in the underdeveloped world, where modernists held out their architecture as a panacea for housing problems. Another critic of modernism, Brent Brolin, noted that attempts to build modern architecture in the Third World were disastrously inefficient, largely due to the high costs of imported industrial materials. Besides, the modernist effort to save human labor with industrial materials made little economic sense in these countries, where skilled labor was in plentiful supply, as were natural building materials adapted to local conditions.[41]

During this period arguments that "backwardness" had its advantages acquired an increasing number of adherents, and not all were grounded in environmental values. Drawing on phenomenological concerns, many young architects argued that traditional building was preferable because it brought humans into harmony with nature. They proposed a new architectural vision of nature as an end in itself, rather than a recalcitrant means to combat. Thus, many during this period looked to preindustrial, vernacular styles for models of an architecture that was both environmentally responsible and meaningful.[42]

The Technological Critique: Modernism as Outmoded

Not all critiques of modernism emerging in the 1960s rejected its ideals of technological progress and the future for a validation of nature and the past. Architectural revolutionaries like Archigram, Superstudio, and Archizoom berated their modernist elders for their sclerotic failure to keep abreast of the latest technological developments. The problem with so-called modern architecture, these hip young technophiles asserted, was not its goals of progress and mass production but its backward technological means for achieving them. For them, modernists remained wedded to a Fordist view of standardized, centralized, and hierarchical technologies, while developments now made possible technologies that were more flexible, decentralized, and individual. Get with the technological times, screamed these young militants. Abandon your standardized skyscrapers, symbols of collective enslavement to work, and get hip to the individual freedom of consumer play made possible by the revolution in communications and electronics.

This critique of modernism as technologically backward was concentrated in countries that came to Fordism late, after the Second World War. The British and Italians were at the forefront, while the Japanese and French were also involved. All had installed Fordist institutions under American tutelage after the war, and were experiencing the first wave of mass consumerism when economic growth slowed in the early 1960s. Because Fordism was still in its infancy, this downturn was experienced not as a crisis of the system, as in the United States, but as a stall on the path to future development. To solve this problem young architects and others called for accelerated technical innovation that shifted focus from the standardized, stable technology of production to the flexible and mobile technology of consumption. Sounding very much like Americans during the Great Depression, many Europeans argued that they could consume their way out of recession by pioneering advanced consumer technologies.

The intellectual progenitor of this technological critique of modern architecture was Reyner Banham, who during the 1950s had been associated with Alison and Peter Smithson's move toward a popular consumer aesthetic. By the 1960s the Smithsons had moved on to more conventional modernism, leaving Banham and others to pioneer a more technological consumer aesthetic. Banham launched the technological critique of modernism with his 1960 book *Theory and Design in the First Machine Age*, which argued that modern architecture was stuck in an early stage of technological development that was inappropriate for the needs of contemporary society. The first machine age, Banham argued, originated in 1912 and was marked by the emergence of machines of individual consumption, like the automobile. Early modernists built their machine aesthetic on the simple, rectilinear forms of mass-produced cars, assuming these were the timeless forms of machine rationality. They ignored the real logic underlying modern technology, which was, Banham asserted, "an unhaltable trend to constantly accelerating change." Already by the 1930s these early auto forms were superceded by the technical demands of streamlining, but they were not completely outmoded until the second machine age emerged after the Second World War. Marked by the invention of new consumer technologies like television, this new stage required rapidly changing products and styles to stimulate consumer demand. Since the modernist aesthetic of standardized and timeless forms could not perform this new economic function, architects should abandon it, Banham argued, and look to the popular culture of consumer technologies for the necessary variety and flexibility. He cited as an example of a technologically up-to-date architecture the buildings of Buckminster Fuller, which were designed like automobiles for mass production and planned obsolescence.[43]

A year after Banham's attack on modernism, a British group named Archigram emerged to implement his critique. David Greene, the group's poet, expressed Archigram's intentions thus in its first newsletter: "A new generation of architecture must arise with forms and spaces which seem to reject the precepts of 'Modern' yet in fact, retains these precepts. We have chosen to bypass the decaying Bauhaus image which is an insult to functionalism." For Archigram and others in this school, the new technologies of the 1960s could improve not only functionalist architecture but also society, laying the foundation for a world of flexibility, individuality, mobility, and leisure. Emerging in the interwar period of material scarcity, modern architecture had idealized and aestheticized the technology of mass production, for it saw in more efficient and productive work the salvation of society. In the postwar era of abundance, however, scarcity was conquered, and economic efforts shifted from the production of goods to their consumption, which was facilitated by the fantastic aesthetic of the suburbs. These rebels of the sixties took mass production for granted and sought to shape the entire environment into a unified landscape of leisured mass consumption modeled on the growing variety and individuality of consumer goods. They took as their task ensuring that the leisure hours liberated by mass-production efficiencies would be fun and fulfilling. Archizoom, an Italian group of radical technophiles, wrote of this new society of play: "To become the master of one's own life, one must first of all *free oneself from work*....Only by rejecting work as an extraneous presence in one's life can one picture a new use for the home: a perpetual laboratory for one's own creative faculties, which are continually being tried and continually being surpassed."[44] To hold the interest of humans increasingly focused on play, the techno-radicals argued that the landscape had to be flexible, changing with the mood and whims of people. They held that with the proper sort of materials, architecture could be just as changeable and disposable as automobiles. Archigram wrote: "'Fashion' is a dirty word, so is 'temporary,' so is 'flashy.' Yet it is the creation of these things that are necessarily fashionable, temporary or flashy that has more to do with the vitality of cities than 'monument buildings.'" The group called for housing to be constructed as an expendable, throwaway consumer product, using the latest, lightweight, space-age materials. An environment of play would also demand a great deal of variety and individuality because, the technophiles asserted, the standardized similarity of modernism led to alienation. Archigram argued that individuality could be achieved by each person using standardized parts to build her own unique dwelling. The extremes to which this consumer individuality could go was revealed by Archizoom, which wrote: "Not a single culture, but one for each individual....Creating culture today is no longer—at least it shouldn't be—the privilege of a few intellectuals....This is an inalienable right to act, modify, form and destroy the surrounding environment." But even conceding to these techno-radicals the point that in a democratic society all should have the right to shape the environment, one could still ask why this right should be expressed in a multitude of individually constructed cultures, instead of a common culture constructed by all. The answer lies in the fact that the new consumer technologies idealized by these architects were already molded by the demands of the marketplace, which invariably conceives of goods as commodities sold to individuals and is incapable of delivering public goods that are appropriated collectively.[45]

This same hyperindividuality was also evident in the distinguishing characteristic of the environment postulated by these young idolaters of technology—mobility. For Archigram, Archizoom, Superstudio, and others, the permanence and immobility of modernist structures were prima facie evidence of their oppressiveness. To be established was to be part of the establishment; to be confined was to be encumbered. The microelectronic revolution obviated the need for permanent structures, and allowed each individual to construct her own environment and carry it with her. For these technophiles, nomadism became the ideal. Archigram's David Greene wrote: "It is likely that under the impact of the second machine age the need for a house (in the form of permanent static container) as a part of man's psychological make-up will disappear. With apologies to the master [Le Corbusier], the house is a appliance for carrying with you, a city is a machine for plugging into." With permanent structures gone, the institutions housed in them would have no place to establish themselves. They would be replaced, according to Archigram, by the "moment-village," the temporary and chance encounters of individual nomads passing in the night of perpetual fun.[46]

Of course, the old avant-garde of the 1920s similarly stressed movement and change to facilitate the restructuring and rationalization of a production system plagued by scarcity. But however well adapted to the movement of labor and capital in early Fordism, modern architecture's approach to mobility was too collective and productivist for these 1960s rebels. The skyscraper and housing estate spoke of masses of bureaucrats and workers circulating as collectivities and focused on production. For these rebels, individuality within consumption was now seen as the salvation of humanity. So they went beyond modernism's collectivized movement of production to the individualized movement of consumption. But their critique never questioned modernism's underlying presumption that the solution to social problems lay in an architecture that pioneered new technological means.

How to Fix Modern Architecture: Aesthetic Cures for Modernism's Ills

All of the critiques of modern architecture emerging in this tumultuous decade carried at least implicit cures, most of which retained many of modernism's achievements. Few proposed a total return to historical styles and methods, for by this period most buildings were constructed of industrial materials manufactured in factories. Most critics of modernism proposed to merely take these established facts and go beyond the machine aesthetic to different styles of building. The major critiques lined up with stylistic solutions as follows:

> The social and political critics, who argued that modernism was elitist, proposed a populist aesthetic based on the mass culture of commerce and entertainment.

> The phenomenological critics, who argued that modernism was meaningless, proposed a historicist aesthetic that tapped the established meanings of architectural types.

> The environmental critics, who argued that modernism was wasteful, proposed a natural aesthetic that reconciled humanity to the environment.

> The technological critics, who argued that modernism was outmoded, proposed a new technological expressionism that captured the individuality and mobility of consumer products.

Although divided by the specifics of their aesthetics, all these solutions shared an aesthetic/spatial fallacy. All of these architectural critics assumed that societal problems were largely caused by the look and arrangement of the material environment, and could hence be solved by rearranging space and its aesthetics. All failed to connect the problems identified with their deeper roots in the social relations of Fordist capitalism. None of the major schools of architectural criticism questioned the hierarchical relations of mass production or the institutions of mass consumption that legitimated them. For the vast majority of architects in this "radical" generation, what most needed revolutionizing were the forms and relations of things in space, not the forms and relations of people in history. Theirs was ultimately the fallacy of reification—mistaking relations between people for relations between things. Of course, revolutionizing society *also* involves reshaping things, for every society realizes its social relations in specific aesthetic and spatial forms. So changing social relations in time also changes the forms of things in space. But it is a fallacy to believe the converse—that changing things necessarily changes society. The ultimate success or failure of these architectural cures for modernism's ailments thus depended upon the social struggles to change Fordist capitalism that emerged after 1973.

Historicism: The Search for Meaning in a Reified Past

For phenomenological critics, who accused modern architecture of being meaningless, the solution lay in introducing into modern buildings and cities the meaningful symbols of the past. They argued that modernism, with its focus on movement and change, failed to fulfill the human values of stability and rootedness, that is, being at home in the world. While the newness of modern architecture sought to express a rupture in time and place, the historical references that these architects proposed attaching to buildings were meant to reassert a continuity of both, thus giving people a sense of rooted permanence in an otherwise rapidly changing society. As Dutch architect Aldo van Eyck wrote in 1967: "Architects nowadays are pathologically addicted to change.... This, I suggest, is why they tend to sever the past from the future, with the result that the present is rendered emotionally inaccessible, without temporal dimension....So let's start with the past for a change and discover the unchanging condition of man." A sense of permanence within the vicissitudes of history was also what Aldo Rossi hoped to capture with his architectural types. Time and again in *The Architecture of the City* he referred to types as "permanent" and "constant," adaptable to many functions as the city changes with the ebb and flow of time. For Rossi the role of the architect was not to invent new forms but to adapt the inventory of forms handed down from history and established in the collective memory to the solution of the new problems presented by the city.[47]

Historicists like Rossi and Van Eyck also advocated establishing a continuity of place, a sense that the landscape was a unified and unique whole with a particular purpose. Modern architecture was said to destroy the existing city fabric, by either replacing it wholesale with a homogeneous aesthetic or creating an incremental newness that clashed with the older buildings around it. The result was either a disorienting sameness or a defiant difference. To reestablish a continuity of place architects of the 1960s pioneered an approach known as contextualism. Advocated in particular by Colin Rowe, this approach held that new buildings must acknowledge the historic architecture of their location by aesthetically referring to its scale, aesthetic, and placement. This did not mean that the new architecture had to reproduce the historic styles of older buildings, but merely that it should make sufficient aesthetic acknowledgment of its neighbors to create a unified sense of place that made people feel at home. With a similar purpose, Aldo Rossi developed his concept of architectural types into a system he called analogical architecture, which required the architect building in an old city to make formal analogies to the archetypes of the architectural surroundings. In this way a city could grow and change, but still retain a unity around which human identities were constructed.[48]

Some straight historical revivals and reproductions did emerge in this period. But most architects did not consider simple revivalism a solution to the problems of modern architecture, for it ignored the changed architectural demands of industrial society. The vast majority of historicists in the 1960s acknowledged the modern demands for new programs and materials, and merely sought to borrow the forms of the old to place on the new in order to recreate the feeling of stability that people associated with history. What was borrowed by the historicists was not the concrete *content* of historical architecture but its abstract *forms*, stripped of the particulars of program and construction. As Giulio Carlo Argan, an advocate of the Italian neoliberty movement, wrote of the formation of types: "In the 'type' they [historical buildings] are deprived of their character and of their true quality as forms; by sublimation into a type they assume the indefinite value of an image or a sign. Through this reduction of preceding works of art to a 'type,' the artist frees himself from being conditioned by a definite historical form, and neutralizes the past." Through abstraction, forms were taken out of the specific social context that produced them, and rendered free-floating signifiers with the ability to evoke timeless feelings. Aldo Rossi himself said of types that their "suppression of precise boundaries in time and space" allowed them to become "archetypal objects whose common emotional appeal reveals timeless concerns." These abstract historical types thus became a kind of formalism, a way of escaping the agonizing vicissitudes of history into a timeless realm of pure forms. Already in 1966 Rossi was citing Claude Lévi-Strauss's structural anthropology of primitive spaces to validate his idea of timeless forms revealed in history. The structural linguistics of Ferdinand de Saussure and its derivative discipline of semiotics were also increasingly used during the decade to argue for the idea of forms revealed in history but originating in some universal cognitive structure outside the flux of time.[49]

Rossi presented an example of these decontextualized and reified historical forms in his Gallaratese apartment block in Milan, begun in 1969. The structure was a long, shallow building of reinforced concrete whose major element was a seemingly endless portico of repeated piers, surmounted by equally long rows of identically square windows. These historical types were from traditional Milanese tenement blocks, Rossi claimed, and the long corridor signified "a life-style bathed in everyday occurrences, domestic intimacy, and varied personal relationships." The architecture of this new residential district in late industrial Milan evoked the intimate lives of the extended families of the poor in the early industrial city. But it did so without conveying any historical sense of either the vitality or poverty of such tenements. The Italian tenement of the nineteenth century would have been more decorated than Rossi's flat concrete facade with punched out windows. Decorative moldings, window boxes, and shutters would surely have been present, alongside signs of poverty, such as

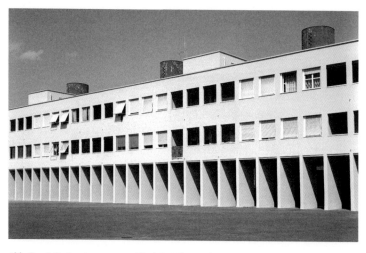

Aldo Rossi, Gallaratese quarter, Block D, Milan, Italy, 1973 (Photograph Arne Maasik)

Aldo Rossi, House of the Dead at San Cataldo Cemetery, Modena, Italy, 1971 (Wolfgang Schwager/ Artur/View)

chipped-off stucco. But Rossi's historical type was emptied of any content that identified the historically situated lives and struggles of a particular period. As Manfredo Tafuri has written, Rossi's reified typologies created "an emptied sacrality: an experience of fundamental immobility and of the eternal recurrence of geometrical emblems reduced to ghosts."[50]

Ghosts of buildings, spectral forms of life from a past emptied of any real content—this was what Rossi and the other historical typologists offered. The same rigidly regular distribution of square windows punched out of a flat and featureless facade was used by Rossi as the typology of his 1971 House of the Dead at the San Cataldo Cemetery. Both buildings, only one of which was actually used as an ossuary, seemed to be dead, timeless memorials to life that existed in some indistinct past. Neither bore any marks of human construction, which would have given clues about what sort of workers constructed them under what sort of production relations. Both replaced the traditional method of masonry construction, which spoke of pre- or early industrial craftsmen working under the quasi autonomy of the guild system, with smooth surfaces of colored concrete that were historically mute. In his poem "A Worker Reads History," Bertolt Brecht challenged such obliterations of the role of labor in history, writing:

Who built the seven gates of Thebes?
The books are filled with names of kings.
Was it kings who hauled the craggy blocks of stone?

Although the names of ancient slaves went unrecorded in the history books, their travails could nonetheless be read in the architecture, which spoke of back-breaking labor massed and commanded by a powerful few. But Rossi's abstract, historical typologies covered over the marks of construction that might have testified to history created through human effort, under hardships, inequalities, and struggles.[51]

The historical typologies of the Italian neoliberty movement sought to reintroduce meaning into modern architecture by creating a sanitized and reified past, a repository of positive images stripped of the social labors and struggles that propel history. They created myths, as defined by Roland Barthes in *Mythologies*. Here he has conceived of myth as a second-order form of signification, in which a sign of one meaning system enters into another as mere form, alienated from its original content as provided by human history. Once stripped of this real content, the sign enters into the second system and adopts whatever meaning is assigned to it. The architects of the neoliberty movement similarly stripped architectural forms of the historical facts of their construction, and then reinvested them with the soothing meanings of stability and place craved by people living in a social system whose only purpose was constant change and universal exchange.[52]

The communication of reified, mythological meanings in architecture was not confined during this period to those drawing on the symbols of the distant past. A group of young American architects sought to make modern architecture meaningful again by turning it into a formal typology. Known as the New York Five, Peter Eisenman (b. 1932), Michael Graves (b. 1934), John Hejduk (1929–2000), Charles Gwathmey (b. 1938), and Richard Meier (b. 1934) were united by an attempt to revalidate the purist aesthetic of early modernism in order to revive the heroism and innocence of the now tainted movement. Eisenman, the most verbose of the group, vehemently rejected the avant-garde's insistence that their aesthetic forms expressed social meanings and values, especially efficiency and functionalism: "The making of form is more than the satisfaction of functional requirements and more than the creation of aesthetically pleasing objects, but rather the exposition of formal relationships." The meaning of his and, by inference, the other Five's architecture, lay, he insisted, not in social and historical analogies but in abstract and universal regularities beyond time and place.[53]

The work of the Five was vaguely and formally reminiscent of Le Corbusier's early work, but lacked his direct references to mass production and technology. Like the early modernists, the Five's work consisted largely of private houses, but the modernists built houses that looked like factories and apartment blocks, while the Five's houses looked like private, bourgeois escapes from such urban collectivities. And while the early avant-garde used simple, rectilinear shapes to express a social concern for efficiency, the American formalists used them as pure, superfluous forms, expressing nothing more than themselves. This was clear in Michael Graves's Benacerraf House addition, in which most of the space formed by the pure white planes was an exterior void, serving no function beyond communicating a trendy retro-avant-garde look. Thus, to validate the modernist avant-garde as heroic and innocent and dissociate it from the commercial taint acquired in the 1950s and 1960s, these young Americans stripped it of its political program of technocracy and left only mute forms. Modernism itself was mythologized and became a part of the historicist solution to its own ills.[54]

Naturalism: The Aesthetic Reconciliation with Nature
Closely related philosophically and aesthetically to the historicists were the architects embodying the rising environmental consciousness of the decade.

Michael Graves, Benacerraf House addition, Princeton, New Jersey, 1969
(Photograph Laurin McCracken/courtesy Michael Graves and Associates)

Their arguments that modern industrialism and modern architecture alienated humanity from nature implied that preindustrial society and its architecture cultivated a closer relation to the natural environment. Like the historicists, the naturalists turned to the past for aesthetic vision. But while the historicists looked to historical architecture to connect humanity to its own history, the naturalists looked to the past to connect humanity to nature. Consequently, the latter generally concentrated on the rural vernacular styles of preindustrial societies, which were thought to embody forms naturally adapted to the physical environment.

The popularity of this naturalist position was indicated by a 1964 exhibit at the Museum of Modern Art. Entitled Architecture without Architects, the exhibit polemically compared, in the words of the accompanying catalog, "the serenity of the architecture in so-called undeveloped countries with the architectural blight in industrial countries." Unlike trained architectural experts, who created a blight upon the landscape with concerns for prestige and profits, the untutored builders of communal architecture "demonstrate talent for fitting their buildings into the natural surroundings. Instead of trying to 'conquer' nature, as we do, they welcome the vagaries of climate and the challenge of topography." The exhibit included vernacular styles that ingeniously made use of natural materials, captured animal wastes for use as fuel and fertilizer, and fought extremes of climate structurally without artificial energy sources. These adaptations to nature's own economy not only saved resources but also made for human habitation that looked and felt like part of nature, not the imposition of an alien rationality.[55]

As the revolt against the machinery of postwar Fordism grew in this decade, the interest in the rural vernacular also escalated, for, as Gene Kavanaugh argued, periods of change "seem always to bring with them a need to get back to the earth, or to connect in some way with the deepest tribal knowledge." Regional styles, evolved in adjustment to local climates and materials, were popular during the 1950s in mass-produced suburban housing, but the 1960s saw their revival in the elite architectural field. One of the most important uses of a regional vernacular in this period was Sea Ranch, a condominium complex by Charles Moore (1925–1993) and associated architects on the coast of Sonoma County in northern California. Completed in 1965, his design drew on the Bay Region style, which was so well adapted to this rugged coastal landscape that the condos seemed to have grown naturally from it. The simple, boxy volumes were reminiscent of the humble barns and ranch houses of the area's past, while the single-shed roofs echoed the gentle

Moore, Lyndon, Turnbull
& Whitaker, Sea Ranch
condominium, Sonoma
County, California, 1965
(Photograph Christopher
Noll/© Turnbull Griffin
Haesloop)

rises of the landscape's meadows and coastal hills. Rough-hewn redwood sid-ing befit an area abundant with this wood, and with age it turned a soft gray that mimicked the rock outcrops on the coast below. In other works of this same mid-1960s period, Moore utilized the white stucco of the Mission style to fit the sunny, Mediterranean climate of southern California. Although both the Faculty Club (1968) at the Santa Barbara campus of the University of California and the Burns House (1974) in Santa Monica had kitschy interiors, their stucco exteriors blended sensitively into their landscapes.[56]

The styles of not only the rural vernacular but also the urban vernacular were revived during this period to achieve a more natural, environmentally friendly aesthetic. The preservationist movement also used an environmental/economic justification for saving old buildings, arguing that it was a waste of resources to build new buildings on open land when old buildings within the urban fabric could be renovated. As Aldo van Eyck wrote, "the world can no longer afford such waste, nor can it afford to overlook the right of people to maintain both the built form and the social fabric of their domicile if that is their choice." Van Eyck's renewal project in Zwolle, the Netherlands renovated existing row houses. Others sought to save old factories and warehouses as well. Joseph Esherick (1914–98) and William Wurster (1895–1973), leaders in the Bay Region style, pioneered such renovations on the San Francisco bayfront. Wurster redesigned an 1850s chocolate factory and turned it into an upscale shopping complex called Ghirardelli Square, while Esherick similarly remod-eled a bayside cannery built in 1894 for retail use. Compared to the sprawl-ing, single-story steel and concrete factories of the Fordist era, the red-brick, multistoried industrial vernacular of these old buildings seemed charming and more compatible with both the natural surroundings and human beings. Such

Moore, Lyndon, Turnbull & Whitaker, Faculty Club at the University of California, Santa Barbara, 1968 (Photograph Tony Mastres/University of California, Santa Barbara)

William Wurster, Ghirardelli Square, San Fransicso, 1965 (Photograph by author)

connotations were possible, however, only because few shoppers remembered the hot, unpleasant work of these factories or the pollution caused when they dumped their wastes into the bay.[57]

The emerging naturalistic aesthetic of this period sought to reconcile humanity not only to the nature outside but also to the nature within. The modernists eliminated all aesthetic references to the human body in their attempt to elevate reason over nature. Modern architecture was a residence for the mind, not the physical body. The 1960s revolt against the rational machine resurrected the body as a legitimate metaphor in architecture. Kent Bloomer and Charles Moore wrote in *Body, Memory, and Architecture* that the human body provided the foundation for the human experience of the environment. The body influenced not just the spaces but also the aesthetics of architecture, they argued, for people felt at home in something that looked like them. So people routinely perceived buildings as having eyes, mouths, and feet. Architects during this period revived the tradition of anatomical metaphors in their revolt against the inhumanity of modernism. One of the most whimsical examples was Stanley Tigerman's Daisy House, commissioned by the owner of several Florida strip clubs. The house was obviously phallic in plan, possessing a long, projecting wing with a rounded end that was flanked by two smaller, testicular protrusions. Although this masculine penetration of the landscape may not have been what the environmentalists had in mind when they spoke of man merging with nature, this whimsical exercise did remind people that humans

Stanley Tigerman, Daisy House, Porter, Indiana, 1978 (Photograph Howard N. Kaplan, Chicago/© Stanley Tigerman, Stanley Tigerman and Associates)

produced and used architecture with their bodies, as well as their minds. Any attempt to create a natural architecture to counter the abstract rationality of modernism would have to recover the natural foundation of humanity and not just the nonhuman environment.[58]

Populism: The Search for Democracy through Popular Culture

The young architects who mounted the social and political critique of modernism were, like phenomenological critics, concerned with meaning, arguing that modern architecture undemocratically imposed its elitist codes on the people. While a few architects proposed a more democratic design process that allowed the people to voice their own meanings, most of the populists believed that they already knew the language of the masses—it was the vernacular of America's consumer market. The populists proposed simply to transfer this commercial code to the high art of building. Although this populist aesthetic found adherents around the world, its main practitioners were Americans. The United States had pioneered the entertainment aesthetic in architecture during the 1920s and kept it alive in the suburbs even as modernism thrived in the cities of the 1950s. When Fordism fell into crisis in the 1960s, dragging modern architecture with it, American architects found a vital alternative just beyond the city limits. Further, unlike Europeans, Americans had little preindustrial history to draw on for aesthetic alternatives to modernism. So many American architects turned naturally to mass culture for popular meanings with which to infuse an increasingly discredited and meaningless modernism.

The ideological justification for this move toward mass culture was offered mainly by Robert Venturi and Denise Scott Brown. Working solo in the mid-1960s, Venturi launched his first critique of modernism in 1966 with the publication of *Complexity and Contradiction in Architecture*. Not yet familiar with the populist influences of Scott Brown and Herbert Gans, this critique followed the historicist tendencies of the Europeans of the day. Venturi took modernism to task for creating a narrow and elitist language that could not "accommodate existing needs for variety and communication." He declared that "I am for richness of meaning rather than clarity of meaning," and, in contradiction of Mies' less-is-more dictum, quipped that "less is a bore." Venturi proposed to enrich the impoverished meanings of modernism by the inclusion of abstract historical forms. Sounding remarkably like Aldo Rossi, he called for lifting architectural elements "abstractly from their historical context," and inserting them into the new, where "they contain in their changed use and expression some of their past meaning as well as their new meaning."[59]

While the bulk of the early *Complexity* argued for the complex and contra-dictory use of historical forms, Venturi anticipated his later populism by also arguing for the inclusion of forms from contemporary commercial culture. Use of such "banal and vulgar" elements was justified, he averred, by their very existence: "Architects can bemoan or try to ignore them or even try to abolish them, but they will not go away." Architects' power to shape the environment was diminishing, Venturi continued, necessitating a lowering of their ambi-tions to accommodate the status quo: "Industry promotes expensive industrial and electronic research but not architectural experiments," he recognized, so realistic architects had to work with the elements handed them by this com-mercial culture. But they could still achieve complex and contradictory forms by using these elements in unusual ways, Venturi argued, citing the example of pop art. Besides, he went on, the seeming chaos of commercial Main Street was actually organized in a complex and contradictory clash of scales and contexts. If architects could blend some historical forms into this honky-tonk landscape, perhaps America could be saved from the boring simplicity of modernism.[60]

At the end of the book, Venturi included examples of his own work that supposedly illustrated his principles of inclusive and complex architecture. The only large-scale project was Guild House in Philadelphia, a six-story apartment building for the elderly commissioned by the Quakers and completed in 1963. True to Venturi's philosophy, the building was a deceptively complex blend of banal commercialism and sophisticated historicism, held in a contradictory

Venturi and Rauch, Cope and Lippincott, Guild House, Philadelphia, 1963
(Courtesy Venturi, Scott Brown and Associates)

unity of form. Guild House accommodated the historical context of its neighborhood of traditional row houses with its dark-brown brick and ordinary,
double-hung windows. Also yielding to the ordinary commercial vernacular of
the city was the large, garish sign over the entrance announcing the building's
name, as if subsidized housing for the elderly required hawking. But a closer
inspection by the architectural cognoscenti revealed a number of sophisticated
historical forms. The wings containing the apartments stepped back symmetrically from the entrance facade in a manner resembling a Renaissance palace.
The entrance facade also elaborated the Renaissance theme by superimposing
on the six-floor building the illusory divisions of three monumental stories.
Directly above this contradictory entrance composition of ordinary commercial and Renaissance forms, was the crown jewel of the building, a nonfunctional television antenna in gold anodized aluminum. Venturi claimed that this
seemingly ordinary reference to America's mass culture itself carried contradictory meanings. "The antenna...can be interpreted in two ways: abstractly, as
sculpture in the manner of Lippold, and as a symbol of the aged, who spend so
much time looking at T.V."[61]

The complex and contradictory juxtaposition of forms demonstrated in
Guild House subsequently became known as double-coding, a defining characteristic of postmodern architecture. Double-coding incorporated elements
from both mass culture and the high art of architecture, thus communicating
simultaneously with architectural professionals and the broader public. At
this stage of his career, Venturi achieved such dual meanings by using true aesthetic forms that maintained a distinction between the material form of communication, the signifier, and the underlying meaning or content, the signified.
Modernists also communicated through this form-content model, using the
forms of machines to express the content of Fordist social relations. Because
they did so, their architecture often inadvertently exposed the class contradictions of this emerging social structure. The same machine forms that appeared
beautiful and orderly to the technocratic class that controlled them appeared
ugly and exploitative to the working masses subordinated to them. Venturi's
early work similarly allowed contradictory interpretations by communicating
social content in aesthetic forms. Putting the form of a Renaissance palace on a
cheap brick building with a TV antenna created a clash of forms that served to
remind people of the clash of classes whose contradictory interests were represented and hierarchicalized in these forms. At the Guild House Venturi's ironic
antenna-cum-sculpture was the center of this clash of interpretations. While
the architectural elite appreciated its form as sculptural, as Venturi advised,

many common folk interpreted it as a mockery of the elderly's immersion in mass media. The Quakers were not amused, and had the antenna removed. But the controversy over the antenna testified to the fact that at this stage Venturi's work was indeed complex and contradictory, exposing through form the contradictory content of the Fordist-Keynesian society, which cared for its no-longer-productive aged in a tenement palace and entertained them with gold-plated kitsch.[62]

In the late 1960s, however, Venturi began to move away from this use of contradictory forms toward an architecture of simple, one-dimensional symbolism. This move was completed in *Learning from Las Vegas*. Here the concern for historical forms was dropped in favor of a full-blown embrace of the type of commercial symbolism represented by the Las Vegas strip. Venturi et al. now justified such symbolism not, as in *Complexity and Contradiction*, by a grudging expediency but by a militant populism that declared it to be the democratic language of the masses. This shift in the political justification of mass symbolism was surely due to the influence of Scott Brown, who learned this populist line from Herbert Gans. But the difference between *Complexity* and *Learning* was not merely in the political justification of popular elements, but also in their aesthetic treatment. While in the early book these elements were treated as forms, that is, as multidimensional spaces defined by program and structure, in *Learning from Las Vegas* they were treated as symbols, one-dimensional icons of direct, depthless communication requiring no interpretation: "This architecture of styles and signs is antispatial; it is an architecture of communication over space; communication dominates space as an element in the architecture and in the landscape."[63]

The authors of *Learning from Las Vegas* clarified this distinction by proclaiming that formal architecture produced "the duck," while symbolic architecture yielded "the decorated shed." The duck was a building in which the meaning was embodied in the overall spatial form. (The name came from a Long Island poulterer whose drive-in store was shaped like a duck.) The decorated shed, by contrast, was a building whose meaning was communicated by applied ornament. Las Vegas casinos were examples of decorated sheds, for their symbolic fronts of Roman columns, Aladdin's lamps, and neon signs hid the standardized hotel buildings behind. Historical architecture, the authors declared, had often been both a duck and a decorated shed. Gothic cathedrals, for example, molded overall space to convey religious meanings, while also appending symbolic facades of portals and stained-glass windows. But modern architecture had righteously purged buildings of direct symbolism and ornament, demanding that form itself be the only communication. The authors declared, however, that modernist forms were dead ducks, and decorated sheds of the commercial vernacular were better adapted to contemporary society.[64]

Their main argument for the simplistic symbolism of commercial sheds was the populist assertion that this was what the "middle-class" masses wanted, and it was undemocratic to force on them the modernist ducks of aesthetic elitists. But the authors appended to this other reasons that were rather functionalist. First, decorated sheds were said to be cheaper to build, for they used standardized building systems for their functional space and slapped cheap ornament on the front. Modernist ducks were more expensive because the whole building was unique. But this "economy" of decorated sheds was peculiar to the wasteful consumer society that the authors took for granted. To attract attention and give consumers individuality, the casinos had to present a unique and changing image. And it was cheaper to differentiate and change the casino image by altering the symbolic facade than restructuring the whole building. Venturi et al. specifically referred to the automobile as the model for such obsolescence in buildings. They also invoked the auto in their second functionalist excuse for the decorated shed. The car accelerated travel to high speeds and separated buildings from the road by parking lots, thus preventing the slow, close inspection required to appreciate the forms in ducks. The vast spaces and split seconds of auto-mediated perception, they argued, demanded large-scale, immediately readable symbols to deliver commercial meanings. To adapt to these "functional demands" of the postwar consumer landscape, the Las Vegas casinos presented flashy, attention-grabbing facades to short-attention-span consumers racing by in their dream machines, hiding the ugly reality of standardized construction behind them. Similar excuses were offered for the facadism found on suburban developers' houses, which were also praised in *Learning from Las Vegas*.[65]

A final functional adaptation of decorated-shed architecture to the economy of consumer illusions was the rigid separation between inside and outside. Modern architecture sought to erase the barrier of the wall, opening up the inner workings of the building to the light of public scrutiny. But in Las Vegas the fragile, chancy consumer dreams manufactured inside casinos could not stand the scrutiny of daylight, so, Venturi et al. wrote, the gambling rooms were always dark and enclosed. This separation had the effect of privatizing and "disorient[ing]" the occupant in time and space." Such a privatized, somnambulant subjectivity was also cultivated by the configuration of the interior. The low, enclosed gambling rooms of the casinos provided, the authors wrote, a new monumentality, "a space for crowds of anonymous individuals without explicit connection with each other," "combin[ing] being together, yet separate." Thus isolated together in a comfortable cocoon that obliterated the external world of social production beyond their control, the consumers/gamblers could fancy themselves rugged individualists determining their own fates by deciding in which slot machine with predetermined odds to cast their coins.[66]

Another architect at the forefront of the populist movement, Charles Moore, also endorsed this new monumentality for a consumer society of privatized individuals. In two key articles of the 1960s, Moore wrote that the old monumentality, represented in the centralized industrial city, depended upon the existence of a social elite which controlled money and taste, and demanded public buildings of importance to testify to its rule. But a new, more decentralized and egalitarian society was emerging that demanded a more decentralized and individual monumentality. Moore argued that electronic media leveled corporate hierarchies into networks of instant communication that could immediately response to market demand. With no more "Establishment" to demand public display of power, the urban landscape became a homogeneous, decentralized fabric of private spaces testifying to individuality, of which southern California was the exemplar. The only monumental, public places in this landscape, Moore continued, were the private entertainment venues, such as Disneyland, and the freeways, where people came together as individual consumers constructing their own private fantasies. But Moore's "public" places were curious indeed, for there was no meeting, no interaction, no consensus formation, but mere movement in channels prearranged and preprogrammed by the designers, with the mere illusion of choice.[67]

The accounts by the populists of the "functions" of the decorated shed were no less ideological than the functionalism of modern architects. Both unquestioningly accepted the economic requirements of the capitalism of their day and adapted architecture to aesthetically meet them. In early Fordism, European modernists idealized the standardized, mechanical look of mass production not only to build cheaply but also to persuade the masses to conform to the requirements of technocrat power. In later Fordism, when stimulating mass consumption took priority over conformity to mass production, the entertainment architecture championed by the populists engineered superficial illusions of individuality to capture consumers. The authors of *Learning from Las Vegas* recognized that the aesthetics of Las Vegas and Disneyland "functioned" to fuel wasteful consumerism, but, like the modernists, they claimed to be neutral technicians of their age. Their role was not to question the values of Las Vegas, they declared, but to merely investigate these "methods of commercial persuasion," which could also "serve the purpose of civic and cultural enhancement." But as Theodor Adorno observed, the idea that society's means are neutral and can be put to a variety of ends is an illusion. What is functional is determined by a historically specific society's ends, but these ends leave their imprint on "the rationality of the means devised to achieve those ends." The means of commercial persuasion investigated by Venturi et al. were hopelessly contaminated with consumer society's ends of individual profits and class domination, and could never serve the common good.[68]

Venturi, Scott Brown, Moore, and other populist architects took the symbolic style of the mass-consumption economy of the 1960s and turned it into an aesthetic in the restricted field of architecture. In doing so they sought not to destroy high-art architecture but merely to, in the words of Venturi et al., "alter high culture to make it more sympathetic to current needs and issues." Through double-coding and irony, they proposed to speak to both the architectural elite and the popular culture, and hoped that such pluralistic expression would ultimately bridge the gap between classes: "Social classes rarely come together, but if they can make temporary alliances in the designing and building of multivalued community architecture, a sense of paradox and some irony and wit will be needed on all sides." One of the most interesting examples of this class-unifying, double-coded architecture was Venturi et al.'s 1967 entry in a competition for the National Football Hall of Fame. The front of their building was dominated by a billboard the size of a football field containing a continuous electronic display, an element clearly lifted from roadside commercial culture. Yet the architects also argued that it could be seen by the cognoscenti as analogous to the facade of a Gothic cathedral, with its similarly persuasive imagery of mosaics and statues. The double-coding continued on the interior, with its barrel-vaulted ceiling that was penetrated, also like a Gothic cathedral, by the buttresses of the billboard. Like their ecclesiastical counterparts, these buttresses created "chapels" along the interior, where football "relics" like Knut Rockne's sweater would be displayed. But on balance the project was so dominated by popular symbolism that the contradiction by historical forms was missed. Even though the vaulted ceiling was historical in form, this reference was engulfed by the images of football movies projected on it. Historical forms were treated as mere projection surfaces for the symbols of commercial culture, which flattened out their space and reduced them to depthless signs. Here art did not raise popular symbolism to the level of form, but was reduced to an empty vessel for commercial symbols.[69]

Venturi, Scott Brown and Izenour, National Football Hall of Fame project, 1967
(Courtesy Venturi, Scott Brown and Associates)

Even more one-dimensional was the entry of Venturi, Scott Brown, and Izenour in the competition for the Thousand Oaks Civic Center, in which they sought to use the aesthetic of commercial persuasion to symbolize community government. As the architects noted in their description of the project, if any community was amenable to expression through roadside commercial symbolism, it was this "sprawling, growing, impermanent California suburb," whose new civic center was to be located on a hill overlooking the Ventura Freeway. Venturi et al. gave Thousand Oaks a decorated civic shed, a group of low, cheap, modular buildings dominated by a couple of gaudy signs whose symbolism, the architects admitted, "even a child could understand and enjoy." The first of these signs was the words "Thousand Oaks" etched on the hillside berm in gigantic letters, which, they wrote, "substitute a symbolic image of Thousand Oaks for a nonexistent civic skyline and for the soon-to-be bulldozed oaks." In other words, this sign was an empty signifier that simultaneously stood in for and obscured the lack of a real community. The empty signifier also stood in for the nature that once defined the region but was a casualty of uncontrolled development. Nature was now only another nostalgic symbol to evoke a nonexistent past of California for commercial purposes. The second sign, which reinforced these simulated meanings, was a tower topped by a flagpole, a traditional symbol of civic centrality. But this touch of historical symbolism was combined with an unabashed gimcrack of commercialism, the neon-light outline of a live oak tree on the tower. Finally, reinforcing this commercial symbolism were large signs identifying government departments on balconies and facias, which were "to be read like today's special on the A&P windows." The message was clear—government too is a commodity, a service sold individually to taxpayers for their private consumption, not a collective enterprise defined by common interests.[70]

The decorated-shed aesthetic of Venturi and Scott Brown eschewed all of the complexity and contradiction of Venturi's earlier aesthetic of ambiguous architectural forms. In the decorated shed these forms became flat, symbolic facades emptied of any meaning beyond consumer hucksterism. Architectural forms thus became myths, floating signifiers stripped of their historical meanings and manipulated by the second-order signification system of extraneous, capitalist intent. And what these mythic symbols of decorated sheds forgot or hid was, as Barthes recognized, the fact that they were historically produced by humans under specific social relations. The eye-catching, differentiated facades visually hid the cheap, standardized construction of the hotels and service spaces behind them, and in doing so obscured the constraining order of production relations that modernists revealed. Class relations were also obscured in the decorated sheds by lowering elite art to the level of commercial kitsch demanded by the working masses. As long as the art forms consumed by the bourgeoisie were distinct and beyond the understanding of the masses, they were a constant reminder of class differences. However, when architects like Venturi, Scott Brown, and Moore stooped down to speak with the vernacular of commercial kitsch, class differences were visually obscured and Americans could be convinced that they were truly living in a classless utopia.

Techno-Radicalism: Liberation in the New Consumer Technologies
Similar in spirit to populism was the aesthetic movement that emerged from the technological critique of modernism as outmoded. With American populists, the largely European technophiles looked for aesthetic solutions in the present and future of mass consumption. But what they found aesthetically fascinating about consumer culture was not its symbolism but its technologies. Their adulation of the new technology of consumption was similar to the romantic modernism of the Depression era, which sought to restart a stalled system of mass production by focusing on the new technologies of mass consumption, such as streamlined cars and planes. In European countries and Japan, a similarly new and incomplete Fordism stalled in the 1960s, leaving some young architects to conclude that the solution lay in a future utopia of consumerism liberated by new technologies of microelectronics and telecommunications.

The technophiles of the 1960s created a new aesthetic for architecture based on the contemporary symbols of technological progress, including spacecraft, oil refineries, pleasure piers, and freeways. All these shared the characteristics of openness, circulation, and loose-coupling, which appealed to a generation of youth rebelling against the rigidly closed, bureaucratic society of mass production. Take, for example, spacecraft. When flight was atmospheric, planes and rockets were designed in unified shells to slip through the air. With the advent of space travel, however, overcoming air resistance was no longer necessary, so aerodynamic envelopes were cracked open to spill their functional elements freely out into space, usually hung on open lattice frameworks. In stark contrast to modernist glass-and-steel skyscrapers, whose oppressively unified envelopes pressed their components into an inflexible whole, such frameworks of parts were visually open and functionally flexible, and thus became visual metaphors for freedom from Fordist bureaucracies. These new technologies also represented the heightened mobility demanded by this generation. While postwar modernist architecture settled down to symmetry and stability, freeways and oil refineries testified directly to a constant, unfettered circulation of people and materials in a refreshingly chaotic freedom. The young technophiles of the 1960s took the light, open, circulatory look of these new technologies and fashioned an aesthetic that became known as megastructure.[71]

As the name implies, these technology-worshiping architects were initially interested in large-scale buildings that addressed the urban housing problems of the day. But their large structures were more varied, flexible, and individual than the modernist mass-housing schemes they criticized. Megastructuralist Moshe Safdie (b. 1938) argued that modernist high-rise projects created a "horrible life" for residents, while suburban single-family housing wasted land and destroyed community. Safdie and other megastructuralists sought a modern equivalent to the Mediterranean village, which combined a high-density community with individual variety. They also wanted their buildings to be joyous playgrounds for people free of the debilitating demands of work. They found that the new aesthetic of open frameworks with add-on elements accommodated all these criteria.[72]

The first architect to conceptually elaborate this solution was N. J. Habraken, in his 1961 book *Supports*. His alternative to modernist mass housing was publicly financed high-rise support structures, within which individuals would build single-family units from standardized parts. Such a scheme would have the economic advantages of high-density and standardized construction while simultaneously allowing individuality, mobility, and flexibility. Individual houses could be built, altered, even moved elsewhere, without altering the support framework. Further, although made of mass-produced parts, the houses could be assembled in different configurations to allow an endless variety, Habraken stated, just like mass-produced cars.[73]

One of the most appealing aspects of megastructure for young architects was that it provided for individuality while also imposing an overarching aesthetic order. Unlike the sprawling chaos of development through the private market, megastructure projects created an organizing framework that defined spaces and created urban unity. But within the bounds of this unity, individuals were given the freedom to build as they chose, allowing them to realize another goal of these architectural techno-rebels—fun and games. Habraken argued that while modernist mass housing was "a military parade" in which all moves were rigidly planned, his support-structure housing would be "a game which must be played to arrive at a result," a game in which everyone participated. Habraken envisioned his collective game of support-structure housing not

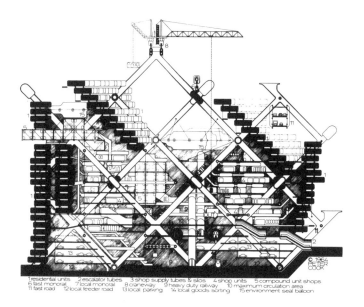

Peter Cook, Plug-In City project, 1964 (© Peter Cook, reprinted, by permission, from Peter Cook et al., *Archigram*. London: Studio Vista, 1972, 37)

replacing the old city wholesale but infiltrating its interstices, where "human diversity can rediscover itself in new relationships and develop its own community atmosphere." Other megastructuralists, like Japanese architect Arata Isozaki (b. 1931), saw their frameworks soaring high above the modernist city. His Space City project of 1960 showed dwellings on huge bridges that surmounted the devastation of the old city. As French megastructuralist Yona Friedman (b. 1923) wrote: "the ancient disorders and discontents of the cities could be overpassed, and a new world created in the sky, purified of the *membra disjecta* of past and exhausted civilizations on the ground below."[74]

Perhaps the most renowned advocates of megastructure were members of the British Archigram group, whose fantastically conceived but meticulously drafted projects of the mid-1960s made utopia seem buildable. Archigram's most famous megastructure project was Plug-In City of 1964, which Peter Cook (b. 1936), its main designer, described as "an investigation of what happens if the whole urban environment can be programmed and structured for change." The predominant feature of the city was a support framework constructed of tubes laid out diagonally to produce diamond-shaped voids. These nine-foot-diameter tubes also contained all circulation for people and goods. On top of the framework, gigantic cranes lifted mass-produced dwelling units into position within the voids, providing a flexible variety of space for offices, shops, residences, workplaces, and recreation. Just like mass-produced cars, which were also the model for this throwaway architecture, these housing units were carefully planned for obsolescence. Bathrooms and kitchens would last for three years; living rooms and bedrooms, five to eight years; workplaces, four years. Because each megastructure framework in the city would contain a different mix of units, depending upon the decisions of residents, each would have a different configuration, creating what Cook called the overriding feature of the design—"deliberate varietousness of each building outcrop: whatever else it was to be, this city was not going to be a deadly piece of built mathematics." Indeed, an axiomatic drawing of the whole city showed a dizzying variety of configurations, all built from the same units.

A second central feature of Plug-In City was mobility, which was objectified in the numerous circulation services and routes. The unstable diagonality of the frameworks themselves connoted movement, both vertical and lateral. And the gigantic cranes on top of the frameworks, which in the drawings were always occupied lifting and repositioning units, dominated the skyline of Plug-In City, reminding viewers that this was a city in motion. In fact, Archigram conceived of the owners of units moving frequently, and taking their obsolescent housing with them, like tent-toting nomads. Archigram's obsession with mobility led to another project in which the entire city was mobile, Ron Herron's (1930–1994) whimsical Walking City of 1964. His drawing depicted gigantic, buglike metal capsules stalking across New York's East River on telescoping legs. With the famous Manhattan skyline in the background, Herron's

Moshe Safdie, Habitat, Montréal, 1967 (Photograph Timothy Hursley/ courtesy Moshe Safdie and Associates)

project dreamed of the new city as a nomad, moving freely across the land-scape, sealed and self-contained against the pollution and corruption of the established modernist city.[76]

Although these fantastic manifestations of megastructure never moved beyond project stage, they did provided the inspiration for actual build-ings, the most famous of which was Moshe Safdie's Habitat housing. Part of the Montréal Expo of 1967, this was an informal agglomeration of precast-concrete room units stacked onto a frame by cranes. Although it was conceived as a model for low-cost housing, the only attempt to build housing based on Habitat was undertaken in Puerto Rico in 1974, and it had to be abandoned due to both technological and economic difficulties.[77] The unfortunate reality of megastructure was that it could not simply transcend the material realities of capitalist real estate development. As Peter Blake recognized, extensive pre-fabrication and standardization was a pipedream within a fragmented, mar-ket-driven building industry. Further, to allow for the flexibility of units, the support frameworks would have to provide a lot of redundant and unprofitable space for expansions and changes. Finally, these technophiles did not recog-nize the patent inefficiencies involved in millions of mobile people transport-ing bulky building components around with them whenever they changed residences. The popularity of megastructure was not driven, however, by eco-nomic realities but by the ideological promise to solve the contradiction inher-ent in Fordist capitalism between the individual and the community. To create the social unity necessary for the interdependent system of mass production, Fordism standardized and leveled individual differences in production and consumption. As part of the 1960s revolt against such standardization and bureaucratization, the megastructuralists promised to return individual free-dom, but within the context of an orderly and authentic community.

To fulfill this popular ideological promise megastructure was gradually reduced from a full-blown housing scheme to a mere aesthetic to add the look of movement and individuality to conventional buildings. This was the case for the megastructural Cumbernauld Town Centre (1967) in Scotland, designed by Geoffrey Copcutt. In an attempt to lend a newly built town the look of orga-nization as well as flexibility, Copcutt designed an open-ended hilltop frame and piled on it an agglomeration of civic functions. But the extendability of the frame was a mere illusion to disguise the reality of self-enclosure. The ideologi-cal promise of individuality and mobility were also on display in probably the most renowned of all megastructure buildings, the Centre Pompidou in Paris, designed by Richard Rogers (b. 1933) and Renzo Piano (b. 1937) and completed

Richard Rogers and Renzo Piano, Centre Pompidou, Paris, 1977 (Photograph Erich Lessing/Art Resource/NY)

in 1977. This art museum's six stories were constructed of a long-span, lattice-truss framework with no fixed walls, allowing for optimum flexibility of space for changing exhibits. All the services and mechanical equipment were hung in an external subframe, thus displaying a maze of color-coded pipes and ducts that looked like an oil refinery. The circulation of people was also externalized and aestheticized in a glass escalator tube that snaked its way up the west side of the center. Visitors inundated the center just to ride the escalator, thus turning an art museum for the edification of the masses into an amusement park ride reminiscent of Disneyland. So the megastructural promise of individuality within a differentiated community was dashed on the shoals of a mass culture that moved homogenized consumers in a meaningless and fragmented circuit of consumption.[78]

It was probably this realization that megastructure did not allow for real individuality but merely furthered the standardization and massification of architecture that pushed techno-revolutionaries like Archigram and Superstudio in the direction of radically individual and mobile structures that spelled the end of the building as such. After Plug-In City, Archigram began to see large-scale building as too collective and constraining, and designed individual shelters that were totally self-sufficient. In 1965 Archigram's David

Greene (b. 1937) declared that "the house is an appliance for carrying with you" and designed the trailerlike Living Pod for one individual. In 1967, Mike Webb reduced this mobile shelter to the Cushicle, a motorcycle/hovercraft with a tent structure that inflated over the frame. By 1968 Greene had done away with the motorcycle and reduced the dwelling to an extension of personal clothing in his Inflatable Suit-Home. Finally, Archigram proclaimed "death to the building," arguing that traditional structures were too authoritarian and stationary. They explained that "our architectures are the residue of a desire to secure ourselves to the surface of our planet, if only they were on wheels, or if some slippery substance could be injected under them, our anchors to the planet, like the aborigine's, should be software, like songs or dreams, or myths. Abandon hardware, earth's-surface anchors. Electric aborigine makes for the moratorium on Buildings."[79]

The realization of this anarchic vision of a totally individual environment with no hardware boundaries was Superstudio's Microevent/Microenvironment project of 1972. In a series of evocative photomontage images, the group depicted humans wandering aimlessly through a landscape totally devoid of built structures. The only artificial feature visible was a ubiquitous grid pattern that enveloped the ground plane and sometimes hovered overhead as well. In the accompanying text Superstudio wrote that the images depicted "the possibilities of life without objects," and that "in substance, the rejection of production and consumption, the rejection of work, are visualized as an aphysical metaphor: the whole city as a network of energy and communication." The grid represented a network of energy and information extending to every inhabitable area of the globe, into which individuals could plug to create their desired microclimates. This supernetwork thus eliminated stationary architectural enclosures and allowed a totally unrestrained, individual nomadism—go anywhere, anytime, with anyone. Superstudio argued that their electronic-network utopia would destroy the object as status symbol imposed by the ruling class and ultimately realize Marx's communist utopia of "from everyone according to his capabilities, to everyone according to his needs."[80]

These self-proclaimed revolutionaries were, however, mere pawns to the ruse of capital, which used them to work out its contradictory development beyond the Fordist stage. Try as they might to move beyond capitalism, these techno-radicals were trapped in the confining web of its deepest assumption— the laws of the marketplace. Like Venturi and Scott Brown, they saw the only escape from bureaucratic society to be the unencumbered individualism of the consumer market, dismissing all organized collectivities and the buildings that housed them as confining and oppressive. These "radicals" who took the automobile as a model for truly liberated housing, ignored the fact that certain goods are indivisible and inherently social, and consequently unattainable through individual market decisions. For example, all individuals might assemble a unique dwelling in a megastructure, but they could not individually buy what made a community—peace, togetherness, cooperation. These techno-radicals did not challenge the atomistic logic of the marketplace but merely pointed the way to the hyperindividualism and market fragmentation of post-Fordist capitalism.

The techno-radicals also unwittingly initiated solutions to another problem at the root of capitalism, that of the commodity. Karl Marx began *Capital* by showing the commodity to be a contradictory unity, at once a concrete use value serving human needs and an abstract exchange value sold on the market to enrich capital. The material container of use value that stored and realized exchange value proved a troublesome burden to capital from the beginning, for it had to be produced, stored, transported, and ultimately consumed by material creatures with physical limits. Capital sought for centuries to overcome these restraints and free the commodity from its use value. The modern movement was an expression of this desire of capital to deobjectify itself, for it used technology to build cheap, light, "almost nothing" containers of space that accelerated the movement of capital around the globe. The technophiles of the 1960s furthered this ruse of capital to overcome the physical limits of the commodity. In proposing to replace the material structure of architecture with information and images, Archigram, Superstudio, and others sought to free capital to circulate effortlessly as ephemeral electrons over suitable conductors. Superstudio's reduction of architecture to a mere network of energy was a brilliant anticipation of global, post-Fordist capitalism, in which capital circulated electronically through computers and satellite communications, and forced homeless workers to chase it to the ends of the earth to upload their labor power into the network, so they might in return download commodities to meet their needs. The "moment-villages" that Archigram dreamed of in the 1960s—those temporary, chance encounters between totally "free" individuals, mobile and self-sufficient—were realized as the nightmare of post-Fordist production—temporary, chance encounters between a homeless, mobilized work force and an incessantly circulating capital, resulting in the production of objectless, ephemeral images and simulations of life to compensate for and occlude the fact that in reality human life and society had ceased to exist. The techno-radicals of the 1960s were laying the groundwork not for the liberation of humanity but for the liberation of capital from its material and social constraints.

The techno-radicals, however, were not the only rebels of the 1960s who provided aesthetic solutions for the new regime of capitalism that would emerge from the ruins of a failing Fordism. Historicism and populism would also be pressed into ideological service to provide legitimation for the transformed social relations and landscapes of post-Fordism. The dissent of the 1960s provided a rich resource to be mined by the new orthodoxy of the 1980s and beyond. However, the ways in which these different aesthetics of anti-modernism were deployed within post-Fordism were not predetermined by some essences within them that awaited unfolding. The development of both postmodern architecture and the post-Fordist regime of accumulation were determined by the class struggles let loose by the death of Fordism, and their correspondences with and contradictions to the aesthetic struggles within the field of architecture.

1. "Detroit Makes an About-Face on Design," *Business*, Feb. 28, 1959. For a full analysis of the Edsel case, see David Gartman, *Auto Opium: A Social History of American Automobile Design* (London: Routledge, 1994), 174–79.

2. *Life*, Nov. 8, 1957, 126, 128. See also Thomas Hine, *Populuxe* (New York: Knopf, 1986), 129–131; Gartman, *Auto Opium*, 168–71.

3. Gartman, *Auto Opium*, 203–5; David Gartman, "Dialectics of the Labor Process, Consumer Culture, and Class Struggle: The Contradictory Development of the American Automobile Industry," in *Rethinking the Labor Process*, eds. Mark Wardell, Thomas L. Steiger, and Peter Meiksins (Albany: State University of New York Press, 1999), 93–109; Emma Rothschild, *Paradise Lost: The Decline of the Auto-Industrial Age* (New York: Vintage, 1974); Samuel Bowles, David M. Gordon, and Thomas E. Weisskopf, *Beyond the Wasteland* (London: Verso, 1984), 84–91.

4. Rothschild, *Paradise Lost*, 26–53; Gartman, *Auto Opium*, 182–211. On the changing relations between primary and secondary workers, see Bowles et al., *Beyond the Wasteland*, 87–88; Frances Fox Piven and Richard Cloward, *The New Class War* (New York: Vintage, 1982).

5. Bowles et al., *Beyond the Wasteland*, 79–84.

6. See Barbara Ehrenreich, *Fear of Falling: The Inner Life of the Middle Class* (New York: HarperCollins, 1989), 57–96.

7. Joan Ockman, introduction to *Architecture Culture: 1943–1968, A Documentary Anthology*, ed. Joan Ockman (New York: Rizzoli, 1993), 13–22.

8. Diana Crane, *The Transformation of the Avant-Garde: The New York Art World, 1940–1985* (Chicago: University of Chicago Press, 1987), 5–9; Erika Doss, "The Art of Cultural Politics: From Regionalism to Abstract Expressionism," in *Recasting America: Culture and Politics in the Age of Cold War*, ed. Lary May (Chicago: University of Chicago Press, 1989), 195–220; Frances Stonor Saunders, *The Cultural Cold War: The CIA and the World of Arts and Letters* (New York: New Press, 2000); Chin-tao Wu, "Embracing the Enterprise Culture: Art Institutions Since the 1980s," *New Left Review* 1st ser., no. 230 (July/August 1998): 28–75.

9. Pierre Bourdieu, *The Rules of Art* (Stanford, CA: Stanford University Press, 1996), 121–27, 225, 239–40.

10. Crane, *Transformation*, 32–36, 65–82.

11. Bourdieu, *Rules of Art*, 127; Andreas Huyssen, *After the Great Divide: Modernism, Mass Culture, Postmodernism* (Bloomington: Indiana University Press, 1986), 142–58, 146–65.

12. Peter Blake, *Form Follows Fiasco: Why Modern Architecture Hasn't Worked* (Boston: Little, Brown, 1977), 9; Peter Blake, *No Place Like Utopia* (New York: Knopf, 1993), 306–7; Philip Johnson, "The Seven Shibboleths of Our Profession," in *Writings* (New York: Oxford University Press, 1979), 146.

13. Hans Hollein, "A Comment," in *Archigram*, by Peter Cook, Warren Chalk, Dennis Crompton, David Greene, Ron Herron, and Mike Webb, (London: Studio Vista, 1972), 6; U.S. Bureau of the Census, *Historical Statistics of the United States. Part 1: Colonial Times to 1970* (Washington, DC: U.S. Government Printing Office, 1975), 140.

14. Stern interview in Barbaralee Diamonstein, *American Architecture Now* (New York: Rizzoli, 1980), 235. See also Magali Sarfatti Larson, *Beyond the Postmodern Facade* (Berkeley: University of California Press, 1993), 246–48.

15. Paolo Portoghesi, *After Modern Architecture* (New York: Rizzoli, 1982), 95–101; "Motion of May 5, 1968 Strike Committee, École Nationale Superieure des Beaux-Arts, Paris," in *Architecture Culture: 1943–1968*, ed. Joan Ockman (New York: Rizzoli, 1993), 456–58; Tigerman interview in Barbaralee Diamonstein, *American Architecture Now II* (New York: Rizzoli, 1985), 230; Robert A. M. Stern, *New Directions in American Architecture*, rev. ed. (New York: Braziller, 1977), 117.

16. Blake, *No Place*, 289–90; Vincent Scully, *American Architecture and Urbanism*, rev. ed. (New York: Henry Holt, 1988), 227, 229. On political alliances built on structural homologies, see Pierre Bourdieu, *Homo Academicus* (Stanford, CA: Stanford University Press, 1988), 156–75; Bourdieu, *Rules of Art*, 251–52.

17. "Critique of Urbanism," in *Theory of the Dérive and Other Situationist Writings on the City*, eds. Libero Andreotti and Xavier Costa (Barcelona: Museu d'Art Contemporani de Barcelona, 1996), 112; Portoghesi, *After Modern Architecture*, 3; Charles Jencks, *The Language of Post-Modern Architecture*, 6th ed. (New York: Rizzoli, 1991), 34; Schnaidt is quoted in Kenneth Frampton, *Modern Architecture: A Critical History*, 3rd ed. (New York: Thames and Hudson, 1992), 287.

18. Scully quoted in Stern, *New Directions*, 81; Peter H. Green and Ruth H. Cheney, "Urban Planning and Urban Revolt: A Case Study," *Progressive Architecture* 49 (Jan. 1968): 154; Paul Davidoff, "Democratic Planning," in *Architecture Culture*, ed. Joan Ockman (New York: Rizzoli, 1993), 443–45; Andreotti and Costa, eds., *Theory of the Dérive*, 44, 92.

19. Herbert Gans, *The Urban Villagers: Group and Class in the Life of Italian Americans* (New York: Free Press, 1962), esp. 263–87, 305–35.

20. On Jane Jacobs at *Architectural Forum*, see Blake, *No Place*, 216, 290–91; Jane Jacobs, *The Death and Life of Great American Cities* (New York: Random House, 1961). The quotes are on 287, 41, 82.

21. Jacobs, *Death and Life*. The quote is on 273.

22. Jacobs, *Death and Life*, 222–29, 239, 372–78.

23. Herbert J. Gans, *Popular Culture and High Culture*, rev. ed. (New York: Basic Books, 1999).

24. Robert Venturi, Denise Scott Brown, and Steven Izenour, *Learning from Las Vegas* (Cambridge, MA: MIT Press, 1972), 104, 106.

25. N. J. Habraken, *Supports: An Alternative to Mass Housing* (New York: Praeger, 1972), 42.

26. Ibid., 25, 12. The Stern interview is in Diamonstein, *American Architecture Now*, 237.

27. Davidoff, "Democratic Planning," 442–45; Giancarlo De Carlo, *An Architecture of Participation* (Melbourne: Royal Australian Institute of Architects, 1972); Venturi et al., *Learning from Las Vegas*, 126–33. The quote is on 127; Anthony Jackson, *Reconstructing Architecture for the Twentieth-First Century* (Toronto: University of Toronto Press, 1995), 169–70.

28. Jacobs, *Death and Life*, 289–90, 313.

29. Denise Scott Brown, "Architectural Taste in a Pluralist Society," *Harvard Architecture Review* 1 (Spring 1980): 41–52; Colin Rowe and Fred Koetter, "Collage City," in *Theorizing a New Agenda for Architecture*, ed. Kate Nesbitt (New York: Princeton Architectural Press, 1996), 283; Tomás Maldonado, *Design, Nature and Revolution: Toward a Critical Ecology* (New York: Harper and Row, 1972), 13–14.

30. Gans, *Urban Villagers*, 326–35. The quote is on 327.

31. Maldonado, *Design*, 64–65.

32. Heinrich Klotz, *The History of Postmodern Architecture* (Cambridge, MA: MIT Press, 1988), 128.

33. Jencks, *Language*, 92.

34. Christian Norberg-Schulz, "The Phenomenon of Place," in *Theorizing a New Agenda for Architecture*, ed. Kate Nesbitt (New York: Princeton Architectural Press, 1996), 414–28. The quotes are on 426, 423.

35. Kevin Lynch, *The Image of the City* (Cambridge, MA: MIT Press and Harvard University Press, 1960). The quotes are on 95, 119.

36. Manfredo Tafuri, "Design and Technological Utopia," in *Italy: The New Domestic Landscape*, ed. Emilio Ambasz (New York: Museum of Modern Art, 1977), 390–400; Ernesto Nathan Rogers, "The Evolution of Architecture," in *Architecture Culture*, ed. Joan Ockman (New York: Rizzoli, 1993), 303–7.

37. Aldo Rossi, *The Architecture of the City* (Cambridge, MA: MIT Press, 1982), 35–41. The quotes are on 128, 130. See also Rossi, "An Analogical Architecture," in *Theorizing A New Agenda for Architecture* ed. Kate Nesbitt (New York: Princeton Architectural Press, 1996), 348–52.

38. Larson, *Behind the Postmodern Facade*, 79, 199–202; Scully, *American Architecture*, 252–53; Gans, *Levittowners*, 185; Sharon Zukin, *Landscapes of Power* (Berkeley: University of California Press, 1991), 190–92.

39. Blake *Form Follows Fiasco*, 20–25, 40–46.

40. Ibid., 69–79, 88–114.

41. Ibid., 51–66; Brent C. Brolin, *The Failure of Modern Architecture* (New York: Van Nostrand Reinhold, 1976), 105, 112.

42. See, for example, Vittorio Gregotti, "Architecture, Environment, Nature," in *Architecture Culture*, ed. Joan Ockman (New York: Rizzoli, 1993), 400.

43. Reyner Banham, *Theory and Design in the First Machine Age* (New York: Praeger, 1967), 10–11, 327–29. The quote is on 327. See also Reyner Banham, "A Throw-Away Aesthetic," in *Design By Choice* (New York: Rizzoli, 1981), 90–93.

44. Peter Cook, Warren Chalk, Dennis Crompton, David Greene, Ron Herron, and Mike Webb, *Archigram* (London: Studio Vista, 1972), 8; "Archizoom," in *Italy: The New Domestic Landscape* ed. Emilio Ambasz (New York: Museum of Modern Art, 1972), 235. See also Constant (Nieuwenhuys), "New Babylon," in *Theory of the Dérice and Other Situationist Writings on the City*, eds. Libero Andreotti and Xavier Costa (Barcelona: Museu d'Art Contemporani de Barcelona, 1996), 155.

45. Cook et al., *Archigram*, 23, 16; "Archizoom," 17.

46. Cook et al., *Archigram*, 52. See also Superstudio, "Description of the Microevent/ Microenvironment," in *Italy: The New Domestic Landscape*, ed. Emilio Ambasz (New York: Museum of Modern Art, 1972), 244.

47. Van Eyck quoted in Frampton, *Modern Architecture*, 298; Rossi, *Architecture of the City*. The quotes are on 40–41, 60, 179.

48. Thomas L. Schumacher, "Contextualism: Urban Ideas and Deformations," in *Theorizing a New Agenda for Architecture*, ed. Kate Nesbitt (New York; Princeton Architectural Press, 1996), 296–307; Rossi, "Analogical Architecture," 348–52.

49. Giulio Carlo Argan, "On the Typology of Architecture," in *Theorizing A New Agenda For Architecture*, ed. Kate Nesbitt (New York: Princeton Architectural Press, 1996), 244–45; Rossi, *Architecture of the City*, 176; Rossi, "Analogical Architecture," 349. See also Umberto Eco, "Function

and Sign: The Semiotics of Architecture," in *Rethinking Architecture*, ed. Neil Leach (London: Routledge, 1997), 182–202.

50. Rossi, "Analogical Architecture," 350; Manfredo Tafuri, *The Sphere and the Labyrinth: Avant-Gardes and Architecture from Piranesi to the 1970s* (Cambridge, MA: MIT Press, 1990), 273–74.

51. Bertolt Brecht, "A Worker Reads History," in *Selected Poems* (New York: Grove, 1959), 109.

52. Roland Barthes, *Mythologies* (New York: Hill and Wang, 1972).

53. Stern, *New Directions*, 117; Peter Eisenman, "House I 1967," in *Five Architects*, Peter Eisenman, Michael Graves, Charles Gwathmey, John Hejduk, and Richard Meier (New York: Oxford University Press, 1975), 15.

54. For a similar analysis of the New York Five, see Tafuri, *The Sphere and the Labyrinth*, 281–84, 295–98.

55. Bernard Rudolfsky, *Architecture without Architects: A Short Introduction to Non-Pedigreed Architecture* (Albuquerque: University of New Mexico Press, 1987), n. pag.

56. Gene Kavanaugh, forward to *Home Sweet Home: American Domestic Vernacular Architecture*, edited by Charles W. Moore, Kathryn Smith, and Peter Becker (New York: Rizzoli, 1983), 12; Eugene J. Johnson, "Performing Architecture: The Work of Charles Moore," in *Charles Moore: Buildings and Projects, 1949–1986*, ed. Eugene J. Johnson (New York: Rizzoli, 1986), 64–67, 212–17, 142–45, 181–83.

57. Jencks, *Language*, 81–84. The quote is on 84.

58. Kent Bloomer and Charles Moore, *Body, Memory, and Architecture* (New Haven, CT: Yale University Press, 1977), 41–42; Jencks, *Language*, 93–94; Larson, *Behind the Postmodern Facade*, 156.

59. Robert Venturi, *Complexity and Contradiction in Architecture* (New York: Museum of Modern Art, 1977), 42, 16, 17, 13, 38.

60. Ibid., 42, 44.

61. Ibid., 116. On the Guild House, see also Venturi et al., *Learning from Las Vegas*, 64–72.

62. On double coding, see Charles Jencks, *What Is Post-Modernism?* (New York: St. Martin's, 1986), 10. On the antenna controversy at Guild House, see Scully, *American Architecture*, 236; Tom Wolfe, *From Bauhaus to Our House* (New York: Pocket Books, 1982), 100–104; Heinrich Klotz, *The History of Postmodern Architecture* (Cambridge, MA: MIT Press, 1988), 149–54; "Interview: Robert Venturi and Denise Scott Brown," *Harvard Architecture Review* 1 (Spring 1980): 238.

63. Venturi et al., *Learning from Las Vegas*. See also Venturi, *Complexity and Contradiction*, 14.

64. Venturi et al., *Learning from Las Vegas*, 64, 73–84.

65. Ibid., 32–42, 87, 4, 9–13, 104–6.

66. Ibid., 44, 46.

67. Charles Moore, "Plug It in Ramses," *Perspecta* 11 (1967): 35–36; Charles Moore, "You Have to Pay for the Public Life," *Perspecta* 9/10 (1965): 57–106.

68. Venturi et al., *Learning from Las Vegas*, viii, 1; Theodor Adorno, "Functionalism Today," in *Rethinking Architecture*, ed. Neil Leach (London: Routledge, 1997), 9.

69. Venturi et al., *Learning from Las Vegas*, 84–87, 108–9, 116. The quotes are on 108.

70. Ibid., 142.

71. Reyner Banham, *Megastructure: Urban Futures of the Recent Past* (New York: Harper and Row, 1976), 17–32.

72. Ibid., 111.

73. Habraken, *Supports*, 59–65.

74. Ibid., 86, 79; Friedman quoted in Banham, *Megastructure*, 207.

75. Peter Cook et al., *Archigram*, 36–41, the quotes are on 36.

76. Ibid., 36, 39, 48.

77. Banham, *Megastructure*, 105–111.

78. Ibid., 168–79, 211–13; Frampton, *Modern Architecture*, 285–86. See also Jean Baudrillard, *Simulacra and Simulation* (Ann Arbor: University of Michigan Press, 1994), 61–73.

79. Cook et al., *Archigram*, 52, 64, 82. The quotes are on 52, 118.

80. Superstudio, "Description of the Microevent/Microenvironment." The quotes are on 242, 244, 245.

6

Disney Goes Downtown:
Post-Fordism, Postmodernism, and the
Collapse of Spatial Segregation

NOTHING IS MORE INDICATIVE of the revolutionary changes that the American landscape underwent after the collapse of Fordism than two events in 2001, both associated with a name that had become synonymous with the suburban entertainment aesthetic. Forty-six years after the opening of Disneyland, which helped pioneer the suburban escape from the city, the Disney name returned to downtown Los Angeles, and the company also brought a simulacrum of downtown to its suburban theme park. In January of 2001 the Disney Company opened adjacent to its Anaheim theme park the Downtown Disney attraction, a public esplanade of shops and entertainment that simulated the excitement of urban night life. At about the same time, in downtown Los Angeles, construction commenced on the Walt Disney Concert Hall, a high-culture venue by architect Frank Gehry (b. 1929). Why was the pioneer of suburban kitsch culture going downtown and sponsoring high-art architecture?

The Walt Disney Concert Hall, which was underwritten not by the company but by its founder's widow, was not the first association of the Disney name with high architecture. When Michael Eisner took over the Disney Company in 1984, he began to commission architects to design the corporation's hotels and office buildings in a new hybrid style called postmodernism, which incorporated aspects of the suburban entertainment culture into the legitimate architecture usually confined to cities. Many of these buildings were in or near urban areas, but the Walt Disney Concert Hall was the first association of Disney with a major city and its legitimate arts. Putting the founder's

Frank Gehry, Walt Disney Concert Hall, Los Angeles, 2003 (© Meredith L. Clausen, Cities/Buildings Database http://content.lib.washington.edu/buildingsweb/)

name and family money into a downtown concert hall was, perhaps, one part philanthropy and one part business acumen. Walt Disney Concert Hall would surely endear the company to a market segment that Disney was desperate to tap, the culture-craving young urban professionals, or yuppies, who were moving back downtown to exercise control over the increasingly global economy. Capturing their attention and consumer dollars was all but guaranteed by the spectacular design of the hall by Frank Gehry, whose soaring, fragmented, sculptural forms seemed to embody the unfettered freedom and individuality of the new post-Fordist capitalism dominated by the culture industry.

The same motives also caused Disney, now a multimedia giant of the culture industry, to capture some of the upscale excitement of the new, culturally based urbanism for its moribund suburban theme park in California. Disney's original version of ersatz urbanism, Main Street, U.S.A., was by the 1990s a quaint curiosity to the yuppies, who were moving back to gentrified downtown districts to take advantage of upscale cultural activities. So Disney executives decided to bring the gentrified excitement of the new downtown out to the Anaheim suburb. Downtown Disney was thus born, a nongated, admission-free pedestrian esplanade located between the gates of the theme park and

Downtown Disney at Disneyland, Anaheim, California, 2001 (Photograph by author)

the Disney hotels. Promising "uptown fun," the promotional web site depicted the district at night in an explosion of color and form against a background of soaring skyscrapers. Despite the lack of real skyscrapers in Anaheim, Disney Imagineers sought to give this outdoor shopping mall an urban ambience by creating second stories above the shops that simulated walk-up apartments. The shops, restaurants, and entertainment venues within Downtown Disney also revealed the soaring cultural aspirations of an exclusive city shopping district, while simultaneously maintaining a down-to-earth popular appeal.[1]

The Walt Disney Concert Hall and Downtown Disney pursued a new kind of urbanism better adapted to the new post-Fordist economy. Both developments broke down the spatial and aesthetic segregation of city and suburb—Downtown Disney by bringing city spaces to the suburbs, and Disney Hall by bringing suburban entertainment to the city. It was thus clear that post-Fordism was destroying the spatial barriers on which both the economy and culture of Fordism rested, creating a new freedom of movement expressed in Gehry's forms. Yet, at the same time that spatial segregation was collapsing, the walls of social segregation were growing ever higher. Despite the appearance of Gehry's forms as open and unconfined, especially in comparison to the modernist skyscraper, the actual spaces of the high-art concert hall were insulated from the increasing poverty and homelessness in downtown streets by bunkerlike walls that restricted public access. Similarly, although the urban forms of Downtown Disney sought to simulate the exciting openness and diversity of city streets, the area was buried deep in the heart of Disney's Anaheim complex and accessible mainly by car. The new landscape that was taking shape under the new economic and class structure of post-Fordism was one of hybridized urbanism, a simulated openness and excitement that concealed the growing confinements and divisions within and between societies. This new landscape found expression and legitimation in a new aesthetic known as postmodernism.

———

The Post-Fordist Revolution

By the early 1970s the Fordist regime of mass production and mass consumption was in dire straits, especially in the United States. The increasing demand of consumers for diverse and changing goods was lowering labor productivity and increasing production costs. But government policies of collective bargaining and demand management prevented capitalists from recouping increased costs through lowering wages or increasing work pace. These problems internal to American Fordism were exacerbated by increased competition from Europe and Japan and increased prices for raw materials from assertive developing countries. These emerging trends came to a head in 1973, when federal government attempts to control inflation converged with soaring energy prices due to the OPEC embargo to induce the deepest recession of the postwar era.[2]

As David Harvey has argued, many of the Fordist regime's mounting problems could be attributed to its underlying lack of flexibility. A standardized labor process prevented changes in products, strong unions prevented adjustments in labor markets, and Keynesian programs prevented adjustments in both labor markets and fiscal and monetary policy. The deep recession stimulated a corporate attack on these constraining institutions that would ultimately create the new regime of post-Fordism, which gave capital the flexibility to respond to the demand for differentiated and ever-changing consumer goods in increasingly competitive and international markets. First, corporate managers launched a campaign of workplace repression, tightening worker supervision and attacking unions. At the same time they initiated programs to render the labor process more flexible, many of which were modeled on Japanese automakers' lean production methods. Lean production replaced mass production's specialized machines run by narrowly trained workers with general-purpose machines operated by broadly trained workers, both of which could be rapidly adjusted for new products. The more flexible pay systems and enterprise-based company unions of lean production also gave employers more power over workers' pay, benefits, and work standards. American employers, especially automakers, seeking flexibility often adopted one or more of these innovations.[3]

Other American capitalists, however, decided it was more profitable to flee from, rather than restructure, the inflexible institutions of Fordism. The 1970s saw an unprecedented wave of capital mobility that caused the loss of an estimated thirty-eight million jobs and devastated the industrial heartland of the United States. Some corporations seeking lower wages, unorganized workers, and a favorable business climate moved plants to Sunbelt states, while others moved offshore to developing countries to take advantage of desperate workers and politicians anxious for investment. The 1970s and 1980s saw an unprecedented explosion of foreign direct investment in the Third World, most of it in manufacturing facilities for American-based corporations. Still other corporations cut labor costs and increased flexibility by decreasing direct employment and "outsourcing" more and more parts of production to outside contractors. Outsourcing not only saved the costs of employment but also forced contractors to absorb the costs of production changes to accommodate product variety.[4]

This post-Fordist restructuring drastically changed the occupational structure of core countries, resulting in a decline of manufacturing jobs and a rapid growth in service jobs. In the United States, the majority of these service jobs were in personal, retail, and business services, the latter of which included accounting, financial and legal matters, management, research and development, design, personnel, technology, advertising, maintenance and cleaning, communication, transport, and security. Saskia Sassen has argued that the geographic dispersion of economic production since the 1970s increased the importance and complexity of corporate central functions like management, finance, and communication, which required highly skilled, specialized services that were increasingly bought from outside firms and contractors. These booming business services also included jobs in image creation, which was crucial to post-Fordist production. In an advanced economy in which most consumer goods were purchased to fulfill not material needs but symbolic desires, the key to selling a product was not its physical composition but its superficial appearance. Thus, the CEO of Starbucks wrote that people did not just come to his stores for the coffee, but for "the romance of the coffee experience, the feeling of warmth and community." So while production of the physical artifacts was often farmed out to sweatshops half a world away, the manufacture of the product's image through design, advertising, and marketing were maintained in-house or contracted out to highly paid service firms. Image-making professions assumed centrality in post-Fordism, especially since many commodities like computer programs and video images involved little physical production at all.[5]

This same sector of business services that produced highly skilled and highly paid jobs in management, finance, and design, however, also produced a large quantity of low-skilled, low-paying service jobs, such as clerical workers, janitors, maintenance workers, and security guards. Further, in the United States most service jobs were created not in business services but in personal and retail services, in which wages and working conditions were notoriously poor. The demands of the large-chain retailers, hotels, restaurants, and security firms for low overhead and high flexibility combined with severe overcrowding in this low-end labor market to spawn the casualization of many of these jobs. Big-brand employers like Wal-Mart, Gap, and McDonald's hired largely part-time workers, often through employment agencies, and offered them low wages and few if any benefits. So the same corporations that contracted the production of goods from low-wage, temporary workers in the Third World sold them with low-wage, temporary workers at home. Thus, the unprecedented mobility and flexibility of capital was purchased at the expense of unprecedented insecurity and instability of employment all over the globe.[6]

Another important consequence of these shifts in employment was the breakup of the large, vertically integrated firms that dominated the age of Fordism. As corporations outsourced the production of both goods and services, these vertically integrated firms were dismantled, leaving lean and flattened firms that relied increasingly on market purchases, not direct employment, for their needs. Although this disintegration and dispersion of production produced a rising number of small firms and self-employed workers, these changes did not undermine the power and concentration of the large corporations. While nominally independent, the small suppliers and self-employed were actually dependent upon the big corporations, whose purchasing power allowed them to play suppliers against one another and appropriate the lion's share of surplus value. Instead of top-down organizations coordinated by bureaucratic power, the new corporations were lean nodes in dispersed networks of market transactions whose strategic position and assets allowed them to siphon off huge profits from the global flows of value.[7]

These moves by capital to restructure the economy would not have coalesced into the new regime of post-Fordism, however, without state assistance. The governments of Ronald Reagan in the United States and Margaret Thatcher in the United Kingdom initiated during the 1980s a neoliberal political movement that began dismantling the Fordist-Keynesian regulatory framework that hindered restructuring. Their ultimate aims were to remove national restrictions on international capital and impose the discipline of global-market competition on the working class. To achieve these goals the regimes first created a recession by tightening monetary policy, and then weakened government protection of collective bargaining, both of which undermined workers' power. Drastic cuts in social welfare programs further weakened labor, while cuts in corporate and personal income taxes served the dual purpose of providing more capital for investment and depriving Keynesian programs of funding. Relaxing governmental regulations, especially in the financial industry, also allowed the freer flow of capital around the globe. In sum, neoliberal policies shifted the state's role in the economy from supporting demand to stimulating investment and supply, with the promise of returning the national economy to competitiveness. By 1983, corporate profitability did begin to rise again, but this recovery was purchased at the cost of an increasingly polarized and unequal class structure.[8]

The rise of the new post-Fordist regime of accumulation profoundly restructured the class relations bequeathed it by Fordism. The dominant class was still, as under Fordism, a technocratic bourgeoisie whose power and wealth rested on knowledge, skills, and bureaucratic position. But post-Fordism changed the nature of technocracy. Fordism's focus on mass production brought to the top of large corporations those with knowledge and experience of production. Even though accountants and finance men also reached the top, they relied on the close collaboration of a second tier of executives with crucial knowledge of production. With the outsourcing of material production and the increasing importance of finance and image creation in post-Fordism, however, the composition of both top and middle technocrats changed. Pierre Bourdieu has captured this shift with his concept of the new bourgeoisie of "cultural intermediaries," the class created by an economy that relied more on symbolic goods than physical goods. Concentrated in occupations like sales, advertising, public relations, fashion, and design, this class's main function was to create the diverse and changing cultural goods through which consumers could express their individuality and fulfill intangible needs for security, excitement, and self. If we also include in this class of cultural intermediaries those who provided corporations with legal and financial advice, which are also largely symbolic, we have defined the ruling class of this dematerialized, spectacular economy of images. During the 1980s the word "yuppies," an acronym for young urban professionals, was coined to identify this group. Members of the rebellious, college-educated generation of the 1960s, these young adults found a lucrative niche in the new economy of the 1980s.[9]

Below this new bourgeoisie was a similarly transformed working class that bore the brunt of post-Fordist restructuring. The corporate search for low-cost, often foreign labor devastated the traditional blue-collar working class, the stronghold of organized labor, and raised substantial barriers to the struggle of the growing number of service workers. Their spatial dispersion and division into small firms made organization difficult, and the casualization of service work prevented them from developing a stake in any job. The consequence of the growing power of a reconfigured technocratic ruling class and the growing vulnerability of a reconfigured working class was a polarization of classes unprecedented since the Great Depression. Middle-income groups declined proportionally, while both low- and high-income groups grew. And the overall distribution of wealth and income became more unequal, as the new post-Fordist ruling class used its unregulated power to appropriate more and more of the world economy's value.[10]

Most advanced capitalist countries followed this post-Fordist trajectory pioneered by the United States, although there were notable differences between them. Walter Clement and John Myles have shown that although nearly all such countries experienced growth in service jobs at the expense of manufacturing jobs, the types of service jobs varied. In anglophone countries like the United States, UK, and Canada, the largest increases in employment were in the low-paying personal and retail services, and in the high-paying business services. In the Western European countries, however, the share of employment in health, education, and welfare services was substantially higher than that of business, personal, and retail services. This was the result of the retention of a much larger welfare state in most Western European countries. Here institutionalized forces like labor unions and social-democratic parties supported welfare spending and prevented the wholesale deregulation of capital and corporations, resulting in less inequality and class polarization than in anglophone countries.[11]

Spatial Reorganization of the Post-Fordist Landscape

The consolidation of Fordism in the postwar era produced a distinctly segregated landscape that maintained and symbolized the social and cultural cleavages of this regime. The downtown core of cities was the home of the command centers of Fordist mass production, while the suburban fringe contained the legitimating culture of mass consumption. But the post-Fordist restructuring of industry uprooted capital and labor and profoundly transformed the landscape. In the suburbs, new corporate headquarters and offices were found cheek by jowl with shopping malls, while in downtown areas new shopping and entertainment complexes crowded close to the skyscraper office buildings serving the globalized economy. The post-Fordist revolution destroyed the segregation of spaces and jumbled production and consumption together in a messy but exuberant tangle of people and places.

Beginning in the mid-1970s, the cities built by Fordism fell into crisis. In the industrial Midwest of the United States, cities were hit hard by the departure of industry to low-wage areas. Cities of the Northeast, which concentrated white-collar employment, were also financially hurt by the migration of many corporate offices to the suburbs, facilitated by new communication technologies. Consequently, declining tax revenues combined with rising costs and falling federal subsidies to create a fiscal crisis in many cities. As the 1970s turned into the 1980s, however, the post-Fordist flood of movement began to subside into predictable channels, and it became clear that urban conglomerations would play a central role in these dispersed and deregulated flows. For corporations operating decentralized activities around the world, control and coordination functions assumed central importance, and there were advantages to centralizing these functions into a few urban spaces. Cities continued to lose corporate office jobs on into the 1980s and 1990s, but firms providing corporations with producer services found great benefits in urban agglomeration. For them, up-to-date information was essential, and this was more readily available in the dense, informal social networks found in cities. Once concentrations of these activities arose—e.g., Wall Street for finance and Madison Avenue for advertising—any firm seeking to remain competitive could not afford to locate elsewhere. Further, to minimize the costs of supplying highly specialized services to clients, producer-service firms often contracted out some services to small, specialized suppliers. The geographic concentration of firms facilitated such contracting and joint-production arrangements. For these reasons, there arose in the 1980s a few global cities that concentrated the services necessary for the management and control of the global economy. While the old industrial cities of Fordism declined, cities providing concentrated services to the globalized, post-Fordist economy, like New York, London, and Tokyo, rose to international prominence.[12]

These post-Fordist global cities offered advantages not only to the production of producer services but also to the consumption of the new class producing these services, the yuppies. This post-Fordist bourgeoisie of cultural intermediaries had a natural affinity for urban living. Their job was to translate new and innovative culture into products that could be marketed by corporations, and large cities concentrated the centers of cultural innovation and diversity. Consequently, in the 1970s this emerging class of yuppies began to migrate back to urban centers from the suburbs where most had grown up. As rebels in the 1960s, they were already denouncing the mass culture of the suburbs as boring and homogenized. So as they assumed leadership in the post-Fordist economy of image production, the yuppies moved closer to the vibrant, diverse culture of city centers. As architect Bruce Graham (b. 1925) stated in a 1982 interview: "Young people are…more interested in filling their lives with meaningful experiences. Those desires cannot be satisfied in suburban bedroom communities. So young people are moving to urban centers, where they have access to simple pleasures like restaurants and movies, but also theaters,

operas, symphonies, libraries, adult education, and the presence of other people who have the same interests."[13]

The yuppies who pioneered this return to the city in the 1970s were usually fresh out of college and just starting their careers as cultural intermediaries.
Unable to afford luxury urban housing, they moved into older neighborhoods
and refurbished the housing, thus creating the gentrification movement.
Historically, struggling artists had often sought out the low rents and large
spaces of poor urban areas, but in this period the bohemian-artistic life style
appealed to a large section of the new class of symbol producers who were as
yet long on cultural capital but short on money. Renovating an old row house
provided an affordable way to live in the cultural action centers. This move
also displayed the yuppies' distinction from the older, Fordist class of professionals and managers, whose suburban mass culture they rejected. Through
meticulously restoring a nineteenth-century row house on the Lower East Side
of New York, for example, a yuppie couple displayed their cultural knowledge
and taste, and hence, their superiority to the Fordist technocratic class that
embraced the mass culture of the suburbs.[14]

These trends of spatial reorganization came to the attention of urban politicians and real estate developers, who were desperate for a strategy to restore
fiscal solvency to their cities. Noticing that the new producers of business services preferred central locations, many cities sought to attract them by providing the necessary infrastructure, such as new communication technologies and
improved transportation corridors. And to persuade the yuppie employees of
these firms to live near their work, cities built entertainment and consumption facilities, along with upscale, often rehabilitated housing. In the 1970s
and 1980s the Rouse Company made billions developing old downtown districts of American cities into upscale shopping and entertainment areas like
Baltimore's Harborplace and Boston's Faneuil Hall and Quincy Market. Often
offices, housing, and entertainment were provided in one huge megadevelop-
ment, like Battery Park City in New York, near Wall Street. As a further lure
to the class of cultural intermediaries, cultural facilities were centralized in
downtown areas. As Mike Davis has stated, developers discovered that "culture
fertilizes real estate," attracting high-income residents and consumers and thus
raising rents. Los Angeles excelled at spreading cultural manure over the ger-
minating investments on Bunker Hill, locating along Grand Avenue a corridor
of museums, theaters, and music and dance venues that was crowned by Frank
Gehry's Disney Concert Hall. The promoters of the latter stated explicitly that
they valued Los Angeles's cultural center not as a public asset in itself but as

"an economic powerhouse" for generating private revenue and rehabilitating downtown.[15]

Under post-Fordism cities were thus transformed from sober centers of production to exuberant spectacles of consumption aimed at attracting not merely gentrifying yuppie residents but also a broad range of consumers from the suburbs and tourists from the region. Many Americans were discontented with the artificially differentiated goods of Fordist mass culture, and more had the cultural capital from a college education to appreciate goods that were self-consciously aestheticized. There was also something about the validation of the city's heritage in these urban consumption spectacles that appealed even to the unschooled masses. In a time of rapid economic restructuring, there was comfort in the security and certainty of the past. So in the 1970s these urban consumer spectacles met with surprising success and spread across the landscape. The 1980s saw such an explosion of historic shopping districts, convention centers, art festivals, renovated urban housing, and new museums that the competition for consumers became intense, and cities searched frantically for some distinction to stand out in the crowded market.

This post-Fordist urban development, like the Fordist urban renewal of the 1950s and 1960s, was undertaken by partnerships between governments and private developers. But in the earlier period the role of government was stronger, for much of the money for financing came from the federal government, which imposed stringent requirements and offset the power of capital. Beginning in the 1970s, however, the public-private partnerships for post-Fordist urban development were dominated by private developers. When neoliberal national governments slashed aid to cities and deregulated the financial industry, they ensured that only capitalists had sufficient funds for large urban projects and thus dominated the planning and development of cities. In many urban areas quasi-public development corporations, packed with unelected representatives from corporations, banks, and developers, were formed to insulate development decisions from public influence.[16]

Much of the public may have been willing to accept the privatization of urban planning because of the disastrous effects of urban renewal in the 1950s and 1960s, in which government played a larger role. But the post-Fordist restructuring controlled by private interests was in many ways worse than Fordist urban renewal, for it inscribed the class polarization of the economy into the urban landscape. The gentrification of downtown neighborhoods increased land values and rents and forced out low-income residents, who were also displaced by office and consumer-spectacle construction. The monumental decline of low-income urban housing during the 1980s combined with unemployment from deindustrialization and deinstitutionalization of the infirm and insane to create an epidemic of homelessness in many American cities. The emerging post-Fordist economy of cities, however, simultaneously exerted a strong pull on lowly paid service workers. The new office complexes for upscale producer services demanded downscale service workers like janitors, clerks, security guards, and maintenance workers. The consumption patterns of gentrifying yuppies were also responsible for the creation of lots of low-paid service work in cities. Yuppie families generally had two income-earners and consequently relied on more paid labor for household reproduction work. Further, the customized cultural goods demanded by these high-income professionals were, unlike mass-produced goods, more likely to be produced in small firms that created unorganized and lowly paid jobs. Finally, the attraction of desperate and vulnerable workers into cities to provide yuppies with goods and services created the labor supply for a degraded manufacturing sector that could compete with the offshore sweatshops.[17]

The outcome of post-Fordist spatial restructuring was the packing together in urban centers of both the exuberant winners and the desperate losers of the new regime. Crowding close against the glittering towers of post-Fordist work and the gentrified zones of upscale consumption were dilapidated and overcrowded tenements. Competing for space along the sidewalks of post-Fordist cities were, elbow to elbow, yuppies in Giorgio Armani and Donna Karan suits and homeless people and low-wage workers in rags. One of the most troublesome tasks faced by post-Fordist developers and their postmodern architects was the visual segregation of the two extremes of the class spectrum that the new economy inextricably integrated in downtown areas. Unlike the technocratic commanders of the Fordist economy, who could avoid the unpleasant urban results of their reign by escaping at night to the suburbs, the post-Fordist yuppies lived and consumed in the cities where they worked, and faced the polarizing consequences of their efforts at every turn. So did the tourists and suburban consumers who made the gentrified city centers their temporary playgrounds and vacation destinations. Visually segregating the activities that Fordism had spatially segregated was a central obsession of postmodern architecture.

Although many of these transformations were experienced by cities across the developed world, there were national variations in urban restructuring caused by variations in the transition to post-Fordism. The anglophone countries, especially the United States and UK, were at the forefront of the neoliberal urban restructuring described above, while these trends were less pronounced in Western European countries. There the states retained more Keynesian spending and a greater commitment to public housing. In the late 1970s, for example, West Berlin initiated the International Building Exhibition (IBA), an ambitious plan to provide 9,000 new or renovated housing units in some of the city's most depressed areas. The French government also remained committed throughout the 1980s and early 1990s to providing social housing, much of it in new town developments on the outskirts of Paris. And beginning in the mid-1970s the government initiated an ambitious public building program to leave a mark on the Parisian landscape, the famous *Grands Projets*. So in Europe, at least, public expenditures and planning were still central, while in the United States private developers reigned supreme. This difference created important distinctions between the architecture of the two zones.[18]

The Profession of Architecture in the Post-Fordist Transition

These post-Fordist changes in the economy and landscape had a tremendous impact on the profession of architecture. First, the economic climate of the mid-to-late 1970s devastated the building industry. Public construction was crippled by cuts in federal aid to cities, and the private market suffered from high interest rates and inflation. The demand for architectural services was thus low, but the supply grew rapidly in this period due to the continued expansion in higher education. In the United States the number of architects per million in population increased from just under 300 in 1970 to 400 in 1980. This mismatch of supply and demand produced a period of underemployment and inactivity for architects. Many earned a living through teaching, writing, and "paper architecture" (drawings, sketches, and models). The more fortunate and prestigious architects got by on small commissions for single-family residences. As a rule, when an artistic field becomes highly competitive due to an oversupply of producers, there is an increase in aesthetic innovation, as individuals seek to stand out in the crowd. The heightened competition in the field of architecture during the slump of the 1970s put the dissenting trends pioneered in the 1960s into a hothouse, accelerating the process of innovation and selecting those best adapted to the changing economy and building industry.[19]

In the early 1980s the building market picked up, stimulated by Reagan's neoliberal policies. But the increasing dominance of private investors and developers entailed by these policies meant that architects lost what little autonomy from the marketplace that they had during the 1950s and 1960s. In that period the larger public sector for institutional buildings and housing provided insulation from the market. Even in the private sector, oligopolistic corporations flush with cash commissioned trophy headquarters like the Seagram Building, giving architects lavish budgets and considerable freedom. But during the transition to post-Fordism, public spending dried up and oligopoly broke down. Competition and efficiency became the watchwords of the entire economy, including the building industry. Developers of downtown office space in the 1980s building boom faced competition from many similar projects, so it was imperative to build quickly and efficiently. The emerging post-Fordist economy also accelerated the flow of finance capital, which demanded an immediate return on investment.[20]

In this fast and competitive environment for building, developers had little time for artistic pretension, which could drive up costs and delay completion. So they began to bypass architects and exercise tighter control of their projects by relying on outside specialists like project managers, structural engineers, and service engineers. In this market-driven specialization of the industry, the architect's role was reduced largely to applying the external image to the container of space dictated by other specialists on the basis of efficiency. These applied forms had little to do with building functions but were skin-deep, cosmetic frills. Yet, such superficial decoration assumed an unprecedented importance in post-Fordism, which was marked by the demand for individualized and distinctive goods. Developers discovered that they could make their standardized, efficient buildings appear distinctive in a crowded and competitive market by attaching appealing images with the assistance of their architectural cake decorators. As one successful architect of the period, Helmut Jahn (b. 1940), stated: "Architects are sought out today both to create a diversity of visual expression and to satisfy the economic goals behind building. Design statements are very much related to marketplace consumption." So in this new era, the aesthetic and social issues that absorbed the profession in the 1960s were abandoned for a new accommodation to the marketplace.[21]

There were, however, great risks involved in applying this marketable architectural decoration. The developer needed an innovative and distinctive image that could be readily consumed, but if the image was too new or different and not agreeable to the consuming public, the entire project could fail. Developers had to balance the benefits of aesthetic innovation against the risks of market failure. One way to minimize risk was to commission an architect whose style had been previously successful. This developer demand for financial certainty pressured architects to create a recognizable style that could be repeated, with variations, from one project to the next. This period thus saw the emergence of "brand name" architects with signature styles that were immediately identifiable. The "branding" of architecture not only gave developers the distinction and certainty they demanded but also gave architects the distinction and differentiation they needed to stand out in the highly competitive field. Once an architect's signature style became associated with success, then his or her name assumed a fetish value that ensured success. To achieve this status of a brand-name fetish, many architects spent considerable time and effort promoting themselves. As Arthur Drexler, former director of the Department of Architecture and Design at the Museum of Modern Art, stated in a 1982 interview, "merchandising rules the universe and the architect trying to establish himself feels he has to think in terms of the novelty of his approach and the maximum public exposure." The transition to the post-Fordist economy thus created a new architectural aesthetic that focused on marketable images and abandoned the contentious social issues of the 1960s. As Robert A. M. Stern, one of the founders of postmodern architecture, wrote in 1980: "We're not reformers or revolutionaries....The social motivations of the sixties are no longer with us....Now architects are more concerned with how buildings look, and how and why to manipulate their appearance." All that survived of the aesthetic innovations of the 1960s were hollow aesthetic shells, emptied of their critical content.[22]

The economic imperatives of quick and profitable development did not, however, determine the type of superficial images employed to distinguish and differentiate buildings. This was determined indirectly by the impact of these economic forces on culture and ideology. The post-Fordist economy created intractable contradictions that all living within it were forced to face and resolve culturally. But these cultural resolutions varied by class position for, as Fredric Jameson has argued, each class tends to see the problems of the age through its particular interests in contest with other classes.[23] The architectural aesthetic of postmodernism was the cultural expression of the political and economic interests of the yuppies, i.e., the new bourgeoisie of cultural intermediaries, of which architects were an important part.

Postmodernism: Symbolic Resolution of the Contradictions of Post-Fordism

Although post-Fordism was a distinct regime of accumulation, in many ways it extended and exacerbated the basic contradictions of Fordism. These contradictions can be categorized under three major dimensions of experience: time, space, and self. But all were manifestations of the underlying contradiction between subject and object that had been unfolding since the beginning of capitalism. From its inception the market sought to subsume the concrete, qualitative labors of humans under the abstract, quantitative category of exchange value, thus treating subjective activity as an objective thing. While Fordism lessened this contradiction by regulating the market, the post-Fordist regime deregulated markets to be governed by the objective laws of exchange, and thus exacerbated the contradiction between subject and object at all levels of experience.

The realm of experience impacted most by post-Fordist restructuring was that of time, or history, in which the subject-object contradiction manifested itself as an opposition between change and permanence. As Marx himself noted, the competitive demands of the capitalist market compel its ruling class to constantly innovate new means of production, creating a society in which "all that is solid melts into air."[24] Yet at the same time, as Terry Eagleton has noted, this dynamic, restlessly changing economy requires in the cultural realm a solid and unchanging morality to stabilize and regulate the social turmoil created by economic change.[25] In the transition to Fordism, the modern movement mediated this contradiction with the ideology of technological progress, which postulated that underneath the objective chaos of restructuring was a human telos or end. But the 1960s undermined the popular faith in progress, especially the consumer variant of the ideology, for style-based "improvements" in automobiles and other products became so rapid and arbitrary that consumers saw through the game. So when post-Fordist restructuring emerged in the mid-1970s, people could thus no longer find peace in the comforting notion of progress. Their sense of history was lost and replaced by a feeling of overwhelming, arbitrary change. Postmodern ideology thus faced the dilemma of finding a source of meaning and stability in this period of senseless change.

In the realm of space, post-Fordist economic restructuring similarly invalidated the cultural resolution of a contradiction that was prominent under Fordism. Here the general capitalist contradiction manifested itself as the opposition between centeredness and dispersion. On the one hand, as Marx recognized long ago, the imperatives of the marketplace drives capital out of centers of development over the entire globe, battering down national and cultural boundaries.[26] Capital lives everywhere, but no place in particular. On the other hand, humans are material creatures centered in the landscape, tied to a community embodied in a particular place. Under Fordism this contradiction had been addressed by a careful physical segregation of the landscape. The restless sphere of the production and administration of capital was concentrated in the urban cores, while the residences of its workers were agglomerated in the stable, centered communities of suburbs. The post-Fordist economic restructuring, however, broke down this spatial segregation. The productive and administrative functions broke out of the urban core and were dispersed out over the landscape, while the new class of cultural intermediaries migrated from the suburbs back downtown to live and consume. Cities turned themselves into consumer spectacles and became centers of community living. The dilemma faced by postmodern ideology in this realm was instilling in consumers a sense of centeredness in an urban landscape marked by reminders of deindustrialization and capital dispersion.

Finally, these shifts in the cultural depictions of time and space ultimately impacted the experience of the self, which is dependent upon a conception of one's position in time and space. An individual knows who she is when she has a firm grasp of her life as part of the collective efforts of humanity in history, as well as part of a human community rooted in a place. The capitalist contradiction specific to the self is the opposition between unity and fragmentation, or identity and difference. On the one hand, as Marx recognized with his concept of alienation, capitalist labor has a tendency to force people to be other than they really are, to go against their nature. The alienated self is necessarily a fragmented self, divided against itself and pulled in different directions by the ever-changing imperatives of capitalist production and consumption. Yet, on the other hand, capitalism demands individuals with a stable identity, since uncoerced, legally free workers must be internally motivated to act in accordance with the demands of capital. Under the Fordist regime, this contradiction was resolved by the separation of production from consumption. At work people were alien and other, fragmented into heteronomous, individual actions dictated by an objective master, capital. By contrast, people were themselves in the realm of consumption, where their identities were unified around the free selection of commodities. To some extent, this consumer identity was a collective one, tied to a concept of "man" or "the nation" which progressed together through the expansion of life-enhancing consumer goods.

With the rise of post-Fordism, however, the spatial solution to the contradiction collapsed. The new regime broke down the segregation, dispersing capitalist production over the landscape and fragmenting identities created in consumption. Increased differentiation of post-Fordist products also threatened the collective nature of this consumer identity. Fordist product hierarchies, distinguished by quantitative differences in features appealing to all, were demolished and replaced by a flattened plethora of goods qualitatively differentiated to appeal to narrow niche markets, thus destroying any sense of a collective subject progressing together. The self now became hopelessly fragmented in consumption as well as production. Postmodern ideology faced the dilemma at this level of creating selves sufficiently unified to motivate and legitimate efforts in the increasingly fragmented production system.

Although these contradictions of time, place, and self pervaded the general society, the postmodern ideological responses to them were specifically, though unconsciously, formulated to serve the interests of the dominant class of post-Fordism, the new cultural bourgeoisie of symbol producers. In his analysis of this class, Pierre Bourdieu has argued that its members' attitude toward culture was caused by a mismatch between aspirations and achievements, which resulted from either downward mobility from the old bourgeoisie or upward mobility from the working class. The downwardly mobile yuppies were said to be the children of the high economic bourgeoisie who acquired high cultural capital growing up in a wealthy family. Unable, however, to convert this cultural capital into the formal academic credentials required for the established bourgeois professions, they were attracted to the new professions of cultural intermediaries, which put their knowledge of high culture to use in the industries of mass culture creating new and differentiated goods. Bourdieu's data reveals that these downwardly mobile individuals showed competence in high culture, but personally preferred works of popular culture, like jazz music and popular movies. However, they brought to these popular arts the aesthetic disposition of high culture, which privileged form over content. For example, the yuppies had an interest in popular movies like those of Alfred Hitchcock, but unlike most movie fans of the working class, they were more interested in the auteur-directors and their techniques than the actor-stars and story lines. These downwardly mobile children of the high bourgeoisie rejected high culture because its class bearers had rejected them in occupational selection. So they culturally allied with the masses, to whom they were forced to cater in their jobs anyway. But at the same time that they legitimated themselves to the masses by embracing and creating their popular culture, the new cultural intermediaries asserted their distinction from them by treating this culture in the formal ways characteristic of high culture.[27]

Bourdieu does not say much about members of this new class whose social trajectory was upward, but I believe this to be the more common trajectory. The expansion of enrollments in higher education drew many working-class and petty-bourgeois people into contact with high culture, stimulating many to aspire to positions in high art. But most could not achieve the cultural aspirations that their educational credentials led them to expect. Their cultural capital, acquired in formal education, was not as strong as those from the high bourgeoisie, whose acquisition by informal socialization gave them an intuitive feel for high culture. Further, as several scholars have suggested, the number of cultural producers that can be sustained by the subfield of restricted production is generally rather small and relatively constant due to the internal dynamics of cultural competition.[28] Thus, many of the upwardly mobile young people educated in the 1960s who aspired to be high artists had their aspirations frustrated in the 1970s and 1980s, and most were channeled into mass culture by the growing demand for differentiated product images. Both downwardly and upwardly mobile yuppies had an ambivalent relation to high culture that was the hallmark of postmodernism. While they were knowledgeable about and aspired to it, they were rejected by high culture and forced into the subfield of mass culture. So taking a stand of symbolic defiance, as Bourdieu calls it, they challenged the cultural hierarchy by validating popular culture, while simultaneously asserting their distinction from the masses by using it in formal ways.

Yet, the specific solutions of this new class to the contradictions of post-Fordism are explained not only by this ambivalent relation to culture but also by its conflict with other classes. As Fredric Jameson has argued, the truth of ruling-class ideology is found in working-class consciousness, for all dominant ideologies attempt to co-opt, deflect, or silence the expressions of working-class interests.[29] This was especially true for the new cultural intermediaries, whose job was meeting the symbolic needs of masses. In the face of the dispersion in space, change in history, and fragmentation of self created by capital during this period, the working masses demanded centeredness, permanence, and unity, that is, the maintenance of the stable, centered communities and unified selves created under Fordism. If the new class of cultural intermediaries wanted to successfully assert their dominance and also sell commodities to the masses, they had to somehow accommodate and defuse these radically conservative demands within a rapidly changing society that undermined them. In the initial stages of the post-Fordist revolution, they did so by symbolically turning to the past to legitimate the new society.

As Marx noted in *The Eighteenth Brumaire*, the revolutionaries of every era initially wrap themselves in the glories of the past, claiming to be restoring the virtues of the old society not creating a new one.[30] And so it was with the revolutionaries of post-Fordism. The rising bourgeoisie of cultural intermediaries initially portrayed their changes to the economy and polity as a restoration of the glories of postwar Fordism. Ronald Reagan, post-Fordism's main political ideologue, wrapped his neoliberal policies supporting the new bourgeoisie in a populist and nationalist language of nostalgic restoration. Free trade, he promised, would restore competitiveness to basic industries and defeat foreign interlopers in American markets. And slashing social programs would restore prosperity to workers and reassert the priorities of God and family that had been destroyed by the 1960s. He thus wrapped programs favoring the redistribution of power and wealth to a new bourgeois class in the language of populist restoration, and garnered support from a substantial proportion of the blue-collar working class.

In cultural fields, there was a similar tendency to respond to escalating contradictions with reactionary and nostalgic forms that appealed to the victims of this vicious capitalist restructuring. On the dimension of time, when people could no longer believe in the future due to arbitrary change, they were offered meaning from the past, and a nostalgia craze struck both high and mass culture. Popular movies like *American Graffiti* (1973) were often set in the 1950s heyday of postwar Fordism, before the problems and dissent of the 1960s. In this film, as in others, earlier eras were stripped of their social relations and historical events, and the past was evoked largely through material artifacts— autos, fashion, household goods. Through such reified nostalgia, history in postmodern ideology lost its meaning as human action and was reduced to a timeless treasure trove of pleasing symbols with which to simulate security and protection. The popular commodity of the automobile was similarly seized by the nostalgia cult, as automakers began to introduce revivals of old models of the 1950s and 1960s, like the Volkswagen Beetle and Ford Thunderbird. In architecture as well, nostalgia was mobilized as compensation for post-Fordist restructuring. The historicist movement that germinated in the 1960s came to full bloom in the 1970s and 1980s to tack the vague image of better times to the surfaces of developers boxes. Postmodern architecture also stripped history of any real content and offered up hollowed out, historic images of stability and prosperity. These images of the past were exceedingly superficial not only because of the cost-cutting concerns of developers but also because of the backgrounds of yuppie architects. Most of these upwardly mobile symbol producers learned historical architecture in school through visual images in textbooks. Consequently, their perception of architecture was largely two-dimensional, a trait they shared with working-class consumers raised on mass media.[31]

On the dimension of space, postmodern ideology offered working people a sense of centeredness or enclosure to protect them from the dispersive activities of capital around the globe. In the political arena, centeredness often translated into trade protectionism in order to maintain the centrality of domestic industrial communities in the face of international competition. Such policies displaced workers' anger from their own employers, who were exporting and outsourcing jobs, onto foreign capitalists. In architecture, this demand for centeredness and protection was symbolically met by reasserting the barrier between inside and outside characteristic of premodern architecture. Buildings were closed off to the outside with opaque surfaces and bunkerlike walls. Such enclosure was especially important in downtown consumer attractions, where the feeling of security necessary to attract consumers required sealing out the sight of deindustrialized districts and homeless people created by the dispersion of capital.

On the dimension of the self, postmodern ideology resolved the contradiction between unity and fragmentation by once again looking to the past. With the collapse of unified, mass identities, postmodern cultural productions argued that identities could be achieved in a multitude of small, tribelike groups characteristic of premodern society. This emphasis on a diversity of identities emerged from the social movements of the 1960s, which criticized the stultifying consensus of Fordist culture in the name of those on the margins of society. Yet, most of these movements maintained a totalizing vision of social change that united all groups behind a common program of participatory democracy. But as the 1960s turned into the 1970s and repression and recession dashed hopes for total change, many movements retreated back into insular enclaves, narrowing their focus to smaller issues and creating separatist identity politics. These fragmented new social movements were quickly co-opted by post-Fordist marketers and image-makers, who provided them with differentiated goods to express their identities and also used styles pioneered by these lifestyle radicals as sources of newness for the rest of the market. As post-Fordist capitalism spread its tentacles around the globe, many indigenous peoples resisted incorporation by reasserting ethnic and regional identities drawn from the past, which provided both a compensation for and a disguise of the totalizing force of global capital. In the real estate industry, which became increasingly international, developers often used such local styles to disguise their global projects, touching off a movement known as the new or critical regionalism.[32]

At the same time that the rising class of cultural intermediaries was struggling to divert and coopt the progressively conservative demands of the Fordist working class and newly incorporated Third World people, it was also contesting the old Fordist technocratic bourgeoisie, whose power was based on knowledge that facilitated efficient production of goods. The rule of this class was legitimated by a bifurcated ideology that simultaneously asserted its superior knowledge of production techniques and its responsibility for plea-surable consumer goods. But discontent with the homogeneity of consumer goods in the 1960s undermined the consumption half of Fordist ideology and also threatened technocratic legitimation of production. The new symbol pro-ducers struggled to give consumers more differentiated goods, but encoun-tered opposition from the old technocratic class. As Bourdieu has observed, in the 1970s these two groups engaged in intrafirm power struggles that were often expressed in cultural struggles. The new bourgeoisie rejected the old's "uptight" art and consumption habits in favor of a more "laid-back" lifestyle focused on spending and enjoying, much like the popular culture of the lower classes. The new symbol producers validated popular art forms like jazz and film, creating an image of greater democracy and less snobbery and besting their opponents in the contest for public sympathy. But at the same time they sought to show they possessed cultural capital at least equal to the old bour-geoisie by appropriating popular culture in aestheticized ways. In architecture, such postmodern populism involved using the familiar symbols of vernacular buildings in formalized ways that referred to high-art architecture or reversed popular meanings ironically. So ideologically, this new bourgeoisie sought to have its cake and eat it too. It legitimated itself to the masses by giving them insulating historical signs, yet revealed to the old bourgeoisie that they were their equals in cultural knowledge by coding into their popular works a high-art subtext.[33]

This brings us to the final characteristic of the general ideology of post-modernism, the illusion of classlessness. Although the rise of post-Fordism greatly increased inequality between classes on a global and national scale, it also made the category of class seem hopelessly outmoded. The objective pro-cesses of post-Fordist spatial restructuring rendered the perception of classes difficult. In Fordism, class and hierarchy were visibly inscribed in the land-scape. The corporate and governmental skyscrapers downtown testified to the commanding heights of ruling-class power, while on the urban outskirts the fuming factories and refineries reminded spectators of the dirty labor of the working class. Yet, in the post-Fordist landscape spatial signs of class inequality were dispersed and often invisible. Corporate headquarters were scattered over the suburbs in low office parks, and the dirty work of the laboring class was dispersed to rural areas and overseas. The dispersion of material production around the globe made it difficult to conceptually represent the existence of opposing classes, for the necessary visual cues were gone.

Also implicated in the post-Fordist illusion of classlessness was the collapse of product hierarchies in the new economy and the creation of a leveled but diversified consumer culture. While Fordist markets of graded commodities obscured the qualitative differences between products that testified to class position in production, their quantitative differences testified that in consumption some people had more of what everyone wanted. Working people could easily see the differences between, for example, their own Chevrolets and Fords and their bosses' Cadillacs and Lincolns. In the 1960s, however, consumers began to see through the artificiality of these hierarchical differences and demanded more real individuality in goods, resulting in a consumer culture in which newness and diversity were so widespread that hierarchical differences could not be maintained. Specific products were no longer seen as better than others, testifying to a higher class, but merely different, expressing a distinct lifestyle identity. So, for example, the under-$20,000 Volkswagen Beetle, a retro revival of the 1960s anticar, driven by the $200,000-a-year, forty-something yuppie advertising executive to recapture her hippie days, was not seen as "better" than the $30,000 sports utility vehicle driven by her $20,000-a-year, twenty-something secretary to accommodate her new family. It was just different, testifying to a different age and lifestyle group, not a superior class. Products aimed at niche markets based on age, region, gender, family status, sexuality, and ethnicity broke down the broader class categories of marketing into micro groups that gave people not merely a sense of individuality but also a sense of community with those sharing their lifestyle. Behind these nonhierarchical consumer categories existed large and growing class differences in production power that went largely unnoticed. However, this did not keep the rising class of symbol producers from subtly asserting their cultural superiority to those who served as gatekeepers in the new economy. The members of the new symbol-producing bourgeoisie appropriated the same leveled products of popular culture in a formal, aestheticized way that allowed them to recognize each other and exclude class outsiders. Postmodern culture allowed them to have it both ways, distinguishing themselves to class comrades, while unpretentiously blending into the leveled culture of the masses.

Postmodern Architectural Aesthetics

This general postmodern ideology found its quintessential expression in the art of architecture. Although postmodernism was also influential in film, video, literature, and music, architecture was more central to the movement for several reasons. First, architecture has always been a hybrid art, positioned on the boundary between the marketplace and the autonomous art world. Even high-art architecture is an expensive material artifact requiring considerable resources, which in capitalist societies usually come from the marketplace. The regime of post-Fordism saw an unprecedented increase in the commodification of art and the aestheticization of commodities. Since architecture epitomized the hybrid status of nearly all post-Fordist products as both art and commodity, it condensed many of the aesthetic trends of postmodernism. Also propelling architecture to the forefront of art forms during this period was the prominence of space in post-Fordist restructuring. As Fredric Jameson, Edward Soja, and David Harvey have argued, post-Fordism displaced historical consciousness with spatial consciousness, because it sought to solve the contradictions of capitalism by rearranging capital and labor in space. Architecture is the preeminent art of space, so it rose to prominence in the period of post-Fordist restructuring.[34]

The specific aesthetic arrangements of space that solved the ideological problems of post-Fordism were to some extent already incorporated in the popular architecture of entertainment centered in the postwar suburbs. Even in Fordism, many new consumers felt some insecurities about the future, so they sought signs of a stable past in the pseudohistorical styling of their homes and amusement venues like Disneyland. This aesthetic also created an image of centered enclosure and helped create in consumers a unified, collective identity as middle-class Americans. In the 1960s critics of modern architecture incorporated aspects of this popular aesthetic into high-art architecture, pioneering the schools of historicism and populism. These schools thrived during the post-Fordist transition, for they fulfilled the needs for differentiated identities, protective enclosure, and comforting nostalgia, which had grown exponentially. The naturalistic aesthetic of the 1960s did not disappear altogether, but was folded into historicism, which had always been its close ally. The fate of techno-radicalism, however, was more uneven, and depended upon the rapidity with which a country moved toward post-Fordism. Since this school evidenced a continued faith in technological progress and collective planning, it survived mainly in Europe, where social-democratic intervention in the economy and the city remained relatively strong throughout the 1970s and 1980s. But even here techno-radicalism lost its revolutionary aspirations in the recession and repression of the 1970s, and became a modified version of modernism that accommodated a less sweeping transition to post-Fordism.

Postmodern architecture was thus composed mainly of populism and historicism, both of which accommodated the cultural requirements of post-Fordist restructuring. Although closely related, the two followed different paths of development. Populism took the degraded symbols of the commercial culture and raised them to the level of art by formalization and aestheticization. Historicism, on the other hand, took the exalted signs of high-art architecture and lowered them to the level of entertainment through pastiche and trivialization. Although in the 1970s the two schools were close competitors for the architectural throne from which modernism had been deposed, by the 1980s historicism had emerged triumphant.

Populism: The Formalization of the Entertainment Aesthetic

The decorated-shed aesthetic that Robert Venturi and Denise Scott Brown developed in the early 1970s provided the basis for the populist wing of postmodernism. This aesthetic matched perfectly the demand of the new building market for quick, economical buildings designed by technical specialists but differentiated with a thin layer of decoration applied by an architect. The decorated shed also made a clear distinction between internal space and the external container, providing the kind of centered enclosure demanded by people trying to have fun in degraded urban environments. The friendly face of commercial signs or popular historical symbols on downtown shopping districts and museums was accommodating and reassuringly familiar to masses coming back to urban centers. As Charles Moore, an important populist, stated: "I get much more pleasure out of trying to figure out what would turn them [consumers] on, what dreams and visions and images they are hanging onto in their heads. Then I try to make those happen in some way that's full of a choreography of elements that interest people....I think the overall requirement of anything that people are going to spend money on is that it should be a pleasant place to be." The populists often held public meetings of prospective consumers of their buildings to sound out their dreams and desires, calling the practice "democratic participation" to disguise what was obviously market research.[35]

At the same time that the populists appealed to the masses with pleasant and popular symbols, they also spoke to the cultural cognoscenti through the language of high art. As Denise Scott Brown stated bluntly: "We are taking a very broadly based thing, which is popular culture...and we're trying to make it acceptable to an elitist subculture, namely the architects and the corporate and governmental decision makers who hire architects." This elite subculture of culturally sophisticated people also included the broader class of symbol producers, who wanted symbols of legitimate art mixed with their consumption to distinguish themselves from common consumers. The populists provided the yuppies with distinction by double-coding their buildings, by speaking simultaneously in a high-art and popular language. Often this involved using popular signs in formal ways, such as abstraction, distortion, and irony. Or sometimes symbols from high-art architecture were simply layered over or juxtaposed to symbols from popular culture. So populist architecture offered something for everyone—the reassurance of popular symbolism for the masses and the distinction of esoteric art for the cultural elite. Consequently, this aesthetic eschewed integration and unity for the clash and confrontation of multiple elements.[36]

The work of Venturi and Scott Brown best represents the populist approach of the 1970s and 1980s. Their decorated-shed architecture resonated with developers' needs in the mid- and late-1970s, and their services were consequently in demand. Their first project of real note during this period was the 1977 addition to Oberlin College's Allen Art Museum, an Italian Renaissance revival building of 1917. This solemn and symmetrical building with a red-tile roof and an arched portico supported by columns was the sort of neoclassical architecture traditionally used to create a grandiose home for high art. Venturi and Scott Brown ironized and deflated this historicist pretension by slamming onto its side an ugly and ordinary decorated shed that mocked the original at every turn. The shed addition was set back substantially from the Renaissance

Venturi, Scott Brown and Associates, Allen Art Museum addition at Oberlin College, Ohio, 1977 (Courtesy Venturi, Scott Brown and Associates)

building, so the facades were not in the same plane. Neither did the flat roof of the addition harmonize with the peaked roof of the original. Venturi and Scott Brown's decorated-shed addition also countered the stable symmetry of the Renaissance original with an asymmetrical entrance set back from the facade on the far end. And the gracefully arched and recessed openings of the portico and niches on the facade of the original museum building were contradicted by the flat, rectilinear ribbon windows set high under the eves, making it look like a high-school gym of the 1940s, as the architects themselves noted.

The only feature of the addition that harmonized with the original museum was its color scheme—the pink and red sandstone approximated the colors of the Renaissance building. But even here the architects could not resist cutely contradicting the original, whose pink stone sections were marked off symmetrically with red, rectangular detailing. On their facade Venturi and Scott Brown arranged the stone blocks in a gaudy, red and pink checkerboard pattern. Was this a reference to the checkerboard square trademark of the Ralston Purina feed company, used to symbolize the farm country surrounding the college and deflate its civilizing pretensions, or was this merely abstract surface decoration? We will never know for sure, since, as Robert A. M. Stern has noted, even when Venturi explained his architectural references, he was often deceptive. What is clear, however, is that the building was double-coded. The architects used the shed construction familiar in the commercial culture to project an accessible image to the masses, who perhaps did not feel comfortable in a museum that proclaimed its high-art distinction with Neo-Renaissance architecture. This gymlike building announced to them that art was just another spectator sport, to be consumed passively like a basketball game. Yet, the elite consumers with the proper stock of cultural capital could laugh at the witty ways that Venturi and Scott Brown countered the pretensions of the old building with their decorated-shed architecture.[37]

Toward the end of the 1970s, however, Venturi and Scott Brown turned toward more historical forms and away from the simple symbols of Main Street and Las Vegas. But they used these high-art historical forms in popular ways so as not to be taken as seriously validating historical styles. Their populist historicism was clearly visible in Gordon Wu Hall (1983). Located on the campus of Princeton University, this building housing a dining hall and social facilities was plainly modern in construction, with flat brick walls and flush, metal-framed ribbon windows. Yet it also bristled with witty references to the historical architecture of the campus. Since many of Princeton's original buildings were in collegiate Gothic style, Venturi and Scott Brown echoed the

Venturi, Rauch, and Scott Brown, Gordon Wu Hall at Princeton University, New Jersey, 1983 (Courtesy Venturi, Scott Brown and Associates)

style by capping each end of Gordon Wu Hall with a semicircular bay window of the type common at Princeton. Along the main facade of the building the architects also included an arched, triple-divided window of the type used by Palladio, and a heraldic gate harking back to the Elizabethan and Jacobean halls of Oxford and Cambridge Universities.

The most striking feature of all this historical decoration was its insistent flatness. Apart from the rounded bay window at either end, the facade of Gordon Wu Hall was a long, flat wall broken only briefly at the second story by two rectangular setbacks. All windows were flush with the brick surface. But perhaps the most insistently flattened decoration was the heraldic marble gate over the entrance door, where the original mannerist compositions of clocks, spires, and arches were stylized to building-block simplicity and added to the flat wall as paper-thin appliqué. Similarly two-dimensional were the large keystones set in the brick above the glass wall of the dining hall. They were probably intended to lend visual stability and weight to the modern construction, but these meanings were contradicted by the lightness of these flush blocks. Even the sculpture of the school's tiger mascot in the plaza terminating the building was reduced to a flattened head, as if the unfortunate animal had been steamrolled by the architects' heavy-handed wit.

At Gordon Wu Hall Venturi and Scott Brown were trying to give people facing post-Fordist restructuring comforting images of historical stability, unity, and centeredness. Yet, in their attempts to show ironic distance from these historical quotations, the architects contradicted the humanistic connotations of their forms, creating instead a decentered and fragmented composition. This long, linear building had no real center, and the historical references were scattered helter-skelter over the hall in a disarray that inadvertently symbolized post-Fordist restructuring. Venturi and Scott Brown seemed here to be celebrating the fragmentation and dispersion of humanity, which may have seemed liberating for the class of symbol producers being educated at Princeton but was frightening to the many losers of post-Fordism. But the fact that these architects did not succeed here in offering comforting illusions may speak to their artistic integrity rather than their failure.[38]

The work of Venturi and Scott Brown in this period culminated in another museum addition, this time to the prestigious National Gallery of London. In their 1991 Sainsbury Wing addition the architects did not slam an ugly and ordinary decorated shed on the side of this institution, for they had been moving away from the symbols of commercial culture toward historicizing decoration. So unlike the Allen Museum addition, the Sainsbury Wing was politely respectful of the original building of 1838, which was built in Corinthian style. The new building, which was separated from the old by a passageway, was its

Venturi, Scott Brown and Associates, Sainsbury Wing of the National Gallery, London, 1991 (Courtesy Venturi, Scott Brown and Associates)

same height, faced with similar stone, and adopted its Corinthian pilasters. So a quick glance by a not-too-knowledgeable public revealed no offensive or condescending gestures. And it was just such a broad, consuming public that the new gallery was trying to attract, for Margaret Thatcher's neoliberal government refused to pay for it, arguing that culture should rely on the market for support. To attract consumer dollars, the Sainsbury Wing contained a large gallery shop, a restaurant, and a coffee bar. So in this art museum, just as in shopping malls, the consuming masses could buy trinkets, eat a meal, and sip a latte. Also like shopping malls, the addition was enclosed on three sides by high, blind walls that sealed out any unpleasant reminders of the surrounding urban fabric. The Sainsbury Wing was also made familiar to consumers of commercial culture by large, commercial-style lettering on the north elevation announcing that this was indeed the National Gallery.

Venturi and Scott Brown here spoke the popular code of consumer culture in order to, as Venturi wrote, "attract a wider range of people, to increase museum attendance…[and] expand its market" beyond the cultural elite. Yet the architects also double-coded their Sainsbury Wing with clever allusions to architecture history to hold the interest of the symbol-producing yuppies of London. While the popular viewer noted only the obvious signs of classicism on the south facade, those with cultural capital saw an amusing mannerist composition blending the old and new. The architects made it clear that their accommodation of the original building was a mere front, a stone package placed over a modern building of glass and concrete. The stone revetment stopped abruptly where the addition turned the corner to the passageway between the buildings, revealing a modernist glass wall. And the stone facade itself was treated in a way that suggested the fading relevance of the classical order. The references to the Corinthian order were strongest in the section closest to the old building, and gradually faded along the length of this wall. At the corner next to the old museum, Venturi and Scott Brown crammed four Corinthian pilasters in the space of a few feet, but then gradually spaced them more widely until they disappeared entirely. The blind windows between the pilasters gradually lost depth until they faded into the wall. As the Sainsbury Wing rounded the corner to the west facade, it unceremoniously dropped the classical stone for ordinary brick reminiscent of the surrounding buildings.[39]

The ultimate result of the double-coding here was a multivocal composition that spoke the languages of old and new, popular and elite. But were these double-coded populist compositions successful in the dual ideological demands of providing the working masses with stability, centeredness, and unity to escape post-Fordist restructuring, while simultaneously giving the class of symbol producers the distinction and democratic aura to legitimate their new rule? This question is best answered by a review of the work of Charles Moore, a pioneer of the populist aesthetic in the 1960s who became one of its most important practitioners in the 1970s and 1980s. His Piazza d'Italia (1979) is especially important, for it embodied an aspect of postmodern populism as yet unexamined—the appeal to new ethnic and lifestyle groups. In this work, Moore sought to provide a center and identity for one of these new social groups, Italian-Americans, and his composition revealed just how deep and enduring such post-Fordist identities were.

In the 1960s Moore's idea of diversity was to use vernacular styles indigenous to an area to blend the building into the landscape. In the 1970s, however, he increasingly resorted to paper-thin, decorative layering to wrap a building in a package acceptable to its intended taste culture. This kind of depthless, stage-set architecture reached its apotheosis in the Piazza d'Italia, a public plaza in New Orleans's old Warehouse District that was intended to be a focus for the Italian-American community of the area. Yet, the real depth of the new ethnic loyalties that were resurrected defensively in the wake of post-Fordist restructuring could be seen in Moore's architecture here. The Piazza d'Italia was a fragmented collage of ahistorical clichés of Italianness extracted from American

Charles Moore, Piazza d'Italia, New Orleans, 1979 (Photograph by author)

mass culture, owing more to the movies than to the authentic history of Italy. The clichés included the Trevi Fountain, Italian columns, Latin inscriptions, a campanile, a pergola, and the boot of Italy. Moore seemed to recognize here that all that immigrants retained of their Italianness after so many years of immersion in American mass culture was a handful of depthless images, simulacra of an Italy that no longer existed. But Moore did not treat these clichés as realistic historical reproductions but as modern media images of a national culture. For example, all five orders of Italian columns were represented, but were laid out around the fountain in short, fragmented sections, like snapshots in a tourist's photo album. Further, these columns used modern materials such as glistening stainless steel and neon lights. Moore was striving here for a syncretistic integration of an old ethnic culture into a new mass culture, but all he seemed to accomplish was to remind people of the superficiality of both. Many people sought to retreat from the juggernaut of totalizing capital into dreams of past diversity, but all that was left to construct their identities were the depthless images of global media conglomerates, who used them to disguise the fact that they had already destroyed the social foundation of these cultures. In the plaza Moore also gave the culturally savvy some high-art references, but his ironies rang hollow, and the inside jokes played on a sincere people seemed more cruel than clever.[40]

Moore's Piazza d'Italia also evidenced another crucial concern of postmodern architecture, the creation of new public spaces within city cores. Charles Jencks, the foremost scholar of postmodern architecture, called Moore's plaza for the Italian-American community a prime example of postmodern public space, but it also revealed the flaws in this concept. For yuppie symbol producers and other consumers to comfortably live and shop downtown, its public spaces had to be insulated from the human and physical wreckage of deindustrialization. Such was the case with the Piazza d'Italia, which, although open to the public, was originally planned to be surrounded by an existing skyscraper and a new Italian-American Federation headquarters. But plans for the latter were downsized, leaving the plaza bordered on two sides by empty lots and frequented by the homeless, a part of the public that planners hoped not to accommodate. This area of New Orleans became gentrified, but the Piazza d'Italia did not thrive because it was too public. Tourists and yuppies preferred their "public space" insulated from the broad public by admission fees and private security guards. In 2002, the Piazza d'Italia's classical architecture, usually symbolic of endurance and stability, was in a shabby state of disrepair, despite being renovated twice, because of its cheap construction. This crumbling classicism stood in stark contrast to the nineteenth-century, red-brick ware-houses across the street, which had been renovated into the types of "public space" that yuppie symbol producers preferred—the consumer spaces of lofts, galleries, hotels, restaurants, and coffee shops, to which the price of admission was economic and cultural capital.

Although this populist aesthetic sought to solve the dilemmas of an emerging post-Fordism from the interests and perspective of its privileged class of symbol producers, it was unable to provide for all of this class's ideological needs, as indicated by its declining popularity in the early 1980s. Venturi and Scott Brown had toned down their populist cant by the mid-1980s. Their brash appropriation of popular-culture motifs turned into a gentle use of historical forms accompanied by a subtle double-coding. In their rush to realize in the 1970s the democratic critique of modernism begun in the 1960s, Venturi and Scott Brown failed to notice that the demands of the populace had changed. Sobered by the loss of jobs, income, and community, much of the public now sought emblems of stability and protection that populists seemed unable to provide. The fragmented ways in which they used all forms, popular and his-torical, prevented people from achieving a feeling of wholeness and stability. As Charles Jencks stated, while Venturi's collage-like use of signs "was important and liberating in 1972 because it reaffirmed the necessity for considering signs, by the 1980s it had led to many dissociated buildings, with caricatured motifs stuck all over them." Even when Venturi and Scott Brown began to use histori-cal symbols, their parodic forms made history look provisional and paradoxi-cal, thus preventing its use as an illusion of permanence. Also undermining the illusion of stability were the shoddy construction methods that revealed the ephemerality of their forms. Finally, the whole process of double-coding was ineffective. The high-art references were too obscure even for trained archi-tects, while the unschooled masses often found them vaguely condescending. Robert A. M. Stern angrily stated that "this obscurantism defended by a pre-sumably populist ideology is finally at the heart of the matter; it sets up the most profound and provoking reaction." Peter Blake agreed that these buildings were ultimately elitist and arrogant: "Ironic name architects designed buildings in the shapes of private jokes that would leave their fellow Yalies rolling in the aisles, but possibly failed to amuse the ordinary people condemned to live and work in (and pay for) those private jokes." So by the 1980s this populist trend faded, and was replaced by another trend that emerged in the 1960s as a cri-tique of modernism, historicism.[41]

Historicism and Disneyfication: Lowering High Art to Upscale Entertainment

Historicism had long been used to provide people with ersatz stability and meaning in their lives. It was revived in Europe and America during the 1930s in reaction to economic collapse, and survived during the 1950s in the segregated suburban realm of mass consumption. But as the Fordist segregation of work and play collapsed, aesthetic segregation fell with it, and suburban pseudohistoricism moved downtown to offer consumers a sense of stability and wholeness to disguise the hypermobility and fragmentation of post-Fordism. But this time the reified, cartoon historicism was applied by trained architects with high-art pedigrees. Unlike the populists, who took the signs of a degraded popular culture and raised them to the level of art, the historicists took the exalted art of historical architecture and lowered it to the level of entertainment, much of which was aimed at well-heeled, overconsuming yuppies.

The major historicists, such as Michael Graves and Robert A. M. Stern, developed an aesthetic that reconciled the present with what they saw as the enduring values of the past, like family and tradition. As Stern wrote, while modernism was a dialectic between things as they are and things as they ought to be in the future, "post-modernism seeks a resolution between...things as they were and as they are." This aesthetic incorporated past forms into present buildings by stripping them of historic detail and turning them into abstract types that no longer required handicraft labor. These types could be quickly applied as decoration to the outside of buildings designed by engineers and developers. As Graves stated, "the standard form of building is its common or internal language...determined by pragmatic, constructional, and technical requirements. In contrast, the poetic form of architecture is responsible to issues external to the building and incorporates the three-dimensional expression of the myths and rituals of society." Besides being easily produced, these historical types had the benefit of being reified, that is, stripped of any unpleasant reminders of the human labor originally required to produce them.[42]

These abstract historical forms gave people not only a sense of history in a period that had destroyed any continuity of time, but also a sense of rootedness in an era that had uprooted everyone. The historicists sought to create a reassuring sense of place out of the abstract, homogenized space to which post-Fordist capitalism reduced the globe. Michael Graves wrote that the "amorphic or continuous space, as understood in the Barcelona Pavilion [by Mies van der Rohe] is oblivious to bodily and totemic reference and we therefore always find ourselves unable to feel centered in such space." To turn amorphic space into a human place, Graves insisted, architectural forms had to contain symbolic reminders of the bodies and landscapes in which people dwelled. Charles Moore, also an advocate of anthropomorphism, similarly argued that when architecture referred to the body, "those of us who lead lives complicatedly divorced from a single place in which we can find roots, can have, through the channels of our minds and our memories, through the agency of building something like those roots re-established."[43]

Other historicists argued that achieving such rootedness required not only natural references but also a sense of enclosure, insulating occupants from outside forces. As Graves stated: "Our culture needs separations between one point and another—outside versus inside.... If we do [not have these], we also dissolve the difference between the private and the public, the sacred and the profane. We destroy enclosive realms that have helped give identity to our society." So Graves and other historicists treated the skins of their buildings as solid, impermeable barriers to a hostile external world, protecting the intimacy and isolation of the interior occupants. Finally, this historicism sought to provide consumers with a comforting sense of integration and wholeness to mask and compensate for the fragmented, contradictory reality of the outside world of post-Fordist restructuring. While the populists often embraced the contradictory elements of the environment—old versus new, popular versus elite—the historicists integrated all elements into a soothing but superficial wholeness devoid of discomforting clashes. As Romaldo Giurgola argued: "It's not for architecture to illustrate the contradictions of life, but rather to come spontaneously from the resolution of opposing forces.... [It's a question] of establishing a continuity so that the city presents itself as history, as a living place, and not as an assortment of competing elements." This attitude resulted in the much-touted "contextualism" of the postmodern historicists, who blended their buildings into the urban fabric by superficially parroting the styles and materials of their neighbors. Such seamless wholeness was also applied at the level of the individual buildings, which often contained an eclectic mix of historical forms but integrated them into a whole so as not to evoke contradictory images of history. Consequently, postmodern historicists could facilely collapse references from thousands of years of architecture into one eternal present of wholeness.[44]

Although this architecture of reified historical pastiche emerged in the 1960s with the work of Europeans like Aldo Rossi, it did not become a dominant aesthetic until the late1970s. In this period Michael Graves abandoned his previous flirtations with early modernism and developed an architecture of historical archetypes, as signaled by his Plocek House of 1977. The first impression projected by its blocky structure was one of massive weight and stability. The modern cladding material was scored and colored to look like stone blocks. And the scarce number of small windows on the house not only emphasized the massiveness of the walls but also sealed off the inside from the outside environment, although it sat in solitude on a bucolic hillside. The major historical references here were to ancient Middle-Eastern architecture. The defensively narrow entrance slit that extended the entire height of the house was guarded on either side by massive, square columns, clearly referring to Egyptian temples. A similar column on the side of the house served as a chimney, but had a base in a stepped, ziggurat form. So here in rural New Jersey, Graves constructed a fantasy of Egyptian defensiveness, standing insular and isolated, perhaps against the economic chaos raging without.[45]

The work that really awoke the architectural world to Graves's new historicism was the Portland Public Services Building, completed in 1982. In this public box of office space with a tight budget, Graves got the maximum aesthetic effect by painting onto its surface flat, scenographic fantasies of ancient architecture. He again used abstract Egyptian motifs in his design, even putting Sphinx-like "feet" on either side of the base. Rising from this base on all sides

Michael Graves, Portland Public Services Building, 1982 (Photograph Paschall Taylor/courtesy Michael Graves and Associates)

were simulated Egyptian columns of brown cladding, which extended halfway up the large building. On two sides the columns were topped by jutting capitals; on the other two, by a flat appliqué of garland. On the sides with the capitals, huge, brown keystones extended from the column tops. In a niche at the top of each keystone Graves inserted the simulation of a primitive hut, and the roof of the building was graced by a simulated temple. The rest of the building surface was covered with tiny square windows and cladding that was scored to simulate stone construction.

All this decoration seemed contrived to lend mass and stability to a modern office building. The tiny windows seemed barely able to penetrate the "stone" walls, the columns strained under their weight, and the massive keystones held the whole thing down. This public building also seemed curiously insulated from its surroundings. The massive, relatively closed base and tiny windows of the superstructure projected protection and defensiveness against the public streets of the city. And all the gratuitous appliqué—Egyptian columns, primitive huts, ancient temples—was used to evoke a sense of continuity with humanity's ancient roots. Although similarly flattened and reified historical motifs could be found in Venturi and Scot Brown's populist works, like Gordon Wu Hall, there the decoration was so fragmented, contradictory, and dispersed that it seemed to simulate the disorder of history and failed to provide the requisite sense of stability. But Graves's carefully integrated and centered ancient imagery at the Portland Building conveyed a sense of historical wholeness of primordial origin. In this period of vicious social change that dismantled the social safety net and regulations of the Fordist/Keynesian order, Graves thus added his architectural voice to the political rhetoric of Reagan, similarly calling for a return to basics and traditional values to obfuscate a ruthless leap forward into the brave new world of global post-Fordism.[46]

A similar simulation of a secure historical past could be found in another public building by Graves, the San Juan Capistrano Library, completed in 1983. Although much smaller than the Portland Building, the architect provided another flat composition in heavy-handed Egyptian proportions. But here Graves wrapped the ancient proportions in Spanish-Mission-style decoration reminiscent of the nearby Mission of San Juan Capistrano. He provided the obligatory red-tile roof, as well as a light monitor over the entrance and a pretty little courtyard with a fountain. But the proportions seemed far too heavy for this indigenous style. For example, a metal pergola along one side of the building was curiously oversupported by closely spaced, massively square columns. This attempt to create an image of historical stability was quickly

Michael Graves, San Juan Capistrano Library, California, 1983
(Photograph by author)

contradicted, however, by the signs of shabbiness and decay that the building bore by 2001. The windows in the light monitor were dingy and fogged,
the stucco was cracked and stained in places, and the bottoms of several door
frames were rotted. Such quick, cheap construction was typical of this post-
Fordist era, in which temporary marketability dominated the building industry. Graves gave the citizens of San Juan Capistrano a reified, marketable image
of "Californianess" to attract tourists to their little town, but did little to provide them with an enduring and useful repository for knowledge.

This obsessive attention to image dictated another failing of postmodern architecture illustrated by the San Juan Capistrano Library. Photos of the
building published in architecture and tourist books were impressive, but
people using it noticed a lack of attention to detail. Up close, Graves's library
was featureless and imprecise—surfaces lacked moldings, lines were inexact,
and planes intersected clumsily. This lack of detail in Graves's flat, cartoonlike
designs connoted a degradation of human dwelling to the one-dimensional
measure of the marketplace. His broad, flat shapes were meant to be consumed
in image alone, so he designed only the outlines of a building in quick, rough
sketches and never got down to detailed drawings. In the system of trademark
architecture that emerged in post-Fordism, star architects like Graves stamped
buildings with their trademarks and then turned the designs over to lower-paid
assistants, who turned their doodlings into models and drawings for construction. This system produced two-dimensional cartoons that could be quickly
built and appealed to consumers from a distance, but lacked the interest and
details that accommodated enduring human occupation.

After Graves, the second great innovator of this aesthetic of pastiche historicism was Robert A. M. Stern. In the 1960s he studied with Robert Venturi and Denise Scott Brown, and absorbed their philosophy of double-coding. But Stern's background and habitus inclined him more to the historical styles of old money rather than the petty-bourgeois kitsch of populism. When he began to build in the 1970s, he thus coded civilized and subtle ironies into the historical styles acceptable to his upscale clients. Stern's ironies were also unlike Venturi's in being carefully integrated on the surface and unnoticeable to the untrained eye. While Stern was more subtle than the brash Venturi, he was more witty than his fellow historicist Graves. The house he designed for himself in 1976, for example, was ostensibly a revival of streamline moderne from the 1930s. The front facade was bowed-out at one end and had speed whiskers at the top. But contradicting this historic style was the podium of fieldstone, which seemed to refer to Wright's Prairie style. And the smooth streamlines of the facade were broken into fragments by changes in height and depth. These ironies were carried off so deftly, however, that they went unnoticed by all but the most culturally sophisticated viewers, so that the transportation back to the good old days of the Great Depression could be effected without interruption.[47]

Such dreamlike transportation to the past to compensate for the denials of the present was even more effectively achieved in Stern's East Hampton Residence on Long Island, completed in 1983. Another in his long line of historical country houses for the new rich seeking a cultural pedigree for

Robert A. M. Stern, East Hampton Residence, Long Island, New York, 1983 (Photograph © Roberto Schezen/Esto)

themselves, this house was designed in Shingle style, which was adopted in the 1880s by the newly enriched industrialists for their resort homes on Long Island. At that time the United States was in the middle of a long economic decline that dampened the commercial enthusiasm of these industrialists, who retreated from troubled cities to bucolic East Hampton where they sought to recapture the old values of colonial America in this simple, unpretentious architecture. Stern revived this style for the nostalgic retreats of the rich in the period of post-Fordist restructuring. The two-story house was a single, massive volume with a peaked roof, onto which Stern scattered a number of semi-detached scenographic features. On one side of the house a tall, overproportioned chimney insistently symbolized the hearth and family togetherness. Floating off the front was a tiny porch with a peaked roof that was supported by six massive Doric columns. As with Graves, Stern's obsessive support elements suggested weight, stability, and protection in precarious times. The back of the house incorporated another protective metaphor, an overproportioned and aesthetically detached tower with a large window looking over the back lawn, perhaps to forewarn of invaders from the outside world. The critic Gavin Macrae-Gibson has argued that Stern's East Hampton Residence was a conscious collage of images, united only by analogy to an underlying emotion: "The forms transport us to Atlantic resorts, to vacations, to American summers by the sea....The house is an album of images that reconstruct this experience for a society wishing to 'play at achieving the ancient values once again.'" These images were, like the elements of a dream, disjunct and juxtaposed yet somehow all associated with an unconscious wish for stability and wholeness, desires denied in a time of fragmentation and mobility.[48]

The careers of both Stern and Graves took an exponential leap through their association with the entertainment corporation that pioneered in mass culture the type of dream-state historicism that they raised to high art: Disney. In the mid-1980s, the company was struggling to reposition itself in consumer markets that were being transformed by post-Fordism. To do so Disney hired as its head in 1984 Michael Eisner, an executive with experience making movies at ABC and Paramount. Eisner immediately began to move the company's products up-market to capture the class of affluent yuppies who were demanding high-quality, culturally sophisticated goods to testify to their growing economic and cultural capital. Evidence of his new strategy emerged on his second day at Disney, when he declared that the drawings for two hotels contracted for Walt Disney World were "horrendous," and that Disney would select architects to redesign the entire project. Eisner later stated that he decided at this point that his legacy at Disney would be architecture that would "have the beauty and strength" to endure over time.[49]

After consulting with a friend on the board of the Whitney Museum of American Art, Eisner proposed a collaboration to design the hotels between Robert Venturi, Michael Graves, and Alan Lapidus. But when Venturi insisted on a competition for the project, not a collaboration, Eisner ended up selecting Graves's dreams of reified historicism over Venturi's fragmented populism. For the first hotel Graves again drew on ancient Egyptian motifs, creating a steep central pyramid with sloping wings, while for the second he used a curving vault form reminiscent of Baroque cathedrals. Eisner liked the mythological forms, but thought their execution too solemn for an amusement park. He told Graves to "lighten up," which he did by theming each with a fairy-tale creature. The hotels, named the Dolphin and the Swan, became focal points for a convention center located at Disney World. Like all of Graves's buildings, both were packed with subtle references to high-art architecture—the giant swans were from Giovanni Lorenzo Bernini's (1598–1680) Palazzo Barberini; the sailboat bridge and pyramid, from Claude Nicolas Ledoux (1736–1806). The yuppie businesspeople staying there could thus distinguish themselves from the masses crowding the theme park by using their cultural capital to pick out these references. At the same time the new symbol producers could distinguish themselves from the old bourgeoisie with Graves's playful attitude toward high culture. The architect deprived his historical forms of the seriousness of tradition by abstracting and flattening them. So, for example, while the huge sculptures of dolphins and swans on the roofs of the hotels were three-dimensional, other decorations were two-dimensional cut-outs, like the dolphins in the fountain in front of the hotel. Similarly flattened to cartoon outlines were the central pyramid and vault, which were impressive viewed frontally but from the side appeared as thin as plywood stage props. The painted cartoons of banana trees and waves on the facades also emphasized their flatness. Graves intended this flatness to generate distance and ambiguity. As he stated: "That two-dimensionality lets you think more broadly. It was a discovery along the way."[50]

If Graves meant that conventioneers with cultural capital could smile knowingly at his ironic distance, surely he was correct. But if he meant that this thinned out architecture stimulated deep thinking, he was wrong, for the stage-set flatness of the forms prevented any penetration into the social depths of the historical allusions. "Just kidding," Graves seemed to say, "no need to get serious," that is, to think about the real origins of those Egyptian treasures, or the social brutality revealed in those fairy tales. Most of the spaces in these hotels, including the interiors, seemed designed precisely to occupy the eye with cloying decoration, so as to divert the mind from the real purpose of both the Disney Company and its business conventioneers—making money. In the Dolphin, for example, ceilings of public rooms were draped with brightly striped tenting simulating cabanas, and the walls were lined with planters sprouting artificial banana plants. Even the guest-room corridors were covered with decorations like carpets simulating beaches. Graves left not one square inch of these hotels unthemed, for a blank space might give the mind an intermission to analyze the scripted performance. And this rested mind might come to the same unflattering conclusion about these hotels as did the architectural historian Vincent Scully: "In general, there is a kind of imperial brutality in the Swan and the Dolphin that serves this newer Disney World well. The movie is *Intolerance*, the set, Babylon. The fountains of this Paradise serve uncouth kings, richly bedecked, whose animal totems, illuminated from below, ride in the black velvet sky."[51]

Eisner's first venture into legitimate architecture to attract upscale consumers was a rousing success. The Dolphin and Swan not only attracted lots of conventioneers to Disney World but also increased the company's cultural capital. But even before Graves's hotels were opened in 1990, Eisner extended his plan by commissioning name architects to design office buildings that would give Disney a commanding cultural presence outside of its theme parks. When Eisner decided to build a new corporate headquarters in Disney's Burbank, California, home, he again turned to Graves to design an attention-grabbing monument to Disney in the entertainment capital. But this time the architect toned down the historicist whimsy for a pompous classicism designed to lend the executives of kitsch the weighty importance of Medici princes. Rendered in Graves's simplified Tuscan style, the Team Disney building was replete with classical references. At front was a long reflecting pool surrounded by a pergola with massive piers that looked more like a Roman peristyle than a garden structure. The front elevation of the building was equally massive, with weighty, red sandstone piers lifting a pediment over the entrance, which was topped by a circular temple that extended down through the building to form a central rotunda. On the roof of the executive wing there were paired barrel vaults that formed the topmost offices and abstractly evoked the mouse-ear logo of the company. Directly behind the rotunda was a narrow courtyard surrounded by four stories of arcades crowded with large, closely spaced columns that lent visual weight to the stucco construction. Graves's initial design was

Michael Graves,
Team Disney,
Burbank,
California,
1991 (Mary Ann
Sullivan, Bluffton
University)

again a bit too ponderous for Eisner, who demanded some Disney characters to advertize the corporation. So the double-coding architect gave the masses gigantic figures of the Seven Dwarfs holding up the classical entablature of the facade. Graves's building seemed to say to the masses "we do not take ourselves too seriously," while simultaneously conveying the weighty influence and cultural importance of kitsch entertainment in the post-Fordist age.[52]

Not long after Graves started designing Team Disney, Eisner solicited the talents of another historicist, Robert A. M. Stern, to design an employment office that would establish a corporate presence near the public realm of Orlando, the city closest to Disney World. Disney wanted to make an impression not only on those applying for jobs but also on the public as a whole, a part of which had become critical of the corporation's heavy-handed control of its politically autonomous Reedy Creek Improvement District around Disney World. Stern set out to culturally legitimate the corporate despot with royal raiments, giving it an employment castle. He designed a Venturi-like decorated shed, a long, sprawling box tarted up to resemble a sixteenth-century Venetian palace. The facade was covered with a harlequin pattern of alternating gold and white diamonds, punctured by Gothic-style windows, and crowned on each end by a glass-and-steel tower. Over the middle of the shed were giant gold letters spelling CASTING, since Disney liked to think of its employees—and liked for them to think of themselves—as cast members in a gigantic stage production. In his second assignment for the corporation, Stern turned away from obfuscating indoctrination for Disney workers toward illusions of grandeur for the upscale consumers of Disney entertainment. For its new hotels near the Epcot Center, Disney was seeking, in the words of one authorized commentator, something "classy yet affable, nostalgic and still somehow trendy." In other words, these yuppie hotels had to be historical enough to lend these upstarts a pedigree but also sufficiently trendy and friendly to distinguish them from the old bourgeoisie. In his Yacht Club and Beach Club hotels Stern offered upscale vacationers a veneer of nineteenth-century civility to validate their twentieth-century success. The former simulated an exclusive turn-of-the-century New England club in Shingle style, while the second conjured up a more accessible mid-Atlantic shore hotel in Stick style.[53]

Over the 1990s Stern and Graves would be joined by a stable of other world-class architects employed by Disney, including Robert Venturi and Denise Scott Brown, Antoine Predock (b. 1936), Charles Moore, Frank Gehry, Jacquelin Robertson (b. 1933), Robert Siegel (b. 1939), Charles Gwathmey, Helmut Jahn, and Aldo Rossi. Eisner's architectural quest for cultural respectability for Disney was rewarded in 1992 by an Honor Award from the American Institute of Architects for the Team Disney building in Orlando by Arata Isozaki. Paul Goldberger, the *New York Times* architecture critic, wrote: "Disney has now made its contribution to the history of architecture." The purveyor of Mickey Mouse cartoons was now a recognized patron of culture.[54]

Just when this purveyor of mass entertainment began to turn its amusement parks into art museums, the purveyors of legitimate art ironically began to turn their art museums into amusement parks for the masses. And like Disney, they used postmodern architecture to do so. The class restructuring that accompanied the rise of post-Fordism also left art museums scrambling to redefine their "markets" to survive in the new economy. In their rush to the unregulated marketplace in the 1980s, neoliberal politicians like Reagan and Thatcher slashed government subsidies for the legitimate arts, forcing

Robert A. M. Stern,
The Beach Club,
Walt Disney World,
Lake Buena Vista,
Florida, 1991
(Courtesy Alan S.
Dalinka)

public museums to turn to the private market for funds. There they found that post-Fordist restructuring had created a broader class of symbol-producing bourgeois who had knowledge of the arts and were interested in using them to legitimate themselves. But this group was used to appropriating art in a different way than old bourgeois museumgoers. Since many had grown up as consumers of mass culture, they were accustomed to treating culture as a purchased commodity, a trait also reinforced by the employment of these yuppies in the commercial market. In order to appeal to this potentially broader market of patrons, cash-strapped museums had to change their assumptions about art. As Pierre Bourdieu has argued, the traditional bourgeois museum was organized around the "pure gaze," the ability to look past the content of the art work to its form. This gaze drew a sharp distinction between art, an object of pure contemplation, and the commodity, an object of immediate sensual pleasure. In order to broaden their audience to the new bourgeoisie of cultural intermediaries, museums found it necessary to eschew the assumption of pure-gaze appropriation and present art as another commodity, appropriated not with active contemplation but with passive, sensual pleasure.[55]

In the 1980s and 1990s, art museums turned to a new mode of presentation to attract more market revenue—the blockbuster exhibit. Taking their cues from Hollywood, whose sales were increasingly dependent on a few heavily promoted, high-budget films, museums mounted highly publicized and expensive exhibitions of art on the popular end of the spectrum of legitimate culture—ancient Egyptian treasures, Impressionists, well-known modernists like Picasso and Matisse. These exhibitions were generally mounted with an eye to not contemplative integrity but dramatic effect, emphasizing the sensual beauty of objects. To defray exhibit expenses, museums enlisted private sponsors, usually corporations, which invested their growing economic profits in legitimate culture in the hopes of reaping symbolic profits. Substantial revenues also came in from ticket sales, which were generally handled through commercial outlets. But in addition, most blockbuster exhibits capitalized on the commodity-oriented art public by selling spin-off products. Once tiny museums shops expanded into veritable shopping malls, where one could buy any manner of mundane commodity emblazoned with reproductions from the exhibit. In the new, privatized museum, art was for sale, and consumers took it home with them on T-shirts and key chains.[56]

The new museum that lowered art to commodified entertainment adopted the same architectural style that Disney used to raise commodified entertainment to an art—postmodern historicism. Accessible historical clichés treated in an abstract way were recognizable and welcoming to the masses seeking cultural stability, while the inside references validated the cultural capital of the yuppie symbol producers. But the specific museum applications of this aesthetic were determined by the urban location of the museums of the 1980s and 1990s. Post-Fordist urban development brought museums back to downtown areas, where they were often neighbors with urban blight and homelessness that undermined the artistic spectacles they sought to create. This problem was solved by one of the primary traits of postmodernism—the visual insulation of inside space from the threatening world without. An architecture of defensive, almost military security infected the public museums downtown, further privatizing public space.

This insularity is apparent in Venturi and Scott Brown's Sainsbury Wing of the National Gallery of Art in London, which was enclosed by high, blind walls. Even more paranoically protected from its urban surroundings was the most critically acclaimed museum of the early post-Fordist period, James Stirling's New State Gallery in Stuttgart, Germany, completed in 1984. The symmetrical, U-shaped building was fronted by an eight-lane freeway and bordered on all sides by an urban fabric of old and new buildings. Most commentators focused on the clever double-coded references that Stirling applied to the sandstone building. Some, like the Egyptian cornices, were ancient, while others, like the undulating glass wall reminiscent of Aalto, were modern. Receiving less attention, however, was the fortresslike protection of the State Gallery from the urban fabric. While the surrounding buildings cordially reached out to meet the road, Stirling's museum was cautiously set back from it and raised on a stone podium. And while its neighbors opened up to city sights with abundant fenestration, the almost windowless, bunkerlike walls of

James Stirling, Michael Wilford and Associates, New State Gallery, Stuttgart, 1984
(© Meredith L. Clausen, Cities/Buildings Database http://content.lib.washington.edu/buildingsweb/)

the New State Gallery turned a defensive face to the city, being punctured only occasionally by narrow gun-port slits. The galleries admitted light mainly from skylights that covered the roof. The round sculpture garden was open to the sky, but this gun-turret of a structure was completely sealed off from the city by high walls. Stirling seemed to imply that art and culture were under siege in the post-Fordist city, and had to be protected from the barbarian hordes without. And indeed, autonomous art, which keeps enough distance from society to be critical of it, was under siege in the new climate of barbaric market competition, in which everything had to pay for itself and only the most profitable survived. But it was not the "dangerous classes" of the dispossessed outside the museum that posed this threat, but the bourgeois yuppies inside, who reduced art to another spectacular commodity.[57]

Theodor Adorno has written that authentic, autonomous art must reveal in its forms the contradictions of the society in which it exists, in the hope of motivating actions to resolve them. The main shortcoming of market-driven postmodern architecture was the abandonment of this obligation and its accommodation to the role of stimulating consumption. Instead of revealing the ugly contradictions of the emerging regime of post-Fordism championed by the new ruling class, instead of making people feel uncomfortable and alien in this new society so they could oppose it, postmodern architects gave people nostalgic illusions of protection and soothing simulations of privacy that obscured the ugly realities of class polarization and created a narcotizing realm of spectacular consumption. Of course, postmodernists like Robert Venturi and Denise Scott Brown could claim that they were merely accommodating people as they were, instead of imposing on them their own idealized conceptions of what they should be. But as Adorno has observed, the bourgeois's tolerance and "love of people as they are stems from his hatred of what they might be," and, in fact, serves to divert them from their historical potentials.[58]

Venturi and Scott Brown might have further objected that their brand of postmodernism was not a seamless, soothing whole but rife with ironies. Through double-coding they claimed to be both tolerant and critical of their era. As Scott Brown stated: "One way to meld respect for, love for, and criticism of your age is through irony. With a sense of irony you can laugh rather than cry about phenomena you both hate and love." But this postmodern irony was not synonymous with Adorno's Marxist concept of contradiction, and this quote reveals why. While contradiction is the clash of opposites that potentially leads to change, irony is the mere coexistence of opposites in a tolerant diversity that generates no change. So postmodernists placed high-art references side by side with popular kitsch, implying that the dominant and subordinate classes could peacefully coexist. By contrast, avant-garde modernists confronted workers in housing estates with the one-sided rule of instrumental reason, revealing both the beauty of a potential rationality and the ugliness of its distortion by existing capitalist society. These modernist displays of contradiction evoked vociferous reactions and led to actions by workers, petty bourgeois, even Nazis. No such reactions were generated by the polite irony of postmodern buildings, which was a private opposition confined to the knowing few and did not threaten the placating public references. Such irony was the coward's criticism, consciously constructed so it could not be publicly prosecuted and thus ensuring it had no effect on the powers that be. Avant-garde modernists were defiant, technocratic revolutionaries who displayed contradiction and evoked confrontation that led to change. The postmodernists were compliant smart alecks, creating ironic compositions that elicited consumer somnambulism and orchestrated the acquiescence to post-Fordism.[59]

New Urbanism: Postmodern Planning and the Myth of Community

The effect of the postmodern historicism extended beyond the aesthetics of individual buildings to encompass the planning of entire communities. The crisis of Fordism in the 1970s undermined modernist urban planning, as the government's role diminished and functional zoning collapsed. In congruence with the rise of post-Fordism, however, a new urbanism emerged that, like postmodern architecture, turned to the past for answers. Postmodern planning sought to recreate an idealized integrated city of the past, before Fordism separated and segregated not merely social functions but people as well. The advocates of this nostalgic vision of urban community organized themselves into a movement they called the new urbanism. This movement found its principal ideas in the 1960s critique of urban planning by Jane Jacobs, who argued for a diversity of people and activities assembled by the vital forces of the market. By the 1980s, it seemed that Jacobs's dream might come true, at least in the United States, where the government pulled out of urban planning and private developers following market incentives were mixing classes and functions in downtown areas. People were also longing for traditional communities of family values and neighborliness, and the new urbanists arose to help developers provide them. At the head of this movement was the architectural team of Andres Duany (b. 1949) and Elizabeth Plater-Zyberk (b. 1950), both of whom had studied at Yale with postmodernists like Vincent Scully, Robert Venturi, and Denise Scott Brown. They took the classical and vernacular aesthetics of their teachers and applied them to the design of entire communities, turning the nostalgic simulations in individual postmodern buildings into collective delusions on the scale of a city.

Unlike Jane Jacobs, the new urbanists focused their criticisms and efforts on the suburbs, not the city. The segregation of city functions had already broken down under the demands of gentrifying yuppies and developers for urban mixtures of production and consumption. It was just such urban diversity, pedestrian scale, and public space that the new urbanists hoped to bring to the suburbs to replace traditional development patterns. So when Duany and Plater-Zyberk published the bible of new urbanism in 2000 after two decades of work. It was entitled *Suburban Nation* and focused on combating suburban sprawl. Although the authors acknowledged urban problems, their main mission was to bring the spatial geography of the city center to the suburbs, where they believed most new growth would occur.

In their preface Duany and Plater-Zyberk claimed "the American Dream just doesn't seem to be coming true anymore.... It seems that our economic and technological progress has not succeeded in bringing about the good society." They blamed the suburbs, those sprawling expanses of single-family homes that segregated and isolated people by age, income, ethnicity, and family type. These fragmented, homogeneous enclaves produced no real sense of civic responsibility to anyone beyond the neighborhood. People now wanted more community and togetherness, and the new urbanists claimed to know how to spatially engineer these. First, they argued, neighborhoods needed different housing types to accommodate people of different income levels. Second, every neighborhood should contain retail stores and office space, so people could shop and work within walking distance of their residences. Once people got out of their cars and on foot, they argued, they would meet face to face and a community would grow. To facilitate such encounters these architects advocated placing houses close to the street and opening them to public intercourse through semiprivate spaces like front porches. The new urbanists also encouraged the development of civic life through including in every neighborhood public spaces where diverse people could meet as equals. Finally, to weave all this diversity and activity into an aesthetic whole they advocated unity of style in a neighborhood. The average suburb contained individualized castles that competed for attention, while real neighborhoods needed aesthetic standards that revealed a cooperative community.[60]

Evident in the program of new urbanism were some of the same demands that underlay the general postmodern aesthetic. Emphasis on community and rootedness developed in response to the uprooting mobilities of the new post-Fordist regime. At the same time, the new cultural bourgeois found the suburbs of their youth boring and longed for the diversity of urban areas. The new urbanists sought to provide people with both diversity and community by bringing aspects of the new, gentrified cities to the suburbs. And they relied upon the marketplace and private developers to do so. Like Jane Jacobs, the new urbanists placed the blame for unlivable suburbs on government regulations and zoning restrictions that steered developers into bad decisions. Their solution was less government, that is, changing restrictive zoning laws so developers could provide people with the housing they really wanted through the marketplace. For the new urbanists, building diverse communities was perfectly compatible with, even contingent upon, the profits of private developers.[61]

By this marketplace standard, the new urbanism was an overwhelming success. By 2000, the firm of Duany Plater-Zyberk and Company alone had designed over 200 new neighborhoods that greatly enriched their developers. Despite their profitability, however, there are reasons to doubt that the new urbanism actually accomplished its goal of diverse communities, and one of the main obstacles to this accomplishment was the free market they embraced. Duany and Plater-Zyberk cited as an example of their success in integrating different income classes their Kentlands development (1991) in Gaithersburg, Maryland, where they built a diversity of housing types—mansions, row houses, and apartments—to accommodate social diversity. But their concept of class diversity was very narrow, encompassing only the difference between a $214,000 middle-class row house and a $500,000 upper-class mansion. The few apartments included at Kentlands rented for $750 a month—not exactly housing for low-income families. The architects themselves recognized that the market prevented the integration of low-income housing into affluent new urbanist developments. When located in upscale neighborhoods, they stated, affordable housing tended to escalate in price, thus eliminating the intended diversity. Nowhere was this problem more evident than in the most famous of all new urbanist developments, the Florida town of Seaside.[62]

Seaside was begun in 1981 by developer Robert Davis, who stated his initial goals as "civil society, social justice, and environment." Collaborating with Duany and Plater-Zyberk, he conceived Seaside as an inexpensive beachfront community, with the best lots initially selling for $12,000. Many of the first houses built were modest cottages, which were guided by the town's architectural code into the vernacular styles of the southeastern United States and

Caribbean. But the overwhelming marketplace success of this development undermined the original goals and turned Seaside into a chic, upscale resort, in which the original cottages sold for nearly $1 million and the Victorian mansions built subsequently sold for up to $4 million. So there was little diversity in Seaside, but was it nonetheless an actual community where people met, interacted, and deliberated? Duany and Plater-Zyberk designed the public spaces required for such a community, like downtown Seaside, a U-shaped block containing a grassy square, amphitheater, shops, art galleries, restaurants, a meeting hall, and a neighborhood school. Further, the Seaside planners initially left a long stretch of public beach devoid of buildings, and placed on it architect-designed public pavilions. To encourage pedestrian activity, they laid out the development so no home was more than a five-minute walk from downtown, and provided ample walks and paths. To further encourage civil interchange, the code mandated that all houses be built a few feet from sidewalks and streets, and have a porch adjacent to the street.[63]

As a result of all this mandated propinquity and public space, Seaside had the look of a close-knit, friendly town. But it was missing one indispensable ingredient of community—residents. In the summer months Seaside's streets were packed with people, but most were not residents but tourists renting the houses of absentee owners, who themselves used them only as vacation homes. The dirty little secret of the Seaside "community" was that no one really lived there, save for about thirty year-round residents. When I visited in December, during the off-season, the highly touted, community-creating streets, sidewalks, and public spaces were absolutely deserted. The only people stirring were workers cleaning, maintaining, and building the vacation houses of

Andres Duany and Elizabeth Plater-Zyberk, Seaside, Florida, 1981
(Photograph by author)

others. And they were not walking but riding around in golf carts. When questioned, one maid answered with a laugh that, no, she did not live in Seaside but commuted from a town some forty miles away. An inquiry at the Seaside Neighborhood School revealed that most of the students were bused in from surrounding communities. Thus, this town that was supposed to address American's longing for tradition and rootedness was just another testimony to the transience of a spatially dispersed post-Fordist society, in which people circulated so incessantly that they could not settle down long enough to relax on the front porch, stroll down a shady path, or pass a kind word to a neighbor. Seaside became just another resort for the wealthy, another place to throw up a trophy house as an economic and cultural investment. With this emphasis on market individualism, it was not surprising to find many of Seaside's original public spaces being reappropriated for the private realm. By 2001 most of the streets, as well as all but one of the beach pavilions, were conspicuously marked with signs declaring them to be "private." So the public was not welcome in the "public" spaces of Seaside, which were, like the new "public" spaces of downtown districts, open only to private consumers who could afford the admission price to paradise.[64]

The new urbanist planning movement, like the broader movement of postmodern architecture, proved the folly of trying to change society through reconfiguring space. No amount of public space, front porches, sidewalks, or cute Victorian architecture could create social ties among a people who were increasingly divided by a yawning class chasm and forced into vicious competition with all others in the global marketplace. Seaside and the rest of postmodern architecture offered only an empty simulacrum of community that prevented people from confronting the social reality that destroyed real communities.

The Exception of European Architecture in the Post-Fordist Age

During the first decade after the collapse of Fordism, European architecture followed many postmodern trends pioneered in the United States. Postmodern historicism was particularly strong in Europe, as Aldo Rossi and others continued to advance this style of abstracted and reified classicism. Many Europeans seemed to agree with Americans that the best way to weather the post-Fordist change was to retreat to a nostalgic fantasy of past stability and wholeness. Yet, the transition to the new economic regime was not identical in Europe and the United States. On the Continent social spending programs were trimmed but not slashed as in America and Britain. And governments generally retained a greater control over urban planning and a greater commitment to public housing. Consequently, state bureaucracies remained strong and committed to the idea of technological progress. This was also the case in Japan, where a state capitalism based on close cooperation between the government and corporate cooperatives called *keiretsus* remained strong throughout this period. In Japan and Europe there thus emerged a new modernist aesthetic that embodied a continued belief in bureaucracy and science as saviors. Often called high-tech architecture, this aesthetic had its roots in the 1960s movement of megastructure, which was well suited to express the European approach to post-Fordist restructuring in the 1970s. Like the early megastructuralists, countries on the Continent also sought to create more economic flexibility to accommodate the market demand for individuality, but within a "support structure" of government regulation and control. The faith in technology and rational planning remained, but in a more decentralized and individualized technocracy. High-tech architecture symbolized this program.[65]

A prescient pioneer in this genre was the Centraal Beheer building in Apeldoorn, The Netherlands, by Dutch architect Herman Hertzberger (b. 1932). Completed in 1972 for an insurance company, this office complex was the materialization of the post-Fordist idea of flexible, nonhierarchical production, in which workers participated in decision-making. Abandoning the standardized uniformity of the monolithic modernist skyscraper, which symbolized hierarchy and bureaucracy, Hertzberger created a low, dispersed building composed of square units stacked to varying heights in an overall pattern, creating the image of a voluntary cooperation of equal individuals. Inside the building this orderly individuality was symbolized by a regular grid of open offices, each of which could be internally arranged by the individual worker. Although Hertzberger's building reflected some of the changes in the post-Fordist workplace, it obfuscated others. For all the appearance of leveled democracy, this was still an insurance bureaucracy, in which all the individual workers submitted to hierarchical power. And the ability to move the furniture around in one's cubicle was not real participation but mere compensation for workers' bureaucratic powerlessness.[66]

British architect Norman Foster (b. 1935) used a similarly decentralized but more high-tech aesthetic in his Distribution Center for the French automaker Renault, completed in 1983. He designed this center in rural England as a shed whose metal roof was suspended from a series of masts by I-beams and guy wires. The roof was composed of identical bays, more of which could be added on any side to facilitate flexible expansion. And to symbolize this

Herman Hertzberger, Centraal Beheer, Apeldoorn, the Netherlands, 1972
(© Herman Hertzberger)

open-endedness, Foster left one end of his generally rectangular structure incomplete, in a stepped pattern. This structure represented the technology of post-Fordism, which was no longer centralized and immobile but dispersed and mobilized, allowing capital to cast its net of exchange widely over the global landscape. This dispersion of economic forces was symbolized by the building's dispersion of roof support over dozens of masts and hundreds of cables and beams. Just like globalized capitalism, there was no center here, no place of spatial concentration but merely a homogeneous network of supports capable of indefinite expansion in any direction. And the mobility of this network was symbolized by the undulating white roof of the Renault Distribution Center, which looked like the fluttering tents of an encampment of nomads. Archigram devised similarly flexible, tentlike structures in the 1960s and conceived of them as maximizing the freedom of individuals to escape the power of "the establishment." But the ruse of instrumental reason turned the tables on the 1960s techno-radicals, and by the 1980s such temporary, mobile structures represented the new-found power of the post-Fordist corporate establishment to escape from individual workers, their communities, and entire nations, to pull up the stakes of their corporate tents and move to greener pastures in the hypernomadic marketplace.[67]

While corporate Europe often turned to high-tech architecture that was symbolically nonhierarchical and dispersed, the state bureaucracies that remained powerful usually preferred a more monumental and monolithic expression of technology and rationality. Unlike these transnational

Norman Foster, Renault Distribution Center, Swindon, England, 1983
(Photograph Richard Davies/courtesy Foster and Partners)

corporations, the state is necessarily rooted in a place, monopolizing the legitimate use of force within a particular territory, as Max Weber defined it. So high-tech state architecture generally employed technology to assert a dominating presence in the landscape, and nowhere was this more evident than in Paris. Beginning in the mid-1970s the French state under the presidencies of Georges Pompidou and François Mitterand undertook an ambitious public building program in the capital known as the *Grands Projets*. This series of grand and architecturally important public structures not only reasserted Paris's prominence as the cultural capital of an increasingly unified Europe but also provided the framework for urban development that shaped private developers' decisions. For these tributes to state power, the French government used a high-tech aesthetic emphasizing transparency and glass.

From the beginning modern architects had asserted the superiority of glass architecture, arguing that it symbolized the triumph of reason and democracy by opening affairs of state to the gaze of the general public. The underside of glass architecture was that it opened the private realm of individuals to the surveillance of instrumental reason, which enforced its standardized will on all. Claiming to protect individuality, postmodernists embraced opacity over transparency, sealing up the interior of buildings as a private refuge. The French state, the self-proclaimed embodiment of Enlightenment rationality, felt it necessary to reassert the primacy of technocratic rationality against what it perceived to be, in the words of architectural scholar Anthony Vidler, "a regressive postmodern tendency of historical atavism." So many of its *Grands*

Projets embraced *la transparence*, perhaps to strengthen the state's tenuous hold on power in a Europe where transnational corporations and transnational governments were weakening its grip. But the type of transparency it pursued departed from the modernism of the 1950s and inadvertently signaled that the time of state-based rationality had passed.[68]

In the *Grands Projets*, the French state sought to attain a monumental but elusive presence with different types of transparency. In one type, a monumental geometric shape was hollowed out with a pure transparency. Examples of this *transparence* included Dominique Perrault's (b. 1953) Bibliothèque Nationale (1996) of four transparent glass towers and the Parc André-Citroën (1992), a landscape park with a glass pavilion. But the most famous manifestation of this vision was I. M. Pei's underground addition to the Louvre Museum, the central focus of which was a large, above-ground glass pyramid that formed the new entrance. This iconic shape that generally denoted solidity and stability was consciously rendered "immaterial," according to Pei, by using the most transparent materials possible. Unlike the conspicuous steel supports of modernist glass buildings, the frame supporting the glass pyramid of the Grand Louvre was composed of a latticework of exceptionally thin rods. And the glass itself was exceptionally white and flat, to give the impression of one monolithic, transparent structure. In Pei's hands, the shape symbolic of timeless stability looked more like a light tent, pitched temporarily in the courtyard of high culture. This state monumentality was ephemeral and seemed to be in the process of disappearing.[69]

A similarly elusive state presence was expressed in another of the *Grands Projets*, the Grande Arche de la Défense, but with a different kind of transparency. The difficulties encountered by the French government in realizing this project hinted at its symbolic significance. When the building was first planned in 1982, it was to be a state center for international communications

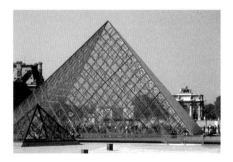

Pei Cobb Freed and Partners, Grand Louvre, 1989
(©Meredith L. Clausen, Cities/Buildings Database http://content.lib.washington.edu/buildingsweb/)

located in the financial district of Paris, La Défense. From entries in a competition President Mitterrand selected the winning design, which was submitted by Danish architect Johann Otto von Spreckelsen (1929-87). But halfway into the project the socialist Mitterrand was defeated by the conservative Jacques Chirac, who stopped state funding for the Grande Arche. To fund its completion the project manager, who headed a large investment fund, organized a joint company with the state holding a minority share, and then converted the building from state functions to a private office building occupied mainly by financial firms from La Défense. The architect, however, seemed to anticipate the fate of the building, for his form symbolized the hollowing out of the French state to the benefit of the finance capital headquartered nearby.

Like the other *Grands Projets*, Spreckelsen's Grande Arche de la Défense was a transparent, monumental shape—a concrete cube 110 meters across. Its transparency, however, was achieved not by glass surfacing but in its form. The monumental cube was hollowed out in the center, thus simulating a triumphal arch like Napoleon's located not far away. Stabilizing this empty cube proved a challenging feat of engineering, requiring a vast array of suspension cables inside the opening. Even then the building swayed back and forth as much as four centimeters. Inside the hollow cube, suspended from the network of cables, was a white, tentlike canopy of fabric covering the public plaza below. Perhaps this hole in the heart of the pristine cube of reason represented the 55 percent investment share that private capital took out of the state project,

Johann Otto von Spreckelsen, La Grande Arche de la Defense, Paris, 1989 (Mary Ann Sullivan, Bluffton University)

thus symbolizing the emptying out of government power by neoliberal policies. Here global finance capital erected its own triumphal arch, revealing in
the form that it had no home but was merely an abstract emptiness, a dematerialized container of exchange value that could hold anything and be anywhere. This placeless power was mobile and transient, as represented again
by the increasingly popular form of the tent. The state, as well as the people
over whom it exerts power, is necessarily tied to a place, a physical locale, but
the competing power of global capital drove through all such places and left a
void. In the French state's attempt to present its continuing power and presence in the capital city with these transparent architectural projects, it ironically revealed its increasing impotence in the face of the power of transnational
corporations and capital. Its presence was increasingly a fragile house of glass,
from which it certainly would throw no stones of discipline at capital, which
now stalked the globe beyond the control of the states and people unfortunate enough to be tied to the materiality of place. The high-tech architecture
of these *Grands Projets* symbolized the triumph of that dispersed, mobile force
that was also revealed in corporate projects like those of Foster.[70]

There was, however, another architectural trend that emerged in the
semideveloped periphery of Europe that defied the high-tech symbolism of
a dispersed and mobile capital embraced by the Continent's capitalist core
countries. The economic integration of Europe under the European Union
threatened these less developed countries' indigenous producers, especially
farmers, with overwhelming competition and ultimate demise. The European
periphery thus saw a backlash against globalization and unification that found
aesthetic expression in a movement known as critical regionalism. In countries
like Spain, Italy, and Greece, architects opposed the forces of globalizing power
by reviving regional and national traditions. Kenneth Frampton, the leading
advocate of critical regionalism, has written that this school was defined by an
attempt to create "place-forms" rooted in local topography and traditions, with
an emphasis on the tactile and techtonic aspects of architecture. The best of
this genre avoided the sentimental clichés of the past employed in postmodern
historicism, as well as the chauvinistic implications of some of the new ethnic
reactions to globalization. For example, in his Museo Nacional de Arte Romano
(1985) in Merida, Spain, Spanish architect Rafael Moneo (b. 1937) evoked the
pride of the region's Roman heritage in a building of arched walls and naves
constructed with bricks of the same dimensions as those in the Roman ruins
nearby. But the Romans' imperialist attempt to unify Europe was contradicted
here by a layout and materials from the regional tradition of the Madrid school

of architecture. These contradictions of past and present prevented a simplistic and chauvinistic identification with either. The pride of a regional past was mobilized against globalization without encouraging the chauvinism that could lead to nationalism and racism, as in Nazi Germany. Some commentators questioned, however, whether this movement in peripheral Europe could effectively steer a path between the Scylla of chauvinistic separatism on the one hand and the Charybdis of capitalist incorporation on the other.[71]

Deconstructionism, or, How I Learned to Stop Worrying and Love Global Capitalism

All postmodernism aesthetics besides high tech were backward-looking retreats from the post-Fordist revolution, conforming to Marx's insight that revolutionaries often legitimate themselves by adopting the raiments of the past. But Marx also stated: "The new social formation once established, the antediluvian Colossi disappeared and with them resurrected Romanity....Bourgeois society in its sober reality had begotten its true interpreters and mouth pieces."[72] And so it was with the new post-Fordist society. Reagan and Thatcher successfully mobilized conservative rhetoric about traditional values and national glories to destroy the Fordist regime, as well as the Soviet-style socialism that was its necessary and defining opponent. But once they swept the stage of history clear of antagonists, they could not seem to find in their remembrances of empire and Hollywood westerns a rhetoric suitable for constructing a new, global post-Fordism. So both players and their ideological scripts exited stage right, to be succeeded from the center-left wings by the true protagonists of global capitalism, Bill Clinton and, eventually, Tony Blair. These advocates of a Third-Way ideological formula between Reagan/Thatcher conservatism and Fordist/Keynesian liberalism promised to combine market efficiency with social solidarity and security in a truly world market, albeit one dominated economically and militarily by the United States. Under the excuse of creating a bright new future, not recapturing a past, Clinton continued Reagan's neoliberal policies of deregulating markets and dismantling Keynesian social programs, and badgered leaders of other capitalist countries to do likewise.[73]

So Clinton and Blair rode the rising tide of post-Fordist globalization, and an exhilarating ride it was for anyone at the forefront of the new economy of digits, symbols, and images. Corporations that had chafed for half a century under the weight of Fordist fetters experienced this era with the heady euphoria of a new, unbounded freedom. Now capital could go virtually anywhere, sell virtually anything, employ virtually anyone. International competition led to cross-national mergers and acquisitions, creating transnational corporations and a transnational capitalist class. Those occupying privileged positions in these newly unfettered corporations were enriched with soaring salaries and stock options, which unleashed a frenzy of conspicuous overconsumption.

In this new atmosphere of triumphant capitalism, the nostalgic aesthetic of postmodernism seemed outmoded. The ruling class of the new regime no longer needed old bottles to disguise its intoxicating new wine, but demanded new ideological bottles that celebrated its freedom and prosperity. One of these new bottles in the ideological pantry of post-Fordism was deconstructionism, an architectural aesthetic that arose in the mid-1980s. Expressing the euphoria of liberation from a rectilinear grid of regulation, deconstruction took the controlled elements of modernism and smashed them open, releasing some enormous pent-up energy. Deconstructionism celebrated a free-for-all world in which there were no more rules.

The exhilarating post-Fordist economy was not, however, the only force creating the deconstructionist aesthetic. Also influential were forces internal to the field of high-art architecture, the most important of which was the cycle of innovation theorized by Pierre Bourdieu. To attain distinction outsiders pioneer innovations, some of which are adopted by the economic bourgeoisie to legitimate its resources. But commercial distribution deflates their distinction, sending the privileged back to the cultural field to find new goods. Post-Fordism, with its focus on differentiation and individuation, accelerated this cycle, ensuring that no aesthetic trend survived for long, including postmodernism. Its meteoric rise in a building market focused on differentiating images ensured its rapid demise. In 1987 the critic who discovered postmodernism, Charles Jencks, wrote that this style had become so widespread and commercially successful that, like modernism in the 1960s, it "suffered from overproduction and vulgarization" and was consequently "middle-aged, if not moribund." The commercialization of postmodernism flooded the landscape with similarly decorated buildings, which deflated its uniqueness and degraded its artistic status. Postmodernism was peculiarly susceptible to vulgarization because it sought through double-coding to be both a popular aesthetic and high art. As it became more commercialized, however, architects reached larger audiences by editing out the irony and appealing mainly to the masses with consoling aesthetic integration.[74]

This vulgarization of postmodernism motivated avant-garde outsiders competing for distinction to reassert the autonomy of architecture by creating a new aesthetic tied to deconstructionism, an esoteric philosophy that was revolutionizing literary criticism and other intellectual fields. Deconstructionism was well suited to deposing postmodernism because, first, it was a difficult, esoteric theory that required considerable academic training. Thus, it reasserted the dominance of architects with more cultural capital than economic capital and insulated the field against commercialism. Further, deconstructionist revolutionaries in architecture were ensured alliances with both the producers and consumers of other fields influenced by the theory, thus increasing the power and market of the movement.[75]

Another internal factor facilitating the downfall of postmodernism and the rise of deconstructionism was the increasing internationalization of the profession of architecture. The rise of global cities in the era of post-Fordism created an international real estate market that attracted foreign capital from around the world. With the financial sectors of all countries deregulated to allow foreign investments, corporations from around the globe began to make major investments in development projects in cities like London, New York, Los Angeles, and Tokyo. This internationalization of the real estate market brought with it the internationalization of the architectural profession. During the 1980s and 1990s big-name architects like Michael Graves, James Stirling, and Renzo Piano became globe-hopping professionals, designing buildings in major cities around the world. Postmoderism was not, however, well-suited to this new international marketplace for architecture. While modernism claimed to use a universal language of progress and technology, postmodernism opposed universalism with an aesthetic that validated history, the vernacular, and the contextual, all of which are necessarily tied to particular nations and regions. In short, postmodernism did not travel well. A style created by an American postmodernist to address the country's traditions and culture, for example, seemed inappropriate in Tokyo. An international real estate industry needed a global aesthetic that had the same meanings for all people in a unified global economy. But architects could not revert to the discredited universalism of modern architecture, which was associated with Fordist bureaucracies and rules. A new international language was required that expressed the global freedom of capital from Fordist limits and restrictions. Deconstructionism or "decon," as it was known, was just such an aesthetic.[76]

On its surface the aesthetic of deconstructionism appeared to owe much more to modernism than to postmodernism. Devoid of decoration and references to historical styles, decon used severe geometric forms rendered in modern materials such as glass, steel, and other metals. But while mature modernism used these forms and materials to create images of order and stability, deconstructionism used them to construct connotations of instability and fragmentation, which were celebrated as the virtues of a new age of freedom. Deconstructionists took their aesthetics loosely from the work of the French founder of deconstructionist philosophy, Jacques Derrida, who in the early 1970s broke with the structuralist tradition by declaring that there was no rational structure or code beneath human signs and actions. There existed only the irrational and variable surface of different signifiers, in all their chaos and fragmentation. The purpose of a critic or philosopher, he held, should not be to impose some singular, totalitarian meaning on a text, but to take it apart, revealing the free play of its internal differences and contradictions.

The implications of deconstructionism for architecture were immediately clear. Modernism's attempt to impose one set of universal, rational rules on all architecture was oppressive and totalitarian. But postmodernism was no solution to this modernist absolutism, for it used simplified images of stability to impose a superficial unity on an era of change and dispersion. The new era required a new language that, in the words of decon architect Bernard Tschumi (b. 1944), "celebrates fragmentation by celebrating the culture of differences, by accelerating and intensifying the loss of certainty, of center, of history." Tschumi and others justified this new architectural language as commensurate with the deregulation of social institutions in the new age of post-Fordism: "First deregulation of airlines, then deregulation of Wall Street, finally deregulation of appearances; it all belongs to the same inexorable logic....There are no more rules and regulations. The current metropolitan deregulation caused by the dis-industrialization of European and American cities, by the collapse of zoning strategies, contradicts any attempt to develop new sets of regulating forces." Not all rules were abolished, however. The end to *state* rules and regulations meant that the rules of the marketplace became more powerful than ever. But market rules were more dispersed and less palpable than the geographically centered rules of states, and they favored the interests of capital and the privileged symbol producers who served it. For this class, post-Fordist deregulation felt like freedom, which they expressed in a deconstructionist aesthetic that shattered and slashed the confining forms of modernism. Deconstructionism was a metaphor for smashing the iron cage of bureaucratic regulation and freeing the prisoner of capital.[77]

Deconstructionism was an attempt to solve the same capitalist contradictions addressed by postmodernism, but in the new era of established post-Fordism. The ideological demands of the established ruling class were different from those of the emerging one, but the dilemmas it faced did not change.

The new cultural bourgeoisie of corporate symbol producers still confronted the contradictions of establishing some sense of permanence during rapid change, some conception of centeredness within increasingly dispersed space, and some semblance of unity among increasingly fragmented individuals. But unlike the earlier postmodernists, they privileged the latter sides of these contradictions.

On the dimension of time, deconstructionist architecture emphasized the excitement and exhilaration of change over the security and serenity of permanence. It promised progress and liberation from the past, but an unconstrained progress, not the regulated advance of modernism. In the unregulated markets of post-Fordism, vicious competition was ubiquitous, and survival required constant innovation. Product cycles thus accelerated to dizzying speeds. But, as Fredric Jameson has argued, product changes became so rapid and random that they undermined the experience of newness, for they seemed to have no direction or goal. So a paradoxical sense of stability arose in an incessantly changing society, and the idea of history faded. The deconstructionists captured this sense of stationary motion in architecture. Frank Gehry, for example, revealed motion in his twisting and turning metal forms that some said reflected the influence of film, which simulates motion through a sequence of still images. Tschumi conceived of his Parc de la Villette as a film strip of still images viewed through movement along prescribed paths. Yet, the simulated movement in this architecture seemed to have no direction, to be going nowhere. Early modern architecture simulated movement that was directional. The arms of the Bauhaus building by Gropius and the planes of Mies's Barcelona Pavilion reached out into the landscape, symbolizing the expansion of a technocratic capitalism from a central, metropolitan core. Yet, post-Fordism incorporated the whole world into the market, bringing the history of capitalist expansion to an end. Now movement merely oscillated in fashion and business cycles, and this directionless movement was captured by deconstructionism. As architectural critic Michael Sorkin has observed, Gehry's rotating masses and tipping facades showed a "frozen motion," like the stationary dynamism of a flickering flame or a cinematic image.[78]

On the dimension of space, the deconstructionist aesthetic emphasized dispersion over centeredness. Eschewing the false sense of centeredness of postmodernism's insular, enclosed spaces, the deconstructionists celebrated the dispersion of space by smashing open enclosures. The decons took the rectilinear shapes of modernism and exploded them from the inside, setting their contained spaces free in a violent dispersion that symbolized the freedom of unregulated capital to spread itself over the entire globe. These deconstructionist explosions left gaps and voids in their buildings, spaces of absence that struggled to represent some "other" or make way for some "event" that had been repressed and was not quite there. This idea of representing absence was derived from Derrida's philosophy, which argued that criticism should decenter the meaning of the text by incorporating the traces of other meanings that had been suppressed by authority. Peter Eisenman applied this idea to architecture, asserting: "Any site contains not only presences, but the memory of previous presences and the immanences of a possible presence. The physical difference between a moving thing (dynamism) and a still one (stasis) is that the moving one contains the trace of where it has been and where it is going. The introduction of this trace, or condition of absence acknowledges the dynamic reality of the living city."[79]

Bernard Tschumi argued that in this decentered, in-between space new activities could take place, unpredictable events that were suppressed by the presence of traditional architecture. Drawing on the ideas of the megastructuralists, he tried to make architecture with an indefinite program, "to design the conditions that make it possible for this nonhierarchical, nontraditional society to happen." But regardless of the deconstructionists' arguments that the absent force expressed in their dispersed spaces was the growing freedom of humanity, in reality it was the freedom of dispersed capital liberated from the humanizing constraints of Fordist regulation. As Fredric Jameson has argued, the dilemma of art in the post-Fordist age was to represent the force of capital that was everywhere in general but no place in particular. This representation was especially difficult in architecture, which by its very nature is constructed in a space. So the deconstructionists represented dispersed capital as a void, the figure of a force that exists but is not here, not present to the senses. What made this representation ideological, however, was the depiction of this force as total freedom, which reflected the particular class viewpoint of the unrestrained, symbol-producing professionals. The ugliness of the absent force of capital, as viewed from the perspective of its many global victims, went unrepresented.[80]

Finally, on the dimension of the self, the deconstructionist aesthetic emphasized fragmentation and difference among people over unity and sameness. While postmodernism countered the fragmentation of self with unified identities in smaller lifestyle groups, deconstructionists embraced the fragmentation of the self. Poststructuralists like Derrida and Gilles Deleuze criticized the unified Freudian subject as an artifact of power and idealized the fragmented mentality of schizophrenia, in which deterritorialized flows of desire triggered by the outside world washed over the psyche in an exhilarating, unorganized delirium.[81] Deconstructionists embraced this dissociated self by gathering together in one space many disjointed, different meanings. Bernard Tschumi carried out such a dissociated assembly of desiring elements in his Parc de la Villette, which he conceived as a place "where fragments of dislocated reality may be apprehended." He called the elements of his park composition *folies* (French for madnesses) because they did not force a unity but left themselves open for an infinite number of reassemblies by the individuals who visited the park.[82]

Deconstructionist architecture thus unabashedly celebrated the attributes of post-Fordism that postmodernism apologetically sought to obscure. This positive perspective on the new regime was conditioned by the position of architecture in the class structure of the new economy. The elite architects of the high-art subfield were part of the rising bourgeois class of yuppies who produced symbols for the deregulated global economy. After the building slump of the late 1970s and early 1980s, the expansionist market of the late 1980s and 1990s greatly increased the demand for market-differentiating architecture, and no design seemed too wild if it attracted the attention of overconsuming yuppies. Deconstructionism was the self-satisfied voice of this new elite of globe-trotting, wealthy architects, whose identification with capital made fragmentation look like freedom, difference look like individuality, and displacement look like home. But for those in the class of embodied labor, who lived in a particular space and time but were subject to the commands of a nowhere master, what the deconstructionists celebrated looked like disaster. The exploded, contorted forms of decon connoted the wreckage left behind by an arbitrary and powerful but invisible force moving irrationally and violently through the landscape. So when the design of deconstructionist Daniel Libeskind (b. 1946) was chosen for the extension to London's Victoria and Albert Museum, one Londoner commented upon seeing photos that it looked like an earthquake site.[83]

Could it be, however, that this frank aesthetic revelation of the dislocating and fragmenting consequences of the new economy was inadvertently progressive, like modernism before it? This may have been true of some deconstructionist architecture, but not most of it, for reasons apparent from a close examination of the work of the most renowned architects in this school. The most successful of the deconstructionists was Frank Gehry, whose signature twisted and fragmented metal forms became so synonymous with avant-garde design and cutting-edge technology that in the early years of the new millennium his buildings appeared in ads for luxury cars and consumer electronics. The success of this Canadian-born and Harvard-educated architect who practiced in the Los Angeles area came only after he moved away the modernist style he used while working for Victor Gruen (1903–1980), the architectural pioneer of the shopping mall. The mall was the product of postwar architectural segregation, which paired the modernist boxes of production downtown with the decorative aesthetic of consumption in the suburbs. Gehry's deconstructionist aesthetic testified to the post-Fordist destruction of this segregation and the dispersion of space by bringing together the joy of consumerism with the materials of productivism.

Gehry's remodeled residence in Santa Monica, completed in 1978, was the first manifestation of his new, dislocated aesthetic that he called "urban junkyard." Here the architect took a pretty pink cottage in this upscale suburb and wrapped it on three sides with a shell of corrugated metal, chain-link fencing, and unfinished plywood. Clearly, this was an ironic reversal of the usual suburban aesthetic of entertainment and obfuscation, in which ugly mass-produced elements were hidden under an obscuring shell of warmth and individuality. Here Gehry placed a pretty cottage inside an angular wrapper of industrial ugliness, turning the heretofore hidden rational core of mass production into a demystified shell. His house was a metaphor for the spatial disorganization and dispersion of post-Fordism, in which industry and production moved into the suburbs and consumption moved back downtown. And where these the two previously separate worlds met symbolically in the intersections of the new industrial shell with the old suburban cottage, the house was disrupted and wounded in violent, disorienting clashes that destroyed its suburban serenity. At back, the shell touched the house and left a crude, unfinished structure of raw two-by-fours, as if the encounter ripped off the original pink sheathing. On the side, a glass cube twisted at a forty-five-degree angle slashed into the house and left a void between it and the shell that became the new kitchen. The house seemed to reveal a violent and intrusive force that destroyed the centeredness of the Fordist individual and exposed her to penetration and dispersion. Since Gehry remodeled his house during the rapid deindustrialization of Los Angeles, this destructive force may be seen as global capital, surging out of urban centers toward the periphery and wrecking havoc in its wake.[84]

A similarly critical edge seemed to permeate Gehry's work of the early 1980s, like the Edgemar shopping complex in Santa Monica, where the urban-junkyard aesthetic of industrial materials in angular, twisted shapes was used in a complex of shops on Main Street. These same distorted, cubist shapes

Frank Gehry, Gehry House, Santa Monica, California, 1978 (© Gehry Partners, LLP)

continued into the late 1980s, but Gehry's junkyard materials underwent a definite transformation. In the Herman Miller Western Regional Manufacturing and Distribution Center in Rocklin, California, completed in 1989, the architect replaced his cheap corrugated steel with expensive galvanized steel and copper siding. Both materials were applied in sheets so thin that they "pillowed out" in the middle, giving the surfaces a soft, accommodating look. Here Gehry no longer defiantly contradicted the prettiness of the suburban dream but created an eccentric beauty that trumped it at its own game. By the late 1980s and early 1990s, Gehry's shapes had also taken on an expressive exuberance that seemed to celebrate, not criticize, the post-Fordist age of mobility and dispersion. At his seminal Team Disney, he gave the side facing the freeway a flat facade of blue-green steel. But on the side of the building facing Disneyland, Gehry gave the executives an entry facade of twisted, curvilinear forms in yellow stucco. Like his early work, this facade seemed to express some powerful external force, but here this force seemed joyous and liberating, not angular and destructive.[85]

This new aesthetic of exuberant movement and expressive rupture culminated in Gehry's two masterpieces, the Walt Disney Concert Hall and the Guggenheim Museum Bilbao (1997). Reversing the geographic movement of the early works, which brought urban realism out to the consumer suburbs, these projects brought his new aesthetic of liberation back downtown to obscure its ugliness and stimulate spectacular consumption. The Disney Hall was part of a concerted effort by developers and politicians to revitalize downtown Los Angeles by creating a cultural center to attract gentrified yuppies.

By lending its name and its funds to the project, the Disney family and company asserted a presence in the upscale cultural center and improved its image with the new symbol producers. By the time Gehry won a competition for the building in 1987, he had abandoned his dirty realism and gave his sponsors a design of exciting, spontaneous movement expressed in curving, twisted forms of limestone. However, members of the governing board for the Disney Hall worried about the contaminating effects of the ugly urban environment on the building. First, they were concerned that the stone would get dirty, so Gehry changed the cladding to stainless steel, ensuring that the crown jewel of Los Angeles's gentrifying downtown would never tarnish. After the 1992 urban riots, the sponsors also worried about the social contamination of this site of high culture by the "dangerous classes" of the area. Gehry responded by turning his open and accessible original design, which included a generous public plaza, into an enclosed precinct surrounded on three sides by imposing, rectilinear stone walls and extensive surveillance. Like the urban compositions of the postmodernists, Gehry's deconstructed Disney Hall became insular and self-contained, with the exuberantly free forms reserved for the inside, and prisonlike walls on the outside. It was difficult to avoid the impression that the spontaneity and freedom symbolized by Gehry's forms were reserved for the few, namely, the moguls of globalized culture corporations like Disney. This was *their* concert hall, representing their freedom in a new economy of deregulated and globalized cultural production.[86]

Changes in design and problems with funding delayed the realization of Gehry's Walt Disney Concert Hall until 2003, by which time Gehry had already achieved superstar status with the 1997 completion of his Guggenheim Museum in Bilbao, Spain. Like the Disney Hall, the Bilbao museum was part of an ambitious scheme to exploit culture to revive an old Fordist city. The Basque Country Administration, the regional authority of this deindustrializing city of steelmaking and shipbuilding, offered to finance a European extension of this New York museum in exchange for receiving its tourist-attracting aura. But what could draw tourists to this drab, out-of-the-way industrial town to see art regularly on display in Frank Lloyd Wright's circular Guggenheim Museum in New York? Perhaps an even more spectacularly space-age museum building by Gehry. For a site on the banks of the Nervion River, Gehry designed a building of projecting, curvilinear forms that looked like a couple of ships had collided at the site. To distract from the dirty urban realism all around it, the Guggenheim Bilbao was clad in one of the most exotic and expensive metals imaginable—titanium, sheets of which were pounded so thin that they actually fluttered in the wind to accentuate the static movement of the forms. As at the Disney Hall, these expressive forms of high-tech exoticism rose out of a rectilinear base of stone. Gehry placed the works of the "dead artists" of twentieth-century modernism in this heavy mausoleum of limestone, reserving the light, metal sections of the museum for "living artists" of the post-Fordist world. This world, which arose on the grave of modernism, was marked by lightness and movement, connoted by the shiny metal in forms reminiscent of airplanes, ships, and mobile homes. Such movement was surely a metaphor for the rapid mobility of capital around the globe, for the Guggenheim Bilbao itself was the product of the movement of cultural capital from the metropole of New York to the semiperipheral Bilbao. Some residents of the city criticized the museum for costing too much public money and displaying international artists, not Basques. While their cries for regional representation might have drawn sympathy from postmodern historicists and critical regionalists, the architect of global deconstructionism dismissed them as backward: "We're in a world culture," Gehry replied. "We better get on with it."[87]

And get on with it Gehry did. The international buzz generated by the Bilbao created a huge demand around the world for the spectacular architecture generated by Gehry. Many old Fordist cities clamored to get their own "Gehry" to attract the trade in cultural tourism. The architect who began bringing an ugly urban realism into the suburbs to undermine its superficial prettiness ended up taking an energetic prettiness to ugly downtowns to stimulate

Frank Gehry, Guggenheim Bilbao, Spain, 1997 (Photograph Erika Barahona Ede/
© FMGB Guggenheim Bilbao Museoa, 2005. All rights reserved. Total or partial
reproduction is prohibited.)

yuppie consumption. For the winners of the post-Fordist world, Gehry's architecture embodied an aesthetic of pleasure, revealing the freedom and exuberance they felt as they moved about the globe as agents of a new ephemeral and dematerialized capital.

That deconstructionism intended to create spaces of pleasure, free of reminders of the destruction wrecked by global capital, is revealed by another of its foremost practitioners, Bernard Tschumi, who was also one of this school's most prolific apologists and philosophers. He began his career in the 1960s as a left-wing critic of modernism, drawing his aesthetic and political inspiration from the Situationist International. This avant-garde group's practice of *détournement* (diversion, embezzlement) took elements of the existing culture and turned them into a construction that anticipated a transformed society. In the embezzled spaces of the Parisian streets in May 1968, for example, the Situationists constructed their "situations" or "events," subversive actions that revealed the possibilities for a new society of freedom and play. Tschumi took as his goal the creation of an "event architecture," spaces of free activity in which a nonhierarchical, nontraditional society could be anticipated. He argued that such spaces could be created only by breaking open the closed grids of modernism and providing for voids in which unexpected events could occur. Over thirty years of practice, however, Tschumi's objective gradually slipped from outright subversion to transgression, from destroying the limits of the existing society to momentarily going beyond them. He argued that the purpose of this "transgressive architecture" was not revolution but pleasure, and went on to compare it to the Marquis de Sade's sadomasochistic sexual practices. This architecture that transgressed the stable boundaries of convention with free activity was an architecture of desire, for it created spaces where desire could dwell. So Tschumi, like many of his generation, transformed himself from a 1960s revolutionary to a 1990s postmodern deviant who played at breaking the rules just for fun.[88]

The realization of Tschumi's transgressive architecture of pleasure was his monumental Parc de la Villette in Paris. One of the government's *Grands Projets*, this open-air cultural park contained music and media studios, museums, theaters, a gymnasium, playgrounds, concert halls, restaurants, and clubs. Tschumi clearly intended to create a park for his generation of revolutionaries turned corporate symbol producers, writing: "The fact that Paris concentrates tertiary or professional employment argues against passive 'esthetic' parks of repose in favor of new urban parks based on cultural invention, education, and entertainment." In other words, yuppies at leisure demanded not old-fashioned rest and relaxation but active consumption of activities to increase their cultural capital. For these yuppies who wanted to celebrate their newfound freedom from Fordist rules with cultural transgressions that left the structure of capitalism intact, Tschumi created an architectural metaphor for freedom *within* a constraining order. The entire 125-acre site was first overlaid with a large-scale grid of points, set at 120-meter intervals. Each point was a 10 x 10 x 10 meter cube of red steel that accommodated one function of the overall program, for example, a music hall. This scheme was a reference to the Cartesian grid that modernists used to express a rational containment of space. But here the modernist grid of lines was broken down to a set of points that formed "an organizing structure," as Tschumi wrote, but "a structure without center or hierarchy." This deconstructed grid freed space to allow different and new events to happen within it, to create an "event city," as Tschumi called it. Each of the red point-cubes was varied to accommodate its particular program, but only by incorporating a different combination of a set of prescribed elements, such as cylinders, triangles, ramps, and stairs. Because of the supposed freedom of activity expressed within and provided for these point-cubes, the architect labeled them *folies* (madnesses), revealing a poststructuralist celebration of madness and schizophrenia as freedom from constraining meaning. The park, Tschumi wrote, "aims at an architecture that means nothing, an architecture of the signifier rather than the signified."[89] The point grid by itself, however, was too static for a deconstructionist like Tschumi, so he destabilized it by superimposing two additional systems, one of lines and another of surfaces. Refusing any attempt to unify the design, the architect merely laid these systems on top of one another to create "something that is undecidable, the opposite of a totality." Especially important for this contradiction was the systems of lines, which formed the pedestrian paths in the park. The two major paths were straight and intersected at right angles, but contradicting this Euclidian space was another system of curvilinear paths. These meandering walkways, called the Cinematic Promenade, provided for movement through a series of thematic gardens that were incomplete, allowing for a plurality of meanings.[90]

For Jacques Derrida, Tschumi's Parc de la Villette was the epitome of his deconstructionist philosophy in the field of architecture. Writing specifically in praise of the *folies*, he argued that they pushed architecture beyond the constraint of norms by dislocating their authority and leaving "opportunity for chance, formal invention, combinatory transformation, wanderings." But this refusal to abide by external norms did not mean, Derrida demurred, that this architecture was critical or negative. The *folies* did not destroy but affirmed, for

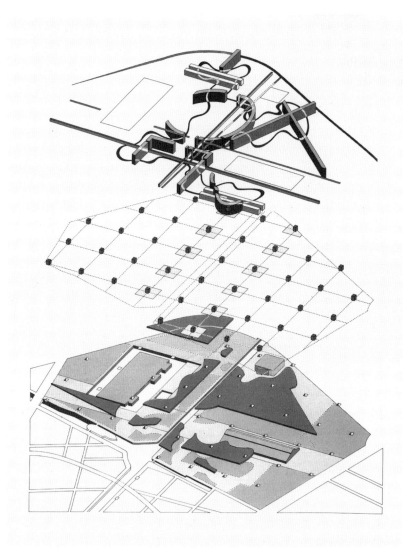

Bernard Tschumi, Parc de la Villette, Paris, axiomatic diagram, 1982
(Courtesy Bernard Tschumi Architects)

they created a "place made for pleasure" that transgressed limits and norms, a pleasure "which previously was anaesthetized, walled in, buried in a common grave or sepulchral nostalgia." Deconstructionist architecture like Tschumi's Parc de la Villette ultimately created, according to Derrida, "places where desire can recognize itself, where it can live."[91]

While the deconstructionist architecture created by Tschumi, Gehry, and others may have created spaces where desire could be fulfilled in the existing society, it did not succeed in changing society but became an integral part of its consumer culture. So trendy did decon become in post-Fordism's culture of consumption that when the ultrachic Italian fashion house of Prada decided to build three new flagship stores around the world, it commissioned Dutch deconstructionist Rem Koolhaas to create spaces where the desire for Prada's exclusive brand of fashion could live.[92] Fulfilling desires within post-Fordist capitalism meant steering them into spectacular commodities for sale on the market, thus diverting their energy from the construction of a society of real pleasure. Bourdieu's theory of cultural capital holds that this appropriation of new artistic styles for capitalist purposes is inevitable, for the dominant class requires ever new and distinctive cultural works to lend it distinction and justify its economic capital. If he is right, then criticizing art for accommodating capitalism is unjustified, since market appropriation is not caused by art's specific forms but merely by its difference and newness, the quest for which is inherent in the field of high art.[93] Theodor Adorno's aesthetic theory, by contrast, holds that the commercial incorporation of art is not ubiquitous and inevitable, but varies by its specific forms. Adorno argues that true art, which by definition is critical and resists incorporation, is the product of the society in which it is produced, but reveals both the beauty and the ugliness of that society. The beauty of true art reflects the potentials for happiness and reconciliation embodied in the society. However, this promise of happiness must always be contradicted by a revelation of ugliness, the fractures and fissures of existing social relations that prevent this promise from being fulfilled. Without this tempering of beauty with ugliness, art risks being incorporated as a commodity that gives people soothing substitutes for happiness to compensate them for their suffering in a repressive society.[94]

Unlike postmodern architecture, deconstructionism reflected clearly the fragments and shards left behind by shattering the old unity of Fordist society. In their dispersed and disorienting forms, the deconstructionists captured the reality of a decentered system in which capital was constantly moving and never located in a particular place. In its early stages, exemplified by Gehry's urban junkyard works, deconstructionism met Adorno's criteria for critical art by refusing artificial reconciliation and revealing the ugly fissures and fractures of the emerging social relations. But somewhere along the road to success this aesthetic's fragmentation became less ugly and more beautiful; its disorientation, less frightening and more exhilarating. As post-Fordism consolidated into the new totality of global capitalism, the beautifully open and free fragments of deconstruction masked this oppressive unity under the cover of individuality and difference. It was just such a celebration of difference and the "other" that post-Fordism demanded in order to differentiate products and create market niches. Because architecture was increasingly integrated into this new global marketplace, it was difficult for architects to resist these demands. The public commissions that had given some dissenters independence from the market under Fordism dried up with the deregulating frenzy, leaving little room for the critical art advocated by Adorno. So the critical ugliness of deconstructionism turned into a celebratory beauty, offering the new society a place where superficial consumer desire could live in the present, without the postponement of social change.

This incorporation was not inevitable, however, as revealed by Peter Eisenman, a deconstructionist whose independence from the commercial market and avant-garde commitment facilitated his creation of an unaccommodating, critical architecture. Eisenman maintained independence from the market by supplementing his practice with teaching, writing, publishing, and directing the Institute for Architecture and Urban Studies. Further, many of his important works were public commissions, like the Wexner Center (1989) at the Ohio State University and the Friedrichstrasse apartment building (1986) in Berlin's IBA program. This independence allowed Eisenman to create a theory and aesthetic of deconstruction that revealed the ugly fragmentation of post-Fordism without losing faith in the promise of a new and different society.

From the beginning Eisenman was committed to creating an architecture that revealed the alienation of humans in modern society. Architecture was traditionally centered on human needs, he argued, symbolizing the idea that humans lived in a world that they created and controlled for their own purposes. With the advent of mass technology in the late nineteenth century, however, "man could no longer maintain his anthropocentric focus or take for granted his centric position and, correspondingly, the 'naturalness' of his social organizations. In the face of the recognition of this fundamental human estrangement, man's sense of himself came into crisis." Modernist architecture tried to cover over this alienation by symbolically reasserting humanity's control over technology. But after the tragedies of Hiroshima and the Holocaust, humanity was forced to confront its basic alienation from the tools it had made. Eisenman's early houses, built between 1967 and 1975, attempted to expose this alienation by "dislocat[ing] the house from that comforting metaphysic and symbolism of shelter in order to initiate a search for those possibilities of dwelling that may have been repressed by that metaphysic." He built these single-family homes as autonomous, nonhuman objects, using a formal structure that, he argued, "would necessarily create anxiety and a distance, for it would no longer be under man's control." The early houses were not deconstructed but overconstructed with a nonhuman logic. In House II, for example, nonfunctionality was exaggerated by the inclusion of two support systems, one of columns, the other of walls, each more than sufficient to hold it up. In House III Eisenman generated a structure of clashing, nonfunctional spaces by superimposing two grids upon one another, one twisted forty-five degrees from the other.[95]

Around 1975, the period in which the controlled world of Fordism fell into crisis, Eisenman became displeased with his formal, structuralist architecture and moved into his deconstructionist phase. He was convinced that the early houses were not sufficiently alienating, because they were still based on a centered structure underneath the architectural signifiers. There was no such center, he asserted, that could form the basis of an autonomous art of architecture. Now adopting the deconstructionist terminology of Jacques Derrida, who became Eisenman's friend and collaborator, he argued that architecture should swear off any definitive meanings or presences and strive to dislocate all meaning by revealing the absences that have been repressed by presence. The architectural object must be simultaneously a presence and an absence. The physical object was present, but it must dislocate itself and point to an absence, "a logic that begins and ends beyond itself, bringing out from within itself things that are other than itself." Although Eisenman adopted the terminology of Derrida, there were major differences in their aesthetic approaches. Derrida's goal was the outright destruction of presence or meaning, since any definitive meaning was a totality that repressed the differences that existed outside of it. Once the presence of meaning was deconstructed by representing the repressed others or absences, the text and all the oppressive social institutions based on it collapsed, and unrestricted pleasure reigned, here and now. Eisenman, on the other hand, stated that he was dislocating or "shifting the boundaries but not obliterating the boundaries of meaning." In architecture, presence could not be decisively destroyed, for the physical presence of shelter was the manifestation of this art. But this architectural presence could be dislocated by representing the absences within it. Unlike Derrida, however, Eisenman believed that the mere representation of absence was not sufficient to bring down the institutions materialized in architecture and allow pleasure in the here and now. For him, art alone could not bring beauty into existence, but could only strive "to be simultaneously a creation and a critique of the institutions it builds." Art destabilized institutions by representing an absence that was not a beautiful difference, as in Derrida, but an ugly logic of oppression. Architecture, Eisenman wrote, "requires a more complex form of the beautiful, one which contains the ugly, or a rationality that contains the irrational." Ultimately, this absent, irrational logic that Eisenman used to destabilize comforting shelter was a metaphor for the displaced logic of global capital.[96]

Eisenman presented the ugly absence underlying the soothing presence of shelter by using what he called "traces," which he defined as "the presence of an absence," the representation in architectural structure of something that was not there. These traces were meant to provoke uncertainty and anxiety by showing a distance or alienation between the subject and object. Eisenman incorporated in his architecture traces of both place and time, each of which dislocated the present structure by placing it in a larger framework or logic. He created traces of place by superimposing on one site analogous elements from other sites. Eisenman sometimes called this superimposition "scaling," for it entailed imposing the scale or relative size of one site on another site of a different scale. In this procedure, he sought to reveal that a place is not identical to itself, but is a location in some larger whole that is not present. Scaling was usually achieved by imposing on a site an overlay of different grids and axes that had little to do with the existing site. For example, at his Wexner Center for the Arts at the Ohio State University, completed in 1989, Eisenman aligned his buildings with the existing campus grid but cut across his complex at an acute angle with a pedestrian passageway covered by a gridlike scaffolding. This passageway, he stated, was oriented to the larger street grid of the city of Columbus, from which the university initially sought to distance itself by skewing its grid 12.25 degrees. By superimposing this urban grid on the campus, Eisenman shattered the sheltered isolation of the university by reminding it that its education and art were inevitably part of a larger world of urban problems that it could not ignore.[97]

The most impressive use of scaling, however, was Eisenman's Friedrichstrasse IBA housing in Berlin, where he superimposed on the facade of the apartment building two grids from maps of different scales. The small-scale white grid represented the Berlin street grid, while the large-scale red grid was said to represent the lines of the Mercator projection map of the world. Further, the plane of the facade representing the Mercator grid cut into the plane representing the street grid at an acute angle and split the building in half. Surely this trace of a global scale that cut into and disrupted the peace of this building was none other than the system of world capitalism, which engulfed every place with its invisible flows of abstract exchange. But it was an *absent* system, existent but not present or representable in concrete terms. Eisenman represented here the absent, homogenizing grid of global capital to prevent people from settling down into a false sense of domestic security. Indeed, the building embodied the new globalization movement's call to arms—"think globally, act locally." It reminded occupants that humans, unlike capital, necessarily reside physically in a specific place, but their embodied lives are determined beyond them by disrupting global forces that they have to combat before their fissured lives are whole again.[98]

The other dimension of Eisenman's displacing traces was that of time. The architect layered on any one site reminders of different times, stating that "any site contains not only presences, but the memory of previous presences

Peter Eisenman, Wexner Center for the Arts at the Ohio State University, Columbus, 1989 (Courtesy Eisenman Architects)

Eisenman/Robertson,
Block 5, Friedrichstrasse,
Berlin, 1986 (Courtesy
Eisenman Architects)

and the immanences of a possible presence." Traces of history dislocated the immediacy and inevitability of the present presence and made way for absent, alternative futures. These liberating traces of history were best exemplified by Eisenman's unbuilt project for the University Art Museum at California State University in Long Beach. Here the architect derived the axes and shapes of the buildings from several contradictory historic structures—the ranch that once existed on the site, a nearby river bed, geological fault lines, the coastline, and the existing campus. In this way Eisenman stated that he incorporated on the site images of the 1849 settlement of California, the 1949 creation of the campus, and the projected 2049 "rediscovery"of the museum (after an earthquake?). The deconstructed, fragmentary forms were reminders of the violent origins of California in the gold rush days, as well as predictors of a future disaster. But there was also a certain beauty precariously balanced on these shards of ugliness. The thoughtful traces of otherness represented something else that was absent—not merely in the sense of not here, but also in the sense of not existent. This nonexistent absence was potential unity, the promise of reconciliation that was denied in the here and now. This force seemed to hold Eisenman's fragments and traces in a tense suspension, neither together nor apart. His compositions were thus not pretty enough to create a place where desire could live, but neither were they so ugly as to cynically deny that the desire for unity was dead.[99]

Eisenman's architecture seemed faithful to Adorno's criteria for true, critical art. It did not offer immediate satisfaction of desires, or reconciliation of humans with each other and the environment. This was the mistake of the postmodernists, who offered images of rootedness and stability to obfuscate the ugly reality of post-Fordism. Nor did Eisenman offer, like high-tech architects, a warmed-over Fordist faith in science and technology. He and the other deconstructionists reflected in their fragmented forms the collapse of Fordist regulation and the emergence of a global capitalist system of dispersed spaces. Most deconstructionists, however, interpreted the lack of unity in the new world as inevitable, even beautiful, reflecting the freedom and joy of the new ruling class of symbol producers. In his fragments, by contrast, Eisenman revealed the ugliness of global capital without abandoning the beauty of a future reconciliation or totality. But the promised totality of Eisenman's architecture was not the repressive obliteration of differences under a homogenizing instrumental reason, as in modernism. The beauty of his architecture promised a liberating unity within differences, in which the obliteration of false differences would allow true differences in human abilities and desires to be expressed within and for society, not against it, and would create, in Adorno's words, "an emancipated society…in which people could be different without fear."[100] Because he combined this beautiful promise of reconciliation with the ugly denial of it in post-Fordist capitalism, Eisenman did not build hotels for Disney, stores for Prada, or housing for yuppies.

Adorno's theory recognizes that critical art like Eisenman's architecture may be a powerful force in society, but not by itself, not isolated from practical activity. Art provides a force for social change only as part of the critical praxis of movements challenging the ugly contradictions of their societies. Such was the case with avant-garde modernism, Depression-era populism, and the 1960s challenge to establishment modernism. Eisenman's critical deconstructionist architecture was also connected to a rising movement, one that opposed the neoliberal project of global capitalism, which obliterated the freedom to be culturally, economically, and politically different. In the 1990s there arose a powerful social movement challenging the unification of the world under the neoliberal policies of the World Bank, International Monetary Fund, and World Trade Organization, all of which pressured countries to roll back social welfare policies protecting people from the ravages of the unregulated market. In 1999 this movement for a different internationalism burst into public consciousness with the protests at the World Trade Organization meeting in Seattle. Eisenman's deconstructed architecture gave formal voice to this protest against global capitalism by recording the traces of difference that were repressed by its imposed homogeneity.

Not only do social movements empower art to change society. They also have the power to change art. As Bourdieu recognizes, these social conflicts often introduce into art fields new kinds of artists, with different social backgrounds and different habitus, who see the world in different ways that unconsciously symbolize different interests. Thus, the technocratic movement in Europe in the early twentieth century introduced into architecture artists from the professional-managerial middle class. Their disposition toward instrumental reason led them to formally resolve the problems of the day with new rationalist forms. And during the 1960s, movements of oppressed minorities and youth attracted sympathy from young architects, many of whom were from the popular classes themselves. Their popular habitus combined with their marginal positions in the field to generate a revolt against modernism and the creation of new aesthetics that combined popular and high-art forms.

Art can play this role in progressive movements, however, only when it is autonomous, when it is free from the market's demand for immediate comfort and the state's demand for legitimation. Only then it is possible for artists to unconsciously express in their forms the clashes and contradictions of a society divided against itself, thus stimulating criticism, not false reconciliation. Thus, insulated from the market by nonintrusive state support, the new technocratic architects in Europe expressed both the beauty and ugliness of their project to rationalize capitalism, thereby heightening awareness of the contradictory social forces of the day. By contrast, the social and architectural movements of the 1960s ultimately resulted in the accommodating postmodern forms of the 1970s and 1980s because of the evaporation of artistic autonomy. The rise of the post-Fordism and its almost totally privatized market for architecture forced 1960s rebels to cater to consumers with an aesthetic that did not reveal but concealed emerging inequalities and social dislocations under reassuring facades of historical stability and popular entertainment.

Although some architects like Eisenman are still able to maintain artistic autonomy from the market and state by drawing on the dwindling demand for public and institutional architecture, the spreading tentacles of neoliberal, post-Fordist capitalism are strangling this demand and enforcing heteronomy. And the voices of protest against neoliberal globalization that have fueled this autonomous art are also increasingly drowned in the icy sea of the market. In the absence of empowering movements and emboldening autonomy, even a critical art like Eisenman's can merely maintain the hope that history has not come to *this* end, that the collective project of human liberation is not now hopeless.

1. Downtown Disney web site at http://disneyland.disney.go.com/disneylandresort/DowntownDisney (accessed November 7, 2001; site now discontinued).

2. This account of the collapse of Fordism draws heavily on Samuel Bowles, David M. Gordon, and Thomas E. Weisskopf, *Beyond the Wasteland* (London: Verso, 1984); and Alain Lipietz, *Mirages and Miracles: The Crisis of Global Fordism* (London: Verso, 1987).

3. David Harvey, *The Condition of Postmodernity* (Cambridge, MA: Blackwell, 1989), 141–47; Bowles et al., *Beyond the Wasteland*, 105–9; Daniel Zwerdling, *Workplace Democracy* (New York: Harper Colophon, 1980); James P. Womack, Daniel T. Jones, and Daniel Roos, *The Machine That Changed the World* (New York: Harper Perennial, 1991); Mike Parker, "Industrial Relations Myth and Shop-Floor Reality: The 'Team Concept' in the Auto Industry," in *Industrial Democracy in America*, eds. Nelson Lichtenstein and Howell John Harris (New York: Cambridge University Press, 1993), 249–74.

4. Barry Bluestone and Bennett Harrison, *The Deindustrialization of America* (New York: Basic Books, 1982); Lipietz, *Mirages and Miracles*; Naomi Klein, *No Logo: Taking Aim at the Brand Bullies* (New York: Picador, 2001), 195–229.

5. On the shift to services, see Wallace Clement and John Myles, *Relations of Ruling* (Montréal: McGill-Queens University Press, 1994); Saskia Sassen, *The Global City: New York, London, Tokyo* (Princeton, NJ: Princeton University Press, 2001); Starbucks CEO is quoted in Klein, *No Logo*, 20.

6. Klein, *No Logo*, 231–57; Sassen, *Global City*, 289–305.

7. Bennett Harrison, *Lean and Mean: The Changing Landscape of Corporate Power in the Age of Flexibility* (New York: Basic Books, 1994); Clement and Myles, *Relations of Ruling*, 40–62; Saskia Sassen, *Cities in a World Economy* (Thousand Oaks, CA: Pine Forge Press, 1994), 24; Andrew Sayer, "Postfordism in Question," *International Journal of Urban and Regional Research* 13 (Dec. 1989): 678–85.

8. On post-Fordist state policy, see Bob Jessop, "Post-Fordism and the State," in *Post-Fordism: A Reader*, ed. Ash Amin (Oxford: Blackwell, 1994), 251–79; Mike Davis, *Prisoners of the American Dream* (London: Verso, 1986); Bennett Harrison and Barry Bluestone, *The Great U-Turn* (New York: Basic Books, 1988).

9. Pierre Bourdieu, *Distinction: A Social Critique of the Judgement of Taste* (Cambridge, MA: Harvard University Press, 1984), 295–315, 354–71. On this class

of cultural intermediaries, see also Mike Featherstone, *Consumer Culture and Postmodernism* (London: Sage, 1991), 28–50.

10. Harrison and Bluestone, *The Great U-Turn*; Sassen, *Global City*, 223–29.

11. Clement and Myles, *Relations of Ruling*, 28–31; Sassen, *Global City*, 223–24.

12. Magali Sarfatti Larson, *Behind the Postmodern Facade* (Berkeley: University of California Press, 1993), 80–82; Sharon Zukin, *Landscapes of Power* (Berkeley: University of California Press, 1991), 35–77; David Harvey, *The Urbanization of Capital* (Oxford: Blackwell, 1985), 211–13; Sassen, *Global City*; Edward Soja, *Postmodern Geographies* (London: Verso, 1989), 190–221.

13. Graham interview in Barbaralee Diamonstein, *American Architecture Now II* (New York: Rizzoli, 1985), 122.

14. On gentrification, see also Zukin, *Landscapes of Power*, 179–215; Neil Smith, "New City, New Frontier: The Lower East Side as Wild, Wild West," in *Variations on a Theme Park*, ed. Michael Sorkin (New York: Hill and Wang, 1992), 61–93.

15. Mike Davis, *City of Quartz* (New York: Vintage, 1992), 70–83. The quote is on 76; www.disneyhall.org (accessed on August 29, 2001; site now discontinued). See also Harvey, *Urbanization*, 211–14; Harvey, *Condition of Postmodernity*, 91–96; Larson, *Behind the Postmodern Facade*, 81–86; Charles Jencks, *The Language of Post-Modern Architecture*, 6th ed. (New York: Rizzoli, 1991), 177–81.

16. Zukin, *Landscapes of Power*, 51–54; Mike Davis, "The Infinite Game: Redeveloping Downtown L.A.," in *Out of Site: A Social Criticism of Architecture*, ed. Diane Ghirardo (Seattle: Bay Press, 1991), 78–99.

17. Sassen, *Global City*, 261–70, 284–305; Neil Smith, *The New Frontier: Gentrification and the Revanchist City* (London: Routledge, 1996).

18. Diane Ghirardo, *Architecture After Modernism* (New York: Thames and Hudson, 1996), 108–112, 200–8; Alexander Tzonis and Liane Lefaivre, *Architecture in Europe since 1968* (New York: Thames and Hudson, 1992), 8.

19. For the ratio of architects per million in population, see Garry Stevens, *The Favored Circle: The Social Foundations of Architectural Distinction* (Cambridge, MA: MIT Press, 1998), 212–13. See also Larson, *Behind the Postmodern Facade*, 247.

20. Larson, *Behind the Postmodern Facade*, 123–24.

21. Jahn interview in Diamonstein, *American Architecture Now II*, 145. See also Peter Rice, "The Dilemma of Technology," in *Architecture in Europe*

since 1968, Tzonis and Lefaivre, 36–41; Bernard Tschumi, *Architecture and Disjunction* (Cambridge, MA: MIT Press, 1994), 140–42.

22. Drexler interview in Diamonstein, *American Architecture Now II*, 71; Stern interview in Barbaralee Diamonstein, *American Architecture Now* (New York: Rizzoli, 1980), 237, 249. See also Larson, *Behind the Postmodern Facade*, 119–20; Stephen Kiernan, "The Architecture of Plenty: Theory and Design in the Marketing Age," *Harvard Architecture Review* 6 (1987): 103–13; Peter Blake, *No Place Like Utopia* (New York: Knopf, 1993), 103–9.

23. Fredric Jameson, *The Political Unconscious* (Ithaca, NY: Cornell University Press, 1981).

24. Karl Marx and Frederick Engels, "Manifesto of the Communist Party," in Karl Marx and Frederick Engels, *Collected Works*, vol. 6 (New York: International Publishers, 1976), 487.

25. See Terry Eagleton, "Capitalism and Form," *New Left Review*, 2nd ser., no. 14 (March/April 2002): 119–31.

26. Marx and Engels, "Manifesto of the Communist Party," 487.

27. Bourdieu, *Distinction*, 357–71. For data on the knowledge and consumption of both high and mass culture by the younger generation of professionals, see Paul Dimaggio and Michael Useem, "Social Class and Art Consumption," *Theory and Society* 5 (1978): 109–32; Richard A. Peterson and Albert Simkus, "How Musical Tastes Mark Occupational Status Groups," in *Cultivating Differences*, eds. Michele Lamont and Marcel Fournier (Chicago: University of Chicago Press, 1992), 152–86; Richard A. Peterson and Roger M. Kern, "Changing Highbrow Taste: From Snob to Omnivore," *American Sociological Review* 61 (1996): 900–907.

28. Randall Collins, *The Sociology of Philosophies* (Cambridge, MA: Harvard University Press, 1998), 37–46 ; Stevens, *The Favored Circle*, 122–25.

29. Jameson, *The Political Unconscious*, 290, 83–87.

30. Karl Marx, "The Eighteenth Brumaire of Louis Bonaparte," in Karl Marx and Frederick Engels, *Collected Works*, vol. 11 (New York: International Publishers, 1979), 103–4.

31. Fredric Jameson, *Postmodernism, or, the Cultural Logic of Late Capitalism* (London: Verso, 1991), 19–21, 170–71, 399–406; Jean Baudrillard, *Simulacra and Simulation* (Ann Arbor: University of Michigan Press, 1994), 43–48.

32. Klein, *No Logo*, 107–24; Jameson, *Postmodernism*, 318–56; Fredric Jameson, *Seeds of Time* (New York: Columbia University Press, 1994) , 40–42, 189–205.

33. Bourdieu, *Distinction*, 295–315.

34. Jameson, *Postmodernism*; Harvey, *Condition of Postmodernity*; Soja, *Postmodern Geographies*.

35. Moore interview is in Diamonstein, *American Architecture Now*, 127, 130, 128. On "democratic participation," see Scott Brown interview in ibid., 234.

36. Scott Brown quoted in Heinrich Klotz, *The History of Postmodern Architecture* (Cambridge, MA: MIT Press, 1988), 172. See also Jencks, *Language*, 97.

37. Stern in "Forum Discussion: Beyond the Modern Movement," *Harvard Architecture Review* 1 (Spring 1980): 200. See also Jencks, *Language*, 70–73.

38. Gavin Macrae-Gibson, *The Secret Life of Buildings* (Cambridge, MA: MIT Press, 1985), 145–68.

39. Venturi quote is from Robert Venturi, *Iconography and Electronics upon a Generic Architecture* (Cambridge, MA: MIT Press, 1996), 229.

40. On the Piazza d'Italia, see especially Jencks, *Language*, 116–19; Ghirardo, *Architecture After Modernism*, 63–64.

41. Jencks, *Language*, 159; Mary McLeod, "Architecture and Politics in the Reagan Era," *Assemblage* 8 (1989): 34; the Stein interview is in "Beyond the Modern Movement," 200; Peter Blake, *No Place Like Utopia*, 297.

42. Robert A. M. Stern, "The Doubles of Post-Modern," *Harvard Architecture Review* 1 (Spring 1980): 87; Michael Graves, "A Case for Figurative Architecture," in *Theorizing a New Agenda for Architecture*, ed. Kate Nesbitt (New York: Princeton Architectural Press, 1996), 86.

43. Graves, "A Case," 90, 88; Moore is quoted in "Beyond the Modern Movement," 208.

44. Graves interview is in Diamonstein, *American Architecture Now*; Giurgola interview is in Diamonstein, *American Architecture Now II*, 104–5.

45. On the Plocek House, see Jencks, *Language*, 113–14.

46. Kenneth Frampton, *Modern Architecture: A Critical History*, 3rd ed. (New York: Thames and Hudson, 1992), 307–8; Macrae-Gibson, *Secret Life of Buildings*, 74–97.

47. Jencks, *Language*, 98–100.

48. Macrae-Gibson, *Secret Life of Buildings*, 98–117. The quote is on 116.

49. This account of Eisner at the Disney Company draws heavily on Beth Dunlop, *Building a Dream: The Art of Disney Architecture* (New York: Harry Abrams, 1996). The quote is on 18.

50. Graves is quoted in Dunlop, *Building a Dream*, 70. For the historical references of these hotels, see Jencks, *Language*, 166.

51. Vincent Scully, "Animal Spirits," *Progressive Architecture* 71 (Oct. 1990): 91.

52. Dunlop, *Building a Dream*, 80–89; Karen Nichols, Lisa Burke, and Patrick Burke, eds., *Michael Graves: Buildings and Projects, 1990–1994* (New York: Rizzoli, 1995), 20–27.

53. Dunlop, *Building a Dream*, 77–83, 108–112. The quote is on 111.

54. Goldberger quoted in Ibid., 97.

55. Bourdieu, *Distinction*, 28–50; Pierre Bourdieu, "Outline of a Sociological Theory of Art Perception," in *The Field of Cultural Production* (New York: Columbia University Press, 1993), 234–37.

56. Chin-Tao Wu, *Privatising Culture: Corporate Art Intervention since the 1980s* (London: Verso, 2001).

57. Jencks, *Language*, 112, 141–43; Ghirardo, *Architecture After Modernism*, 88–90.

58. Theodor Adorno, *Minima Moralia* (London: Verso, 1974), 38–39. The quote is on 25.

59. Scott Brown interview is in Diamonstein, *American Architecture Now II*, 239.

60. Andres Duany, Elizabeth Plater-Zyberk, and Jeff Speck, *Suburban Nation* (New York: North Point Press, 2000). The quote is on xii.

61. Ibid., 113–14.

62. Ibid., 48–49.

63. Robert Davis, "Seaside at 20," *Seaside Times*, special twentieth anniversary issue (2001), 2; Peter Katz, *The New Urbanism* (New York: McGraw-Hill, 1994), 3–17.

64. Rob Walker, "Making a Pilgrimage to Utopia-by-the-Sea," *New York Times*, May 3, 2002, late edition.

65. Tzonis and Lefaivre, *Architecture in Europe*, 13–15; Frampton, *Modern Architecture*, 300–5.

66. Tzonis and Lefaivre, *Architecture in Europe*, 48–51; Ghirardo, *Architecture After Modernism*, 211–13.

67. Tzonis and Lefaivre, *Architecture in Europe*, 116–19.

68. Anthony Vidler, "From *The Architectural Uncanny: Essays in the Modern Unhomely*," in *Architectural Theory since 1968*, ed. K. Michael Hays (Cambridge, MA: MIT Press, 2000), 753.

69. Tzonis and Lefaivre, *Architecture in Europe*, 226–29.

70. Ibid., 224–25; Ghirardo, *Architecture After Modernism*, 201–5.

71. Kenneth Frampton, "Towards a Critical Regionalism: Six Points for an Architecture of Resistance," in *Labour, Work and Architecture: Collected Essays on Architecture and Design* (London: Phaidon Press, 2002), 76–89; Frampton, *Modern Architecture*, 314–27; Tzonis and Lefaivre, *Architecture in Europe*, 17–19, 148–51. For a questioning of critical regionalism, see Jameson, *Seeds of Time*, 189–205.

72. Marx, "The Eighteenth Brumaire," 104.

73. This analysis draws heavily on Perry Anderson, "Testing Formula Two," *New Left Review*, 2nd ser., no. 8 (March/April, 2001): 5–22.

74. Jencks, *Language*, 149, 163, 165. The quote is on 149.

75. Stevens, *The Favored Circle*, 113–15.

76. On the internationalization of real estate and architecture, see Sassen, *Global City*, 190–95.

77. Tschumi, *Architecture and Disjunction*, 237, 218, 224.

78. Jameson, *Seeds of Time*, 15–19; Bernard Tschumi, *Cinegramme Folies: Le Parc de la Villette* (Princeton, NJ: Princeton University Press, 1987), i; Michael Sorkin, "Frozen Light," in *Gehry Talks: Architecture + Process*, ed. Mildred Friedman (New York: Rizzoli, 1999), 30–32, 39.

79. Peter Eisenman, "Architecture and the Problem of the Rhetorical Figure," in *Theorizing a New Agenda for Architecture*, ed. Kate Nesbitt (New York: Princeton Architectural Press, 1996), 180.

80. Tschumi, *Architecture and Disjunction*, 258; Jameson, *Seeds of Time*, 69–70; Jameson, *Postmodernism*, 399–418.

81. Gilles Deleuze and Felix Guattari, *Anti-Oedipus: Capitalism and Schizophrenia* (Minneapolis: University of Minnesota Press, 1983).

82. Tschumi, *Cinegramme Folie*, 17.

83. "London Asks: 'Is This a Joke," *Mobile Press-Register*, May 18, 1996.

84. Macrae-Gibson, *Secret Life of Buildings*, 2–28; Jameson, *Postmodernism*, 107–29.

85. Friedman, *Gehry Talks*, 60–65, 78–93.

86. Ibid., 148–63; Ghirardo, *Architecture After Modernism*, 100–2.

87. Gehry quoted in Cathleen McGuigan, "Basque-ing in Glory," *Newsweek*, Jan. 13, 1997, 70; Friedman, *Gehry Talks*, 176–93.

88. Tschumi, *Architecture and Disjunction*, 5–22, 254–59; Bernard Tschumi, "The Pleasure of Architecture," in *Theorizing a New Agenda for Architecture*, ed. Kate Nesbitt (New York: Princeton Architectural Press, 1996), 532–40.

89. Tschumi, *Cinegramme Folie*, 1, iv. See also Tschumi, *Architecture and Disjunction*, 176–89.

90. Tschumi, *Cinegramme Folie*, vii.

91. Jacques Derrida, "Pointe de Folie–Maintenant L'Architecture," in *Rethinking Architecture*, ed. Neil Leach (London: Routledge, 1997). The quotes are on

331, 328. The final quote is from Jacques Derrida, "Architecture Where the Desire May Live," in ibid., 323.

92. Rem Koolhaas, *Projects for Prada, Part I* (Milan: Fondazione Prada Edizioni, 2001).

93. For such a viewpoint on deconstructionism in particular, see McLeod, "Architecture and Politics," 53–54.

94. Theodor Adorno, *Aesthetic Theory* (London: Routledge and Kegan Paul, 1984).

95. Peter Eisenman, *House of Cards* (New York: Oxford University Press, 1987), 170, 172, 177.

96. Ibid., 186, 185, 182–85; Peter Eisenman, "En Terror Firma: In Trails of Grotextes," in *Theorizing a New Agenda for Architecture*, ed. Kate Nesbitt (New York: Princeton Architectural Press, 1996), 568.

97. On traces and scaling, see Eisenman, "En Terror Firma," 560–70; Eisenman, "Architecture and the Problem of the Rhetorical Figure,"179–81; Peter Eisenman, "From *Moving Arrows, Eros and Other Errors: An Architecture of Absence*," in *Architecture Theory since 1968*, ed. K. Michael Hays (Cambridge, MA: MIT Press, 2000), 582–85. On the Wexner Center, see Peter Eisenman, *Recent Projects* (Nijmegen: SUN, 1989), 63.

98. Ghirardo, *Architecture After Modernism*, 129–22.

99. Eisenman, "Architecture and the Problem of the Rhetorical Figure," 180; Eisenman, *Recent Projects*, 25.

100. Adorno, *Minima Moralia*, 103.